D1547038

THE PIRAEUS

The Lion of the Piraeus (see p. 147). By courtesy of Al. N.
Oikonomides and the *Classical Bulletin*

The Piraeus

From the Fifth to the First Century B.C.

Robert Garland

Cornell University Press
Ithaca, New York

© 1987 by Robert Garland

All rights reserved. Except for brief quotations in a review, this book, or parts thereof, must not be reproduced in any form without permission in writing from the publisher. For information address Cornell University Press, 124 Roberts Place, Ithaca, New York 14850.

First published 1987 Cornell University Press.

Librarians: Library of Congress Cataloging in Publication Data pending.

International Standard Book Number 0-8014-2041-5
Library of Congress Catalog Card Number 87-47596

Photoset in North Wales by
Derek Doyle & Associates, Mold, Clwyd.
Printed in Great Britain by
Ebenezer Baylis & Sons Limited, Worcester

Contents

For Roberta

Κατέβημεν χθὲς εἰς Πειραιᾶ

Stones make a wall, walls make a house, houses make streets, and streets make a city. A city is stones and a city is people; but it is not a heap of stones, and it is not just a jostle of people.

Jacob Bronowski, *The Ascent of Man*

Illustrations

Introduction

There are a growing number of 'histories' of individual towns, Greek and Roman, from the archaic age to the end of antiquity. With scarcely an exception, however, they lack a conceptual focus or scheme: everything known about the place under examination appears to have equal claim – architecture, religion and philosophy, trade and coinage, administration and international relations. The city *qua* city is flooded out. The approach is usually descriptive and positivistic, 'collecting evidence and interrogating it with an open mind': the unexpressed assumptions about the economy are usually 'modernising' ... In the end, I believe that the history of *individual* ancient towns is a *cul-de-sac*, given the limits of the available (and potential) documentation, the unalterable condition of the study of ancient history ... But what questions do we wish to ask about the ancient city, whether they can be satisfactorily answered or not? That is the first thing to be clear about, before the evidence is collected, let alone interrogated. If my evaluation of the current situation is a bleak one, that is not because I dislike the questions being asked but because I usually fail to discover any questions at all, other than the antiquarian ones – how big? how many? what monuments? how much trade? which products?

M.I. Finley, 'The Ancient City' in
Economy and Society in Ancient Greece (1981, 20).

The wisdom and value of writing a book on the Piraeus* could scarcely be more authoritatively challenged. Moreover, if writing histories on individual towns is a cul-de-sac, *a fortiori* the history of a section of an ancient town, as the Piraeus effectively became, is an even more ill-judged undertaking – arguably very much like a critical commentary on *Hamlet* without the prince.

I have chosen to ignore Sir Moses Finley's warning partly on romantic grounds. The foundation and development of the Piraeus is, for me, one of the great adventure stories of history, there being

---

* The normal Greek spelling of Piraeus is 'Peiraieus' but orthographically this is cumbersome and I have adopted the Latin form instead. See Meisterhans and Schwyzer (1900, 30-3) and Rhodes (1981, 439). The continuity of the name through history is indicated by a Turkish map of Piri Reïs dated 1520 (Herzog 1902, pl. 15).

little in Athens' past to suggest that in the fifth century* her countrymen would, in Thukydides' memorable phrase (1.93.4), 'attach themselves to the sea'. Her previous relations with that element had been distinctly cool: she had not participated in the great colonising movement of the eighth to sixth centuries, and, despite an increasing naval role in the sixth century, even in the early fifth still had difficulty in safeguarding her littoral from piratical raids. Her western ports, which border on the Saronic Gulf, were for a long time hemmed in by Megara, Salamis and Aegina. Indeed in the location of the Asty,† 4km from the coast, it is tempting – but tendentious – to detect a certain shrinking avoidance of the sea.

The decision to build a naval port in the Piraeus, taken in the early years of the fifth century, amounted to a radical and audacious leap forward, equivalent to a collective identity crisis on the part of the state. It is to history's immense loss that we have no record of the extent of the opposition to Themistokles' bold initiative adopted in 493 to build a war fleet instead of dividing the recently acquired profits from the silver mines at Lavrion among the citizen body as a whole. Though the ancient view that Themistokles singlehandedly altered the whole course of Athenian military and political history is certainly a gross over-simplification of a complex issue, full credit must none the less be accorded his powers of oratory, for it was he primarily who bullied, coaxed, cajoled and inspired the Demos into forsaking the pleasure of the moment for what must have seemed to many a very dubious use of public funds.

It is my belief that Themistoklean strategy *logically* called for the abandonment of the Asty in favour of a settlement on the coast. Such a move, had it been effected, would have permitted an exclusive concentration of military resources in one centre. But the Asty was not abandoned and Athens' military forces were thereafter divided in the defence of two communities. Thus by strengthening Athens' offensive capability Themistokles ultimately undermined her defences, her Achilles' heel being the distance between the Asty and the harbour town, linked from *c.* 456 onwards by the umbilical Long Walls. These walls, approximately 7km in length, are for me the symbol par excellence of the Asty's schizophrenic identity as an

---

* All dates are B.C. unless otherwise stated.

† Following the practice of classical authors, I use 'Asty' *passim* to denote the city of Athens in distinction to the city of Piraeus. Cf. Arist. *Pol.* 5. 1303 b 12; Thuk. 2.13.7, 2.94.1 and 8.92.7. See Musiolek (1981, 137). For the Piraeus as asty, see Appendix I no. 14.

inland city with a coastal suburb.

But the Piraeus deserves its own history not only because its foundation was an imaginative feat of the first order and remained a palpable reminder of Athens' huge self-confidence around 490, but also because its very existence was the product and cornerstone of Athenian democracy. Understandably, therefore, the Piraeus, the headquarters of that fleet, constituted and ever remained the democratic heartland of the Athenian state. Though its population rarely finds a spokesman in literary sources, it did at least once in history become vocal, not to say vociferous, both as the focus for oligarchic reform, and as the spearhead and acting headquarters for the democratic resistance to that reform, hence justifying Aristotle's claim (*Pol.* 5.1303 b 10-12) that its population was 'more democratic' (*mallon dêmotikoi*) than that of the Asty.*

Aristotle's observation implies a further reason for attempting a history of the Piraeus. Attike was no monolith in terms of its social, economic, political and religious structures, and it is only by analysing the links between its periphery and centre that its composition can be properly understood. Borrowing a phrase from another context, 'The more a system is specifically defined in its forms, the more amenable it is to historical criticism' (Barthes 1957, 112). Perhaps the most engrossing questions raised by this study are the extent to which the Piraeus was idiosyncratic and how that influenced Athenian history. It was while I was investigating the diversity of religious choices peculiar to the port community that I first became interested in the Piraeus for its own sake.

Extracting the Piraeus from the Athenocentric material surrounding it (if indeed I have fully succeeded in achieving this aim) is analogous to the task of splitting molecules into atoms. Molecular Athens, it seems to me, has exerted an excessive fascination over the mind of the historian. So I have tried to write a history of the Athenian state whereby its economic, political and military advance is perceived primarily in terms of a radical decision taken in the first two decades of the fifth century which brought into being a highly progressive urban entity. I believe that that same decision, which at first acted as a social and political catalyst,

* No English word adequately covers the range of meanings implied by *dêmotikos* but in this instance it should certainly be translated 'democratic' or 'committed to the principles of democracy'. For this meaning elsewhere in Aristotle, cf. *Pol.* 4.1292 b 13-16. Similar examples in other authors include Ar. *Clouds* 205, Dem. 21.209 and Isok. 16.37. For *dêmotikos* used in a more restricted sense to mean 'deme-minded' or 'concerned with the welfare of the deme', cf. Lys. 20.22.

subsequently served to inhibit and constrain; and that from 322 onwards the distance of the Piraeus from the Asty had become such a handicap and liability that it rendered Athens as vulnerable to political pressure as a patient on a life-support system is to the flick of a switch. And this remained her condition until 86 when the switch was finally thrown.

This book could never have been written without the benefit of previous researches undertaken in the same area. In particular, I would like to record my debt to M. Amit's (1965) useful outline sketch of the Piraeus, to A.R. Burns' (1976) assessment of Hippodamos' originality, to P. Krentz's (1982) fundamental revision of the politics of the Thirty, to B. Jordan's (1975) investigation of the Athenian naval administration, to D. Whitehead's (1977) evaluation of the identity and role of Athenian metics, to S. Isager's and M.H. Hansen's (1975) summary of Athens' foreign trade in the fourth century, to P. Gauthier's and C. Habicht's work on Hellenistic Athens, to W. Judeich's (1931) exemplary discussion of the topography of the Piraeus, supplemented by G.R. Culley's (1973) investigation (in unpublished thesis form) of the topographical issues raised by *IG* II² 1035, and to P.J. Rhodes' (1981) magisterial commentary on the Aristotelian *Athênaiôn Politeia*. David Whitehead's book on the demes of Attike (1986) only came out while I was revising my manuscript but it will be obvious how much, even at this late stage, I benefited from his fine scholarship, particularly in the writing of Chapter 2 (a) and (b). His description of the Piraeus as a 'super deme' was particularly welcome at a moment when I was doubting whether I knew enough about other demes to justify making such a claim myself, though I inherently believed it to be correct.

To the best of my knowledge, only one other scholarly investigation of the Piraeus has been attempted, namely that of Panagos (1968). The neglect of the region is due partly to the fact that it has only been fairly recently that classical archaeologists have devoted as much attention to the Attic countryside as to the environs of Athens. Partly, too, it derives from the absence of striking physical remains and from the fact that the most important excavations in the Piraeus were carried out at a time when archaeological techniques were still rudimentary. But it is also a reflection of the way we select and order our data. In this book, rightly or wrongly, these have been organised in such a way as to justify the judgement of Plutarch (*Them.* 19.4) that Themistokles did not ' "knead the Piraeus to

Athens" as Aristophanes in the *Knights* alleges (l. 815); rather he kneaded Athens to the Piraeus, thereby making the land subservient to the sea'. In function and ideology, I believe the Piraeus to have been the quintessential Athens, and it is from this fundamental premiss that my investigation proceeds.

The besetting sin of all who write books on any 'unjustly neglected' topic is to exaggerate its importance in order to justify their own eccentricity. While aware of the dangers of myopic vision, I have resisted the advice of one reader to 'play down' the antithesis between the Asty and the Piraeus, which forms a thread throughout the narrative section of this work – though by 'antithesis', I wish to emphasise, I do not mean political antipathy. So far as an ancient historian may reasonably speak of having convictions, that is mine. As Arnaldo Momigliano commented in a review he wrote over forty years ago, the decisive quality in any author is his courage to be wrong.

My system of spelling Greek names is, like everyone's system, inconsistent. The fact that I adopt the Latin form 'Piraeus' but retain the proper Greek form 'Peiraieis' for the demesmen of the Piraeus will, I hope, seem less irritating to readers if it is borne in mind that official documents, even the same official document, tolerated variants (cf. Appendix II no. 6 where '*Peiraieôn*' is used at l.4 and '*Peiraiôn*' at ll.10-11). Current English usage seems undecided about whether to name the port 'Piraeus' or 'the Piraeus', and I have therefore adopted the latter form purely from preference. The = sign, which I adopt when listing epigraphical works, is understandably irksome to epigraphers, as Robin Osborne has pointed out to me, but, like him, I know of no preferable alternative.

The assistance which I have received from other scholars through correspondence and in conversation has been immense, and I would like to thank in particular Sarah Aleshire, John Davies, Phillip Harding, Peter Krentz, Jon Mikalson, Robin Osborne, Antony Spawforth, David Whitehead and Zeph Stewart, each of whom read parts of the manuscript at various stages. My greatest debt, however, is to Judith Binder of the American School of Classical Studies in Athens who disabused me of more ignorance and linguistic inaccuracy than I like to recall and who has the ability to produce a much more scholarly book than I have done here. The faults and weaknesses which this work contains are clearly my responsibility alone. Three grants, two from the British Academy and one from the Keele Research Fund, enabled me to stay at the

British School in Athens in order to study the topography of the Piraeus. The friendly encouragement which I received from its director Hector Catling and fellow students was of immense benefit, as always. The book was completed at the Center for Hellenic Studies in Washington D.C. where I was a junior fellow from 1985-6, and I should like here to record my deep affection and regard for its director, Zeph Stewart, who made the experience so fruitful and rewarding. Finally, I would like to thank my wife Roberta, who walked beside me every inch of the way.

Washington D.C.,   R.G.
June 1987

1. History

(a) Physical description

Once upon a time, as Strabo (*Geog.* 1.3.18) informs us, the Piraeus peninsula was an island which lay opposite the mainland. This, he explains, is the origin of its name, which derives from *peran*, meaning 'opposite'. Confirmation of Strabo's claim that the Piraeus was once cut off from the mainland is provided by geology and by the fact that the names of a number of the regions which lie round about, such as Halai, Halipedon and Halmyris, have as their root *hals*, meaning 'sea'. Even in classical times the Piraeus was probably connected to the rest of Attike by only a narrow strip of land, as is indicated by Plutarch's statement (*Kim.* 13.7) that the work of constructing the Long Walls, which ran through Halipedon to the northeast of the Piraeus, was hampered by 'wet and marshy ground', and could only be effected by laying large quantities of gravel and rocks to serve as secure foundations.

The Piraeus is a rocky limestone peninsula about 3.7km in length situated in the Saronic Gulf some 7 or 8km southwest of the Asty, towards the northern end of the west coast of Attike (Fig. 1). It is enclosed by two masses, Mounychia, a steep hill which attains a height of 86m above sea-level to the northeast, and Akte, a low plateau which rises gradually on all sides to a height of 58m to the southwest. The two are linked by an isthmus 17m above sea-level, formed from the alluvial deposit of the Kephisos River which discharges into Phaleron Bay to the east.

In its lack of natural assets, other than limestone used for building material, the Piraeus may justly be described as one of the least hospitable regions in all Attike. Its hills are steep, barren and practically waterless, and its climate, both in antiquity and probably as late as the nineteenth century, was most unhealthy owing to the proximity of the Halipedon Marsh. The development of this desolate region in the early decades of the fifth century, therefore, owed

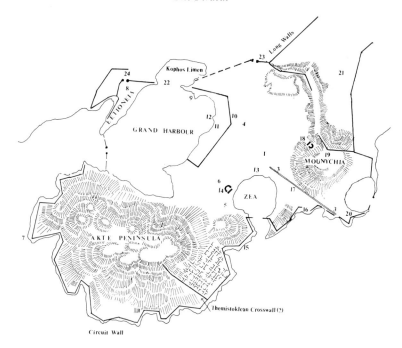

Fig. 1. The Piraeus

1. Hippodamian Agora
2. Remains of houses
3. Conjectured road to the sanctuary of Bendis
4. Sanctuary of the Dionysiastai
5. Metroon
6. Roman Forum
7. Tomb of Themistokles (?)
8. Aphrodision
9. Jetty or *Chôma*
10. Diisoterion
11. Emporion
12. Display area or *Deigma*
13. Arsenal of Philon
14. Zea Theatre
15. Phreattys
16. Serangeion
17. Asklepieion
18. Theatre of Dionysos
19, 20. Sanctuaries of Artemis and Bendis
21. Theseion (?)
22. *Dia mesou chôma*
23. Asty Gate
24. Aphrodision Gate

everything to the unrivalled protection which its three landlocked harbours afforded to Athens' naval arm.

The correct apportionment of ancient names to these three harbours caused endless disagreement among eighteenth- and nineteenth-century topographers and antiquarians which was finally resolved in 1843 with the publication of Ulrichs' 'Topographie der Hafen von Athen'. The largest of the three, the Megas Limen or Grand Harbour, known today as Kentrikos Limen, lies on the western side of the isthmus. It is a completely landlocked basin with an opening some 300m in length created by a detached ridge called Eetioneia to the north and by the northern coast of Akte to the south. Another name for the Megas Limen in antiquity seems to have been Kantharos or Goblet, though conceivably this term merely designated its southern bay. It is thus probable that many of the references in ancient texts simply to 'Piraeus' are intended to denote the Megas Limen. There have been significant changes in the shape of this harbour since antiquity due to a rationalisation of the configurations of the natural coastline, particularly around the peninsula of Eetioneia and also along the harbour's southern flank, where the modern shoreline of Akte Alkimou now obscures the remains of 94 shipsheds.

On the eastern side of the isthmus lies Zea Port, modern Limen Zeas or Pasolimani, a small mushroom-shaped harbour enclosed between Akte to the southwest and Mounychia Hill to the northeast. Mounychia Port, modern Tourkolimani or latterly Mikrolimani, the smallest of the three, is oval-shaped and lies directly below Mounychia Hill. Further to the east lies the wide, open bay of Phaleron which fulfilled the role of harbour in an earlier stage of Athenian history, being 'the place where sea and city are nearest' (Paus. 1.1.2). Into this bay flowed Athens' two main rivers, the Kephisos and the Ilisos (Str. *Geog.* 9.1.24).

The submerged condition of archaeological remains around the coast, including quarries and rock-cut tombs, led Négris in 1904 to the conclusion that there had been a rise of approximately 3.5m in the sea-level over the last two and a half thousand years as has been registered in other parts of the Mediterranean. Estimates of the exact rise have since varied, but it now seems likely that it should be put at under 2m.

(b) Before 500

In the Bronze Age the Piraeus appears to have been insignificant. The only evidence of any Mycenaean settlement comes from the remains of a single burial dated to Late Helladic IIIb found in the Charavgi area to the northeast of the peninsula. This solitary find contrasts strikingly with the abundant evidence from other coastal towns of Attike in the Mycenaean period, most notably from the Late Helladic IIIb-c cemetery at Porto Rafti Bay on the east coast, which has yielded over 220 burials showing indications of contact with Egypt and the Levant. Porto Rafti is probably to be identified with the later deme of Prasiai, and the memory of the era when this bay was perhaps the chief port on the Attic coast is preserved in the myth of Erysichthon, son of Kekrops and Agraulos, who sailed thence to Delos on a sacred mission and to whom a grave monument was erected on the shore. Phaleron Bay (Fig. 2) is also likely to have been important in the Bronze Age, being celebrated in mythology as the embarkation point from which Theseus set sail for Crete and Menestheus for Troy (Paus. 1.1.2; cf. Hom. *Il.* 2.552). Though few Mycenaean remains have been found along its coast, some moderately prosperous chamber tombs are reported from the

Fig. 2. Phaleron Bay looking east.

vicinity of Palaio Phaleron and Kalamaki to the southeast. Early Geometric settlements were confined to Athens and its immediate surroundings. In Middle Geometric I, however, there was a movement out into the countryside and towards the coast, as reflected in the Piraeus by a cemetery at Palaia Kokkinia to the north of the peninsula, whose earliest graves date to *c.* 850. In the Late Geometric period Attike experienced a marked economic decline, especially around her coast, and her population appears to have increasingly turned its back on the sea, devoting itself to agriculture instead. New settlements none the less sprang up around the coast, notably at Phaleron, Trachones, Helleniko, Aliki, Voula, Vouliagmeni and Vari. The cemetery at Phaleron, which was used continuously from *c.* 715 down to the close of the seventh century, has yielded 87 graves, 26 of which were cremations. A striking indicator of acute impoverishment in this region is the fact that the pottery is of extremely inferior quality and that many graves contained no offerings at all.

Shortly before Solon came to power in 594/3 Athens is alleged to have launched her first substantial naval expedition which resulted in the seizure of Sigeion on the south side of the entrance to the Hellespont. Some scholars would see in this venture the tentative beginnings of a commitment on Athens' part to a maritime role in the Aegean, on the grounds that a navy was essential for the defence of such a distant possession. Even if the expedition and conquest did take place, however, it cannot be assumed that Athens intended to treat Sigeion as an imperial possession. She may simply have established a colony for land-hungry Athenians, which subsequently flourished independent of its mother city. A further contention, that the alleged enterprise reveals an interest or dependency on Euxine trade, is also unlikely, since Sigeion is not strategically placed to control entrance to the Dardanelles. Even Athens' successful bid to re-capture the island of Salamis from Megara, which took place during Solon's ascendancy, cannot certainly be taken as evidence of Athens' increasing confidence in her naval arm, not least in view of the fact that the assault on the island took place with the assistance of only a single triakontor (Plu. *Sol.* 9.2).

It was perhaps as a direct result of the acquisition of Salamis that ports on the west coast such as Eleusis, Keratsini, Aixone (Voula) and Sounion now became important for the first time, though there is no evidence to indicate that the Piraeus was among them. Athens' principal port throughout the sixth century was Phaleron Bay.

Described by Herodotos (6.116) as a naval station or *epineion*, it was here that the Peisistratids, aided by the Thessalians, defeated a Spartan attempt to disembark and drive them out. Here, too, the Kybernesia, probably the oldest Athenian naval festival, was celebrated in honour of Theseus' steersmen sons, the pilot Nausithoos and the steersman Phaiax (Philochoros *FGrH* 328 F 111 ap. Plu. *Thes.* 17.6).

During the period of Peisistratid rule Athens extended her links throughout the northeast Aegean. The Thracian Chersonese on the

Fig. 3. Finial of sphinx *stêlê*, *c.* 540.

Fig. 4. Painted marble disc, *c*. 500.

northern shore of the Propontis was re-settled by the elder
Miltiades, who established there a minor dynasty (Hdt. 6.34-7).
Sigeion, which had apparently been re-occupied by the Aeolians,
was captured by Peisistratos in *c*. 550 (Hdt. 5.94), and about the
same time Athenian settlers appear at Elaious, situated at the tip of
the broad promontory which lies to the north of the Hellespont.
Finally in *c*. 500, the younger Miltiades, who had succeeded to his
uncle's position in the Chersonese, took control of the islands of
Lemnos and Imbros, which command access to the Hellespont
(Hdt. 6.39-41).

There is, however, little evidence to justify the belief that by the
end of the sixth century Athens had in any real sense become a naval
power. Although she had achieved a certain dominance over Megara,
and was establishing connections with the northeast Aegean, she
remained extremely vulnerable to piratical raids around her coast.
The exposed position of Phaleron and its lack of permanent port
facilities are further testimony both to the limits of her naval
aspirations and to the low priority attached to maritime enterprises.
The existence of local districts known as *naukraroi*, a word which may
possibly derive from *naus* and *krainô*, has been taken to indicate that
Athens possessed a formidable navy in the late Archaic period, but

the supporting evidence for this view is largely lacking. Athens was, moreover, overshadowed by Aegina, whose importance as a sea power in the sixth century is well-attested.

The Piraeus seems to have figured little in early Athenian history, though there are some indications that its settlement may not have been negligible. In the first place, Lewis' contention (1963, 33) that the Tetrakomoi, an association of four villages comprising Piraeus, Phaleron, Xypete and Thymaitadai, might possibly have constituted one of the twelve ancient poleis of Kekrops would, if correct, certainly demonstrate the antiquity and prominence of the settlement in the post-Mycenaean era. The fact that the cult of Artemis Mounychia (below p. 113) was administered by a hereditary priesthood strongly suggests that as early as the seventh century there was at least one powerful genos in the region. An Archaic gravestone with sphinx finial dated to the mid-sixth century constitutes some evidence for the region's prosperity before the Classical era (Fig. 3), as, too, does a painted marble disc dated *c.* 500 (Fig. 4). There are, moreover, strong indications that before the end of the sixth century the Piraeus was already a deme of more-than-average size (below p. 59). Though few physical remains predating the fifth century have come to light, this may simply be due to the fact that the site of the Geometric and Archaic settlement has yet to be identified.

The Piraeus first enters the historical records in *c.* 510 when the tyrant Hippias, judging that his position in Athens was becoming increasingly untenable following the murder of his brother Hipparchos, set about fortifying Mounychia Hill. His intention according to the Aristotelian *Athênaiôn Politeia* (19.2) was to establish it as the seat of his government, but he was driven into exile before effecting the transfer.

(c) The Themistoklean fortification

Despite her lack of a proper navy, by the beginning of the fifth century Athens was reckoned to be the second most powerful state in mainland Greece (Hdt. 5.97.1): her largely agricultural economy was buoyant, aided by the silver mines at Lavrion; trade was increasing, as indicated by the wide dispersal of Athenian pottery; and the reforms of Kleisthenes passed in 508/7 had set Athens firmly on the road to democracy. All three aspects of Athens' progress – military capability, economic viability and adherence to democracy – were soon to be reinforced and radicalised by the decision to develop the Piraeus. As if to demonstrate the shape of things to come, when Aristagoras of Miletos came to Athens in 499 to request help for the Ionians in their revolt against Persia, the Athenians agreed to send 20 ships (Hdt. 5.97.3). In the ensuing war with Aegina they had 50 ships of their own and had to request assistance from the Corinthians who supplied an extra 20 (Hdt. 6.89).

Thukydides, the earliest authority for the development of the harbour town, provides the following description of how the project had been initiated, interrupted and subsequently resumed (1.93.3-7):

> Themistokles persuaded the Athenians to finish constructing the walls (?) around the Piraeus (*tou Peiraiôs ta loipa*) which had been begun during his archonship (i.e. 493). It was his belief that the Piraeus with its three natural harbours offered a splendid location and that if the Athenians became a sea-faring nation (*nautikoi*), this would greatly assist them in extending their sphere of influence. Indeed Themistokles was the first to have the audacity to suggest that the Athenians should attach themselves to the sea (*tês thalassês ... anthaktea*) and in so doing laid the basis for their empire (*archê*). In accordance with his policy, the Athenians built the walls around the Piraeus ... Themistokles attached particular importance to the navy because, in my estimation, he recognised that it would be easier for the Persian king to launch a naval rather than a military offensive. He was of the opinion that the Piraeus was more useful than the upper polis, and he frequently urged the Athenians that if ever they were hard-pressed on land to go down to the Piraeus and resist all their enemies with their fleet.

All ancient sources agree in attributing the inspiration for developing the Piraeus to Themistokles but are in less than perfect accord about the details. That the plan was not entirely due to the vision of one man is obvious on a priori grounds, though our evidence does not provide us with any insights into the political complexities surrounding the decision. The initial proposal seems to have been to build a naval port, presumably to be provided with dockyards, mooring sheds and other naval facilities, though the main labour probably went into the construction of a fortification wall around the Piraeus peninsula to guard it against sudden attack (Figs. 5 and 6).

Thukydides suggests that the primary motive behind the scheme was a defensive one: Themistokles believed that the Persians were

Fig. 5. *above, below and opposite above* Three views of remains of the Themistoklean Wall on the west side of Zea Port.

Fig. 6. *below* Model of a section of the Themistoklean Wall with ditch in front.

considering launching an attack on Greece which Athens could more easily repulse by sea. Other sources, notably Herodotos (7.144), point to the unresolved conflict with Aegina which many Athenians probably judged a more immediate threat than that posed by Persia. Defensive considerations, however, almost certainly combined with offensive ones and the sources indicate that the underlying intention was to achieve unchallenged supremacy over all Greeks. If this tradition is true, as is probable, the Piraeus project would have been seen by its architect as playing a decisive role in the furthering of this aim. Whether there was an accompanying economic motive behind the scheme is very unlikely. Certainly the destruction of Miletos by the Persians in 494 must have changed patterns of trading in the eastern Mediterranean, but Boersma's contention (1970, 38) that the Athenians 'must have quickly understood that the annihilation of their greatest rival for the eastern trade offered them vast opportunities' is tendentious on a number of counts. It presupposes in the first instance that cities on opposite sides of the Aegean were capable of competing for the same commercial markets and, equally tendentiously, that politics and trade were interrelated. Nor is it likely that the Athenians decided at this early date to develop the Piraeus in order to protect essential imports. Even allowing for some insight on the part of the demos into potential economic benefits deriving from the project, it has to be emphasised that there is no evidence that the original blueprint design contained any provision for commercial shipping. However, a further factor, namely growth in the size of cargo vessels in this period, cannot be completely ruled out, since Phaleron Bay did not enable large vessels to ride at anchor.

The most intriguing question of all, however, is whether the demos fully envisaged the political implications, and if so, whether that was also a part of the design. It is often remarked that Themistokles' appearance on the political scene coincided with other important changes that strengthened Athenian democracy: sortition, in place of direct election, was either introduced or re-introduced for the archonship in 487; the board of strategoi, annually elected but eligible for repeated re-election, now replaced the archons as the foremost officers of state; and finally, the year 487 witnessed the first attested use of ostracism. The decision to convert Athens into a naval power served in effect as a guarantee that these reforms would never be repealed, thereby justifying the claim of Pseudo-Xenophon (*AP* 1.2) that 'it is the demos who man the ships and hold the power in the polis'. In similar vein Plutarch (*Them.* 19.4) put forward the view that Themistokles 'increased (sc. the power of) the demos against the *aristoi* and filled them with boldness, since power (*dunamis*) now passed into the hands of sailors, boatswains and pilots'. These comments derive from the belief that – whatever the importance of Athens' fleet before 480 – by developing the Piraeus, Themistokles made the state permanently dependent upon the *thêtes*, the lowest property-holding group in Athenian society, who constituted the bulk of the rowers in the fleet. This intimate association between democracy and naval power lies at the heart of the political events in which the Piraeus exercised a shaping hand, for it was always the rowers, and hence the Piraeus, which through thick and thin remained rootedly committed to democracy. Hence, whenever Athens fell a victim to oligarchical oppression, it was natural and inevitable that the democratic resistance should focus on the Piraeus, the region where loyalty to democracy was staunchest.

The fortification of the Piraeus took many years to complete. Either because the state had more pressing concerns or because it encountered opposition from Miltiades on his return to Athens from the Chersonese after the Ionian revolt in 493-2, the project was left in abeyance for several years. Thus it was that in 490, immediately after the battle of Marathon, the Persian fleet dropped anchor in the bay of Phaleron to the east while considering whether to launch a further attack on Athens, because 'Phaleron was at that time the naval station (*epineion*) of the Athenians' (Hdt. 6.116).

Before the Piraeus project was resumed, Athens had taken the historic decision to reserve the proceeds of a new silver strike at Lavrion to finance an ambitious shipbuilding programme. According to the Aristotelian *Athênaiôn Politeia* (22.7), the strike was made in 483/2 and yielded a surplus of 100 talents. At the instigation of Themistokles a recommendation was put forward the following year to devote this sum to the building of a fleet of at least 100 (less probably 200) triremes. The decision by the Athenian Demos in 482 to adopt the proposal of Themistokles instead of distributing the windfall among the entire population has been justly hailed as 'one of the most important events in the history of western civilization' (Meiggs 1982, 122). Ancient sources agree that the immediate purpose for which the ships were built was the war with Aegina; in the event they were to be first tested against Persia, when, at the battle of Salamis two years later, the Athenians were

able to muster a fleet of 200 ships, more than half the size of the
entire Greek contingent. Probably Themistokles also took the first
step in setting up the administrative apparatus necessary for the
running of Athens' naval establishment, though for this we have no
direct evidence.

To build a fleet of between 100 and 200 ships requires huge
supplies of timber which were not readily available in Attike itself.
Where did the wood come from? Macedon, Athens' chief supplier in
later periods of history, is unlikely to have risked provoking Persia
whose preparations for an expedition against Greece were well
under way. Thrace and Asia Minor can be ruled out for the same
reason, leaving south Italy, with which Themistokles is known to
have had strong links, as the probable main source, perhaps
supplemented by supplies from Euboia (cf. Meiggs 1982, 124). Since
the Piraeus did not as yet have any facilities for shipbuilding, most of
the ships were probably built at Phaleron, though some may have
been constructed at other ports around the coast.

Shortly before the Persians arrived, the population of Attike was
evacuated to Troizen, Aegina and Salamis in what was surely the
largest naval exercise ever to be mounted from the Piraeus.
Plutarch's description of the scene in the harbour on the day of the
evacuation is evocative, if historically suspect (*Them.* 10.5):

> The event filled those witnessing it with pity and admiration as the
> Athenians dispatched their dependants in one direction and
> themselves crossed over to Salamis, oblivious to the shrieks, tears and
> embraces of their nearest and dearest. The elderly, who had to be left
> behind on the mainland, aroused compassion, and pets, too, added to
> the commotion by choosing this moment to display heartrending
> affection for their masters, howling beside them as the latter went on
> board.

The extent to which in two brief years Athens had come to be
identified in the eyes of the Greek world as a naval power is
illustrated by an anecdote also related by Plutarch (*Them.* 11.3-5).
Following the evacuation described above, Themistokles was
taunted by the other Greeks as being 'a man without a city (*apolis*)'.
He replied that the Athenian navy was the greatest polis in all
Greece and that if the Greek contingent withdrew to the isthmus of
Corinth, the Athenians would sail away and found a new city
elsewhere. No one, it seems, least of all the Spartan Eurybiades,
commander of the Greek fleet, seriously doubted their ability to do
just that.

When Xerxes' fleet arrived off the coast of Attike a few days later, it docked at Phaleron, presumably because the naval installations of the Piraeus were still only half-completed (Hdt. 8.66.1). In the ensuing battle, which was probably fought towards the end of September, the Athenian fleet fought best after the Aeginetan (8.93.1). The outcome, an overwhelming victory for the Greeks, set the seal upon Themistoklean defensive strategy based on command of the sea.

No date is preserved for the completion of the Piraeus fortification but the impetus almost certainly derived from the devastating events of the Persian wars and from the confidence generated by the victory at Salamis. The year 479 would therefore have been an appropriate moment for Themistokles to introduce a second proposal to the assembly regarding the resumption of the Piraeus project. On this occasion he was probably just an ordinary citizen when he spoke in the assembly, though his status as an ex-archon would have given him considerable authority. Diodoros Siculus (11.41.2), who, like Plutarch (*Them.* 19.2), places the whole project after Xerxes' invasion, dates its completion to 477/6, which may, for all we know, be correct.

In the autumn of 478 the Athenian naval commander Aristeides, allegedly under pressure from the Chians, Samians and Lesbians, agreed to take over the leadership of those Greek states in the Aegean and along the coast of Asia Minor which had participated in the struggle against Persia (Plu. *Arist.* 23.4-5). The following year, after heralds had been dispatched issuing invitations, an alliance was formally inaugurated. According to Thukydides (1.96.1), its professed purpose (*proschêma*) was to ravage the territory of the Great King in order to exact vengeance for the injuries that its member states had suffered. That Athens in 477 could pose as the leader of a maritime alliance is merely further proof of the esteem in which her fleet was now held.

As stated in the Introduction (p. 2), it is my belief that the Themistoklean project in its purest form demanded the total abandonment of the upper city in favour of wholesale migration to the harbour town – though it is, of course, in the highest degree unlikely that such a suggestion was ever put forward. Logic certainly demanded such a radical upheaval, since from now on Athens' offensive and defensive capability was to become concentrated upon the Piraeus. Given this condition, it was a military nonsense to have to defend two urban centres situated within 8 km of each other.

Fatally for Athens, as Bury-Meiggs (1975, 204f.) noted, the Asty was close enough to the coast to enable fairly rapid communication with the port town. Had the distance been greater, the case for abandoning the old city would have been unanswerable and the future course of Athenian history would have been very different. That such a move does not seem to have been contemplated was due to emotional attachment, vested interest, religious scruples and the sheer force of public inertia.

(d) The linking of the Asty to the Piraeus

According to Thukydides (1.98.1), the first military action to be undertaken by the newly formed Delian League was the capture of Eion on the River Strymon from the Persians in 476. This was followed by the seizure of the island of Skyros, which now became an Athenian cleruchy. Tradition records that it was on Skyros that Kimon, in obedience to an oracle received from Delphi, discovered the bones of Theseus which he conveyed back to Athens amid much pomp (Plu. *Thes.* 36; *Kim.* 8). The elevation of Theseus from local to national hero, an event which postdates 508, was a direct consequence of Athens' newly assumed maritime role and a reflection of a profound re-evaluation of national identity, symbolic of which is the removal of his bones from an island notorious for piracy. Equally suggestive is the fact that Theseus now acquires a second father in Poseidon, whose promotion at this date to front-rank Athenian deity is no less meteoric than that of his son.

Within twelve years of the League's foundation its professed purpose had been achieved. The occasion of its fulfilment was the great land and sea battle fought at the mouth of the River Eurymedon in southern Asia Minor in *c.* 466, when a Persian fleet of two hundred triremes was captured and destroyed. The commander-in-chief of the Greek forces was Kimon who is said to have used a new-style trireme capable of transporting more hoplites than its predecessor (Plu. *Kim.* 12.2). At Delphi the victory was commemorated by the dedication of a bronze palm supporting a golden Athene (Paus. 10.15.4); in the Asty by the building of a new south wall to the Acropolis (Plu. *Kim.* 13.6); and in the Piraeus by the establishment of a cult in honour of the hero Eurymedon, the deified essence of the river who was believed to have played a decisive role in the outcome of the battle (below p. 126).

The history of the Piraeus from *c.* 460-445 was as much

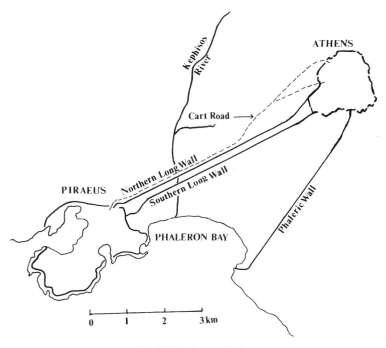

Fig. 7. The Long Walls.

determined by struggles on the mainland as by ambitions abroad, and the focus of this section is upon the manner in which the port came to be perceived as playing a determining role in those struggles. Athens' weakness in respect of her distance from her primary means of defence and supply had already been revealed by the Persian sack of the Asty in 480 and was to have far-reaching consequences for the entire future course of Athenian history. To mitigate that weakness, which could never be eliminated, the decision was taken in 458/7 to link the Asty to the coast by means of two diverging walls, one of which, the Northern Long Wall, extended to the northwest shore of the Grand Harbour, and the other, the Phaleric Wall, to the east coast of Phaleron Bay (Fig. 7).

Thukydides (1.107.1) states that this project was commenced soon after an Athenian naval victory over Aegina and a successful incursion into the Megarid. Plutarch (*Kim.* 13.8), however, reports that the original foundations for the Long Walls were laid down by Kimon, who paid for the work from the spoils of his victory at Eurymedon. Since this tradition conflicts with Plutarch's own picture of Kimon as an arch-conservative, it seems inherently implausible, because the consequence of their construction was to privilege further a strategy based on naval defence over one based on military defence – and hence of the radical *thêtes* over the conservative hoplites. No other political figure is, however, associated with the work and the tradition, for all its improbability, should not be rejected outright. If Kimon had no part in the original decision to join Athens to the Piraeus, he may still have contributed towards the scheme financially, perhaps as a way of regaining popular support following his return from exile (Garlan 1974, 48). But whatever the truth of Kimon's involvement with the scheme, there can be no denying that the conception of the Long Walls is an ideological and democratic response to Athens' defensive weakness from *c.* 477 onwards.

The wedge-shaped area thus enclosed effectively sealed off the Asty, Phaleron and the Piraeus from the rest of Attike, the military thinking being that so long as Athens retained mastery of the sea, her population could never be starved into submission. More than that, their construction signalled to the world outside that Athens' pursuit of an expansionist role in the Aegean was not to be curbed by pressures from the mainland. That this was how they were interpreted is clearly indicated by Sparta's first peace proposal made at the end of the Peloponnesian War that they and the Piraeus fortifications, but not the circuit wall of Athens, should be razed to the ground.

The Long Walls were completed in the autumn of 457, following a spectacular Athenian victory over the Boeotians at Oinophyta (Thuk. 1.108.3; D.S. 11.81-83.3). Soon afterwards Aegina was forced to become a tribute-paying member of the Delian League, assessed at the punitive level of thirty talents, the highest figure on the tribute list. Her harsh treatment indicates that there was no longer any place in the Aegean for a rival to Athenian maritime power, least of all if it lay a mere 25km from the Piraeus.

Athens was fast becoming the most powerful mainland state when in 454 she and her allies suffered what Thukydides (1.109-110) alleges to have been a catastrophic defeat in Egypt, involving the loss of the greater part of a fleet of 250 ships. The primary aim of the Egyptian expedition seems to have been to cripple Persia, but it may in part have been inspired by the desire to secure a monopoly on Egyptian corn, since the earliest evidence of a corn shortage in Athens is contemporary with this event.

The linking of the Asty to the coast by the building of the Northern and Phaleric Long Walls, though successful as a means of preserving contact with the sea, none the less left Phaleron Bay perilously exposed to invasion. Events on the mainland at the end of the so-called First Peloponnesian War which resulted in the loss of Boeotia and Megara in 447-6, as well as the revolt and reduction of Euboia, underscored Athens' vulnerability to attack from her neighbours. The re-thinking of Athenian defence strategy and foreign policy consequent upon this development can be clearly detected in the decision, doubtless taken on the initiative of Perikles, to construct the so-called Middle Wall parallel to the already existing Northern Long Wall. According to both Andokides (3.7) and Aischines (2.174), the work commenced immediately after the conclusion of the Thirty Years' Peace with Sparta in 446/5. It may well have been prompted by the Peloponnesian invasion of Attike under King Pleistoanax which preceded its signing.

The new project wholly eliminated Phaleron from the fortified area. What had previously been a broad wedge terminating in an extensive and open shoreline was now reduced to a narrow corridor of communication between two walled cities. The building of the Middle Wall or *Dia mesou teichos*, otherwise known as the Southern Long Wall, reflects yet greater confidence in the power of the fleet to keep Athens' population adequately provisioned at all times. Whereas the Northern and Phaleric Walls had enclosed the fertile area to the north of Phaleron, the new arrangement accepted the possibility that Athens under siege might become wholly dependent on her imports.

It also lends credibility to the belief that from the mid-fifth century onwards Phaleron as a port had ceased to function other than in a marginal capacity, with the result that its protection was no longer an intrinsic part of Athens' strategic defence. The architect of the Middle Wall was Kallikrates, Iktinos' partner in the building of the Parthenon, a further indication that it was regarded as a project of first-rate importance. Yet despite its importance, and for reasons that are wholly obscure, the work proceeded so slowly that Perikles was ridiculed in Comedy on account of his dilatoriness in bringing it to completion.

The linking of the Asty to the coast marks the moment when the Piraeus came of age. The total length of the circuit walls of both towns, combined with the Long Walls and Phaleric Wall, was greatly in excess of 30km. The construction of such an elaborate system of fortification in such a brief period is a staggering achievement, especially when it is remembered that the Athenians were at war for most of the period and consequently capable of diverting their manpower into constructive work only during the brief intervals afforded by peace. And yet that vast length of trailing wall, by far the most extensive and elaborate of its kind in fifth-century Greece, merely serves to underline Athens' fatal weakness in the distance of the Asty from its source of supply.

(e) The Periklean expansion

The initiative of Themistokles extended only so far as the transfer of the naval port of Athens from Phaleron to the Piraeus. Not until long after Themistokles' eclipse did the Athenians convert the Piraeus into one of the leading commercial centres in Greece. Thukydides, who is our principal source for its fortification, does not describe how it subsequently grew up into a densely populated urban centre since his concern is with the events that led up to the Peloponnesian War. What almost certainly happened, however, is that the demos appointed a commission of land-distributors (*gêonomoi*) to supervise its layout, as it did in *c.* 445 when founding a colony at Brea.

Since the Piraeus was not an entirely new foundation, it may well be that the implementation of the commissioners' plan necessitated the expropriation of certain pre-existing structures. Evidence from elsewhere suggests that the order to expropriate had to be passed by the state, compensation being awarded to those who suffered loss on the basis of an expert decision reached by official assessors (*timêtai*). Only sacred land could not be appropriated in this way, since it retained its sacredness in perpetuity as is indicated by the decree establishing Brea wherein it is laid down that 'the *temenoi* which are reserved should remain exactly as they are.' Which *temenoi* pre-dated the appointment of the Piraeus commission cannot be ascertained, but certainly those of Artemis Mounychia, Demeter and Dionysos all have a strong claim to being ancient.

The most influential member of the commission was Hippodamos of Miletos who is credited by Aristotle (*Pol.* 2.5.1267 b 22 – 1268 a 14) with having 'invented the art of cutting up cities (*diairesis*) and cut up the Piraeus'. What particularly struck Aristotle about Hippodamian town-planning was its underlying theoretical basis which established an inter-relationship between social classes and land distribution (below p. 140f.). The originality of his invention thus seems to have been the concept of determining in advance of its development the overall layout of a city according to the functional structures which it was intended that it should contain.

The problems concerning Hippodamos' contribution to the Piraeus in the light of the scanty archaeological data and the ambiguous testimony of Aristotle will be discussed in Chapter 4. We can do no more than speculate as to when he began his assignment. The Scholiast on Aristophanes' *Knights* (1. 327) states that he divided up the Piraeus 'at the time of the Persian Wars (*kata ta Mêdika*)'. Since Strabo (*Geog.* 14.2.9) attributes the foundation of the new city of Rhodes in 408/7 to 'allegedly the same architect who built the Piraeus', it is unlikely, if this latter testimony is to be believed, that he began the earlier project much before *c*. 450. Very possibly Hippodamos arrived in Athens in the early 440s at the invitation of Perikles and soon after completing this, his first commission was called upon to design the layout of Thourioi, a panhellenic colony founded on the east coast of the toe of Italy.

It is also impossible to tell how long it took to implement the decisions of the Hippodamian planning commission, but such meagre and disjointed scraps of information as we possess indicate that over the next fifteen years both naval and commercial facilities in the Piraeus were greatly improved. Andokides (3.7) alleges that new shipsheds were built following the conclusion of the Thirty Years' Peace in 446/5, and one of the financial decrees of Kallias, which may have been passed just over a decade later, regulated that when all outstanding debts had been repaid to the treasury of Athene and the Other Gods, 'the Athenians should expend remaining funds on the *neôrion* and the walls'. Moreover, the Scholiast to Aristophanes' *Acharnians* (1. 145) reports that the Alphitopolis Stoa in the Emporion was erected under the guidance of Perikles. Its construction is firm evidence of Athens' increasing dependency on imported corn and of her recognition that stocks must be maintained at a high level in order to safeguard her population in time of war. Whether the Piraeus acquired any other monumental public architectural works at this date cannot be determined.

Perikles' interest in the commercial potential of the Piraeus can be gleaned from the Funeral Speech where he proudly declares: 'The products of the whole earth flow to us on account of the greatness of our polis and we enjoy them just as naturally as we do our own' (Thuk. 2.38). But there was a more sinister aspect to this boast. By

432 Athens had converted the Aegean into what Finley (1978, 119)
calls 'a closed sea' with the capability of controlling both the entry of
essential imports and the circulation of all merchandise among its
member states. This control was exercised by the *Hellespontophulakes*
or 'commissioners of the Hellespont'. These officials are known only
from an inscription dated *c.* 426 granting Methone the right to
import corn from Byzantion, but the origins of their office may well
antedate the outbreak of the Peloponnesian War. Their existence
argues a state of affairs whereby the majority of Athens' allies,
themselves denied access to the source of supply, were forced to
travel either to the Piraeus or to other Athenian depots in order to
purchase supplies of corn.

   Athens' ability to regulate the flow of traffic within the boundaries
of her empire was brutally demonstrated in 432 when Perikles
excluded the Megarians 'from the harbours of the Athenian empire'
and was to find a prominent place in Athenian strategy during the
Peloponnesian War. Thus, while one aspect of the Periklean
expansion was to equip the Piraeus with improved commercial and
naval facilities, another was to exploit its potential for the
advancement of Athenian imperialism.

(f) The port in the Peloponnesian War

When war broke out with Sparta in 431, the Piraeus represented the
cornerstone of Perikles' fatally flawed *Kriegsspiel*, the rules of which
were to avoid land-battles, maintain sea power, and adhere strictly
to a non-expansionist policy in regard to the allies (1.143.3-144.1).*
Foreseeing a possible threat from Aegina, which still retained its
inveterate hatred for Athens, Perikles expelled the entire population
from the island and re-settled it with Athenian colonists (2.27.1).
The move was a sound one, Aegina being in Perikles' felicitous
phrase 'the eyesore of the Piraeus' (Arist. *Rhet.* 3.10 1411 a 15; Plu.
Per. 8.5) and well-placed to serve as a Peloponnesian naval base.

   Less than felicitous was Perikles' recommendation that all
Athenians living in the countryside should abandon their homes and
migrate to the Asty (1.143.5; cf. 2.13.2). Since this constituted the
majority of the citizen body (2.16.1), the population of the urban
centre probably doubled overnight. The refugees, for whom not even
minimal facilities may have been provided, were allocated lots 'in

---

* Unless otherwise stated, all references in this section are to Thukydides.

the space between the Long Walls and most of the Piraeus' (2.17.3). The majority probably camped out in tents, especially on the uninhabited southern half of Akte peninsula. It is not surprising that within a year Athens' population was riddled with the plague. The epidemic first spread through the harbour town where the concentration of refugees may have been densest and which was almost wholly dependent on easily polluted wells. Its inhabitants were under the impression that the Peloponnesians had poisoned their wells (2.48.2). No one, not even Thukydides, seems to have understood the precise connection between over-crowding and disease.

In the winter of 429/8 the Spartans displayed rare tactical initiative in planning a bold attack against the Piraeus which at this date was open and unguarded. A fleet of forty triremes set sail from the Megarian dockyards at Nisaia with the intention of making a direct assault on the port. Cold feet and a contrary wind diverted it to Salamis instead, however, where it surprised an Athenian guard-post at Boudoron and contented itself with laying waste the island. The inhabitants of Salamis managed to light beacons to warn Athens of the attack, thereby causing 'a panic greater than any that had occurred in the war' (2.94.1): those living in the Asty believed that the Spartans had already attacked the Piraeus, while those in the Piraeus imagined that Salamis had been taken and that the Spartans were about to sail into the port (see below p. 80). This, comments Thukydides drily, the Spartans might easily have done, if faintheartedness had not got the better of them. As a result of this scare the Athenians took immediate steps to improve security by converting the Piraeus into a closed port (*kleistos limên*). This they did by extending the circuit walls on either side of each harbour's mouth by means of moles known as *chêlai*, thereby decreasing the width of the entrance passage. The moles terminated in fortified towers to which a chain was attached, a device enabling the port to be completely sealed off in time of danger.

Further to safeguard the Piraeus and Athenian shipping, in the summer of 427 Nikias led a successful expedition against the tiny island of Minoa off the coast of Megara. His object was not only to forestall any repetition of the abortive raid of 429, but also to prevent Minoa being used as a base for piratical activity. Henceforth, the island served as an Athenian look-out station and garrison, similar to the one which already existed on Salamis (3.51).

Athens and Sparta made peace in 421 and the Piraeus does not directly feature again in Thukydides' account of the Peloponnesian War until the launching of the Sicilian Expedition in June 415. His description of the feelings among the crowd which watched its departure on that ill-omened day is justly celebrated (6.30.2):

> The Athenians and any of their allies who happened to be in Athens at the time went down to the Piraeus at dawn on the day the expedition was due to set sail in order to launch their ships. Virtually everyone else in the city, including both residents and foreigners, went down there with them. Those of them who were native Athenians were giving their own people a send-off, whether friends, relatives or sons. They came with emotions of hope and sadness inextricably bound up, speculating upon the conquests which they expected to achieve, but reflecting, too, that there were those upon whom they would never set eyes again, bearing in mind that they were being dispatched on such a lengthy journey. At this instant, as they were on the point of separating from one another with risks on both sides, the dangers facing the expedition came home to them more than they had at the time when they had voted in favour of its dispatch. None the less their spirits revived both because of their naval strength and at the sight of the armaments which they possessed in such abundance.

Two years later the expedition ended in failure. The Athenians' first reaction was fear of an immediate Syracusan attack upon the Piraeus, now almost wholly bereft of ships (8.1.1-2). The expected invasion did not materialise, however, and in the course of the next winter the Athenians succeeded in building a new fleet. Following the Spartan occupation of Dekeleia which prevented the transportation of essential supplies of corn overland from Euboia via Oropos, the demes of Rhamnous, Sounion and Thorikos were fortified so that corn could be transported by sea instead. In order to combat Athens' financial crisis the annual tribute (*phoros*) exacted from her allies was now replaced by a 5 per cent tax (*eikostê*) on all goods transported by sea which passed through the harbours of the empire (7.28.4).

It is sometimes alleged that interstate trade was seriously disrupted during the Peloponnesian War. Thukydides (2.67.4), for instance, refers to the seizure and slaughter of some *emporoi* by the Spartans off the coast of the Peloponnese in 430, but there is nothing to suggest that this action formed part of a concerted drive against Athenian trade. Again, the scene in Aristophanes' *Acharnians* (819f.; 911-14), where a sycophant denounces a Megarian and a Boeotian for trading with Dikaiopolis, is often used to support the theory that the Athenians imposed a complete embargo on the import of foreign goods, but without justification. While trading between individual members of hostile states probably did decline during the Peloponnesian War, it is hard to imagine by what means foreign imports could have been banned altogether, nor, if they were, how that could advantage the state imposing the ban. Certainly the archaeological evidence for the study of trading contacts during the Peloponnesian War does not warrant the conclusion that economic links were severed.

The final incident involving the Piraeus recorded in Thukydides (8.90-94) occurred in 411, at the time of the oligarchic revolution which established the Council of Four Hundred. The initial success of this body in attaining political dominance was largely due to the absence of the Athenian fleet, which was stationed off Samos at the time. This upheaval coincided with a democratic revolt on Samos itself which deposed the ruling oligarchy. Upon the fleet declaring its independence from the Four Hundred and constituting itself into the democratic city of Athens, the extreme oligarchs began building a wall along the peninsula at Eetioneia to the north of the Grand Harbour (Fig. 27). The moderates, who were under the leadership of Theramenes, declared that the purpose of this fortification was 'not to keep out the fleet at Samos if it should try to enter by force' – evidently judged to be a reasonable and even laudable objective – 'but to let in the enemy with fleet and infantry, whenever they (i.e. the extremists) might wish'.

The wall on Eetioneia abutted onto 'the largest and nearest of the stoas', which was used as a storehouse for corn. The extremists, who were clearly prepared to starve the democrats into submission if they put up any armed resistance, sent envoys to Sparta in the hope of obtaining favourable peace terms. None were forthcoming, and in the wake of the assassination of the leading extremist Phrynichos, Theramenes felt sufficiently emboldened to attempt a coup. After the arrest of the moderate Alexikles by the hoplites building the fort of Eetioneia, Theramenes and his supporters set off for the Piraeus. There followed a news blackout characteristic of other crises in the port's history: those domiciled in the Asty thought that the extremists had already seized the Piraeus, while those resident in the Piraeus imagined that they were about to face a hoplite assault. On his arrival in the port, Theramenes was given a hero's welcome and succeeded in persuading the hoplites working on the wall to tear down what they had already built. A meeting of the ekklesia in Mounychia theatre was fixed for the next day, the choice of location being clearly determined by the political stability of the region. At the assembly it was resolved to march on the Asty and oppose the Four Hundred (Thuk. 8.93), thereby establishing the precedent that opposition to oligarchy could most effectively be mobilised from the Piraeus.

Later the same year Euboia revolted, a catastrophe which, according to Thukydides (8.96.1), produced among the Athenians 'the greatest panic so far ever experienced'. Their chief fear was that an attempt might be made to capture the Piraeus, since it was now bereft of naval cover. The Peloponnesians could easily have done this, comments Thukydides (8.96.4) in words which closely echo his judgement upon the failed attack on the port in 429, if only they had been more daring.

Not long after the revolt of Euboia, the Four Hundred were replaced by the Five Thousand, a government destined to prove transitional to the restoration of extreme democracy. Six years later, at the end of the summer of 405, the sacred trireme Paralos sailed into the Piraeus, bearing tidings of Athens' crushing defeat at Aigospotamoi. The news was relayed to the Asty by the keening of the bereaved which travelled the length of the Long Walls. That night, as Xenophon (*Hell.* 2.2.3) reports, no one slept for fear that their city would be destroyed. Next day an assembly was held which took the decision to block up two of the Piraeus' three harbours and to place the city in readiness for a siege. Shortly afterwards the Spartan navarch Lysandros, having completed the subjugation of the Athenian Empire in the Hellespont, sailed into the Piraeus with a fleet of 150 ships and sealed off its harbours to all merchant shipping. Bereft of ships, allies and food, the Athenians proposed peace on condition that they could retain 'the walls and the Piraeus' (Xen. *Hell.* 2.2.11). The offer was summarily dismissed, but the vital importance of the physical attachment of the Piraeus to the Asty and the determination of the Demos that the corridor connecting the two communities should remain intact is indicated by the passing of a decree, probably at the recommendation of Kleophon, outlawing any proposal recommending the destruction of the Long Walls (2.2.15).

(g) The men of the Piraeus versus the men of the Asty

The determination of the democrats notwithstanding, in March 404 Athens was forced to surrender on terms which included the loss of all but twelve triremes along with the destruction of the Long Walls and Piraeus circuit. Three to four weeks later, Lysandros entered the Piraeus and the work of demolition got under way. It was carried out to the accompaniment of the music of flute girls and amid scenes of wild enthusiasm in the mistaken belief on the part of Sparta's allies that 'this day signalled the beginning of freedom for Greece', as Xenophon (*Hell.* 2.2.23) sardonically remarked. By late summer or perhaps early autumn the walls had been destroyed.

Sparta's intention in physically dividing the Asty from the Piraeus was to deracinate the source of Athens' military might. But the political consequences of the separation were no less significant than the military ones. The demise of the fleet and the hoped-for decay of the Piraeus signalled in effect an attempt on Sparta's part to roll back the tide of political progress. When the oligarchy of the Thirty assumed the reins of government in the late summer of 404, a number of their measures were aimed directly at the Piraeus, not only because it was the heartland of radical democracy, but also because it symbolised the exact antithesis of the oligarchic value-system which both they and the Spartans espoused, and had served in the ninety-odd years of its existence as a forcing-house of social and political change. Significantly, too, Xenophon (*Mem.* 2.7.2) speaks of a mass migration to the Piraeus on the part of Athenian citizens consequent upon the revolution of 404: it may well have been the belief of those who took to their heels that in the Piraeus they would be out of harm's way.

The Thirty put the Piraeus under the authority of the Ten who were parallel in authority and equal in importance to the Eleven in the Asty. The Piraeus Ten included Charmides son of Glaukon, a participant in a number of Platonic dialogues, and an otherwise unknown Molpis. According to Plato's *Seventh Letter* (324c), it was the duty of the Ten and the Eleven 'to administer the Agora and all other matters pertaining to their respective poleis'. Their powers of enforcement, if not unlimited, were evidently extensive, for neither group was included in the amnesty announced by the restored democracy in 403.

Under the Thirty the assembly auditorium on the Pnyx was altered. The second assembly place differed from its predecessor in one important particular: whereas the first took advantage of the natural slope of the hillside and faced northeast overlooking the Agora, the new one was reversed so that the auditorium faced uphill (Fig. 8). According to Plutarch (*Them.* 19.4), the reason for this reversal of orientation was purely symbolic. He writes: 'The

Fig. 8.   Models of the Pnyx before and after the remodelling by the Thirty Tyrants, from the northwest. *above* Period I, *c.* 450. *below* Period II, *c.* 400.

speaker's platform (*bêma*) on the Pnyx, which had originally been constructed to look across the sea, was turned by the Thirty towards the land, in the belief that the naval empire was the origin of democracy and that farmers had fewer objections to oligarchy.' Until recently, most scholars rejected Plutarch's explanation as pure invention, convinced that the real motive for the reversal was the practical one of providing ekklesiasts with shelter from the wind that swept over the exposed hillside. Recent examinations of the problem have tended to be less dismissive, largely on the grounds that such symbolism accords well with the tenor of the oligarchs' overall programme of social reform. In view of the fact that the Pnyx affords a very poor view of the sea, however, it seems highly improbable that the Thirty would have wasted so much labour and expense on a project that could only marginally assist in asserting a new dominant ideology, if that were their sole or primary aim.

Although at least 1,500 deaths took place during the rule of the Thirty, the oligarchs were not perpetrators of mindless violence. Their intention was not primarily to capture the constitution, but rather to overhaul the social system. Accordingly, they drew up a register of 3,000 citizens whom they invited to share in the government and expelled 5,000 of the remainder from the Asty. These social rejects were compelled to seek refuge in the Piraeus, by which action the Thirty signalled their intention to downgrade the political status of the harbour town. Other measures with far-reaching implications for the Piraeus community included the arrest and execution of at least ten wealthy metics; the revoking of several grants of *proxenia*, an action which deprived the foreign communities concerned of recourse to legal redress against injury; and finally, as a visible demonstration of their outright hostility to everyone and everything connected with the sea, the demolition of the dockyards. Considered to be one of the chief architectural legacies of the Periklean era, the latter had been constructed at a cost of 1,000 talents and were now auctioned as scrap for a mere three talents.

Resistance to the Thirty was led by Thrasyboulos who in March 403 left his encampment at Phyle and descended to the Piraeus where he succeeded in seizing Mounychia. Having previously been fortified by Hippias, the hill probably still retained some of its ancient walling. A tradition that the exiles received divine assistance in the course of their historic march from Phyle to Mounychia (a distance of some 22 km) is preserved in a legend reported by

Clement of Alexandria (*Strom.* 1.24.162) which underlines not only
the importance of the undertaking but also the dangers involved:

> When Thrasyboulos was leading the exiles from Phyle he was eager
> not to be discovered. A column (*stulos*) acted as their guide enabling
> them to avoid the main roads. Thrasyboulos made the march by night
> in bad weather but a fire appeared before them and guided them
> safely as far as Mounychia where it left them at the place where today
> is the altar of Phosphoros.

In response to Thrasyboulos' initiative, the Thirty and their
supporters mustered in the Hippodamian Agora before forming into
battleline 'not less than fifty shields deep' on the road leading to the
temple of Mounychian Artemis and the Bendideion' (Xen. *Hell.*
2.4.11), and then began their assault on the enemy position. In the
battle which took place on the southwest slope of Mounychia the
democrats, having the advantage of higher ground, easily succeeded
in defeating their opponents. The former now constituted 'a large
and heterogeneous body' (Xen. *Hell.* 2.4.25) which controlled not
only the harbour town but also the surrounding countryside. This
they ravaged for wood and provisions, since no commercial shipping
could safely enter the port.

Thus for some six months, from about April to September in 403,
the Athenians had two political centres, one in the Asty and the
other in the Piraeus, both claiming to be the legitimate
policy-making body of the Athenian state. The separate political
identity of the Piraeus at this period is indicated both in Xenophon
and Lysias by the formulation 'the men of the Piraeus (*hoi en
Peiraiei*)' which is used in distinction and opposition to 'the men of
the Asty (*hoi en tôi astei*)', who remained subject to the edicts of the
Thirty and the Ten.

After an indecisive battle fought in the region of Halipedon Marsh
in which the Thirty were assisted by the Spartans, the two sides
agreed to negotiate and representatives of the men of the Piraeus,
accompanied by others appointed by the men of the Asty, journeyed
to Sparta to discuss terms. As a result a general amnesty was
announced for all with the exception of the Thirty, the Asty Eleven
and the Piraeus Ten, though even these were to be pardoned if they
submitted to the due processes of law and were acquitted of the
charges laid against them. In the case of the Piraeus Ten, the
examination (*euthunê*) was to take place before the men in the
Piraeus, a *de facto* recognition of their autonomy and separate
identity. It is not known whether any availed themselves of this offer.

Two years later in 401/0 a final reconciliation was achieved and the democrats staged a triumphal entry into Athens under arms, which culminated in a sacrifice to Athene performed on the Acropolis (Xen. *Hell.* 2.4.39). This highly charged and no doubt deeply moving public spectacle not only symbolised the restoration of unity throughout Attike, but also gave recognition to the part played in it by the men of the Piraeus who hereby served notice that their separate identity now ceased.

(h) The fourth-century revival

Shortly after the re-integration of the Piraeus into the Athenian state, Thrasyboulos put forward a proposal to grant Athenian citizenship 'to all those (sc. metics) who had joined in the return from the Piraeus'. This proposal, which was consistent with a pledge made by the democrats after the battle of Mounychia (Xen. *Hell.* 2.4.25), was thwarted by Archinos, leader of the moderate democrats, who invalidated it on the grounds of procedural irregularity (Ps.-Arist. *AP* 40.2; cf. Plu. *Mor.* 835f-836a). Probably in 401/0, however, a decree was passed bestowing honours, including perhaps in some cases full citizenship, on approximately 1,000 non-Athenians in recognition of their outstanding contribution to the war of liberation. As a further indication of the esteem in which foreigners were held by the restored democracy, it was declared that all *xenoi* who had given their lives in the war against the Thirty should receive a public funeral 'and be granted in perpetuity the same honours as those belonging to citizens'. This gesture probably did much, as it was no doubt intended to do, both to restore Athens' reputation for *philoxenia*, and to encourage metics to re-settle in the Piraeus.

The Middle Comedy poet Philiskos, in an obvious allusion to the loss of Athens' fleet, described the Piraeus in *c.* 399 as 'a big nut with no kernel' (*FAC* II, p.11 fr. 2). It is abundantly clear that Athenian recovery in the decade after the Peloponnesian War went hand in hand with a determination to restore the Piraeus to its fifth-century glory and importance, a practical and essential aspiration in view of the fact that Athenian supremacy was once again to be based on the sea. Palpable proof of this determination is provided by the fact that the first major building project to be undertaken after the war was the reconstruction of the Piraeus circuit and Long Walls (Fig. 9). The reconstruction, largely subsidised by a Persian grant, was

Fig. 9. *above, below and opposite* Remains of fourth-century fortifications on Akte peninsula attributed to Konon.

begun in 394 a few weeks before Konon's naval victory over the
Spartans off Knidos. It was completed in 391 with assistance from
the crews of his eighty triremes who served as labourers. A number
of states who were friendly to Athens assisted in the project, in
particular the Thebans – 'those very Thebans who in 404 had
clamoured for the utter destruction of the city', as Tod (*GHI* II p.23)
wryly observes – who made available the services of 500 craftsmen
(Xen. *Hell.* 4.8.10). In celebration of his victory, Konon either
constructed a shrine to Aphrodite in the Piraeus or else expanded an
already existing one which had been dedicated after the battle of
Salamis. It may have been soon after the battle that Themistokles'
political reputation underwent rehabilitation, in consequence of
which he was honoured with an imposing tomb on Akte peninsula
(Fig. 26).

Probably in the same year that the fortification circuit was
repaired Athens passed a decree to re-build her navy, having till
then possessed only the twelve triremes that she was allowed to keep
by the terms of her surrender in 404. Thrasyboulos, who was sent
out as commander of the new fleet perhaps later the same year, was
initially successful in re-establishing domination over the Propontis.
Since Athens was now no longer in receipt of financial assistance
from Persia, however, he was forced to introduce measures aimed at
increasing her revenue, including a 5 per cent tax (*eikostê*) on
merchandise passing through the Bosporos, similar to the toll which
had been levied in 413 (above p. 30). The violence of Thrasyboulos'
methods of collection cost him his life. Worse was to follow. In 387,
with the assistance of Syracusan as well as Persian auxiliaries, the
Spartan fleet was able to blockade the Athenians in the Hellespont
and thus prevent corn from being shipped to the Piraeus (Xen. *Hell.*
5.1.28).

It was in this same year that the Spartan navarch Teleutias,
commander of a small fleet based on Aegina, launched one of the
most daring raids ever made on the Piraeus. Calculating on taking
the Athenians completely off guard, he sailed into the Grand
Harbour at daybreak with twelve triremes and succeeded in
capturing a number of merchant ships lying at berth on the east side
of the harbour. With apparently no other object in mind than to
create a scare, some of his men jumped ashore at the Deigma where
merchandise was displayed and abducted a number of traders either
too stupefied or too stupid to run away. What followed, as reported
by Xenophon (*Hell.* 5.1.22), reads more like a French farce than

Greek history: 'Those Athenians who were inside their homes at the time ran out to discover what all the shouting was about, whereas those who were outside ran in to their homes to fetch their armour, while others still ran to the city to spread the news.' Eventually a detachment of Athenian cavalry, assisted by hoplites, came to the rescue, in the mistaken belief that the Piraeus was under hostile occupation. By the time these reinforcements had arrived, however, Teleutias had made his getaway to Aegina, taking several captured cargo vessels with him. Though the raid had no direct military consequences, it is probable that the Athenians now again converted the Piraeus into a closed port as they had done previously in 429/8.

Teleutias' raid may well have been intended primarily to undermine Athenian morale by demonstrating the ease with which a Spartan navy could penetrate Athens' defences, but it will also have had the practical consequence of discouraging foreign traders from bringing their wares to the Piraeus. Faced with the prospect of no longer being able to guarantee her essential supplies, Athens agreed to make peace with Sparta in 387/6. Her allies, Thebes excepted, were forced to concur. The terms were dictated by the Persian king, who now claimed sovereignty over the Greek states in Asia Minor, while permitting Athens to retain Lemnos, Imbros and Skyros.

It may also have been a condition of the King's Peace that the Piraeus should henceforth remain without gates. This would explain Xenophon's observation (*Hell.* 5.4.20) that when Sphodrias, the Spartan harmost of Thespiai in Boeotia, set out to attack the Piraeus early in 378, the town was at the time ungated. Sphodrias' raid, if such it deserves to be called, was a very lacklustre affair compared with the spirit and dash of Teleutias' adventure. Xenophon alleges that it was instigated by the Thebans in the hope of driving a wedge between Sparta and Athens, but Diodoros Siculus (15.29.5-6), whose account is more plausible, asserts that the harmost was acting under orders from the Spartan king Kleombrotos. Sphodrias and his band set out at night from Thespiai, intending to make a pre-dawn raid from the land side. Having only covered half the distance to the coast by sunrise, however, they had to content themselves with cattle-rustling in the vicinity of the Thriasian plain.

This unprovoked aggression had a profound effect upon Athenian policy. Not only did the Athenians now provide the Piraeus with gates, but they also began expanding their fleet and forming closer links with the Thebans (Xen. *Hell.* 5.4.34). A further consequence may have been the establishment of permanent garrisons,

watchtowers and relay stations especially in the northwest region of
Attike, an indication of the high priority now placed on frontier
defence. Henceforth, Athens' defence strategy was to be of the mixed
variety, combining frontier protection with a formidable naval
capability.

Shortly before the raid of Sphodrias, the Second Athenian
Confederacy had been formed. It was almost certainly Spartan
nervousness at the prospect of a revitalised Athens which was in fact
the dominant motive behind the failed raid. The charter was
promulgated in 378/7 and it was decidedly anti-Spartan in tone.
Soon numbers had swelled to seventy, of which the most important
was Thebes. To the following year dates the earliest surviving naval
inventory, which lists 106 triremes in the dockyards of the Piraeus.
Over the next twenty-five years the rate of shipbuilding increased
dramatically, so that by 353/2 the total stood at 349.

The house of the Athenian admiral Timotheos which overlooked
the Hippodamian Agora was the scene of a memorable incident in
373. Corcyra, which was being besieged by the Spartan fleet, had
sent an urgent request to Athens for assistance (Xen. *Hell.* 6.2.5-14;
D.S. 15.46-7). Timotheos was appointed commander of a task force,
though without adequate crews to equip it. So he sailed up into the
north Aegean in the hope of recruiting mercenaries from Thrace.
His tardiness cost him his commission and on his return he was put
on trial. As proof of his outstanding service to the state, Timotheos
called as witnesses the Epirot king Alketos and the Thessalian
despot Jason of Pherai, whose membership of the Confederacy had
been due to his diplomatic initiatives (D.S. 15.36.5; *GHI* II 123.111).
The story is told that when these two potentates arrived one evening
at Timotheos' Piraeus residence, he was obliged to send out for
bedding, cloaks and two silver bowls in order to entertain his royal
guests in style (Ps.-Dem. 49.22).

In June 371, anxious at the growing power of Thebes, Athens and
her Confederacy made peace with Sparta. A month later Sparta was
crushingly defeated by Thebes at Leuktra. Military operations over
the next nine years were largely confined to the mainland until
Theban supremacy came to an end at the battle of Mantinea in 362.
The next five years were particularly troublesome ones for Athens.
Following an attack on Athens' ally Peparethos in 361, Alexander of
Pherai made a raid on the Piraeus in what appears to have been an
exact re-run of Teleutias' daring escapade. Sailing straight for the
Deigma, his men disembarked on the quay, grabbed the money on

the bankers' tables, and then departed as rapidly as they had come. As before, the Athenians were taken completely off guard. They apparently had no forces stationed in the Piraeus and lacked any adequate signalling system, for a hasty message had to be dispatched to the strategoi in the Asty requesting urgent assistance (Polyain. *Strateg.* 6.2.2). The blame for this lapse in security was subsequently put on those trierarchs who had sold their trierarchic obligations (Dem. 51.8). Then in 360 Sestos, 'the breadboard of the Piraeus' (Arist. *Rhet.* 3.10 1411 a 14-15) was lost to the Thracian king Kotys, while two other allies, Pydna and Methone, ominously fell victim to Philip of Macedon.

In 357 Athens recovered control of the Chersonese along with the island of Euboia. The same year saw the outbreak of the Social War, precipitated by the revolt of Chios, Rhodes and Kos. When it ended in 354 all that remained in Athens' possession was, in Aischines' memorable phrase (2.71) 'a few wretched islanders', from whom a mere 60 talents were exacted annually in tribute. The Athenian state was in effect bankrupt, her entire revenue comprising only 130 talents (Dem. 10.37). A revealing indication of the level of anxiety regarding the state of Athens' finances at this time is provided by Xenophon's *Poroi* (3.13) which contains recommendations for the improvement of trading facilities in the Piraeus based on the observation that a substantial proportion of the metic population had left Athens. Possibly this document served as the inspiration for some of the financial measures soon to be implemented by Euboulos who in 354 was put in charge of Athens' finances. It was certainly due to Euboulos' initiative that a high priority was now placed on the re-building of the Piraeus shipsheds as well as on the construction of a monumental naval arsenal in Zea Port. There is also slight evidence to suggest that Euboulos may have been responsible for refurbishing the commercial quarter of the Piraeus. At the same time steps were taken to expedite the procedure adopted in lawsuits involving traders (*dikai emporikai*), and a new type of maritime loan was introduced.

The entry of Philip II into mainstream Greek affairs is marked by his capture of Amphipolis in the autumn or winter of 357, an event critically timed to coincide with Athens' involvement in the Social War. His use of siege machinery to breach a section of the enceinte wall heralds the beginning of a new era in the history of Greek warfare in which elaborate fortification systems such as those linking the Asty to the Piraeus were to be rendered increasingly obsolete. A further sign of the times was the ineffectiveness of Athens' navy, now totalling 300 ships, which Philip largely neutralised by confining his campaigning to the winter months. His capacity for lateral thinking is further revealed by the fact that in the autumn or winter of 346 he allegedly suborned a disenfranchised Athenian called Antiphon to set fire to the Piraeus dockyards (Dem. 18.132-3). On Demosthenes' initiative, Antiphon was arrested in the Piraeus, and after acquittal before the ekklesia was subsequently re-arrested and condemned to death by the Areopagus.

In the spring of 338 Philip descended into Greece in answer to an appeal from the Amphiktyonic League. Athens' defeat at Chaironeia later the same year marked the culmination of twenty-five years military build-up and diplomatic manoeuvring by Philip during which Athens had been constantly outflanked and outclassed, not least due to the rigidity of her political and military thinking. Fearing an immediate invasion the Athenians abandoned the countryside in preparation for a final effort to defend the Asty and the Piraeus. It was probably at this time that a defensive ditch was dug around the outer perimeter of the Piraeus circuit in preparation for the expected final assault (cf. Ps.-Plu. *Mor.* 851a; cf. 847d). A minor incident involving the Piraeus which sheds an illuminating light upon the plight of the Athenians in these dark days is preserved in a speech by Lykourgos (*c. Leok.* 17-18). In order to forestall a general exodus in the wake of Philip's advance, the Athenians passed a decree forbidding anyone to leave Attic territory. A certain Leokrates, however, succeeded in slipping out of the Piraeus via one of the postern gates and setting sail in a fishing boat for Rhodes. This he did, the plaintiff remarks in a phrase calculated to stir the deepest passions in the jury, 'untouched by pity for the city's harbours ... and within view of the temple of Zeus Soter and Athene Soteira'. Belated recognition of the impossibility of defending both the Asty and the Piraeus is implicit in a proposal now put forward by Hypereides to grant citizenship to metics and slaves 'and convey sacred objects (*hiera*) along with women and children to the Piraeus for safekeeping.' The decree was passed but subsequently indicted as illegal. Though Hypereides himself was acquitted, it was never put into effect since peace was concluded shortly afterwards.

Even after Chaironeia Athens continued to strengthen her naval arm. The man most responsible for the city's remarkable recovery after her humbling defeat was Lykourgos who had been appointed minister of finance (*ho epi tēn diokēsin*) a few weeks before the battle took place. In addition to building triremes, he brought to completion the construction of the naval arsenal and the shipsheds, and carried out repairs on the Piraeus' defences. Probably partly in order to ensure that Athens had a steady supply of grain at a time when Greece was facing a famine, Lykourgos encouraged the settlement of Egyptian and Cypriot merchants in the Piraeus by proposing that they should be allowed to establish shrines to their native gods.

The revival of the Piraeus from the mid-fourth century onwards was merely one aspect of Athens' general economic recovery in this period. It was, however, very limited in scope and at no time did Athens become more than the ghost, financially speaking, of her former Periklean self. The fact that the refurbishment of the port was one of the principal sources of state expenditure merely indicates how dramatically priorities had changed since the fifth century. The last surviving naval list, dating to the time of the Lamian War when Athens in alliance with other Greek states made a forlorn bid to shake off the Macedonian yoke after the death of Alexander, records the existence of over 400 ships in her shipyards. In 322, however, the Macedonian admiral Kleitos inflicted two severe defeats upon the Athenian navy, first at Abydos in the Hellespont and later that same year off the island of Amorgos in the Sporades. Henceforth the Aegean was Macedonian. The heroic days of the Piraeus had come to an end.

(i) The Macedonian garrison

The year 322 marks the beginning of a period of Athenian history in which the Piraeus played a pre-eminent role both as a centre for Macedonian domination and as a rousing yet painful reminder of former glory for the nationalist resistance. Since the port's foundation over 150 years before the whole structure of Athenian society, her domestic and foreign policy, her military security and economic viability, had depended crucially upon the Piraeus. Now that Athens' naval might had been destroyed, she no longer had the means to safeguard her vital supply route. Hence virtually overnight she found herself at the mercy of whichever power could guarantee or withhold the import of her essential supplies. For almost a century that power was to be Macedon, who found it both militarily convenient and politically expedient to control Athens not by outright occupation but by installing a garrison on Mounychia Hill

Fig. 10. Mounychia Hill from Mounychia Port. On the right are remains of
the ancient (eastern) sea wall or *chêlê*.

(Fig. 10). According to Plutarch (*Solon* 12.6) a powerful prevision of
the strategic potential of Mounychia for Athens' conquerors was
accorded to Epimenides of Crete, a contemporary of Solon and one
of the seven sages of the ancient world. Foreseeing the fateful role
that the hill was to play in later Athenian history, he commented to
some bystanders on his visit to Athens: 'If the Athenians only knew
with what pains Mounychia would afflict them, they would devour it
with their own teeth.' The observation is not the less pertinent for
being apocryphal.

As a result partly of the Macedonian occupation and partly of new
trading patterns consequent upon the conquests of Alexander the
Great, the Piraeus now rapidly lost its position as trading capital of
the eastern Mediterranean. Her population dwindled accordingly,
as is indicated by a sharp decrease in the number of metic
gravestones found in the region (Table 1, pp. 64-5). A further
development of enormous significance was the fact that the Piraeus
now became increasingly detached from the Asty, not least by
reason of the deteriorating condition of the Long Walls, always the
symbolic and actual link between the two communities. On a
number of occasions during the Macedonian period the Asty and the
Piraeus were completely cut off from one another, notably in

319-317, *c.* 295-294 and *c.* 287- *c.* 261. Though nothing is known about the administration of the harbour town during these periods of severance, it may be safely inferred that an autonomous legislature and judiciary of necessity evolved (see below p. 83). This tendency to decentralisation was by no means confined to the Piraeus, though it was here that the social and economic consequences of devolution would have been most keenly felt. Eleusis on three occasions during the Macedonian era issued its own coinage and the so-called Marathonian Tetrapolis, which comprised the demes of Marathon, Trikorynthos, Oinoe and Sypalletos, now for the first time legislated as a corporate group.

By the terms of her surrender at the end of the Lamian War, Athens had to put her navy at the disposal of Antipatros, who became regent of Macedonia on the death of Alexander the Great. In addition, she agreed to replace her democracy by an oligarchy, limiting the franchise to those with property worth 2,000 drachmas or more. Despite strong protests from Phokion, the leader of the embassy which concluded peace terms with Antipatros, a Macedonian garrison under the *phrourarchos* Menyllos was installed on Mounychia in order to ensure that the disenfranchised accepted loss of citizenship. In Plutarch's words (*Phok.* 28.1), this move was 'regarded as a display of insolence (*exousia*) intended to humiliate the Athenians, rather than as an occupation of a strong point brought about by force of circumstances.' Apart from a few brief periods of intermission, the Macedonian garrison was to remain for nearly a century, being finally bribed to depart in 229.

Information about the Piraeus throughout this long stretch of time is largely confined to the tactical and strategic role which it played in Athenian military history. The presence of the foreign garrison, as Gauthier (1979, 355) has demonstrated, did not in itself interfere with the regular bilateral exchanges which took place between the Asty and the port. Except during those periods when the two communities were under separate governments, citizens resident in the Piraeus were debarred neither from exercising their political rights in meetings of the ekklesia held on the Pnyx, nor from participating in the numerous religious festivals that were staged in the Asty. However much its economic prosperity declined overall during this period, the Piraeus continued to function as a centre for shipbuilding, even though its products now served the needs of the Macedonian fleet. Plutarch (*Demetr.* 43.3), for instance, states that in the time of Demetrios Poliorketes the Piraeus participated, along with Corinth, Chalkis and Pella, in the construction of a fleet of 500 ships.

Immediately after Antipatros' death in 319, Polyperchon, whom the former had appointed to succeed him as regent in preference to his own son Kassandros, announced that he intended to restore democracy in Athens. Nikanor, who had replaced Menyllos as *phrourarchos* of Mounychia, called a meeting of the boule in the Piraeus, hoping to win popular support for the occupation. He failed to do so, and narrowly escaped with his life. Realising that he could only keep control by force, Nikanor made a sudden sortie and seized the Piraeus fortifications and harbour walls. Not only had the Athenians failed to recover Mounychia, as Diodoros (18.64.4) observes, but they now lost the Piraeus as well. Thus for the second time in Athenian history the unity of the Asty and the harbour town was breached, and the Piraeus passed wholly under the control of the Macedonian garrison.

Shortly afterwards, Polyperchon's son Alexander arrived in Attike at the head of an army and pitched his camp in the neighbourhood of the Piraeus (D.S.18.65.5). The Athenians perceived Polyperchon as a liberator, but his real intention was to secure the garrison for his own use in the belief that it 'could be extremely useful to him in regard to the needs of war' (D.S.18.68.2). Lack of adequate supplies prevented him from taking Mounychia, however, and eventually his forces withdrew.

Kassandros now set about subjugating the whole of Attike by seizing the Long Walls, Salamis and the fort of Panakton (Paus. 1.25.6). When peace was concluded in the spring of 317, he installed Demetrios of Phaleron as overseer, backed up by the garrison which was now under the command of its third *phrourarchos* Dionysios. Demetrios, who ruled Athens for ten years, reunited the Piraeus to Athens and limited the franchise to those whose property amounted to at least ten minai.

In June 307 Antigonos Monophthalmos, former satrap of Phrygia and aspirant to the whole of Alexander's empire, sent an expedition of 250 ships under the command of his son Demetrios Poliorketes with instructions to liberate Athens. When his fleet arrived within sight of the Piraeus, it was mistaken for that of Athens' Egyptian ally Ptolemy and permitted to enter unmolested. Hearing that it was his intention to expel the garrison and restore democracy, however, the Athenians threw down their weapons and hailed Poliorketes as their saviour. Demetrios of Phaleron capitulated and was granted safe conduct to Thebes. Kassandros' *phrourarchos* Dionysios defiantly held out on Mounychia for about three months until being forced to capitulate. Consistent with his pledge to liberate Athens, Demetrios now razed the Mounychian fortress to the ground and restored the democratic constitution (D.S. 20.45; cf. Plu. *Demetr*.10.1). In addition, he undertook to ensure that the city would receive 15,000 *medimnoi* of corn along with sufficient timber to build 100 ships, evocative proof that Athenian priorities and aspirations had in no way changed since her defeat in the Lamian War. Alert to the sensibilities of the Athenian people, Demetrios assiduously nurtured the belief that they might once again be a power to be reckoned with. Extensive repair work was now carried out on the circuits of the Piraeus and the Asty and, more significantly, on the Long Walls.

How Demetrios Poliorketes imposed his will on Athens during his frequent and extended periods of absence is not known, owing to an almost complete absence of documentary evidence concerning the institutions of Athenian government during his ascendancy. Such evidence as exists, however, tends towards the conclusion that 'there was no far-reaching change in the basic democratic forms of government' (Shear 1978, 55). Athens' military resistance to Kassandros, who sought repeatedly to regain control of Attike, was spearheaded by the strategos Olympiodoros who in *c.* 305 may possibly have repulsed a Macedonian attempt to recover the Piraeus. Then in *c.* 296 civil disturbance broke out among Athens' strategoi which led to the establishment of a tyranny under a leader of the mercenary soldiers called Lachares, branded by Pausanias (1.25.7) as 'the most brutal towards mankind and the most impious in the eyes of the gods'. Some troops from the Piraeus responded by seizing the Acropolis. On being ejected from their stronghold by Lachares, the Peiraikoi, as these freedom-fighters are designated, retired to the Piraeus, and, in circumstances which recall the events of 404-3, established a government which saw itself as representing the legitimate political aspirations of the Athenian people. Those who died trying unsuccessfully to overthrow the tyranny were accorded state burial in the Demosion Sema, in recognition of their devotion to the cause of liberty (Paus. 1.29.10).

Demetrios Poliorketes returned either in the spring of 295 or 294 and began to lay siege to the Asty in order to eject Lachares. According to Polyainos (*Strateg.* 4.7.5), he won the support of the inhabitants of the Piraeus by appealing to their democratic sentiments and claiming that he and they had a common enemy in

Lachares. Deprived of access to all its ports, the Asty soon faced utter starvation. By the terms of their surrender in 294, the Athenians accepted back a Macedonian garrison on Mounychia. Another was installed on the Mouseion, the hill near the Acropolis. Once again Demetrios presented the city with a large gift of grain. This time, however, he established what was in effect an oligarchy. The naked reality was that he had become the occupying power.

The chronology of the next few years is extremely difficult to follow. Probably in the early summer of 287 or less likely 286, after Demetrios had lost control of Macedonia, Olympiodoros was appointed to lead an attack against the garrison on the Mouseion. Demetrios, who was campaigning in the Peloponnese at the time, immediately moved north to blockade the Asty, while the garrison in the Piraeus began laying waste the countryside in order to starve it into submission. Shortly after the siege had begun, however, as the famous decree in honour of Kallias of Sphettos (270/69) reveals, Demetrios was persuaded, thanks to the timely intervention of Ptolemy I of Egypt, to hold peace negotiations with the revolutionaries in the Piraeus. As a result, he agreed to relinquish his control over the Asty, which now reverted to being a democracy. The Piraeus, however, remained in his hands. As a consequence, Athens was now deprived of access to the Emporion and had to rely on other Attic ports for the import of her essential foodstuffs. It would hardly have been surprising if a number of the inhabitants of the Piraeus now chose to abandon their homes, preferring instead a life of freedom in the Asty. Those who remained presumably formed themselves into a separate but subjugated polity, retaining an oligarchic constitution under the supervision of the *phrourarchos*.

The situation which now prevailed was very different from the one which had existed in 322. Then the Piraeus and the Asty had been a united political entity, now they were separate, and the inhabitants of the Piraeus were of necessity compelled to acknowledge their shared predicament with the Macedonian garrison. Both were cut off from communications with the rest of Attike and both were wholly dependent upon essential supplies arriving by sea. Self-evidently, citizens resident in the Piraeus could no longer attend meetings of the Athenian Assembly, become elected to the boule or hold any office of state. A no less devastating and traumatic consequence of partition was the fact that the two populations could no longer engage in joint worship of their shared deities (below p. 122).

Given the military and economic importance of the Piraeus coupled with its emotive value as a potent symbol of democracy, it is hardly surprising that a number of Athenian decrees dating to the period 286-81 regularly incorporate phrases which reveal that the very highest priority was set upon its recovery. This desire for reunification culminated in an abortive attempt to liberate the harbour town. The tactics employed were exactly the same as had earlier been adopted to storm the fortress on the Mouseion. A secret approach was made by two strategoi to Hierokles, leader of the mercenary division of the garrison, who agreed to open the gates at a pre-arranged time. Unlike the faithless Strombichos, however, Hierokles revealed the plot to his commanding officer, Herakleides, so that when the storming party had been duly admitted to the fortress, it found itself ambushed. Like the thirteen who lost their lives during the storming of the Mouseion, the 420 Athenian hoplites who now perished were accorded state burial in the Demosion Sema (Paus. 1.29.7; cf.1.29.10).

One of the most serious gaps in our knowledge of third-century Athenian history is that we do not know for certain whether the garrison on Mounychia was eventually expelled in the 280s. Recent investigations of the question have failed to produce any consensus. Shear (1978), on the one hand, believes that after the débacle described above the Athenian Demos launched a subsequent, successful attack in the spring of 280, once again under the command of Olympiodoros. Gauthier (1979), on the other, has proposed that the Piraeus was recovered in 281 by bribery. A third view, that the garrison remained at Mounychia uninterruptedly from 287 until the Chremonidean War and beyond is held by both Osborne (1979, 193) and Habicht (1979, 101). It is this last theory which carries most weight, not least in view of the fact that Hierokles, the *phrourarchos* at the time of the failed raid on the Piraeus, still held that post in the 270s, an unlikely occurrence, as Ferguson (1911, 152 n.4) long ago pointed out, had he been ousted by the Athenians in the 280s.

The probability that the Piraeus remained in Macedonian hands throughout this period is further suggested by the course of the Chremonidean War, so named after the Athenian statesman Chremonides who passed a decree in the archonship of Peithidemos (probably 268/7) recording an alliance between Athens, Sparta and Ptolemy II of Egypt, the stated object of which was to free Greece from Macedonian tyranny. The fact that Patroklos, commander of the Egyptian fleet, chose to operate from a number of different ports around the coast of Attike, including the island which bears his name near Sounion, strongly suggests that the Piraeus was not available to him as a base for naval operations. The coalition proved ineffective, possibly because the Egyptian fleet was unable to mount a land attack against Antigonos Gonatas' military placements. Athens' surrender in *c.* 261 effectively marks the end of half a century of repeated attempts to recover her independence.

Given the immense symbolic as well as strategic importance of the Piraeus, Tarn's hypothesis (1934, 37) that Athens' primary objective in the war was the recovery of the Piraeus fits neatly into the framework of her aims from 322 onwards. The failure to achieve this objective, coupled with the acceptance by her of loss of independence consequent upon her final defeat in *c.* 261, are both indicated in the fact that *Atthides*, local chronicles of Athens with distinctly political overtones, now cease, the latest in the series being that of Philochoros, whose *Atthis* extended to the end of the war, or perhaps just slightly beyond.

By the end of the war Macedonian garrisons had been set up all over Attike – on the Mouseion, in Mounychia and the Piraeus, on Salamis, at Sounion and in the frontier garrisons at Panakton and Phyle. The period from *c.* 261-229 was a humiliating one for Athens. She had to wait thirty years before gaining her liberty which was ultimately achieved thanks to the intervention of Aratos, strategos of the Achaean League, who sought her support in his war against Macedon. Realising that this depended upon the expulsion of the Macedonian garrison from the Piraeus, Aratos made repeated assaults upon the port, notably in 240, 'like a lover with a broken heart, not desisting despite many failures, and taking courage from the fact that he always came within an ace of success' (Plu. *Arat.* 33.4). With the co-operation of Eurykleides of Kephisia, the leading Athenian statesman of the day, he eventually succeeded in bribing the *phrourarchos* Diogenes to give up all the Attic forts for the sum of 150 talents, 20 of which he contributed himself (Plu. *Arat.* 34.4; Paus. 2.8.6). By the summer of 228 Athens was at last free, and as a mark of their gratitude her citizens established a cult in honour of Diogenes, bestowed on him the title Euergetes, instituted a festival in his honour, and built a gymnasium for ephebes which was named the Diogeneion. He was to be venerated as a hero for centuries to come. Aratos' high hopes that Athens would now join the Achaean League were not to be realised, however. Under cautious leadership she determined henceforth to pursue a policy of absolute neutrality (Pol. 5.106).

(j) The Roman domination

From 228 onwards direct evidence for the condition of the Piraeus becomes increasingly difficult to obtain as Athens ceases to play any significant or independent part in Greek history. Athenian history of the second century is presented as something of a sideshow in the surviving historical records, occasionally rescued from oblivion when the state becomes caught up in the swell of events over which it exercises no control. Any statement about the condition of the Piraeus will therefore tend to be crude to the point of fatuity. Though its ports continued to function, the century and a half down to the sack of Sulla in 86 may be said to have been characterised overall by an increased attachment to the hinterland, to the detriment of her attachment to the sea.

Archaeology can tell us little about the economic condition of the port in 228. Following the departure of the Macedonian garrison, major repairs were carried out to the circuit walls of both the Asty and the Piraeus under the direction of Eurykleides and Mikion. Particular attention was probably paid to the strengthening of the seaboard defences, since Athens now possessed only a handful of triremes. Significantly the Long Walls were not included in this refurbishment, either because they were no longer regarded as integral to Athens' defences, or because she lacked the manpower adequate to defend them. With the decay of the Long Walls, the unity of the two communities was finally breached. Henceforth they existed as disconnected urban entities, a development marked in the epigraphic record by the fact that each is now described as a polis, a designation not previously accorded to the Piraeus.

The period from 228 to the end of the third century was a relatively prosperous and uneventful one for Athens. She enjoyed the protection of Ptolemy III Euergetes who became the eponymous hero of a new tribe Ptolemais in 224/3, and at the same time remained scrupulous in avoiding antagonising the Macedonian king, Antigonos Doson. During the Social War (220-217), fought between Philip V of Macedon and the Achaean League against her allies Elis and Sparta, Athens remained strictly neutral, while taking the precaution of maintaining a strong frontier guard to protect her boundaries against incursion. Likewise in the First Macedonian

War (211-205), when Rome in alliance with Aetolia fought against Macedon, Athens took no part.

Athens' close alliance with Rome dates to the year 200 when the Second Macedonian War broke out. Livy (31.22.6-8) implies that the Athenian fleet during this period comprised a total of three *naves apertae* (i.e. ships which did not afford protection to the rowers in the topmost bank of oars) which she used to guard her coastline from piratical raids from Chalkis. The Piraeus, its naval installations evidently intact, served as a base for the Roman and allied fleet throughout the war (cf. Li. 31.26.5, 31.45.1, 31.47.1, 32.16.9). Its continuing strategic value is indicated by the fact that an unsuccessful Macedonian land attack was made against it in 200, when it was defended by only a small garrison (Li. 31.26.6). Philip then marched on the Asty and a battle took place in the narrow space between the ruins of the Long Walls, after which he withdrew from Attike, destroying tombs, temples and statues along the way.

The advance of the Seleucid king Antiochos III to the Hellespont saw the return of the Romans to mainland Greece in 192. Tempting offers from Antiochos led to the formation of an anti-Roman faction in Athens. To prevent Athens from deserting the Roman cause, the general Flamininus ordered the establishment of a garrison of 500 auxiliaries in the Piraeus, presumably on Mounychia (Li. 35.50.3-4). In the ensuing so-called Syrian War (192-188) there is only one reference to the participation of Athenian vessels and then merely in a routine capacity: in 190 they were used to convey the Roman general Lucius Aemilius Regillus to his command in Samos (Li. 37.14.1). The same year Antiochos was heavily defeated at Magnesia and peace was concluded in 188.

If Athens had wavered in declaring for Rome against Antiochos, she had no hesitation in siding with her against Philip V's son Perseus in the Third Macedonian War (171-168). In return for her loyalty, in 166 she received the territory of Haliartos in Boeotia, together with the islands of Delos and Lemnos. Delos was ceded to Athens with the stipulation that it was to be 'free of taxes (*atelês*)', an expression which is generally taken to mean that no harbour dues could be exacted from merchandise by the Athenian authorities (Pol. 30.31.10; Str. *Geog.* 10.5.4). The degree to which Athens thus benefited from her new acquisition is much debated. Rostovtzeff (1953, 64f.), on the one hand, claims that it was as ruinous to the commerce of the Piraeus as it was to that of Rhodes. Will (1967, II p. 334), on the other, argues that it led to a revival in its prosperity. In reality the undoubted decline in the commercial importance of the Piraeus was occasioned by many circumstances and is not attributable to any single factor. If an underlying cause must be sought, it perhaps lay in a shift in the main east-west trade route, a development which had begun at the dawn of the Hellenistic era when Rhodes first entered into competition with Athens for the title of foremost emporion in the eastern Mediterranean.

The period after 166 witnessed an architectural revival in the Asty made possible by generous benefactions from Hellenistic kings. Of significance for the present study is the fact that in *c.* 150-125 the so-called Tower of the Winds was erected in the Roman Agora in the Asty (von Freeden 1983). The building, which was equipped with an elaborate weathervane intended to provide information about conditions at sea, clearly demonstrates the Piraeus' continuing commercial significance. There is also evidence of building activity in the Piraeus around the middle of the second century in the form of an impressive new theatre overlooking Zea Port. The fact that there is no record of any other major public construction in the port dating to the post-Macedonian era may merely be fortuitous, but the Piraeus was no Athens, and since it possessed none of the glamour which attached to the latter name, it would hardly have been regarded as a fitting object of royal patronage. Hence, a disjunction in architectural appearance between the two towns may well have become striking at this date.

Since Athens remained neutral during the war between Rome and the Achaean League (146-140), she was spared the consequences visited upon those states which had sided with the Achaeans. The period between the conclusion of the Achaean War and the outbreak of the Mithridatic War in the first century was one of continuing prosperity for Athens, during which she exercised considerable prestige as cultural leader of Greece. In the Piraeus this is indicated by abundant epigraphical evidence from *c.* 120 onwards which reveals that several major religious festivals were now being celebrated on a particularly grandiose scale (below p. 114).

In 89 Mithridates VI Eupator, king of Pontos, broke with Rome and set himself up as the liberator of all Greeks under Roman domination. In the Asty, where an oligarchic faction was seeking the support of Rome in order to effect right-wing changes, the democratic opposition seized the opportunity to invite him to liberate the Greek mainland from Roman rule. In the summer of 88, following the massacre of 80,000 Romans and Italians, the king sent a naval detachment across the Aegean under the command of his general Archelaos. Archelaos plundered Delos along the way and then arrived in Greece. There can be little doubt that Mithridates envisaged the Piraeus as an important military base for his operations on the mainland.

Next year Sulla, who had been appointed in charge of the war with Mithridates, landed at Epiros in northern Greece with five legions. He marched immediately south into Attike, meeting with little resistance on the way. On arrival, he detached half his army to besiege the Asty and marched down to the Piraeus which was under the control of Archelaos. Using the ruins of the Long Walls, he proceeded to build a ramp (*chôma*) to the height of the fortifications. The Asty, cut off from her port and deprived of all supplies, was starved into surrender in the spring of 86, though the Piraeus managed to hold out longer. Even after its circuit wall had fallen to the invader, Archelaos succeeded in resisting Sulla's assaults from his stronghold on Mounychia. His position was hopeless, however, and he eventually made his escape by sea in order to join Mithridates' army in Macedonia. The Piraeus, which had shown much more spirited resistance than the Asty, was now burned to the ground with characteristic Roman efficiency by Sulla who spared 'neither Philon's Arsenal nor the docks nor any of its other famous architectural works' (App. *Mith.* 41). It is perhaps not too fanciful to suppose that its terrible destruction was in part inspired by loathing for the democratic sentiments which its population had consistently espoused and probably continued to uphold - sentiments so objectionable to a man of dictatorial leanings.

As luck would have it, the Sullan holocaust has chanced to preserve for posterity several statues of major artistic and historical significance which were discovered in 1959 when the ruins of a burned-down warehouse were excavated. The destruction of the warehouse had resulted in its contents being overlooked by Sulla's agents who were under strict orders to plunder all they could. The cache comprised a bronze Apollo, a bronze Athene, two bronze statues of Artemis and a possible third in marble, two stone herms and a bronze mask. A shipwreck off Mahdia on the Tunisian coast is also very likely to be connected with the events of this year. Its cargo included marble columns, bronze and marble statues, statuettes and reliefs, together with furniture and other items. Inscriptions reveal that several objects had been plundered from sanctuaries in the Piraeus.

Sulla was not the last Roman to inflict damage on the Piraeus. In 48 Caesar's legate Calenus captured the port easily 'because it was unwalled' (Dio Cassius 42.14.1). Three years later Cicero's friend Servius Sulpicius Rufus made a damning criticism of Roman intervention in the Greek world which may serve as a fitting epitaph on the Piraeus:

> At sea ... on my way back from Asia, I was looking at the shores round about. Astern lay Aegina, before me lay Megara, on my right the Piraeus, and on my left Corinth – all once teeming cities and now they lie ruined and wrecked before our eyes (Cic. *ad Fam.* 4.5.4; cf. Str. *Geog.* 14.2.9).

2. Population, Trade and Commerce

(a) Demography

The title of this chapter inevitably suggests a degree of analytical sophistication which it cannot fulfil. What we know about the demographic profile of the Piraeus is, arguably, less than what we know about that of the Asty, concerning which practically nothing uncontroversial can be said. The many upheavals over the 400-year period covered by this survey must (there is no avoiding this presumptuous auxiliary) have produced sudden changes in the size of the population, though they hardly ever rise to the level of explicit testimony and have to be inferred from the general course of events. Because a large proportion of the population of the Piraeus were metics, attracted by the incomparable commercial advantages which it offered, it is a reasonable inference that numbers would have fluctuated very sharply, in line with the changing political stability and economic prosperity of the state. Given Thukydides' observation (2.16.1) that at the time of the outbreak of the Peloponnesian War the majority of the population was domiciled in the countryside, and in view of the current estimate of 200,000-300,000 for the total population of Attike from c. 450 to 320, a very conservative reckoning for the Piraeus in the same period would still be above the 30,000 mark. It should be borne in mind, however, that the port swelled and emptied according to a rhythmic cycle which began in the early spring and ended in late autumn, in line with Greek sailing practices. Like all towns before the nineteenth century the Piraeus probably exacted a heavy price from those who sought a livelihood within its walls: deaths almost certainly exceeded births, so that a constant stream of new residents was necessary merely to keep the population up to strength.

As a provisional guide to the growth and decline in population from c. 493 to 86, I propose the following:

(1) A rapid expansion from c. 480 onwards as a result of the development of the naval, and later commercial zone.

(2) A sharp reduction in numbers of metics immediately prior to the outbreak of the Peloponnesian War.

(3) A large influx of refugees from the countryside in 431, in line with Perikles' policy of abandoning Attike.

(4) A reduction in population of about one-tenth as a result of the plague in 430-426.

(5) A further decline following the departure of refugees in 421.

(6) A reduction in the size of the metic population as a result of the policy of the Thirty in 403, balanced to some degree by an influx of citizen refugees expelled from the Asty.

(7) A decline following the departure of those same refugees consequent upon the restoration of democracy in 403.

(8) A gradual increase in the metic population from 403 onwards and an accelerated increase after *c.* 350.

(9) An overall and immediate reduction in population, particularly of metics, as a result of the installation of the Macedonian garrison in 322, followed by a continual but more gradual dwindling throughout the occupation.

(10) An increase in population from 228 onwards in line with the liberation of the Piraeus and the growth of more settled conditions throughout Attike.

(11) A general slaughter of the Piraeus population by Sulla followed by the migration of many of the survivors to Athens.

Evidence of a sharp decline in the port's population from 322 onwards is provided by the fact that 69 per cent of sepulchral inscriptions which commemorate citizens buried in the Piraeus are dated to the fourth century, 21 per cent to the third to first centuries B.C., and 10 per cent to the first to third centuries A.D.

The population of the Piraeus comprised five elements. In descending order of political representation and legal protection these comprised: demesmen of the Piraeus, Athenian citizens registered in demes other than the Piraeus, metics, short-term visitors and slaves. It is a severe limitation upon the value of this investigation that our sources tell us virtually nothing about the last two groups. The settlement of the Piraeus did not, as noted above (p. 14), wait upon the development of the harbour. Traill (1975) assigns the deme a bouleutic quota of nine or 1.8 per cent of all bouleutai. This suggests that the Piraeus may already have been one of the most populous of the 139 demes at the time of the Kleisthenic reforms (508/7), exceeded by only nine others and equalled by another four. By the middle of the fifth century, however, the Peiraieis or demesmen of the Piraeus represented only a fraction of the total population, which had now been supplemented both by metics and by Athenians registered in other demes. That is because, like any urban centre at any period of history, the Piraeus offered unrivalled opportunities for employment which were simply not available in the countryside; it may even be doubted whether they were quite so available in the Asty itself, given the large workforce needed to staff and maintain the fleet. I strongly suspect that one of the chief motives for the initial development of the Piraeus as an urban settlement was identical to the one which induced all the countries in the developed world to colonise themselves in the eighteenth century, and to settle hitherto unpopulated or underpopulated areas within their own territory: namely a dramatic and unprecedented rise in the native population. Regrettably the recording of the find-spots of sepulchral inscriptions has not in the past been sufficiently accurate to enable us to compare statistically the scale of migration to the Piraeus with that to other parts of Attike, notably the Asty. None the less, the extent to which the Piraeus was populated by Athenians registered in other Attic demes may be appreciated by the fact that out of 240 sepulchral inscriptions commemorating citizens who were buried in the Piraeus, a mere eight commemorate Peiraieis. Though the Piraeus absorbed most of the surplus, an increase occurred at other major sites in Attike as well. This increase is likely to have been particularly pronounced from *c.* 450 onwards, contemporary with the earliest evidence for the import of foreign corn into Attike, and to have reached its peak in 432. Given the structure of the Athenian economy, the population of the Piraeus at this date may well have equalled that of the Asty.

The only testimony which has bearing upon its settlement is provided by Diodoros Siculus (11.43.3) who claims that Themistokles persuaded the Demos 'to make metics and artisans (*technitai*) exempt from taxes (*ateleis*) so that a great multitude would come to the polis and readily establish many crafts'. The passage is problematical on a number of counts, including the precise nature of the *ateleia*, the identity of the *technitai*, and the length of time that the measure remained in force (cf. Whitehead 1977, 148f.). A further difficulty concerns the exact dating of the decree. Diodoros, whose chronology is notoriously inaccurate, puts it at 477/6. More plausibly, it should be placed in the late 480s so as to coincide with

Themistokles' naval bill, since metics were needed to assist in the shipbuilding programme and also to serve in the fleet at the time of Xerxes' invasion. Though serious doubts remain as to the exact nature of the concessions which the state offered to encourage immigration, there are, therefore, insufficient grounds for rejecting Diodoros altogether in view of the fact that Athens' decision to divert her energies in a new direction required the injection of specialist craftsmen from abroad.

On commonsense grounds it is to be suspected that the number of metics resident in Athens and the Piraeus after the repulse of Xerxes' invasion in 479 was small, but that by the middle of the fifth century, thanks to the developing role of the port in international trading, it had reached an unprecedented level (see Meiggs 1972, 263). It is against this background of a swelling metic population that Perikles' citizenship law of 451/0, restricting Athenian citizenship to those of Athenian parentage on both the female and male side, should be set. Some estimate of the total size of the metic population at the outbreak of the Peloponnesian War can be obtained from the fact that 3,000 metic hoplites served alongside an Athenian contingent during the invasion of Megara in 431 (Thuk. 2.31.2). Since it cannot be assumed that this represents the total complement of metic hoplites, and since the number of metics who did not qualify for hoplite status is likely to have greatly exceeded those who did, 28,000-30,000 is generally given as an estimate of their total strength at this date. Of the 366 metics whose deme residence is known, 69 (or 19 per cent) were registered in the Piraeus, as compared with 223 (or nearly 61 per cent) in demes located in or around the Asty (Whitehead 1986, 83f.). In the size of its resident alien population the deme of Piraeus may thus have been exceeded only by Melite in northwest Athens, for whom 75 metics are attested. If we combine this percentage with the figure of 28,000-30,000 for the total number of Athenian metics in *c.* 432, we may calculate, very roughly, that the Piraeus in this period accommodated some 5,000-6,000 resident aliens.

While some of the metics who left at the time of the Peloponnesian War returned when peace and democracy were restored, Clerc's assertion (1893, 375f.) that the foreign population never again reached its pre-432 peak may well be correct. Isokrates' claim (8.21) that at the end of the Social War Athens was 'bereft of *emporoi, xenoi* and metics' is certainly an exaggeration, but the general tenor of his remark finds circumstantial support in the set of proposals put forward by Xenophon (*Por.* 2.2-6) which were designed to attract socially desirable settlers from abroad.

In one respect at least the fourth century witnessed a tightening up of the regulations governing alienage. Legislation was probably now introduced requiring all those resident in Athens beyond a statutory (unknown) number of days to file their names in a public register and to pay the metic tax (*metoikion*). Those, on the other hand, whose sojourn was of shorter duration were now termed *parepidêmoi* or *parepidêmountes*. Around the middle of the fourth century, however, there does seem to have been an improvement in the social, if not political status of aliens. First, decrees honouring metics become more common. One, passed in 301 on behalf of the metics Nikandros and Polyzelos, states that these two voluntarily contributed towards the special tax (*eisphora*) which was levied for the building of the shipsheds and the arsenal every year from 347/6 to 323/2, that they rendered financial assistance to the navy during the Lamian War, and that they subsequently made donations for the repair of fortifications. It thus sheds an illuminating light upon the extent to which the revival of the port was made possible by the goodwill of its metic population. Grants of *enktêsis* were now awarded to metics for the establishment of shrines in the Piraeus and the procedure regarding maritime lawsuits (*dikai emporikai*) was revised in *c.* 350 for the benefit of traders from abroad. We may reasonably suppose that these measures resulted in a sizeable increase in Athens' metic population, soon further to be increased by the arrival of refugees from Macedonian oppression. A telling indication of the very considerable wealth in the hands of one metic family in this period is provided by the grave monument found in Kallithea of Nikeratos and his son Polyxenos, metics from Histria (Fig. 11). The politician most influential in bringing about this substantial improvement was probably Lykourgos. His concern and involvement with metics is demonstrated by the fact that it was he who moved the proposal to grant *enktêsis* to the *emporoi* of Kition in 333/2, who allegedly came to the rescue of the philosopher Xenokrates of Chalkedon when he was unable to pay the metic tax, and who proposed honouring the Plataian Eudemos for his contribution to Athens' finances in 333/2.

As Whitehead (1977, 112) observes: 'The fundamental division in Greek ethnology from at least the sixth century onwards was between Hellenes and *barbaroi*'. For that reason we should not seek, and certainly do not find, plentiful testimony concerning the ethnic

Fig. 11. *Peribolos*-tomb of Nikeratos and Polyxenos, metics from Histria, *c*. 330.

Table 1. Sepulchral inscriptions commemorating foreigners domiciled in the Piraeus as listed in *IG* II² 7882-10530

Place	4th cent B.C.	3rd-1st cent. B.C.	1st-3rd cent. A.D.
Aigai	1		
Aigina	4		
Ainos, Thrace	2		
Aitolia	1		
Akarnania	2		
Antioch		4	3
Arkadia	1		
Bithynia	1		
Boeotia		1	
Bosporos	1		
Byzantion	2		1
Chalkedon	2		
Chersonese		1	
Dardanos			1
Elis	1		
Ephesos	4		1
Eretria	1		
Erythrai	1		
Gela	1		
Halikarnassos	1		
Herakleia	5	6	3
Histiaia	1		
Histria	1		
Iasos, Turkey	1		
Kardia	1		
Karyanda, Turkey	1		
Karystos	1		
Kassandra		1	
Kea		1	
Kerkyra	1		
Kition	3		
Klazomenai	1		
Knidos	2		
Kolophon	1		
Korinth	3		
Kos	1		
Krete	1		
Kromma	1		

origins of metics, an issue which clearly did not preoccupy the average (literate) Athenian to any marked degree. The one exception is Xenophon (*Por.* 2.3) who comments upon the numerical predominance of barbarians from the Levant, chiefly Lydia, Syria and Phrygia, in *c.* 350. It might seem that the best evidence for the

Place	4th cent B.C.	3rd-1st cent. B.C.	1st-3rd cent. A.D.
Kypros	2		
Kythera	1		
Kyzikos	1		
Laodikeia			1
Lykia	1		
Lysimacheia		1	
Maiotis	1	1	
Megara	5	1	2
Methana		1	
Melos	1		
Miletos	4	8	17
Mysia	1		
Naxos	1		
Naukratis	1		
Olynthos	5		
Oria		1	
Paphlagonia		1	
Pella			1
Phaselis, Turkey	2		
Phokis	3		
Plataia	1	1	
Prokonnesos	2		
Rhegion	1		
Rhodes	3	1	
Salamis	3	1	8
Samos	5		
Sidon		2	
Sikilia	1		
Sinope	2		
Siphnos	2		
Smyrna	1		1
Soli, Cyprus	2		
Tegea	1		
Teos	5		
Torone	1		
Total no. of metics	110	34	38
Total no. of states	60	18	10

study of metic ethnicity is provided by sepulchral inscriptions in which metics and, presumably, in some cases *xenoi* who die in Attike are commemorated as 'X, son of Y, of city Z', where the *ethnikon* (of city Z) stands in place of the *dêmotikon* (of deme Z) which is added in the case of Athenian citizens. Sepulchral inscriptions must be treated with caution, however, because the numbers they record are

small and because the illiterate and economically depressed groups
are likely to be seriously under-represented (Davies, *CAH*² VII.1 p.
267). A mere six (3 from the Piraeus) commemorate Kitians, though
they are likely to have formed a sizeable community. In addition,
there are very few Thracians commemorated, though these were one
of the most prominent foreign groups in the Piraeus.

What the inscriptions do fully reveal, however, is that by the third
century at the latest Greeks from all over the eastern Mediterranean
had come to take advantage of the Piraeus' unique commercial
advantages. They include citizens from the Peloponnese, northern
Greece, Chalkidike, Propontis, the southern shore of the Black Sea,
the Aegean islands, Crete, Cyprus, Rhodes, the inland as well as
coastal cities of Asia Minor, and Alexandria. The western
Mediterranean, by contrast, is represented by only a few names
from Italy and Sicily, evidently reflecting the fact that the Piraeus
was better situated for trading with the east than with the west.

Of 182 funerary inscriptions from the Piraeus commemorating
foreigners which date from the fourth century B.C. to the third
century A.D., 110 belong to the fourth century B.C. (Table 1). The
third to first centuries B.C. are represented by a mere 34. The
remaining 38 mostly date to the first and second centuries A.D.,
though a handful may belong to the third. Overall, men
outnumbered women in the proportion of 2:1. It would be unwise to
conclude from this fact alone, however, that the proportion of male
to female metics domiciled in the Piraeus was necessarily similarly
weighted, since a count of sepulchral inscriptions commemorating
Athenian citizens reveals a comparable imbalance. A mere 20
inscriptions commemorate two or more metics, but here again it
would be hazardous to argue from this evidence alone that the
majority were either single or had families outside Attike, since only
the wealthiest metics would have been able (if specially permitted)
to purchase land on Attic soil on which to erect family enclosures.
The contracting role of the Piraeus from 322 onwards is further
revealed by the fact that in the fourth century B.C. 60 different states
are represented by inscriptions found in the port, whereas in the
period from the third to first century B.C. the number has dwindled
to a mere 18. The virulence of the Sullan destruction is indicated by
a very sharp decline in the population of the port from the first
century B.C. onwards: out of 24 sepulchral inscriptions commemorating Peiraieis which date to the Roman era, no fewer than
22 came to light outside the Piraeus itself.

Xenophon's claim that Athens' metic population in the mid-fourth century originated mainly from the Levant is borne out by a study of foreign cults in the Piraeus, which correspondingly reveals a strong bias in favour of that region (see Table 3). Of these the most distinctive were the Phoenicians, in particular the Sidonians, who preserved intact the organisation of their native city when living abroad, and who set up bilingual inscriptions in Phoenician and Greek. Evidence for the existence of a Jewish community is by contrast virtually non-existent.

Metic status as a legally defined category seems to have disappeared around the middle of the third century. In 317-307 a census (*exetasmos*) carried out by Demetrios of Phaleron (cf. Ktesikles, *FGrH* 245 F1) had put Athens' total metic population at around 10,000, though as Hansen (1985, 32f.) has pointed out, it is unclear whether this figure comprises all metics or merely those eligible for military service. It is not known to what extent the presence of a Macedonian garrison on Mounychia led to a reduction in the number of aliens resident in the Piraeus from 322 onwards, but it can hardly have made Attike attractive to foreigners. By the same token, there was perhaps a slight increase in their numbers when the garrison finally departed in 228. Foreign religious associations continued to prosper and multiply in both the third and second centuries, particularly those associated with Caria, Egypt, Lydia, Phoenicia and Phrygia. Foreigners' names also appear in lists of persons who made voluntary contributions (*epidoseis*) to the state for a variety of public needs, including the repair of fortifications in the Piraeus.

The intermingling of nationalities in the Piraeus no doubt played a major part in eroding the distinctions which existed in the Greek world between citizens and non-citizens. Politically speaking, however, the metics and citizens who engaged in commercial ventures did not, except at moments of crisis, constitute a group whose common interests could be opposed to those of a more traditional, conservative kind. There is nothing to indicate that merchants operated as a pressure group within the ekklesia, and it is highly improbable that if they did they would have championed the interests of their foreign trading rivals in public debate. Further, the odium attaching to foreign extraction, which formed part of the stock political invective of the fifth and fourth centuries, provides clear evidence of a very real and abiding distrust of *xenoi* on the part of some members of the citizen body. All this is not to deny that the existence of a large foreign population in the Piraeus would scarcely have been possible without a considerable degree of religious and racial tolerance. Nor do I wish to suggest that the host nation resolutely set its face against all forms of acculturation. As a merchant in a speech written by Demosthenes (33.5) states: 'Travelling about the world and spending my time in the market has made me familiar with most of the men who sail the sea'. The inhabitant of the Piraeus could well have said the same, though to describe him as cosmopolitan in the true sense of that word is, I firmly believe, unwarranted.

Consideration should next be given to sources of livelihood available to the inhabitants of the Piraeus. Commerce was handled by *emporoi, nauklêroi* and *kapêloi*. The first were merchants who transported their cargo in ships other than their own; the second were shipowners or captains who transported their wares on board their own ships; and the third were dealers based in the Piraeus who traded with *nauklêroi* and *emporoi*. Hasebroek's thesis (1933, 21) that it was metics and aliens who constituted the majority of Athens' trading community is scarcely borne out by the evidence of forensic speeches, which feature only fourteen metic or alien merchants in comparison with fifteen citizens (cf. Isager and Hansen 1975, 71f.). In addition to the merchants, there were also the bankers and accountants who arranged loans and kept records of ships entering and leaving port. The earliest known Piraeus *trapezitai* are Antisthenes and Archestratos who in *c.* 394 handed over the charge of their affairs to their freedman Pasion (Dem. 36.43 and 48; 49.6; 52.8 and 14). Another Piraeus banker was Charion, whose gravestone depicts the deceased holding what is possibly an oblong or cylindrical book-roll.

In addition to being a trading centre, the Piraeus was ideally located to serve as an industrial centre since Athens had to import many of her raw materials from abroad and since road haulage was slow, costly and labour intensive. Foremost of her industries was shipbuilding which required a workforce perhaps totalling some 20,000 (below p. 98). Small manufacturing businesses also flourished here, such as the shield factories (*aspidopêgeia*) of Pasion and Polemarchos, the latter employing a very considerable workforce. The orator Demosthenes inherited two *ergastêria* from his father, both probably located in the port: one was a sword factory which employed 32 or 33 workers, the other a bedstead factory which employed 20. The Piraeus was also a major source of supply for limestone, its quarries (*lithotomeia*) using slaves and prisoners of war. The productivity of one such quarry is indicated by the fact that it was rented out in the middle of the fourth century at the very high figure of 115.5 dr. per month. Arable and pastoral farming were both carried out in the vicinity of the Piraeus, while the marshy Phaleric plain was well-suited to the cultivation of the Attic cabbage (*raphinos*). Fishing, too, was a source of livelihood, the local delicacy being Phaleric eels or sprats (*aphuai*) which were caught in the bay throughout antiquity.

The economic and social status of the population of the Piraeus was extremely varied. Many prominent and wealthy Athenians and metics are known to have owned property in the town. One such was the metic Polemarchos whose house, the setting for Plato's *Republic*, was a favourite port of call for distinguished visitors from abroad. Other wealthy residents include the metic Kephisodoros, a member of the group charged with the mutilation of the herms whose confiscated property was auctioned for 2,500 dr.; and the merchant Diodotos from whose estate 5,000 dr. were earmarked for the erection of a lavish funerary monument (Lys. 32.8 and 21). At the other end of the scale there were the urban poor, attracted to the Piraeus as to a magnet. It may have been their presence here in large numbers that inspired Plato to put into the mouth of Sokrates (*Gorg.* 519a) the claim that those who were popularly praised for having made Athens great, namely Themistokles, Kimon and Perikles, in fact did no more nor less than 'unwittingly reduce the polis to a swollen and pustular condition by filling it with harbours and docks and walls and all that kind of silliness, thereby leaving no space for temperance (*sôphrosunê*) and justice (*dikaiosunê*).' The ideal polis according to the view put forward by Plato in the *Laws* (11.919d) should be a minimum distance of 80 stades from the sea, which is, perhaps not wholly fortuitously, exactly double the actual distance of the Asty from the Piraeus. For, as he says elsewhere in the same dialogue (4.704d-705a):

> If the polis were to be on the sea-coast, well-supplied with harbours but lacking the essential commodities of life and not at all productive, it would need a mighty saviour and divine lawgivers if it were not to be afflicted with a vicious and depraved character (*êthê poikila kai phaula*).

Clearly there is no means of telling whether the incidence of criminality and immorality was higher in the Piraeus than in other parts of Attike, but there is no doubt that, like any thriving port, it

Fig. 12. Grave-*stêlê* of a seated woman holding a bird, *c.* 430.

Fig. 13. Grave-*stêlê* of Aristylla, *c.* 430. The deceased, who is standing, holds a bird in her left hand. She is shaking hands with her mother, who is seated.

possessed its sleazy underworld. The singularly repellent spectacle of a man defecating in a brothel which catches Trygaios' eye as he flies over the Piraeus was evidently intended by Aristophanes to capture the distinctive and unmistakable flavour of the region (*Peace* 164f.). We also learn of a 'gang of scoundrels (*ergastêrion mochthêrôn anthrôpôn*)' allegedly engaged in crooked business deals (Dem. 32.10). Male as well as female prostitutes plied their trade in the Piraeus, one of the former being Timarchos, a medical student who gained his credentials in the oldest profession (Aischin.1.40).

Like any densely populated urban area, the Piraeus had its cranks and half-wits. Athenaios (*Deipn.* 12.554ef) tells the story of one such crank called Thrasyllos who was regularly to be found standing in the Emporion with a register book in hand. Thrasyllos deludedly believed that all the ships which docked in the port were his and that he would shortly be enjoying the profits of their voyages. Eventually

Fig. 14. Banqueting Hero votive relief, *c. 400*.

his brother arrived from Sicily and placed him in the care of a physician. Having recovered his wits, Thrasyllos claimed ever afterwards that he had never in all his life been more happily employed than when he stood on the quayside in the Emporion watching his ships come home.

It should be borne in mind that the majority of Athens' foreign visitors, whether men of culture and learning, foreign diplomats, statesmen, kings, tourists or even gods, first stepped onto Attic soil by disembarking in the Piraeus. Being uniquely available to foreign influence, the Piraeus may well have had a more broadly based cultural life than that of the Asty, though because so little of its material remains has survived this proposition is impossible to test. None the less, it may not be accidental that some of the very earliest surviving grave reliefs from Classical Attike were discovered in the Piraeus, including what is possibly the earliest *dexiôsis* or 'handshake motif' in Attic funerary art, as, too, was an early Attic example of a Banqueting Hero votive relief (Figs. 12-14). But the case for a culturally self-contained or even culturally distinct Piraeus should not be pressed, for it is clear that Athenians were quite prepared to undertake daily the one to one-and-a-half hour walk from the Asty to the Piraeus or even the round trip. The elderly Sokrates walked to the Piraeus in order to witness the first performance of the Bendideia – and would have returned the same day, had not Polemarchos inveigled him to stay overnight (Pl. *Rep.* init.); and Antisthenes, a resident of the Piraeus, is said to have commuted to the Asty on foot every day for the privilege of listening to Sokrates (D.L. 6.1).

As noted in the Introduction, Aristotle (*Pol.* 5.2 1303b 10-12) described the population of the Piraeus as 'more democratic than that of the Asty' and I firmly believe this judgement to be true. A priori it commands credence in view of the fact that the majority of the 'naval riffraff (*nautikos ochlos*)', that element among the citizen body which had a particularly strong vested interest in the preservation of extreme democracy, are likely to have settled near their place of work. Other than at times of crisis, however, it was politically mute, being divided and dissipated bouleutically among all the ten tribes instead of comprising the membership of a single huge constituency which could, if it so chose, have exercised its political leverage en bloc. Inevitably as well the frequent absence of the *thêtes* on naval expeditions limited the participation of the *nautikos ochlos* in public debate. Thus structural safeguards within the mechanism of Athenian democracy prevented the hijacking of its policy-making body by one or other interest group. In conclusion, other than in the civil war of 404-3 the population of the Piraeus does not appear to have played a determining role in Athenian politics.

(b) Administration

Several factors lead one to suppose that on a priori grounds the Piraeus was a distinctive, indeed unique administrative entity within the Athenian state:

(1) It was a very densely populated residential settlement.

(2) It constituted the headquarters of the Athenian navy.

(3) It incorporated the Emporion which handled the overwhelming majority of Athens' imports.

(4) It accommodated a very large number of metics and *xenoi*, many of them short-stay visitors whose residency was none the less subject to strict supervision.

(5) Its military security was arguably more critical to Athens' overall defence strategy than that of any other region of Attike.

(6) It functioned as a single large deme, even though the majority of its population were not Peiraieis.

The main source of evidence for this chapter is the Aristotelian *Athênaiôn Politeia* which I take to have been written between 334 and 322 (cf. Rhodes 1981, 51f.), supplemented by deme decrees dated in the main to approximately the same period. Since there is no comparable body of evidence for the earlier or later periods, it follows that this investigation will have to focus chiefly upon the second half of the fourth century. Before *c.* 480, the Piraeus merely possessed the bureaucratic apparatus of any deme but the increase in the complexity of its administration may well have advanced hand in hand with its conversion into a naval and later commercial port. By the period of composition of the *Athênaiôn Politeia* at the latest, however, and probably at least half a century earlier, this apparatus had come to rival, and now kept pace with, that of the Asty itself.

The deme of Piraeus, along with the neighbouring demes of Thymaitadai and Korydallos to the northwest, and Keiriadai and Koile in the southeast quarter of Athens, constituted a city trittys designated Piraeus, which belonged to the tribe Hippothontis, its fellow-trittyes being coastal Eleusis and inland Dekeleia (Fig. 15). With a bouleutic quota of nine it was the second largest of the seventeen demes in its tribe, being exceeded only by Eleusis. Together these two demes accounted for no fewer than twenty of the fifty bouleutai of Hippothontis.

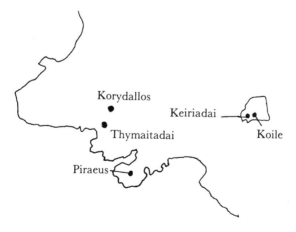

Fig. 15. The trittys Piraeus.

It would be natural to suppose that the boundaries of the deme were co-extensive with the circuit wall encompassing the peninsula, but the existence of a fourth-century marker stating '*horos* of the territory of Peiraieis' suggests that its limits were not so neatly defined (*IG* II² 2623). Its territory may possibly have included the district to the northeast enclosed within the Long Walls, since Xypete, the next nearest deme in the direction of Athens, lay 2km away. Slight evidence in support of this view is provided by the fact that remains which have come to light within the Long Walls have been identified as sanctuaries administered by the deme (below p. 162). The existence of a ploughing festival known as the Plerosia proves that the deme incorporated a significant amount of arable land within its boundaries (Appendix III no. 107) and there is evidence that it owned pastoral land as well (no. 4)*. Its territory was thus far larger than that occupied by the Asty, which by contrast administered its internal affairs through five urban demes.

The deme of Piraeus is aptly described by Whitehead (1986, 122 n. 5) as 'a law unto itself' and one of the clearest indications of its anomalous nature is the fact that by the middle of the fourth century at the latest its *dêmarchos* was, uniquely, a state official; that is to say, whereas all other *dêmarchoi* were appointed by and in their demes, this officer was appointed by lot by the Athenian Demos (Ps.-Arist. *AP* 54.8), a tacit acknowledgement both of his importance and of the sensitivity attaching to his post. It is not clear whether the post was available to all Athenians or exclusively to Peiraieis, but the only known holder of this office, Phrynion, was certainly a demesman for he appears in a deme decree without any demotic. Epigraphical data reveal that he was required to escort persons honoured by the deme to reserved seats (*proedriai*) in the deme theatre at festival time and proclaim their privileges to the assembled crowd (no. 6); to see to the setting up of deme decrees, in conjunction with the deme treasurers (*tamiai*); and to maintain order in the local Thesmophorion, in conjunction with the priestess of Demeter, 'according to the ancient laws (*archaioi nomoi*) pertaining to these matters' (no. 1). I strongly suspect that the demarch's supervisory role in relation to the Thesmophorion as described here was not exceptional and that he was responsible for ensuring that other, if not all, sanctuaries relating to deme cults were similarly maintained. Whenever any violation of the rules of proper conduct in that

---

* Unless otherwise stated, numbers in brackets in this chapter refer to Appendix II.

sanctuary took place, he had the authority to impose a summary fine on the offender. This circumstance clearly reveals that he was regarded, probably uniquely among all demarchs, as the holder of a state office or *archê* 'with enhanced powers accordingly' (Whitehead 1986, 396). From Pseudo-Aristotle (*AP* 54.8) we learn further that he was in charge of the Piraeus Dionysia and responsible for the appointment of its choregoi. Like other demarchs, he presumably combined in his person the roles of president of the assembly, eponymous magistrate, law enforcement officer and collector of revenue. In particular, the collection of the *enktêtikon*, or tax on non-demesmen holding property within the deme, and probably as well the *metoikion*, fell to the lot of this overworked official, tasks of an immensely burdensome nature in a region with as mobile a population as the Piraeus. Other deme officers attested for the Piraeus include a herald (*kêrux*), treasurers (*tamiai*), valuers (*epitimêtai*) and boundary-setters (*horistai*). Though there is no other evidence for either *epitimêtai* or *horistai* at deme level, it is unlikely that they were unique to the Piraeus.

Deme inscriptions in general shed little light upon the detailed handling of deme affairs, and those from the Piraeus are no exception. Of the six surviving inscriptions listed in Appendix II, two are leasing agreements, two are honorific decrees, one refers to the policing of the Thesmophorion, and the sixth is apparently to do with public works. Some indication of its status and importance is provided by the fact that it was one of only fourteen demes for which a theatre is attested (Whitehead 1986, 219f.). More significant is the fact that it is one of only three – the others being Eleusis and Halimous – known to have possessed a shrine dedicated to Hestia, the personified essence of the communal hearth whose foremost sanctuary was in the prytaneion in the Asty (below p. 141). The presence of this goddess in the port surely underscores the fact that 'the deme ... was structured in such a way as to encourage the development of a community spirit which called forth symbolic spaces similar to those which served in the life of the polis' (Giangiulio 1982, 951), and constitutes strong grounds for concluding that the Piraeus, though formally it had no more political importance than any other Attic deme, was none the less perceived as a major urban settlement which had far outstripped almost every other deme. Peiraieis are, moreover, on one occasion recorded as having assigned a special seat of honour (*proedria*) in the deme theatre to a non-demesman who was presumably domiciled in the port (no. 6). The honorand in question was Kallidamas of Cholleidai who was accorded this distinction in *c.* 261 'on account of his virtue (*aretê*) and goodwill (*eunoia*) towards the Demos of the Athenians and the Demos of the Peiraieis' (ll. 31-3) – a particularly suggestive and telling distinction in view of the Piraeus' separate political identity in this period.

Like other demes the Piraeus imposed taxes (*telê*) on demesmen and perhaps an additional tax on non-demesmen. As we have just seen, it also derived an income from the *enktêtikon* and the *metoikion* (no. 6.25-8). It further supplemented its income by leasing out the deme theatre which in 324/3 earned it the tidy sum of 3,300 dr., thanks largely to the initiative of a certain Theaios who 'so managed matters that the theatre earned 300 dr. more' – more, presumably, than it normally earned in a year (no. 3). In addition, the deme issued ten-year leases for the use of its sanctuaries (*temenê*) and pastureland (*ennomia*) at what appears to have been a very moderate fee and with the further proviso that if any special tax (*eisphora*) were imposed by the state, the deme, and not the lessee, would be liable (no. 4). Given these varied sources of income, it is probable that the Piraeus qua deme had an abnormally large income. Whether this in turn implied that it was particularly prosperous is another matter altogether, since the running of its affairs must have required an abnormally large budget. The fact that it relied at times upon voluntary donations (*epidoseis*) to defray the cost of building projects suggests, however, that expenditure did occasionally exceed income (see above p. 67).

Being a densely populated urban area, the Piraeus could not exercise the same degree of autonomy in the running of its internal affairs as demes of lesser size and importance. The upholding of municipal law was in the hands of a number of elected commissions or *archai*, answerable exclusively to the Athenian Demos. Chief among these were the *astunomoi* whose ten officers were equally distributed, five apiece, between the two urban centres. Pseudo-Aristotle (*AP* 50) states that it was their duty to prevent the occurrence of a wide range of possible abuses. They had to ensure that female musicians did not overcharge for their services; prevent dung-collectors (*koprologoi*) from depositing dung within a radius of ten stades of the circuit wall; prohibit the construction of buildings which encroached upon the streets either with gutters which discharged onto pathways or with window-shutters which opened outwards; and finally, take care, with the assistance of public slaves, that the bodies of those who expired on the public highway were duly collected for burial.

Until 320 the Piraeus *astunomoi* were also responsible for the upkeep of its major thoroughfares at festival time. From that date onwards, however, as an inscription found in the Piraeus indicates, this duty was transferred to the market controllers or *agoranomoi*. According to the restoration proposed by Vatin (1976, 557), their responsibilities included prohibiting 'defecation in the Agora and in the streets', as well as the depositing of earth and waste material along major thoroughfares. A more agreeable task of this second decemviral board, five of whose members likewise operated exclusively in the Piraeus, was to supervise commercial activity. They were thus responsible for ensuring that merchandise was sold in an unadulterated condition and that no fraudulent goods appeared on the market (*AP* 51.1). Together with the *pentêkostologoi*, they kept a register of all imports, issuing small lead tokens when market dues had been paid. Only after importers had made a declaration before both sets of officials as to the value of goods being offered for sale were they then free to sell their goods 'at neither a higher nor a lower price than that stated in the declaration before the *pentêkostologoi*'. *Agoranomoi* are first mentioned in 425 in Aristophanes' *Acharnians* (ll. 723, 824 and 968) where they are depicted as maintaining order in the Agora and inflicting corporal punishment on foreigners. Both the Asty and the Piraeus possessed an office of the *agoranomoi* known as the *agoranomeion*, which co-ordinated their administrative activities. The *agoranomoi* were assisted by a junior inspectorate of weights and measures called *metronomoi*, again five apiece for both the Asty and the Piraeus, whose duty was to check the accuracy of all weights and measures used by retailers and wholesalers in the market places (*AP* 51.2). The officials of these three decemviral boards were probably chosen on the basis of one from each of the ten tribes. Each board had two secretaries, one of whom was elected (*hairêtos*) and the other chosen by lot (*klêrôtos*).

The sale of corn, which included barley-meal, barley, wheat and bread, was overseen by the guardians of corn or *sitophulakes* who are first attested in *c.* 386 (Lys. 22). Their duties included ensuring that 'millers sold barley-meal at a price which corresponded to that which they themselves had paid for the barley, and that bread-sellers sold loaves at a price which corresponded to that which they themselves paid for the wheat' (*AP* 51.3). They were also required to keep records of the total volume of corn imported into Athens (Dem. 20.32) and to see that retail corn-sellers (*sitopôlai*) neither amassed large reserves of corn nor made a profit of more than one obol per unit measure (Lys. 22.5 and 8). Athens' perpetual insecurity about her corn-supply should have guaranteed their vigilance: for failing to check the rapacity of the corn-dealers Lysias, (22.16) informs us, they were frequently put to death. According to the Athenian currency law of 375/4, charges were laid before them of all offences committed in the Corn Market. Originally there were five *sitophulakes* for the Piraeus and five for the Asty, but probably in the 320s their numbers were increased to fifteen for the Piraeus and twenty for the Asty (*AP* 51.3).

In the mid-370s, as the currency law referred to above makes clear, *sitophulakes* supervised the retail as well as the wholesale trade in grain. Sometime before the composition of the Aristotelian *Athênaiôn Politeia*, however, control of the wholesale trade passed into the hands of ten *epimelêtai tou emporiou* or supervisors of the Emporion, an *archê* exclusive to the Piraeus whose duties included ensuring that two-thirds of all seaborne corn was unloaded and not shipped to destinations outside Attike (*AP* 51.4). They received denunciations for offences committed 'in the Emporion and in the Piraeus' seated in the Emporion beside the *stêlê* of Poseidon. Nearby, for their reference, laws regulating market activities were displayed. They were assisted in their duties by an inspector of silver coins or *dokimastês em Peiraiei*, a public slave nominated by the boule who tested silver currency for its purity.

In striking contrast to the abundance of officials handling trade, only a single fountain supervisor or *epimelêtês tôn krênôn* existed for the whole of Attike (*AP* 43.1). A decree of the demos dated 333/2 honours a certain Pytheas of Alopeke for repairing a fountain belonging to the Amphiareion in Oropos and for building a new one at the shrine of Zeus Ammon, the latter probably located in the Piraeus.

Supervision of the naval zone of the Piraeus was in the hands of the boule which 'inspects triremes after they have been constructed, along with their rigging and the shipsheds (*neôsoikoi*), and is responsible for the construction of new triremes or quadriremes, whichever the demos has voted for, along with their rigging and the shipsheds' (*AP* 50). The fulfilling of the annual quota of new ships was such an important part of the boule's duties that: 'if the bouleutai had not managed to complete the naval programme by the time they handed over to their successors, they were not entitled to receive the honorarium which they traditionally obtained within the lifetime of the incoming boule'. The boule was particularly active whenever a naval expedition was on the point of dispatch: a decree dated 325/4 regarding the sending out of an Athenian colony to the Adriatic instructed the boule to 'take full charge of the expedition (*epimeleisthai tou apostolou*), punish disorderly trierarchs in accordance with the laws, and meet on the Jetty (*Chôma*) every day until the fleet sails.' In addition to supervising major expeditions, the boule probably held an annual inspection of Athens' entire fleet (cf. Dem. 51.4). Supreme authority in naval matters rested, however, with the ekklesia for whom the boule acted merely in an executive capacity. Thus it was the ekklesia and the ekklesia alone which determined how many ships should be built annually, took decisions regarding the improvement of naval installations, and passed *psêphismata* relating to the launching of naval expeditions.

The day-to-day running of the naval establishment was administered by the ten supervisors of the dockyard. The earliest evidence for this board, which is not mentioned in the *Athênaiôn Politeia*, is dated after *c.* 450 but it may well be that its establishment was contemporary with the build-up of Athens' fleet in the 480s. In the fifth century these officials are known as *neôroi*, whereas in the fourth, which has yielded the most plentiful evidence for their existence, they are commonly referred to as *epimelêtai tôn neôriôn* with no indication that the change in title reflects any corresponding change in their duties. The dockyard supervisors acted as custodians for the triremes and their tackle, and for all other naval equipment which the dockyards contained. Hence it was these officers who issued trierarchs with 'hanging gear (*skeuê kremasta*)' at the beginning of their trierarchy and who attempted, with varying degrees of success, to recover it at its close. They prepared annual accounts known as *diagrammata* which recorded in painstaking detail what they had received from their predecessors and what they handed on to their successors, together with a list of the outstanding items yet to be recovered. In the fourth year of each Olympiad the *epimelêtai* in office engraved their records on stone. *Diagrammata* are most plentiful for the middle quarters of the fourth century and provide a unique insight into the running of Athens' naval establishment. The boule doubtless scrutinised them very closely, particularly when naval equipment was in very short supply. It is most likely that the dockyard supervisors had premises in Zea where several *diagrammata* have come to light.

Security arrangements within the port seem to have been pitifully inadequate, as is indicated by the fact that the Peloponnesians could contemplate making a surprise attack in 429/8. Following the conversion of the Piraeus into a closed port, security was tightened and probably remained at a high level throughout the rest of the Peloponnesian War. However, perhaps as a direct consequence of the two unopposed raids made in the fourth century, dockyard security was placed in the hands of five hundred guardians of the docks or *phrouroi neôriôn*, whose large number reflects the high level of public concern. The fort of Boudoron on Salamis, which the Spartans attacked in 429/8, was evidently intended to safeguard the port against seaborne attack from shipping in the waters off Megara, though as Eliot (1962, 131) notes its signal code must have been extremely limited in view of the fact that the signallers in the Piraeus who relayed the message to Athens were 'unable to make the clarifying addition that the message had as its origin a place other than the Piraeus'. To give advance warning of the movement of hostile shipping off the southeast coast of Attike, a network of signal stations may have been set up between Sounion and the Piraeus, as is indicated by remains of fortifications along the coast at both Anagyrous and Atene.

Initially there was only one military commander for the whole Piraeus. From the mid-320s onwards, however, there were two, one in charge of Mounychia, the other of Akte (*AP* 61.1). The strategos responsible for Mounychia retained the old title 'strategos of the Piraeus' and the new military commander became known as the 'strategos of Akte'. Before 95 a further restructuring took place and their number was increased to three. The old *stratêgeion* in the Piraeus was evidently their military headquarters, though in times of war it may also have served for meetings of the whole strategic board.

The Piraeus strategoi commanded the ephebes, Athenian youths aged between 18 and 20 who underwent two years of military service (Aischin. 2.167). These cadets resided in barracks on Akte and Mounychia and were subjected to training in both hoplite warfare and light-armed weaponry. At the end of their first year a review was held in the deme theatre, where each ephebe was formally presented with a shield and a spear. In their second year they did garrison duty at the various border fortresses scattered throughout Attike (*AP* 42.2-4). By the end of the second century the institution had become militarily defunct, though it continued to play an important part in the religious life of the community. To this period belong the earliest inscriptions referring to naval races (*hamillai tôn ploiôn*) between teams of ephebes held in the Piraeus, which now came to form a major feature of the Diisoteria and Mounychia festivals. On such occasions ephebes were also required to carry out nautical manoeuvres which included 'beaching their ships and pulling up into their docks, carrying out the orders of their strategoi'. The institution did not finally die out until the second century A.D.

Trial by jury also took place in the Piraeus. At least one court, known popularly as 'the one in Phreatto', held its sessions at an uncertain location close to the mouth of Zea Port. Demosthenes (23.77-8) describes the jurisdiction and judicial procedure of this court as follows:

> The law ordains that here trials should be conducted by 'anyone who, having gone into exile through committing unintentional homicide, and being not yet reconciled to those who secured his banishment, stands accused of a second murder, this time wilful ...'. The author of this law devised what was consistent with piety (*eusebia*), without depriving the accused of the right of defence and a trial. How did he do this? He took those who were going to act as judges to a place which the accused could approach, pointing out an area on the mainland but beside the sea called 'in Phreatto'. The defendant sails up in a boat and makes his defence without setting foot onto the land, while the judges listen and pass judgement from the shore.

Manifestly few offenders can have satisfied all three conditions for trial defined in the law and it may be that in the course of time other cases came to be judged here as well. A further source of evidence regarding judicial activity is provided by a series of ten well-worn bronze ballots which were discovered in the last century in a well near Zea (Efstratiades 1872, 400). All are pierced with the legend *psêphos dêmosia* (public ballot) and it is almost certain that they are dikastic in nature. Boegehold (1976, 16f.) has suggested that they may be connected with the court which passed judgement on *dikai emporikai*: since the function of this branch of Athenian law was to expedite judicial procedure in order to cause the minimal delay to *emporoi*, it would be entirely appropriate that the court empowered to hear such cases held its sessions in the Piraeus.

The Piraeus occasionally served as an alternative venue for meetings of the ekklesia and boule. The earliest attested meeting of the ekklesia took place in 411 when the hoplites held an assembly in the deme theatre at which it was resolved to march on the Asty and oppose the Four Hundred (Thuk. 8.93). As already noted (p. 31f.), the Piraeus was evidently chosen because it was felt to be beyond the oligarchs' sphere of absolute control. Again, during the rule of the Thirty at least one meeting of the ekklesia was held in the Piraeus, presumably because the auditorium on the Pnyx was out of commission at the time.

Whether any regular sessions of the ekklesia took place during the fifth century is not known. Demosthenes (19.60 and 125) indicates that an assembly was held in the Piraeus in 347/6 whose purpose was to discuss 'dockyard business (*peri tôn en tois neôriois*)'; it is not unlikely that this was a routine occurrence whenever naval matters constituted the principal item on the ekklesiastic agenda. The same source (19.209) reports that a meeting of the ekklesia was also held in the Piraeus in 343, but in this case it is not suggested that naval matters were under discussion.

No further meetings of the ekklesia in the port town are recorded for well over a century, reflecting the Piraeus' subjection during this period. From 208/7 until 137/6, however, there is a steady stream of epigraphical evidence for the *ekklêsia em Peiraiei*. Since all the recorded meetings took place in the last third of the prytany, it is very likely, as McDonald (1943, 54) has suggested, that throughout these years the Piraeus served as the regular venue for the third of the four regular meetings held every prytany. Finally, a prytany inscription dated 131/0 refers to 'an ekklesia in the theatre which had been transferred from the Piraeus in accordance with the decree'.

The earliest evidence for a meeting of the boule in the Piraeus dates to 426/5. A decree passed by the Demos in that year granting permission to the Methoneans to import a fixed amount of corn from Byzantion deferred similar requests from other allies until 'immediately after the sessions (*hedrai*) in the dockyards'. A century later in 325/4 the boule was instructed to meet in constant session on the *Chôma* in order to superintend the dispatch of a naval expedition. Since an old *bouleutêrion* is epigraphically attested for the Piraeus, however, it is likely that the boule also met there regularly during the last third of the prytany just before a session of the ekklesia, particularly in view of the fact that the only preserved date in the prytany for such a session happens to be the twenty-third (McDonald 1943, 143). An irregular meeting of the boule was held here in 319, the venue having been selected in conformity with the wishes of the Macedonian *phrourarchos* Nikanor who would have felt beleaguered if he had had to attend the *bouleutêrion* in Athens.

From *c.* 320 onwards the administrative machinery of the Piraeus presumably dwindled in accordance with its diminished economic and naval role. A law concerning weights and measures dating to the end of the second century, which assigns to an official known as the harbour supervisor or *epimelêtês tou limenos* the task of ensuring that its provisions were upheld in the port, is one of the few sources of evidence regarding administrative personnel in this period.

Under normal circumstances the Piraeus was not able to exercise any more control over the running of its affairs by virtue of its size, complexity and importance than any other deme. On the contrary, these factors made it subject to more, not less, centralised surveillance than any other region of Attike, with the single exception of the Asty. But there is surely a missing register. We have seen that on at least four occasions its population either chose, or was compelled, to constitute itself into a separate civic entity and to run itself without reference to Athens. Though there is virtually no evidence as to how the port conducted its affairs during these periods except in 404-3, the following circumstances suggest that the severance was achieved with relative ease and that only minor adjustments to its normal functioning were necessary:

(1) The commercial affairs of the Piraeus were quite independent from those of the Asty.

(2) The principal executive offices of the state had premises in the port.

(3) The land defences of the Piraeus were independent from the rest of Attike, while its naval defences were exclusive to it.

(4) Given the complex infrastructure belonging to a commercial and naval port, the region must inevitably have possessed a much higher-than-average incidence of persons equipped with expert skills and specialised knowledge.

(5) The affairs of the deme were sufficiently complex at all times to ensure that its local officials, pre-eminently its demarch, were capable of managing them in times of crisis.

(c) The Emporion

The commercial port of the Piraeus, known as the Emporion, was an exclusively economic zone situated along the eastern and northern shoreline of the Grand Harbour, demarcated from the rest of the town by a set of boundary markers. It comprised several stoas which

served as warehouses, together with a feature known as the Deigma
or Display-area where merchandise was set out for sale. The
Emporion dealt exclusively with overseas commerce; merchandise
conveyed by land was handled in the Hippodamian Agora. Given

Fig. 16. *left and above* Replica of the *Kyrenia*, a fourth-century cargo ship berthed in Zea Port.

the deplorable condition of most Greek roads, however, it would be a reasonable inference that most interstate trade was conveyed by sea. The major reason for segregating the commercial port from the rest of the Piraeus was in order to minimise the disruption caused to the community as a whole and to the naval zone in particular, and in order to facilitate the port authorities in their task of checking merchants and merchandise.

Since Greek shipping came to a virtual standstill during the winter, it is likely that the Emporion hummed and buzzed with frenzied activity for about six months of the year and was virtually idle for the rest. How the population supported itself during the off-season period is not known, but that at least a proportion of it suffered some economic dislocation would seem indisputable (Casson 1971, 271 n. 4). Isager and Hansen (1975, 62) have calculated that in the high season a minimum of six grain ships had to unload at the Piraeus daily in order to meet Athens' huge requirement (cf. Fig. 16). Probably that figure should be doubled to allow for other imports and transit goods. The volume of traffic arriving constantly at the wharves must therefore have required an extremely efficient system of loading and unloading to prevent a backlog of ships and spoiled cargoes from clogging up the harbour, but of the organisation and personnel we know little. The majority of the dockers are likely to have been slaves hired out by their owners on a contract-basis.

The most efficient method of unloading is by lining up a ship's hull parallel to the quayside, but if the example of Roman shipping is anything to go by, it may be that Greek merchant vessels usually docked by the stern (cf. Virg. *Aen.* 6.3; Aus. *Ep.* 23.128). As is the practice in modern ports, larger cargo ships may have remained at anchor in the harbour basin while their merchandise was transferred onto barges (*hupêretikai skaphai*) which anchored alongside. Most commodities were transported either loose, or else in sacks (e.g. grain) or amphorai (e.g. wine). Cranes were used for unloading the heaviest commodities, such as timber and marble, from the end of the sixth century, though pulleys may not have been invented before the fourth. A simple swing-beam (*kêlôneion*) with a weight on one end and a bucket on the other, facilitated the removal of loose grain from the hold. Amphorai had to be removed one at a time, sometimes with the assistance of a pole supported by a man at either end. With the exception of grain, which constituted a highly specialised and closely regulated import, most cargoes were probably mixed. Many ships unloaded only a portion of their cargo in the Piraeus before sailing off to other ports of call.

Merchants began selling their wares as soon as they had unloaded a sample at the Deigma and would have been under considerable pressure from the harbour authorities to conclude a hasty sale. Having disposed of their cargo, they did not usually sail away empty-handed. A part of their hold would be filled with merchandise purchased in the Piraeus and the rest of their storage space would be sold to the highest bidder.

The administration of the Emporion has been discussed above (p. 72ff.). All that need be added here is that ships under a certain tonnage were almost certainly debarred from using its facilities. A fragment of the port regulations of Thasos dated to the second half of the third century states: 'No ship whose cargo is valued at under 3,000 talents (approximately 80 tons) could haul up within the *horoi* of the first (i.e. smaller) harbour, and no ship whose cargo is valued at under 5,000 talents (approximately 130 tons) within those of the second.' Likewise in the case of the Piraeus, small merchantmen were probably required to beach and unload in Phaleron Bay rather than ride at anchor in the Grand Harbour.

The Emporion was not merely a centre for import and export. At the latest by the fourth century and possibly already by the outbreak of the Peloponnesian War it had become the major entrepôt for numerous Greek states which found it more convenient to sail to the Piraeus than to deal direct with the source of supply. The unrivalled advantages of the Emporion for redistribution and transshipment were the subject of admiring comment by several fourth-century writers. Isokrates (4.42), for instance, described Athens in *c.* 380 as 'an emporion in the centre of Greece from which could be obtained produce not readily available elsewhere', while Xenophon (*Por.* 5.3) in *c.* 355, confident of receiving no rejoinder, challenged: 'Where will those who want to buy or sell many items quickly have more success than at Athens?' Indirect evidence for the Piraeus as an entrepôt is provided by an Athenian decree dated *c.* 430 which granted leave to the people of Methone in Macedonia to import grain from Byzantion, the unmistakable inference being that the majority of Athens' allies were required instead to sail either to the Piraeus or to Athenian depots in the Aegean.

To appreciate the importance of the Emporion it is necessary to comprehend the extent to which Athens' economic prosperity and viability depended upon its existence. A comprehensive list of all possible motives for developing the commercial harbour must include the following: (1) to facilitate and guarantee the import of essential goods; (2) to increase revenue to the state by tariffs and other charges; (3) to boost imports and thus promote the interests of producers and merchants; (4) to enhance Athenian influence and prestige and thus indirectly advance the cause of Athenian imperialism; and finally, (5) to threaten and undermine the economies of Athens' commercial rivals.

Regarding (5), there is no evidence to justify the belief that any Greek state consciously operated an export policy or that its behaviour was ever determined by economic considerations of the kind that influence modern nation states. More fundamental still, the Greeks did not regard the economy as an autonomous category over which the state might and should exercise control, so that the notion of a commercial policy based on some kind of fiscal strategy would have been alien, if not abhorrent to their thinking. As Hasebroek (1933, vii) classically phrased it: 'The interests of national production, or of a class of producers, never determined the policy of the autonomous Greek state ... The so-called commercial policy of the ancient state was not concerned with trade, but with the supply of necessities, such as grain and timber, and with the enrichment of the treasury by means of tolls and duties.' To accept Hasebroek's thesis is not to deny that the Emporion was a source of enrichment to producers and merchants alike; it is merely to acknowledge that this was of no concern to the state and did not constitute a factor in its deliberations. Thus, while introducing extremely tight legislation in order to safeguard the import of corn, the state remained indifferent to the profits made by its trading community, many of whom were metics and slaves.

Probably the major source of income derived from a duty of 2 per cent known as the 'one-fiftieth (*pentêkostê*, sc. *meris*)' which was levied on all cargo entering or leaving the port. As was regularly the case in the ancient world, the tax was not recouped directly by the state. Instead its collection was leased out to a consortium by a board of officials known as *pentêkostologoi*. A separate consortium probably collected the 2 per cent levy on grain. Andokides (1.133-4) states that in 399 the right to collect the *pentêkostê* was sold for 30 talents and that the consortium which purchased the contract made a profit of 6 talents on the deal. Since in 399 trade in the Piraeus can have barely recovered from the crippling effects of the war, the value of goods passing through the Emporion in an average year was evidently considerably in excess of the 18,000 talents which is indicated by this figure. In 414 Athens abolished the tribute (*phoros*) imposed upon her allies and replaced it with a 5 per cent levy (*eikostê*) on all allied goods travelling by sea in the confident expectation that her revenue would thereby increase (Thuk. 7.28.4). An official known as a 'five-per-center (*eikostologos*)' was responsible for the collection of this new tax which probably remained in force until 405 (Ar. *Frogs* 363).

It is unclear what other harbour dues, if any, were imposed. There are references in both Aristophanes (*Wasps* 658), Pseudo-Xenophon (*AP* 1.17) and a decree dated *c.* 420-414 to a 1 per cent tax (*hekatostê*), but this may simply be a less inflated form of the *pentêkostê*. In addition, Eupolis (*CAF* I, fr. 48 p. 269 ap. Poll. 9.29) speaks of a passenger tax (*ellimenion*) 'which must be paid before one goes on board', presumably levied on passengers unaccompanied by a cargo. It is not to be forgotten that a further source of revenue to the state, or more accurately to the deme, was the *metoikion*, levied at 12dr. per annum for a man and 6dr. for a woman.

The importance of the Emporion is not, therefore, to be assessed primarily in terms of its financial contribution to the Athenian exchequer. Athens needed an efficient and well-equipped commercial harbour chiefly because she was dependent upon essential imports, principally corn, timber and slaves, as well as iron, tin and copper. Of these the most crucial was corn, since Attic soil, being extremely light and shallow, was unable to produce this commodity in sufficient quantity (cf. Thuk. 1.2; Str. *Geog.* 9.18; Plu. *Sol.* 22; Men. *Dysk.* 3, etc.) . The corn trade was controlled by the board of corn-guards known as *sitophulakes* who supervised prices and ensured fair trading (see above p. 77). In times of crisis, however, state-appointed corn-buyers known as *sitônai* were responsible both for its purchase and distribution, either free or heavily subsidised. The level of public anxiety regarding corn is indicated by the fact that it was an obligatory subject for discussion on the agenda of the ten plenary meetings of the ekklesia (Ps.-Arist. *AP* 43.4) and the only import subject to state intervention. Regulations controlling its movement included the following: it was a capital offence for persons resident in Athens to ship corn to harbours other than the Piraeus; no maritime loan could be extended except to merchants under contract to convey corn to the Piraeus; and finally, corn ships putting in at the Piraeus were required to unload at least two-thirds of their cargo before being permitted to depart. From time to time small convoys of triremes were sent out to accompany grain ships into port. A vivid insight into the extremity of Athens' dependency on imports in years when her harvest failed is provided by Lysias' speech *Against the Corndealers* (22.2), which reveals that in *c.* 386 popular fury against the *sitopôlai* or corn dealers had run so high that they were very nearly executed without trial.

Athens' need for imported corn did not predate the middle of the fifth century. It greatly exceeded that of any other Greek state, as was publicly acknowledged (Dem. 20.31), and may well have been a leading factor in the decision to develop the Emporion. Most of Athens' grain came from around the Black Sea area, particularly the Bosporos, whose ruling house, the Spartokids, gave her substantial trading concessions from *c.* 433 onwards, for which they were rewarded with Athenian citizenship. Some of her supply was probably stockpiled at Byzantion, either to safeguard against a shortage in Athens or for distribution among the troops in that area. Other major suppliers were Egypt, Libya, Cyprus, Phoenicia, Sicily and the Po Valley. Towards the end of the Peloponnesian War Euboia became an important supplier of corn, which, after the Spartan occupation of Dekeleia, now had to be transported by sea

around Sounion to the Piraeus (Thuk. 7.28; cf. 8.4). During the
fourth century Athens repeatedly suffered grain-crises. The worst
and most extended crisis was in the 320s when a series of decrees
were passed honouring metics for making free gifts of corn, selling it
below the market price, or merely providing it in quantity to be sold
at the prevailing market price. Free or subsidised, it was then
distributed to the population of the Piraeus 'in the dockyards and
Long Stoa' (Dem. 34.37). Other commodities such as olive oil are
also likely to have been subject to state intervention at times of crisis,
their purchase being in the hands of *elaiônai*.

Athens also had to import virtually all her shipbuilding supplies,
including timber and Kean ruddle (*miltos*) for the painting of
triremes. Her chief timber supplier was Macedonia, supplemented
by Thrace and South Italy. Her need was so great in the fifth
century that she attempted to compel her allies to convey timber and
other shipbuilding supplies to the Piraeus. Slaves were also
imported. Though some were bred in captivity and others became
enslaved as a result of war, Hansen (1975, 32) has calculated that in
the fourth century Athens needed to import some 6,000 annually –
probably about half her total slave population – in order to maintain
her workforce at full strength. The majority of these came from
Thrace, the Black Sea and the hinterland of Asia Minor.

A mutilated decree dated *c.* 176/5 honouring a merchant for his
eunoia towards Athens when she was experiencing a chronic shortage
of olive oil sheds a fascinating light upon trading practices in the
Emporion at times when demand exceeded supply. The merchant in
question had purchased 1,500 measures of oil with the intention of
exchanging it for corn in the Pontic region and then selling the corn
in the Piraeus. In the course of his voyage, however, he registered as
a *parepidêmos* in Athens where he saw for himself the extremity of the
crisis. Whereupon:

> He hastened to import the oil which he had purchased into our
> Emporion and having paid what was due in taxes in the Emporion, on
> being approached by the *agoranomoi* (?) who thought it fit (*axiountôn*)
> that he should hand over the oil to the polis and [proposed ?] a lower
> price for the oil than that which had been fixed by him, he had the
> courage to sell ... (ll. 12-16).

The document, which breaks off here, probably ended with some
such phrase as 'at the price fixed by the city'. It is tempting to

speculate whether events fell out precisely in the manner described. Was the merchant's *eunoia* prompted wholly by his 'courage' or was he responding in some measure to pressure from the port authorities? Doubtless the *agoranomoi* and *epimelêtai tou Emporiou* were empowered to exclude undesirables from the Emporion if they suspected them of overcharging, and when a particular commodity was in short supply merchants were probably under strong pressure to comply with requests to sell at the 'recommended' price.

Athens' essential imports were by no means her only ones. Perikles' boastful claim (Thuk. 2.38) that 'all the produce of every land comes to Athens' is echoed in Pseudo-Xenophon (*AP* 2.7) who, half with a sneer and half in admiration, wrote: 'Whatever desirable commodity is available in Sicily, Italy, Cyprus, Egypt, Lydia, the Pontic region, the Peloponnese or anywhere else, is brought together at Athens on account of her mastery of the sea.' An impressive list of the exotic commodities for sale in Athenian markets is provided by the comic writer Hermippos in a fragment from a play dated *c.* 430 or 420 (*CAF* I, fr. 63 p. 243 ap. Ath. *Deipn.* 1.27e-f). The list includes silphion and ox-hides from Cyrene; mackerel and salt fish from the Hellespont; pork and cheese from Syracuse; sailcloth, rigging and papyrus from Egypt; cypresswood from Crete; ivory from Libya, raisins and dried figs from Rhodes; pears and apples (or sheep?) from Euboia; slaves from Phrygia, mercenaries from Arcadia; tattooed and untattooed slaves from Pagasai; acorns and almonds from Paphlagonia; dates and wheat-flour from Phoenicia; and finally, rugs and cushions from Carthage.

The most valuable Athenian export from the time of the Persian Wars onwards was silver. When mining activity reached its peak in *c.* 360, production may have stood at over 1,000 talents per year (Hansen 1975, 44). The industry was, however, very much subject to war and other external pressures. Production virtually ceased during the Dekelean War and when it terminated at the end of the fourth century, it was not resumed for over a century. Other exports included olives, olive oil and honey. It is unclear whether Athens was a wine-exporting state, and with the exception of pottery there is no evidence that she exported manufactured goods (cf. Finley 1973, 134).

The chief features of the Emporion may be summarised as follows:

(1) It facilitated the exchange of goods between a host nation which was Greek and itinerant traders, also primarily Greek.*

(2) It served not only as the principal port of entry for goods that were imported into Attike, but also as a redistribution centre for goods which could not easily be procured at the source of supply.

(3) It was a non-residential zone and so played little part in preserving the cultural integrity of the host nation against infiltration by outsiders.

The Emporion conformed to the Polanyian model of a 'port of trade' primarily because it facilitated the juxtaposition of two separate economic systems which none the less remained discrete. By 'economic systems' I mean no more than 'rules governing commercial exchanges', since trading in the Emporion was qualitatively and quantitatively different from trading conducted elsewhere in Attike. Its existence thus raises fundamental questions about the precise nature of the commercial exchanges that took place within its boundaries; the relationship between the Emporion and other market places in Attike; and the type of controls and tariffs to which imports, exports and goods intended merely for transshipment were subject. To none of these problems can a full or even a satisfactory answer be given, but the following conclusions may be tentatively put forward:

(1) All the activities of the Emporion were supervised by the *epimelêtai tou emporiou* who in the first instance were probably answerable to the *agoranomoi*.

(2) Trade conducted within the Emporion was subjected to much tighter surveillance than that which governed commercial exchanges elsewhere in Attike.

(3) While transactions involving transshipment were probably liable to a harbour tax, only goods destined for import were subject to an import tariff.

(4) The right to avail oneself of the facilities of the Emporion was extended to Greeks and non-Greeks alike, irrespective of nationality and social status, whereas the right to trade elswhere in Attike was restricted to those who had been granted metic or at least 'parepidemic' status.

* John Davies points out to me in a letter dated 6/4/1986 that the Piraeus was by no means unique in this respect 'being not essentially different from 6th cent. Samos or 7th-6th cent. Corinth or even from the *emporion* envisaged by Chiots as threatening them at Oinoussai in 546' (Hdt. 1.165).

Fig. 17. Neo-Attic reliefs found in the Piraeus harbour dating to the second century A.D. The scene depicted is a part of the Amazonomachy, copied from the shield of the chryselephantine statue of Athene Parthenos by Pheidias of *c.* 440.

Fig. 18. Neo-Attic reliefs found in the Piraeus harbour, dating to the second century A.D. They are thought to depict the Three Graces, based on an original of *c.* 470.

(5) The Emporion existed primarily to facilitate wholesale, rather than retail trade, and probably set a minimum limit upon the value of goods that could be offered for sale within its boundaries.

(6) Like any agora or public meeting place, the space enclosed by the Emporion was regarded as sacred.

It is impossible to assess the frequency with which merchants sought to evade the regulations laid down in the Emporion or with what ease they might have succeeded. The commonest violation is likely to have been non-payment of harbour dues and the failure to unload two-thirds of grain cargo. Such are the allegations against a Phaselian *nauklêros* made in one of the private speeches of Demosthenes (35.28-9), put forward on the grounds that the accused berthed his cargo ship outside the Emporion at Thieves' Cove.

It has to be conceded that nothing is known about the economic relationship between the Piraeus and the countryside round about, though it is inherently probable that the neighbouring demes found it more convenient to purchase wares in the Piraeus rather than in the more distant Agora in Athens. Presumably the port also functioned as a market for the surrounding countryside, attracting local produce for consumption within its walls.

The Piraeus ceased to be the leading commercial centre in the eastern Mediterranean at the beginning of the Hellenistic period. From the third century onwards that role came increasingly to be filled by Rhodes and to a lesser extent by Delos. Though the economic condition of the Piraeus in the Roman imperial era lies outside the scope of this book, I would briefly note in conclusion that the port served as a major centre for the flourishing traffic in mass-produced Neo-Attic sculpture which the Roman market demanded. Examples include identical sets of reliefs such as those depicting an Amazonomachy (Fig. 17) or those depicting the Three Graces (Fig. 18) found where a merchantman had sunk in the Piraeus harbour (cf. Bass 1966, 78; Vermeule 1977, 12).

(d) The naval zone

Athens' navy occupied the southern shore of the Grand Harbour, and had exclusive use of the ports of Zea and Mounychia. Naval inventories reveal that Zea was the largest naval port in the fourth century, housing no fewer than 196 shipsheds, while the Grand

Harbour accommodated 94 and Mounychia 82. The naval
headquarters, however, are most likely to have been concentrated in
the Grand Harbour at the *Chôma*, which was probably a jetty
projecting westwards from its eastern shore. At some date in the
history of the Delian League, most probably in 454, the Athenians
instructed allied flotillas to muster in the Piraeus before expeditions
set sail (And. 3.38). From the discovery in Zea Port of a circuit wall
marking off the harbour from the rest of the town, it is likely that the
naval zone, like the Emporion, formed a self-contained unit, entry to
which was perhaps reserved for naval personnel.

Plato preserves the tradition that Athens' earliest permanent
shipsheds date to the time of Themistokles. What other amenities
existed at this date is not known, but the first warehouses for the
storage of naval gear and tackle may also have been built under his
supervision in view of the fact that a lost play of Aeschylus
contemporary with the port's foundation refers to *skeuothêkai*. There
is no external evidence for the date of the subsequent increase in the
number of Athens' shipsheds, but as noted above (p. 27) this is most
likely to have occurred after the conclusion of the Thirty Years'
Peace in 446 when the state constructed an additional 100 ships,
bringing the total strength of the fleet up to 300. Ranked by
Demosthenes (22.76) alongside the Parthenon, the Propylaia and
the stoas as among the finest architectural achievements of the
fifth-century democracy, the Periklean shipsheds allegedly cost
1,000 talents to build (Isok. 7.66). Their destruction by the Thirty
was a calculated act of sabotage intended to scupper Athens' navy,
since triremes required a thorough overhauling in dry docks during
the six winter months that they were not on active service. Less than
ten years later, however, *neôsoikoi* are again mentioned in a literary
source, intimating that the reconstruction of the perimeter
fortifications and Long Walls was accompanied by some
refurbishment of the naval quarter (*Hell. Oxyrh.* 1.1 *OCT*). There is
no explicit evidence of any development of the port between *c.* 390
and 360, but a naval list dated 377/6 suggests that by that date there
were enough *neôsoikoi* to accommodate over 100 ships. Shortly before
the middle of the fourth century, and probably at the instigation of
Euboulos, the reconstruction of Athens' shipsheds became a central
political issue. The lists of the dockyard supervisors indicate an
uninterrupted growth in their number over a period of some 25
years, reaching an all-time peak in 325/4. The naval quarter of the
Piraeus continued to function, though presumably in a state of

increasing dilapidation, under both Macedonian and Roman domination, before it was finally destroyed by Sulla. Even then, however, it was not completely obliterated, for ruins of the *neôsoikoi* were still visible to Pausanias (1.1.2) when he visited the port in the second century A.D.

The rowers in the Athenian navy were a full-time professional body drawn largely from the *thêtes*. Since Athens generally maintained a fleet of at least 100 ships on active service during the fifth and fourth centuries, and since the crew of a trireme comprised approximately 200 men, it may be estimated that the fleet provided employment for some 20,000 men. The majority were citizens, though metics and mercenaries were also permitted to serve. According to Plutarch (*Per.* 11.4), Athens' naval training programme was initiated by Perikles, who annually dispatched 60 triremes manned by raw crews for exercises which lasted eight months. The rate of pay for sailors reflected changing economic circumstances. When the Sicilian Expedition was dispatched in 415, for instance, the top wage was one drachma per day, whereas in the last decade of the fifth century, when Athens' reserves were exhausted, that figure was cut by half.

At the outbreak of the Peloponnesian War Athens had a fleet of 300 seaworthy triremes (Thuk. 2.13.8; cf. Xen. *Anab.* 7.1.27). The Athenian navy sustained no major losses during the Archidamian War and its strength remained at around 300 after the conclusion of peace (Aischin. 2.175). In 415 an expedition of 100 ships was sent to Sicily, supplemented by a further 70 a year later (Thuk. 6.43.1, 7.16.2 and 20.2). The entire complement was lost in the battle that took place in the Grand Harbour at Syracuse in 413. Less than two years later, however, Athens succeeded in building up a fleet of 104 ships which had its base on Samos (Thuk. 8.30.2). Then, in 406, upon learning that this fleet was blockaded in Mytilene, the Athenians made their most spectacular shipbuilding effort and within a month of the news reaching Athens a fleet of 110 new triremes set sail, though probably not from the Piraeus but from Macedon, the source of timber supply (Xen. *Hell.* 1.5.20).

At the end of the Peloponnesian War Athens was required to surrender all but twelve triremes. Ten years later she was already re-arming. When the Second Athenian Confederacy was founded her navy was 100 ships strong (Pol. 2.62.6; but cf. D.S. 15.29.6-7). Thereafter the naval lists show a steady build-up: 106 triremes in 377/6, 283 in 357/6 and 349 in 353/2. The last surviving list, that of

325/4, puts the total at no fewer than 360 triremes, 43 *tetrêreis* and 7 *pentêreis*.

Athens' re-armament from 392 onwards raises important questions as to the value and effectiveness of naval power in fourth-century Greece which can only be touched on here. In the fifth century control of the sea had been essential to Athens for three main reasons: first because it provided her with the means of collecting allied tribute; secondly because it enabled her to protect her vital supply lines; and thirdly because it was her primary means of defence. In the fourth century the situation was very different. The Second Athenian Confederary, unlike its fifth-century predecessor, was not a major source of financial gain to the Athenian state, while the decline of Persia coupled with the rise of Macedon rendered military strength more critical than sea power. Athens' fourth-century naval build-up proceeded, therefore, somewhat in defiance of military logic, constrained as she still was to safeguard her essential supplies.

To have the capability of building and maintaining at full strength a fleet of upwards to 400 ships, her shipbuilding industry must have been extremely efficient, particularly in view of the fact that the most important materials, including timber, flax and ruddle, had to be imported. The annual quota was decided by the ekklesia, which also elected the naval architects (*architektones epi tas naus*). The work was then sub-contracted, its progress being monitored by ten trireme-builders (*triêropoioi*), who were elected by the boule and answerable to it (Ps.-Arist. *AP* 46.1). Our sources tell us very little about the large and highly specialised workforce of carpenters, joiners, fitters, ropemakers, painters, and sail-cloth makers employed in the industry, but it presumably provided out-of-season work for many rowers who would otherwise have been laid off in the winter months. The site of the Piraeus dockyard (*naupêgion*) has not been located, but it is most likely to have been situated either on the east coast of Eetioneia or the southern coast of the Grand Harbour.

Only very scanty evidence is available for the rate of shipbuilding in the Piraeus. According to Diodoros (11.43.3), Themistokles persuaded the Demos to build 20 triremes a year, though it is not clear how long this annual rate was maintained. Kolbe (1901, 408) believed that it was abandoned soon after the threat from Persia had been allayed, but given the limited lifespan of a trireme, generally put at around twenty years, it would have been necessary to build a number of new ships each year merely in order to ensure the replacement of old ones. After the battle of Eurymedon the annual rate was perhaps lowered to 10-15 ships and may have remained at that level until the outbreak of the Peloponnesian War, though on at least two occasions there seem to have been extraordinary bursts of shipbuilding energy, notably in *c.* 451 and 431/0, when no fewer than 100 extra triremes were built. As noted, the most spectacular crash building programme of all was that of 406 which was probably carried out at the source of timber supply. In the middle quarters of the fourth century, when Athens again began a naval build-up, the shipbuilding rate must have risen sharply, perhaps to 25 ships per annum.

The size of Athens' fleet was one matter; the number of ships which could at any moment put to sea quite another. A major and recurrent problem in the fourth century was the dearth of naval equipment held in the *skeuothêkê*. The naval inventory for 357/6, for instance, which lists 283 triremes, indicates that there were sufficient oars for only 233, ladders for 232 and main masts for 185. Some wealthy trierarchs probably provided their own equipment (Dem. 47.23; cf. 51.5), but many were unable to meet the expenses demanded of them (cf. Dem. 20.18-21). As a consequence, these latter leased out their obligations to contractors (Dem. 21.80 and 155; 51). In 357/6 Periandros introduced a reform of the trierarchy intended to spread the burden more evenly by dividing the 1,200 most wealthy citizens into twenty tax groups known as *summoriai*. These were further subdivided into *sunteleiai*, each of which was responsible for the maintenance of one ship. Proof that this elaborate system was no more successful than its predecessor is provided by a speech of Demosthenes (4.35) delivered in 351, in which he enquires of his audience:

> Why do you think, Athenians, that all our naval expeditions are too late for the emergencies of war? ... In the conduct of war and the preparations leading to it everything is in disarray, disorganised and ill-defined ... We spend the time for action on preparation, but the emergencies do not last as long as our caution and hesitation.

This state of affairs did not radically improve until *c.* 340 when the naval establishment reaped the benefit of Athens' improved economic condition. Shortly before that date the private equipment of trierarchs had been nationalised and conscription introduced to provide adequate rowers for the fleet. It was probably in 340 that Demosthenes reformed the trierarchy by reducing the number liable to the liturgy from 1,200 to 300. The next year repair work was carried out on the walls at Eetioneia and Mounychia. The same decade saw the completion of Philon's Arsenal, which greatly facilitated the handing out and recovery of naval gear and which was perhaps intended to alleviate a situation which had become insupportable.

Probably as a direct consequence of these reforms the size of Athens' fleet increased and the efficiency of her naval administration improved. By 322 she possessed over 400 ships, and in that same year dispatched what may well have been her largest naval expedition ever, a fleet of 170 ships. It is one of the ironies of history that at precisely the moment when the Piraeus was better equipped to serve the needs of the navy than ever before, Athenian sea power suffered a fatal reverse.

As Aristophanes (*Ach.* 550-2) informs us, when a naval expedition was on the point of despatch, the Piraeus shipyards reverberated with the sound of oars being fitted into place, accompanied by the shouts, flutes and whistles of naval officers giving orders to their crews. This brief but graphic picture of the corporate bustle of the Piraeus contrasts starkly with Aeschylus' image of Ares as the 'gold-broker of corpses' who exchanges soldiers for the ashes which are sent back to their families in cinerary urns (*Ag.* 433-44). Just as it was from the quayside of the Piraeus that Athenians waved goodbye to their loved ones as each fleet set sail, so too it was here on the quayside that they anxiously awaited the grim return of a dispatch boat bearing cinerary urns in place of men, a melancholy ritual that was consummated with near-seasonal regularity.

3. Religion

(a) General

Archaeological and epigraphical evidence do not enable us to determine how many cults existed in the Piraeus before the Hippodamian period. All that can be said with a fair degree of certainty is that its deme cults were both numerous and ancient; that the cult of Artemis Mounychia was one of the most venerable in the region; and that Mounychia Hill was a hallowed spot long before the fifth century. It is clear from *c.* 430 onwards, however, that the introduction of new deities was beginning to reflect the composition of an increasingly mixed population. During the next two centuries this influx rapidly gathered pace as more and more settlements of foreigners came to dwell around the harbour from places as far apart as Caria, Cyprus, Egypt, Phoenicia, Phrygia and Thrace. Among the most distinctive were the Egyptian gods, notably Isis and Sarapis, who became increasingly popular from the third century onwards.

By the end of the third century the cults in the Piraeus available to both demesmen and non-demesmen, Greeks and non-Greeks, men and women, slaves and free, were extremely numerous and varied. Mercenaries, metics and merchants from all over the eastern Mediterrranean had established themselves in small groups, each of which served as a focus for activity of a social and commercial as well as religious nature.

Aristotle asserted that Hippodamian town-planning required the division of the land into three parts, one of which was sacred, but the present state of archaeological knowledge of the Piraeus does not permit us to determine conclusively whether its shrines were concentrated in specific areas. Though the existence of a large number of them is known from epigraphical and literary testimonia, the siting of the majority is at best only approximately determined, while only three have been excavated and published in detail. None the less, it is perfectly feasible to conceive of the demarcation of specific areas of the Piraeus for religious use, not least because the

naval and commercial zones were so demarcated (see above p. 85
and below p. 156).

The most abundant source of evidence is provided by the
epigraphical testimonia assembled in Appendix III.* A total of
about 150 inscriptions recording dedications, honorific decrees,
sacral laws, and, occasionally, lists of members of religious
associations or clubs have survived. Since the wording of these
inscriptions is highly formulaic, the majority tell us little about cult
practices. Dedications, which constitute the majority (some 60 in
all), normally contain a maximum of three words: the name of the
deity in the dative case either followed or preceded by the dedicant
in the nominative with the verb 'he/she dedicated (*anethêke*)' an
optional extra. Honorific decrees, the next largest category (over 30)
record with monotonous frequency the decision by society X to
praise official Y and crown him (or her) with a wreath of olives (less
commonly of gold) because of his virtue (*aretê*), piety (*eusebeia*) or
propriety (*dikaiosunê*) with respect to deity Z. Sometimes an
association openly states that its purpose in honouring its officials is
to encourage similar manifestations of piety in the future, the
formula being 'so that the *orgeônes* (or *thiasôtai*) may be shown to be
giving due thanks to those who have exercised public spirit
(*philotimia*) on their behalf'. More informative because they are more
individualised are the sacral laws passed either by the Athenian
Demos or, in the case of private cults, by the cult associations
themselves. In addition to the epigraphical testimonia, there are the
archaeological data, extremely patchy in view of the fact that well
over half the temples and shrines which are known to have existed in
the Piraeus have so far not been located. Thirdly, there are a few
literary references to foreign cults, almost all of them hostile,
proceeding as they do from authors who are undisguisedly
contemptuous of the allegedly immoderate behaviour which their
exotic rites engendered.

Broadly speaking three categories of religious activity existed in
the Piraeus, which, judged together, contributed to a spiritual life of
considerable scope, just as colourful, varied and exotic (if not more
so) as that which was available in the Asty. First there were the state
cults, such as those of Artemis Mounychia, Asklepios and Zeus
Soter. Secondly, constituting the largest category, there were the
private cults whose membership in each case generally numbered

---

* Numbers in brackets in this chapter refer to Appendix III, unless otherwise
indicated.

less than 50, and which were chiefly though not exclusively established in honour of foreign deities such as Syrian Aphrodite, the Phrygian Mother Goddess and Egyptian Isis. A few of these foreign imports, such as Isis and Sabazios, were to gain eventual acceptance in the Asty, but the majority were confined to the harbour town and remained the concern of privately organised associations. Thirdly, there were the deme cults. Some of these, such as those of Demeter and Dionysos, are likely to have been established before the port's foundation, but the paucity of physical remains predating the fifth century leaves it unclear whether many were of high antiquity.

The religious year of the Piraeus was very full, as may be seen from the calendar of festivals listed in Table 2. No fewer than four – the Asklepieia, the Bendideia, the Dionysia in Piraeus and the Thesmophoria – were *heortai* (see Mikalson 1982, 218), i.e. were provided with a particularly elaborate festival structure. The Piraeus was also the scene of the great sacrifice in honour of Zeus Soter, one of the very largest *thusiai* held in all Attike. Probably all these celebrations were *dêmoteleis*, i.e. state-funded and therefore in part state-administered. There is good reason to believe, moreover, that we know the names of only a fraction of the total number of festivals celebrated at deme level. Each festival will be considered under the heading of the deity concerned, but it may be noted here that the Piraeus also served as a venue for those in honour of deities whose shrines were located elsewhere but who at festival time required access to the sea. The Panathenaia, held in honour of Athene in Hekatombaion, for instance, included a boat race which probably followed the shoreline from the Grand Harbour to Mounychia Port. In Boedromion, on the second day of the Mysteries of Demeter and Kore, known as the day of *halade mustai*, initiates drove in carts either to Phaleron or to the Piraeus in order to purify themselves and their piacular pigs by immersion in salt water. In Thargelion was staged the Plynteria or Washing-festival of Athene Polias when the goddess' old wooden statue was carried down to Phaleron and given a ceremonial scrub-down. Lastly there was the Aianteia, strictly a Salaminian festival which in the Hellenistic period included a boat race from the Piraeus to Salamis. It should also be borne in mind that in addition to annual festivals, there were regular monthly festivals celebrated in the Piraeus as elsewhere in Attike.

Table 2. Calendar of festivals

Month	Festival
Hekatombaion	Sacrifice to Zeus Ammon?
	Naval regatta as part of Panathenaia
Metageitnion	None attested
Boedromion	*Halade mustai* in Eleusinian Mysteries
	Epidauria
Pyanopsion	Oschophoria
	Plerosia (deme)
	Thesmophoria (deme)?
Maimakterion	None attested
Posideon	Dionysia in Piraeus (deme)
Gamelion	Diasia (deme)
Anthesterion	None attested
Elaphebolion	Asklepieia
Mounychion	Mounychia
Thargelion	Bendideia
	Plynteria
Skirophorion	Skira (deme)
	Diisoteria

Unknown date: Adoneia, Aianteia, Attideia, Paralia and Peiraia (deme).

Of the Olympian deities the most popular was Zeus. Aphrodite, Apollo, Artemis, Athene, Demeter, Dionysos and Hermes all enjoyed worship here, but there is no evidence for a cult of Ares or Here. The sea god Poseidon was not prominent, a circumstance which can probably best be explained by the fact that there was a multiplicity of deities who were regarded as protectors of seafarers. The most important of these were Zeus Soter and Athene Soteira, to whom it was customary to make an offering after the successful conclusion of a voyage; Artemis Mounychia, who, in addition to her association with young girls approaching puberty (see below p. 113f.), came in time to preside over the port area as 'watcher of harbours' (*limenoskopos*, cf. Kall. 3.259); the hero Paralos, whose worshippers constituted the crew of the sacred trireme of that name; Apollo Delios, to whose cult *nauklêroi* contributed a levy of 1 dr. after each voyage (no. 14); Egyptian Isis, and others.

Offerings were made by sailors both upon boarding (*embatêria* sc. *hiera*) and upon disembarking (*apobatêria*). The departure of a naval expedition was attended by a particularly elaborate ritual involving those on the quayside as well as those on board ship. When the Athenian fleet was on the point of departure for Sicily in 415, silence was proclaimed by the blast of a trumpet, the customary prayers for the success of the mission were spoken by a herald, libations poured, and, after the singing of a paean, the ships sailed off (Thuk. 6.32.1).

The Piraeus was the primary entry point in Attike for new cults, being subject to foreign influence not only by virtue of its trading community, but also, during the period of Macedonian domination, in consequence of the mercenary garrison on Mounychia Hill. It was not, however, the only entry point. An inscription that has been dated to the first century records the establishment of a cult of the Phrygian-Anatolian goddess Agdistis at Rhamnous. Roussel (1930, 8) has attractively suggested that the cult should be attributed to the presence of a mercenary garrison here during the Macedonian era, but it is also possible that small communities of foreign traders regularly existed in ports other than the Piraeus, particularly in those periods when it was cut off from the Asty.

The impetus behind the introduction of foreign cults into the Piraeus from the final decades of the fifth century onwards was essentially a consequence of the cultural diversity of a multi-ethnic society. Foreign cults were an important feature in the social life of *xenoi* and *metoikoi*, providing them with a natural outlet through which to express their sense of national identity, so vital to any expatriate community. An instructive parallel can be drawn with the Hellenistic burial societies of Rhodes, of which Fraser (1977, 60) writes:

> They provided foreign residents ... with the same type of social environment, the same modes of advancement, and the same opportunities for lavish benefactions, as were provided by the civic organisations for Rhodian demesmen, who themselves rarely, if ever, belonged.

Unfortunately the abundant epigraphical data available for the study of private religious associations in the Piraeus tell us little about the religious rituals which distinguished one cult from another. Mostly what we learn about, in interminable and repetitious detail, are such mundane matters as the admission and subscription of new members, the duties and privileges of the various elected officers, the appointment of new officers and the honours awarded to them at the end of their period of office, the dates of the periodic assemblies, the upkeep and maintenance of the sanctuary, the introduction of new laws and the penalties imposed on members

who seek to contravene or subvert them, the proper celebration of
the regular religious assemblies, and so on.

In most cases the chief officiant* was either a priest or priestess or
occasionally both (cf. no. 38), sometimes assisted by an attendant or
sacristan known as a *zakoros* (no. 91). A *tamias* or treasurer collected
membership dues and disbursed funds for setting up *stêlai*, holding
sacrifices, and paying for repairs to the sanctuary (no. 115). The
association's decrees and ordinances were recorded by a *grammateus*
or secretary. An *epimelêtês*, or alternatively a board of two or three
such supervisors, assisted by junior officials called *hieropoioi*, took
care of the *hieron*, convened assemblies known as *agorai*, announced
honours awarded to outgoing officers, and were responsible for
setting up the *stêlai* on which such honours were recorded.

All major decisions were taken at a meeting of the *agora kuria*
which met on a fixed day in each month. Most officials were elected
for one year and where appointment was by a popular vote (e.g. no.
86.5f.), a successful candidacy probably depended largely upon an
individual's *philotimia,* in effect, his ability and readiness to
contribute to the running expenses of the association and, especially,
to finance its building projects (cf. nos. 9, 62, 90-1 and 112). The
rewards for loyal and devoted service to outgoing officers included a
disbursement from the sanctuary treasury to the honorand for the
purpose of making a dedication or *anathêma* (nos. 9.50f. and 144.9);
the installation of their portrait (*eikôn*) on a wooden plaque (*pinax*)
within the sanctuary precinct (no. 146.17f.); and the proclaiming of
their generosity and other sterling attributes 'whenever the *thiasôtai*
make sacrifice or pour libations' (no. 86.14f.). A *stêlê* conferring these
and suchlike honours was erected in the *hieron* itself. Failure on the
part of the official responsible to comply with the resolutions thereon
inscribed was punishable by a fine made payable to the deity (no.
86.21ff.). Those who sought to violate a society's laws or *nomoi* faced
fines or possible expulsion (no. 39.13).

Though their records tell us nothing of the social benefits of
membership in such exclusive organisations, we can be certain that
the proceedings were occasionally enlivened by activities of a
convivial nature. In addition, it would be surprising if members did

---

* The following extrapolation is based on evidence taken primarily from the
associations organised in honour of Bendis and the Mother Goddess, as well as the
Dionysiastai, who supply the most information about their structure. As Jon
Mikalson points out to me, the devotees of Isis, for instance, might have arranged
themselves quite differently.

not from time to time unite in joint business ventures. Finally, some groups acted as corporations in matters that had to do with death and burial (nos. 61, 90 and 143), and one at least recognised social obligations that extended beyond its own membership (no. 92).

The earliest associations for which we have epigraphical data styled themselves *orgeônes*. From the end of the fourth century onwards, however, the commonest title for a religious club was *thiasos*. Later, in the third and second centuries, the names *eranos*, *koinon* and *sunodos* became standard, while some groups, such as the Sarapiastai, dispensed with any more formal designation altogether. Many scholars are of the opinion that this varied nomenclature reflects the varied composition and constitution of the clubs themselves. It is often alleged, for instance, that *orgeônes* were at first bands of citizens linked in worship to a common deity who only later extended their membership to include metics and slaves, whereas *thiasoi* were essentially composed of 'compatriots in a foreign land united primarily for the worship of their national deities' (Tod 1932, 74). Our present state of knowledge does not in my estimation, however, support such a clear-cut distinction. In the first place, the earliest known Attic *orgeônes*, those constituted in honour of Bendis, were composed in part of emigré Thracians; and secondly, the records of the votaries of the Mother of the Gods demonstrate that at least on one occasion the terms *orgeônes* and *thiasôtai* were used indiscriminately (no. 85).

Initially the composition of most religious associations is likely to have been ethnically homogeneous. Later some at least proselytised from the population as a whole. Size of membership varied but was probably never considerable. The largest of which we have record, an unidentified association in Athens, had 93 members; the smallest, the Dionysiastai in the Piraeus, as few as 15 (no. 60). Probably the average strength fell somewhere between, as in the case of the Sabaziastai whose register comprised 53 names (no. 110). Membership was in some cases hereditary, but more commonly determined by a vote of the whole association. An entrance fee was required, supplemented by an annual subscription. A minority admitted women. Of the club with 93 members referred to above, 34 were women. All the 53 Sabaziastai were, however, male as too were the 15 Dionysiastai. Children were probably encouraged to join, as is suggested by the statutes of the Athenian Iobacchoi.

In the fifth and fourth centuries the Athenian Demos monitored the entry of foreign cults very closely. Metics wishing to acquire a plot of land in Attike on which to erect a shrine to a foreign god were required to find a sponsor and to submit a formal request to the ekklesia for a grant of *enktêsis chôriou*. The first known instance of such a grant was given 'exclusively to the Thracians of all races (*ethnê*)' in *c.* 429 for the worship of Bendis (no. 43). In 333 the merchants of Kition in Cyprus were given *enktêsis* to build a shrine to their national goddess Aphrodite (no. 6). In such cases application was made first to the boule who determined whether it should be referred to the ekklesia. The petitioners addressed the assembly in support of the proposal and afterwards any Athenian could reply 'to the best of his judgement' (no. 6.25). The inscription recording the decree of the Athenian assembly acceding to the request of the Kitians cites as a precedent the foundation of a *hieron* of Isis by the Egyptians to whom *enktêsis* had been granted previously. The Thracians, Egyptians and Kitians are the only metics known to have sought and obtained official permission to establish *hiera*. That none of the many cults which made their entry subsequently allude to the privilege of *enktêsis* is probably due to the fact that by the end of the fourth century it was no longer seen as an exclusive privilege.

Not all cultic associations were so favourably endowed as the three just mentioned, as is indicated by the fact that a number of sacred properties were owned and leased out by the Athenian state. Such properties are classified according to their agricultural usage as either *chôrion* (tilled land), *eschatia* (undeveloped borderland) or *kêpeion* (garden or orchard), and were rented out to an individual lessee for periods of ten years at a time, probably with the option of renewal when the original contract expired. Two such leases refer to *kêpeia* whose location in each case is given as 'on the right hand as you go towards Mounychia'. These leases, like the grants to the Egyptians and Kitians, date principally to the third quarter of the fourth century and should probably be interpreted as falling within the general revision of Athens' finances and religious structure which took place under the direction of Euboulos and Lykourgos. Not only the state but also the deme could issue a lease of this kind, as is indicated by an inscription regarding the letting of 'the Theseion and all the other *temenê*' by the demesmen of Piraeus in 321/0 (Appendix II no. 4).

It remains to inquire whether the presence of so many foreign cults in the Piraeus can be taken as unambiguous testimony of Athenian *philoxenia*. My own suspicion is that the Athenian attitude is more complex than it at first sight seems. A large quantity of inscriptions relating to foreign associations came to light in the last century on the southern part of Akte peninsula at a place called Myloi or 'The Mills' (e.g. nos. 7, 8, 86, 88, 90, 142, 145 and 151). Others have been found on or near the peninsula of Eetioneia to the north (e.g. nos. 36 and 69). This concentration of foreign shrines on the outskirts of the residential area is presumably in the main a reflection of the density of settlement on the Piraeus peninsula, though it is also possible that the state was reluctant to allow foreigners to purchase land in a central location. Moreover, it is highly revealing that of all the religious inscriptions that have been discovered in the Piraeus only those which refer to Phoenician cults are in a language other than Greek (nos. 36 and 100). What is remarkable about these bilingual documents is not merely the fact that they are in Phoenician but that the Phoenician transcribes the formulaic phrases adopted by the whole genre of religious honorific decrees. The motive behind such uniformity was not, I would suggest, wholly spontaneous. Structurally identical, yet ethnically distinct (at least in their initial membership), foreign cult associations may have provided the Athenian state with the means to liaise with its foreign community, not least because their internal affairs were administered strictly in accordance with the democratic principles espoused by the state itself.

Table 3. Foreign deities worshipped in the Piraeus

Deity	*Place of origin*	*Earliest testimony*
Ammon	Egyptian	*c.* 400-350
Aphrodite Euploia	Carian	*c.* 394
Artemis Nana	Phrygian	end of the 2nd cent.
Aphrodite Ourania	Syrian	333/2
Baal or Bel (?)	Phoenician	3rd cent.
Bendis	Thracian	*c.* 429/8
Isis	Egyptian	before 333/2
Kabeiroi	Phrygian	*c.* 420
Men	Lydian or Phrygian	3rd cent.
Mother of the Gods	Phrygian	4th cent.
Nergal	Phoenician	3rd cent. (?)
Sabazios	Thrako-Phrygian	late 5th cent.
Sarapis	Egyptian	end of 3rd cent.
Zeus Ammon	Egyptian	*c.* 400-350
Zeus Labraundos	Carian	beginning of 2nd cent.

For the Peiraieis themselves, who constituted a minority among the population perhaps as early as the mid-fifth century, deme religion had a particularly significant and vital role to play, by serving to reinforce unity and collective identity among those families whose connections with the region were at least as old as the reforms of Kleisthenes. To judge by the sacred calendar of Erkheia, a more-than-average size deme, an estimate for the Piraeus of forty to fifty gods and heroes receiving worship under deme control would not be excessive. Heroes who were the object of cult include Akrapotes, Eetion, Mounychos, Phreatos and Serangos. Deme festivals include the Diasia, which was held in honour of Zeus Meilichios, the Dionysia in Piraeus, the Plerosia, a ritual ploughing to appease the *theoi proerosiai*, the Skira, held in honour of Athene Skiras, and the Thesmophoria (see Table 2 above). Little is known about any of these festivals with the exception of the Piraeus Dionysia, but they no doubt resembled state festivals in all but popularity and size. The exclusiveness of the deme as a corporate entity is indicated by the fact that whereas some of its religious rituals were public (*koina*) and so open to all Athenians, there were others which only demesmen could attend (Appendix II no. 6 ll. 14-17). Just as state priests were answerable to the Athenian Demos, so deme priests were answerable to their deme. This is demonstrated by the decree of the Piraeus (Appendix II no. 1.1-2) which orders the priestess of the Thesmophorion, in association with the demarch, to ensure that the sanctuary was not violated by sacrilegious or unseasonal practices (see Whitehead 1986, 182 for other examples from other demes).

The vitality of the religious life of the Piraeus remained undiminished by the economic decline of the harbour in the third and second centuries. Indeed the epigraphical testimonia support the tentative conclusion that the number of religious associations substantially increased in the Hellenistic era – tentative because of the overall increase in inscriptions which this period also witnessed. Private cults whose earliest attestations postdate *c.* 300 include Agathe Tyche, Artemis Nana, Baal (or Bel), Men, Nergal, Sarapis and Zeus Labraundos. The departure of the Macedonian garrison in 228 probably encouraged the entry of new cults. Of special interest are the Sarapiastai, whose emergence in the last decades of the third century may reflect the close ties which currently existed between Athens and Egypt. Another prominent group who established themselves in *c.* 200 were the Dionysiastai, a prestigious guild which erected a large and imposing *hieron* in a prime locality to the west of the Hippodamian Agora. It is in connection with the Dionysiastai that there exists the only evidence found in the Piraeus for the widespread Hellenistic practice of according heroic status (*aphierôsis*) to a deceased former associate (no. 61). The names Sarapiastai and Dionysiastai, as Stewart (1977, 519) points out, seem to assert 'a definite commitment on the part of the members to the god' and should perhaps be interpreted as evidence of the emergence of exclusive personal ties between man and god, judged to be a marked feature of Hellenistic religion.

Whether public cults flourished to the same degree as private ones in the Hellenistic era is less clear, though there are numerous references in ephebic decrees belonging to the period from *c.* 120 to 86 to the Mounychia, the Dionysia in Piraeus and the Diisoteria. Possibly these references reflect a revival of interest in state cult prompted by a return to more settled conditions following Athens' absorption within the Roman sphere of influence.

It is often alleged, and with some justification, that the dissolution of the Greek city state in the Hellenistic period is directly attributable to the growth of the various clubs, guilds, fraternities and associations which sapped the collective heart out of the polis and fragmented the communal spirit of its citizenry. Such a theory, which may possibly explain the decline of the polis as an effective political force, certainly fails to do justice to its versatility as a medium through which new concepts and foreign influences could be disseminated. Mumford's claim (1961, 236) that the variety of non-Greek religions and philosophies that spread through Greece from the Archaic period onwards 'revealed a profound disillusion with the fundamental premises of civilization' is itself profoundly wrong-headed. What their presence in fact reveals, and nowhere better than in the present instance, is the continuing vitality of the polis as receiver and transmitter. I have concentrated in this chapter upon religion because it is religion which happens to have left most traces upon our records. But there can be little doubt that the material culture and intellectual life of the port were similarly diversified and stimulated by the presence of its heterogeneous community.

(b) Cults

I conclude this chapter with an investigation of cults and foundations arranged alphabetically.

Aphrodite

A temple of Aphrodite was set up on Eetioneia some time in the fifth century, possibly at the instigation of Themistokles as a thank-offering for the victory at Salamis in 480.

Aphrodite Euploia

A sanctuary to Aphrodite was dedicated by Konon after his naval victory off Knidos on the west coast of Karia in 394 (Paus. 1.1.3). Aphrodite, as Pausanias informs us, was held in high esteem by the Knidians who worshipped the goddess under the title of Euploia (Of the Safe Voyage) and it is very likely that Konon's *hieron* was erected in her honour.

Aphrodite Ourania

The cult of the Syrian goddess Aphrodite Ourania (Heavenly) and her paramour Adonis received unfavourable mention in both Aristophanes and Diphilos, the latter sneering that it was particularly popular among courtesans and whores (*hetairai* and *pornai*). It probably arrived in the Piraeus in 333, well over a century later than its first arrival in the Asty. To 333 belongs the grant of *enktêsis* to the *emporoi* of Kition for the acquiring of a plot of land to erect a *hieron* to Aphrodite (no. 6). The decree, which was found in the Piraeus, was probably displayed within the temple precinct. Though it does not specify which Aphrodite is to be so honoured, a fourth-century dedication by a Kitian to Aphrodite Ourania found 'in the southern part of the Piraeus peninsula' (no. 7; cf. no. 8) should probably be associated with this shrine.

Three honorific decrees dated to the end of the fourth century and another belonging to the middle of the third may also belong to the same cult (nos. 9 and 10). If this attribution is correct, they indicate that other Cypriots, notably Salaminians, subsequently enlisted as *thiasôtai*. These decrees contain references to the Adoneia or festival of Adonis, a central feature of which was the placing of small 'Adonis gardens' containing swiftly germinating seeds on flat roof-tops. An effigy of the god was then laid out on this simulated bier, later to be thrown into the sea. It was during the Adoneia that the Athenians dispatched the ill-fated Sicilian Expedition in 415.

Since its climax involved loud lamentation for the dead Adonis, understandably the timing was regarded as very ill-omened (Ar. *Lys.* 390-7; Plu. *Nik.* 13.7).

Artemis Mounychia

The cult of Artemis Mounychia may well have been one of the earliest to be established in the Piraeus. Its foundation myth, which explains the origin of the custom of sacrificing a goat in the goddess's honour, is explained in the Suda (s.v. *Embaros eimi*) as follows:

> After the slaughter by the Athenians of a bear which had broken into the sanctuary of Artemis Mounychia, a plague ravaged Athens. The god (i.e. Apollo) prophesied that its expulsion would only come about if an Athenian sacrificed his daughter to the goddess. A certain Baros (sic) agreed to do so on condition that the priesthood should henceforth be hereditary among his own genos. He then sacrificed instead a ram which had been disguised to resemble his daughter.

Artemis Mounychia is the only example of a Piraeic cult known to have been gentile, that is to say, one whose priesthood was reserved among the (female) members of a single genos. This fact alone argues strongly for a foundation date well before the reforms of Kleisthenes in 508/7. The allusion to human sacrifice is also suggestive of high antiquity, though the tale that in historical times a goat was substituted for a human victim does not necessarily permit the conclusion that in earlier times a human victim had been required (cf. Henrichs 1981).

There are several indications that the cult was closely allied to that of Artemis Brauronia. First, both comprised rituals which were explained by the slaughter of a she-bear which had incurred the wrath of Artemis. They differ in the fact that whereas in the Mounychian *aition* the sacrifice of a virgin was required in expiation of the crime, in the Brauronian version Athenian virgins were ordered to perform an annual ritual known as the Arkteia which involved 'playing the bear *(arkteuein)*'.

Secondly, excavations conducted at Mounychia have yielded an example of a *krateriskos* or small mixing-bowl, which has been found in greatest profusion at the sanctuary of Brauronian Artemis. *Krateriskoi* are sometimes decorated with scenes of girls either performing a solemn dance or running towards an altar. They belong mainly to the first half of the fifth century, though the shape of the vase is at least protogeometric in origin. Kahil (1965, 25) has suggested that the females are *arktoi*, young girls who performed the Arkteia. The ceremony is believed to have been one of initiation for those approaching marriageable years, intended to ensure the goddess's protection and avert her anger. Whether it is legitimate to conclude that the Arkteia was performed at Mounychia is a matter of continuing controversy.

The Mounychia, which took place on 16th Mounychion, is likely to have been one of the most important festivals held anywhere in Attike, not least since it gave its name to the month. The main ceremony was performed at night when worshippers brought to Artemis small round cakes called 'objects-shining-on-all-sides' (*amphiphontes*), so named because they were decorated with torches like the cakes which were offered to Hekate at crossroads. On the same day, and conjointly, the Athenians commemorated the anniversary of their naval victory at Salamis, since, according to Plutarch (*Mor.* 349f), 'on that day the goddess shone with a full moon upon the Greeks as they were conquering at Salamis'. Inscriptions dating from *c.* 120 onwards indicate that in this later period the festival included a naval race for ephebes in sacred ships from the Grand Harbour to Mounychia Port, upon completion of which the participants ascended to the goddess's shrine and performed a sacrifice in her honour (nos. 17-20). The Mounychia is the only festival celebrated in the Piraeus which is known to have retained its importance well into the Roman imperial period: as late as A.D. 192/3 there is a reference to ephebes performing a sea-battle (*naumachia*) at the festival (no. 21). A cult of Artemis Mounychia is known also to have existed in the deme of Thorikos, south of Brauron on the east coast of Attike.

Artemis Nana

A single inscription dated to the close of the second century testifies to the existence of a cult of the Semitic deity Artemis Nana or Nanaia. Nana was the mother of Attis, whom she conceived from the severed genitals of the androgynous Kybele. In origin she was an old Babylonian goddess whose main temple was in Uruk in Southern Iraq. She appears in a hellenized form both as Artemis and as Aphrodite. There is no evidence for the cult in the Greek world outside the Piraeus. Very possibly, she may have been introduced at the same time as the Mother Goddess and even have received worship in the same sanctuary (cf. Clerc 1893, 142).

Asklepios

Asklepios first entered Attike at Zea Port . The spot was marked by a sanctuary in which he was worshipped along with a number of minor deities also connected with the healing art. Previously in Attike the healing art had been confined to a number of relatively insignificant shrines. When Asklepios subsequently arrived in the Asty under the patronage of a certain Telemachos in 420/19 or 419/18 he found temporary accommodation in the City Eleusinion and later a second shrine was established on the south side of the Acropolis, adjoining the Pelargikon Wall.

The Asklepieion in the Piraeus was probably contemporary in foundation with its counterpart in the Asty. The date when the cult first entered Zea is not recorded, but Mikalson (1984, 220) has attractively suggested that the unsuccessful Athenian attack in 430/29 on Epidavros, the site of the god's foremost sanctuary, was in part inspired by the desire to secure 'access to or control of the leading healing deity of the period' (cf. Thuk. 2.56.4). The attack was repulsed and since no further attempt was made on Epidavros during the Archidamian War it is probable that Asklepios' entry to Attike took place shortly after peace had been concluded in 421, with no more than a year's delay before his subsequent establishment in Athens.

The two *hiera* of Asklepios each had their own annually elected priest. It is impossible to determine whether the two branches of the cult were of equal status and how the priests divided responsibilities in the staging of the Epidauria and Asklepieia, the two Athenian festivals held in the god's honour. It is, however, a priori likely that the Piraeus sanctuary took a leading role in the staging of the Epidauria, which constituted a re-enactment of the god's original arrival.

A sacral law (no. 26) found in the Piraeus dating to the fourth century indicates that Asklepios shared his shrine with a collectivity of other deities known as 'temple sharers *(sunnaoi theoi)*'. These included Maleatas, Apollo and Hermes, who were all credited with medical powers, and Iaso, Akeso and Panakeia, personifications of the healing art who were conceived of as the daughters of Asklepios. Those seeking the god's assistance made preliminary offerings *(prothumata)* in the form of cakes to the *sunnaoi theoi* as well as to the sacred dogs and *kunêgetai* (dog handlers?). They then sacrificed a pig

Fig. 19. Head and fragmentary torso of a god identified as Asklepios, second century B.C.

to Asklepios and awaited the cure through incubation within the sanctuary.

Fig. 20. Votive relief of *c.* 350 depicting Asklepios treating a patient with an injured or diseased shoulder. On the left, reduced in scale, the patient's family looks on.

The most impressive find from the Asklepieion is the head and torso of a fragmentary colossal statue of the god (Fig. 19) which is dated to the second century B.C. (Stewart 1979, 48-51). Several votive offerings set up by grateful patients have also been discovered (Fig. 20), along with two decrees commemorating a priest called Euthydemos. There is evidence for cultic activity in the shrine well into the Roman imperial era as is indicated by an inscription set up in A.D. 212/3 by the Paianistai of Mounychian Asklepios (no. 32).

Baal or Bel (?)

A bilingual inscription in Greek and Phoenician (no. 36) which probably belongs to the third century reveals the presence of a *koinon* of Sidonians devoted to the worship of their civic god who is probably Baal or Bel.

Bendis

The cult of the Thracian goddess Bendis provides the earliest
epigraphical evidence for the existence of a major foreign cult in the
Piraeus. Not much is known about her identity other than that she
probably had close connections with Artemis. Cult images depict
her as a girl clad in Thracian hunting gear accompanied by a hound
and holding a spear (Fig. 21). On votive reliefs she is often
associated with a hero called Deloptes who is depicted as an old man
leaning on a staff (no. 42; cf. no. 46).

Regulations regarding the public worship of Bendis are preserved
in a fragmentary *psêphisma* passed by the Athenian demos which is
variously dated between 432/1 and 411 (no. 38). The decree lays
down conditions for the appointment of a priest and/or priestess
who is to be democratically elected 'from all the Athenians'. It also
regulates the details of the public sacrifice in the goddess's honour,
apportioning the parts of the sacrificial victims. There are references
to an offering of first-fruits (*eparchê*) to the goddess and to an
all-night festival (*pannuchis*). Whether the inscription records the

Fig. 21. Votive relief in honour of Bendis, *c.* 400-350. The scene depicts a
team of victors in the torch-race standing behind their trainers who are
offering a libation to the goddess.

actual inauguration of the public cult as Ferguson (1949, 132) supposed, or whether it merely deals with supplementary measures as Bingen (1959, 35) later suggested, remains a matter for conjecture. What is certain is that the public cult was fully established by 429/8 at the latest, since the first two letters of the name of Bendis occur in the treasury account of the Other Gods for that year (no. 37).

There existed two bands of *orgeônes* of Bendis in the Piraeus, one for citizens, the other for Thracians. The existence of the two groups is proved by a reference to Athenians serving as *hieropoioi* in an inscription dated 337/6 (no. 40) and to Thracians worshipping as an *ethnos* in another dated 261/0 (no. 43). There is also slight evidence to suggest that they occupied separate shrines in different parts of the Piraeus (see below p. 162). As Ferguson (1949, 153 n. 65) has pointed out, the citizen *orgeônes* met on the second day of the month (no. 39), whereas the Thracians met on the eighth (nos. 43-4). The latter probably included slaves among their number, since their names sometimes lack patronymics (e.g. nos. 42 and 46). The Thracians claim to have been the first ethnic group to be honoured with a grant of *enktêsis* for the purpose of setting up a *hieron* in which to venerate their national goddess. If, as is likely, the state's desire to incorporate Bendis within the official pantheon was prompted in part by the presence in Athens of Thracian worshippers of the goddess (see below), then probably this grant either accompanied or preceded the establishment of the public cult, both decrees being authorised by an oracle from Dodona. No later than 261/0 a further development took place with the formation of a splinter band of *orgeônes* in the Asty for the convenience of those Thracians who were resident in Athens (no. 43). There is no evidence that the citizen *orgeônes* ever divided in this way.

The introduction of the cult of Bendis represents a remarkable but by no means unique example of the influence of foreign policy on domestic worship, as Nilsson (1951, 45-8) correctly surmised. It is evident from Thukydides (2.29.4) that at the outbreak of the Peloponnesian War the Athenians attached considerable importance to the advantages to be derived from an alliance with the Odrysian Thracians. The granting of a site on which to worship their deity would surely have been seen as a highly effective way of consolidating such an arrangement.

The Bendideia is known chiefly from Plato's famous description at the beginning of the *Republic,* written probably in *c.* 380. It included two processions, one of citizens (*epichôrioi*), the other of Thracians; a large sacrifice; an equestrian torchlight race (*lampas aph' hippôn*) in which the competitors passed torches to one another as they raced (cf. Fig. 21); and finally, a *pannuchis*. It is worth noting that this was the only Athenian festival in which an ethnic group was permitted to retain its national identity; at the Dionysia and Panathenaia, in which metics also participated, they assembled as an amorphous, undifferentiated body of emigrés. The Bendideia was, therefore, a unique event in the Athenian festal calendar, first because it was devoted to the worship of an outlandish barbarian goddess, and secondly because citizens and aliens each had a leading role to play.

After Plato's description, there is no mention of the festival for some fifty years. To the late 330s, however, date the accounts of the proceeds from the sale of hides of animals sacrificed at Athens' major state festivals, and these testify to Bendis' popularity during this period. In 334/3 they amounted to 457 dr., a figure only exceeded in the surviving records for that year by the City Dionysia and the Olympieia (no. 41) and suggesting that a hecatomb had been slaughtered. A political motive behind the attention which the goddess now receives can again not be excluded since Athens is likely to have been sympathetic towards the Thracians in this period owing to their mutual hatred of Macedon. Nilsson would even go further and argue that the cult ceased to be patronised by the state precisely at the moment when Athens' political influence declined in 322. It is, however, quite unwarranted to assume that lack of information from *c*. 380 to 340 necessarily reflects lack of public interest.

The study of Bendis is especially problematic because it uniquely involves consideration of an Athenian state cult existing alongside privately organised bands of foreign worshippers. Among the questions raised are whether the Demos consulted either officially or unofficially with the Thracians over the establishment of the public cult; whether the citizen and Thracian *orgeônes* co-operated in the everyday management of the cult; and finally, what part the latter played in the staging of the Bendideia, other than providing their own contingent for the procession. Regarding this last issue, it is interesting to note that participation in the procession was not simply an honour conferred upon a privileged ethnic minority. A decree of the Thracian *orgeônes* dated *c*. 261/0 refers to a law which 'bids (*keleuei*)'* them to provide their own contingent in the

---

* In a letter dated 16 April 1986, Sterling Dow writes to me: '*Keleuô* in *LSJ* does

procession. The same decree further informs us that the procession is to commence 'from the shrine of Hestia in the *prutaneion*', a further indication of the importance attached to the cult, since the *prutaneion* in the Asty was the symbolic centre of all Athenian civic and religious authority (Ferguson 1944, 103).

The cult of Bendis throws a valuable light upon conditions in the harbour town at several moments in its history. That the goddess should have first settled in the Piraeus where the majority of Thracian metics are likely to have been domiciled is understandable enough, and her entry and acceptance may have been further facilitated by the existence on Mounychia of a cult of Artemis, with whom Bendis had close connections. The decision to include in the festival a procession from the Asty to the Piraeus may have been determined partly by the fact that from 431 onwards, following the abandonment of the Attic countryside during the Peloponnesian War, other processions, such as those connected with the Brauronia and the Eleusinian Mysteries, had either to be suspended or at best much reduced in size. The journey from the Asty to the Piraeus, all of which could be accomplished within the security of the Long Walls, thus provided the only safe route for a leisurely sacred procession. Though hardly compensating for the decline in religious activity elsewhere in Attike, still less for the wholesale abandonment of holy places (Thuk. 2.16.2), the celebration of the Bendideia may have served as a morale-booster for the population penned up within the city walls, while at the same time emphasising the primary and essential attachment between the upper city and the lower harbour town.

Political determinants may also have provided the stimulus behind the passing of the sacral law of 261/0, referred to above. The preamble to the decree states that its introduction was prompted by a decision recently taken by the *orgeônes* in the Asty to set up their own *hieron* to the goddess. It alludes to negotiations between the Asty and Piraeic *orgeônes* which had recently resulted in the decision to form a joint contingent in the *pompê*. The *epimelêtai* of the Piraeus branch are instructed to meet the procession on its arrival at the Bendideion and to entertain its members to lunch, having first provided them with facilities for washing after their long journey.

---

include the range of meanings from 'request' through 'bid' to 'command'. But I think it needs to be be re-written in part so as to include, more definitely, frequent epigraphical use vaguely in the middle, cf. French *demander.*'

Why such negotiations should have taken place at this time is not hard to discover. As Gauthier (1979, 396) has pointed out, the procession from the Asty to the Piraeus must inevitably have been suppressed in the first half of the third century when the political unity of the two communities was severed. The new law probably signalled its revival following Athens' defeat in the Chremonidean War when the two communities were again re-united. Something of the anguish of estrangement that had been experienced by the divided Thracian community during this troubled period seems to be contained in the expressive wording of the injunction laid upon the priest and priestess

> to pray, in addition to the prayers which they [normally] pray, in the same manner as the *orgeônes* in the Asty, so that, this being accomplished and the whole *ethnos* being in harmony (*homonoöuntos pantos tou [eth] nous*), the sacrifices and related rites can be made to the gods in accordance with the customs (*ta patria*) of the Thracians and the laws(?) of Athens, and so that everything may proceed well and piously (*eusebeiôs*) for the whole *ethnos* in matters pertaining to the gods.

– a clear indication of the fact that, whatever the state's interest in the cult at this date, the goddess none the less remained a vital and enduring focus for Thracian ethnicity abroad.

This is the last surviving reference to the Attic cult of Bendis. Though the cult may conceivably have continued to exist down until the sack of Sulla, it is noticeable that the Bendideia is neither included among those festivals to which allusion is made in the ephebic inscriptions of the late second century, nor merits any lexicographical entry.

Demeter

The popularity of the cult of Demeter in the Piraeus is indicated by the fact that the Thesmophorion or sanctuary of Demeter became so over-crowded in the fourth century that the deme ruled that private sacrifices and other unauthorised activities were not to be performed in it unless conducted in the presence of the priestess (no. 48). Moreover, the Thesmophoria festival was sufficiently grand in scale to be classified as a *heortê* (above p. 103). Several votive offerings to Demeter and Kore have been discovered in connection with the shrine (cf. Fig. 22).

Fig. 22. Fragmentary votive relief depicting Kore holding a torch in either hand and standing beside an altar, *c.* 350. To the right of the altar is the raised arm of a diminutive worshipper.

Dionysiastai

Our knowledge of the Dionysiastai in the Piraeus derives from three honorific decrees and one short honorific poem, all dating to the early years of the second century (nos. 60-2). Each applauds the generosity of Dionysios, son of Agathokles (I), priest and treasurer of the cult, who financed the establishment of a shrine to Dionysos, adorned it with dedications, set up a trust of 1,000 dr. to subsidize monthly sacrifices, and paid for a statue of the god. Upon Dionysios' death in 176/5 the Dionysiastai accorded him the supreme distinction of heroisation (*aphierôsis*) and set up a statue of him 'next to the cult statue of the god ... in order that he should have the fairest memorial (*hupomnêma*) for all time' (no. 61.45-8). At the same time they conferred the title of priest upon his eldest surviving son Agathokles (II), who had previously been treasurer and who thus followed the same career pattern as his father. From this it would seem that the Dionysiastai functioned de facto if not de jure as a genos-organised cult.

It is not known when the Dionysiastai first constituted themselves into a corporate body, but it is likely, as Jon Mikalson has suggested to me, that it was 'a creation of Dionysios himself, to accord special and perhaps exclusive worship to his namesake'. Other than that they performed monthly sacrifices, we know nothing about the group's activities. The preface to one of their decrees (no. 60) lists a total of 15 members, all of them Athenian and all of them male. Their social exclusiveness is confirmed by the size and location of their *hieron* which remained in use until 86. Given these facts, it is extremely unlikely that the Dionysiastai were in any way connected with the *technitai* of Dionysos, a guild of dramatic and musical performers who are well-attested in Athens. Dionysiastai are also found at Tanagra and on the islands of Teos and Rhodes.

Dionysos

In view of the antiquity and popularity of rural Dionysia in Attike, it is very likely that the cult of Dionysos in Piraeus predates the Hippodamian development. The Piraeus festival, which took place in the winter month of Posideon, was the most important of all deme Dionysia. Though essentially a local event placed under the direction of the demarch, it was of sufficient importance to be

counted alongside such major state festivals as the Lenaia, the City
Dionysia and the Thargelia as an occasion 'when it is unlawful to
distrain or seize any debtor's property' (Dem. 21.10). Since, as Jon
Mikalson reminds me, property could not be seized unless the
debtor was himself present, the implication behind this ruling is that
the Dionysia was extremely well-attended. The festival, which lasted
four days, began with a procession through the streets of the Piraeus
during which the god's image and other objects, including most
probably, a giant phallus, were borne aloft (cf. Plu. *Mor.* 527d). It
terminated in the deme theatre, where bulls were sacrificed to the
god. Though the Rural Dionysia is attested for no fewer than
fourteen Attic demes, that celebrated in the Piraeus is the only one
at which both tragedies and comedies are known to have been
performed (Dem. 21.10; cf. Whitehead 1986, 216 n. 235 for other
deme Dionysia). As at the City Dionysia a crown was awarded to
the successful choregos (Appendix II no. 6.29). At least one
Euripidean drama was performed here in the fifth century and
reputedly witnessed by Sokrates (cf. Ael. *VH* 2.13). In 307/6 the
state decreed that ambassadors from Kolophon should be assigned
seats in the theatre so as to witness the Piraeus Dionysia (*IG* II²
456.32f.). The status of the festival is further indicated by the fact

Fig. 23. Votive relief depicting Dionysos reclining on a couch or *klinê* in the
company of actors holding masks and drums *c.* 410. The seated woman is
perhaps Paideia, the personification of culture.

that in 329/8 the *epistatai* of Eleusis made a contribution towards the sacrifice performed at it (*IG* II² 1672.106). It was among those festivals which experienced a revival in *c.* 120, as is indicated by frequent allusions to it in ephebic inscriptions (nos. 54-9).

A votive relief dating to the end of the fifth century probably once stood in the shrine of Dionysos (Fig. 23). It depicts a troupe of actors holding masks and tympana approaching the god who reclines on a couch. Beside Dionysos is a seated woman who, as seems to be indicated by the fragmentary inscription beneath, is perhaps the goddess Paideia, the personification of culture. A colossal bronze mask found in a warehouse in the Piraeus may originally have been dedicated here as well.

Eetion (?)

Likely to have been of considerable antiquity is the cult of Eetion (?), the eponymous hero of the Eetioneia peninsula (see p. 217). A dedication by a '*thiasos* of Etionidai' (sic) dated *c.* 450, found between Moschaton and the Piraeus, is possibly connected with his worship (no. 63).

Eurymedon

A cult of the hero Eurymedon was established in *c.* 468 in commemoration of Kimon's double victory by land and sea over the Persians at the River Eurymedon in Pamphylia (no. 64).

Hermes

The worship of Hermes is attested by an early Classical base which was dedicated by a certain Python of Abdera (no. 69). Reference to a sacrifice to Hermes Hegemonios is preserved in the record of monies raised by the sale of pelts for the years 334/3 and 333/2 (no. 41.84f. and 115f.; cf. no. 71). An important statue of the god probably stood at the Asty Gate (see below p. 166). In view of Hermes' intimate association with commerce, it is hardly surprising that he should have been honoured alongside the road which bore wheeled traffic between the Piraeus and the Asty.

Isis

At a date before 333/2 the Athenians gave permission to the

Fig. 24. Funerary monument of a woman in Isis dress with servant.

Egyptians to establish a *hieron* to Isis (no. 6). The *hieron*, possibly the earliest to be set up to an Egyptian deity in Greece, may well have been situated in the Piraeus.

Isis, known as 'she of innumerable names', became one of the leading deities of the Mediterranean world in the Hellenistic period with temples at Epidavros, Kyme, Samos, Halikarnassos and Miletos. In her hellenized and Romanized form, she offered mystic union through a rite of initiation which mainly appealed to women. In sculpture she is often depicted holding a steering oar, an allusion to her association with navigation. A festival in her honour known as the Ploiaphesia (Launching of the Sacred Ship of Isis), which was celebrated widely throughout the Graeco-Roman world, marked the beginning of the sailing season in March.

Over one hundred grave reliefs of women in Isis dress survive from Attike (cf. Walters 1985). They portray the deceased wearing a fringed shawl knotted between the breasts, holding a rattle (*seistron*) in one hand and a bucket containing Nile water in the other (Fig. 24). None of the reliefs can be dated earlier than the Augustan era and the majority are later, evidence of the goddess's immense popularity in the Roman period.

Kabeiroi

Aristophanes' *Peace* (277ff.) indicates that knowledge of the soteriological cult of the Kabeiroi had reached Athens by *c.* 420 at the latest. The Kabeiroi, who were perhaps Phrygian in origin, were four in number and served as both promoters of fertility and protectors of navigation, being capable of rendering their initiates immune to the dangers of the deep (A.R. *Argon.*1.915-8). They were worshipped especially on Samothrace, Euboia, Imbros and Lemnos, and in the coastal towns of northern Asia Minor. Their cult was believed to be of great antiquity (Hdt. 2.51).

Whether the Kabeiroi received cult in Athens or the Piraeus remains uncertain. As protectors of sailors they were widely worshipped in the Hellenistic world, though Athenians do not appear on lists of *theôroi* to Samothrace until the second century A.D. (Cole 1984, 43). A reference in an ephebic inscription dated 122/1 to a procession in honour of the Megaloi Theoi (*IG* II² 1006.29) evidently held in the Piraeus may possibly denote the Kabeiroi, since this is their title in inscriptions found on Samothrace.

Men

Epigraphical evidence indicates that a *hieron* of the Asiatic Moon-god Men was set up in the Piraeus sometime in the third century (nos. 75 and 76). On Attic reliefs Men is commonly represented sitting on an animal and wearing a Phrygian cap. There is usually a rooster in attendance and a crescent moon above. Inscriptions suggest that the god's adherents were predominantly, if not exclusively, metics and slaves. The cult was particularly prominent in Lydia and Phrygia, especially at Antioch-in-Pisidia where there existed the only temple of the god which has so far been discovered (Str. *Geog.* 12.3.31). No trace of the cult has yet been found on the Greek mainland outside Attike.

Mother of the Gods

The *Mêtêr Theôn* or Mother of the Gods was a deity who delighted in the beating of drums, the clash of cymbals and the trilling of flutes (*h. Met.*). Her cult, whose origins can be traced back to the early Iron Age in Mesopotamia, enjoyed singular popularity in the Piraeus where her votaries have supplied us with more information about their religious activities than any other association based there. Notwithstanding, it remains one of the most problematical to study, its inception and the official reaction to it being particular areas of difficulty. Archaeological evidence indicates that the cult arrived in Athens from Phrygia-Anatolia at the beginning of the fifth century when a small temple was erected on the southwest side of the Athenian Agora, close to the Tholos. The private cult, however, was quite separate from the state cult and seems to have been established independently around the middle of the fourth century. As Ferguson (1944, 222) suggested, probably we should think in terms of an essentially new and alien divinity, more barbarous in aspect than her hellenized predecessor. Her subsequent promotion in the Greek world was largely due to Attalos of Pergamon's conquest in *c.* 230 of Pessinous in Galatia, a city famous for its great shrine of the Mother of the Gods, as is indicated by the fact that inscriptions found in the Piraeus become most prolific from *c.* 220 onwards (cf. nos. 86-9).

The deity's official title is problematic. A number of decrees passed by her votaries simply refer to her as 'the goddess' (e.g. nos. 85, 88, 89, 91 and 94). In at least one instance, however, there is mention of 'the goddesses' (no. 92), while on another occasion it is 'gods' to whom sacrifice was made (no. 90). In dedications, however, the goddess is accorded her full title of 'Mother of the Gods' (e.g. nos. 80, 83, 95-8). Though no explanation can fully account for this inconsistency, it is just possible that the reference to 'gods' was intended to include her son and lover Attis, while 'goddesses' may contain a reference to a second, lower-ranking female deity (e.g. Nana, see above p. 114) closely allied to the Mother of the Gods.

The status and identity of her votaries are also problematic. Of their nine surviving decrees, five emanate from the *orgeônes* and instance proposals put forward by Athenian citizens (nos. 88-92); a sixth was passed by a group calling themselves *thiasôtai* who all appear to have been metics (no. 86); and the seventh, the only other decree containing a reference to their title, was promulgated by an association which dubbed its members *orgeônes* in the body of the decree but *thiasôtai* in the honorific crowns carved above and below the text.

At the head of the cult was an annually elected priestess whose duties included officiating at sacrifices, administering the *hieron*, recording dedications, and organising the Attideia or festival of Attis, in which last-mentioned activity she was sometimes aided by her husband (nos. 88, 89 and 91). Initially the priestess was liable to a supplementary donation (*epithetos dapanê*) which was levied on occasions presumably determined by the votaries as a whole. However, a motion passed in *c.* 175/4 at the request of the ex-priestesses apparently acting en bloc released them from any further obligations of this sort, while at the same time urging stricter economies upon the *orgeônes* so as to render such donations unnecessary (no. 91). An outstanding distinction paid to a priestess called Onaso at the end of the second century was the setting up of her picture in the sanctuary as soon as her period of office had expired (no. 94). The priestess of the *orgeônes* was aided by a *zakoros* who was at first appointed annually, but after *c.* 175/4 for life (no. 91). In addition, there was also a treasurer and secretary who were permanent appointees, and a board of *epimelêtai* which appears to have been elected annually. Minor personnel included cupbearers (*phialêphoroi*) and ladies-in-waiting (*hai peri tên theon*) who periodically circulated through the streets of the Piraeus bearing a silver tray and making a collection (*agermos*) on behalf of their deity. Such collections were not intended merely to swell the coffers of the goddess, for we hear of charitable disbursements known as *philanthrôpa* made by the sect on behalf of indigent citizens or *dêmotikoi* (no. 92).

The cult of the Mother of the Gods seems to have been spread through the Greek world by mendicant priests known as *mêtragurtai* who aroused loathing when they first made an appearance in Athens. From literary sources we know that a prominent feature of the goddess's worship was the use of percussion instruments or *tumpana* to induce a mood of frenzied ecstasy which could culminate in an act of self-castration: it was almost certainly an adherent of the Mother of the Gods who is alleged to have mutilated himself on the altar of the Twelve Gods on the eve of the departure of the Sicilian Expedition (Plu. *Nik.* 13.2).

As in the case of Isis, devotees of the goddess were commemorated with gravestones which allude to their devotion to her cult. Two such have survived from the Piraeus in which the deceased is depicted either holding or being presented with a *tumpanon* (nos. 81-2). The laying out (*strôsis*) of a funerary bier (*klinê*) on which reposed an image of the dead Attis, the goddess's lover who was killed by her in a fit of jealous rage, constituted a central feature of the Attideia. Votive offerings found in the Metroon in the Piraeus indicate that the cult of the Mother of the Gods lasted well into the imperial era.

Nergal

A bilingual funerary inscription in Greek and Phoenician dating probably to the third century commemorates a priest of the Assyrian god Nergal who presided over battles, plagues and the world of the dead (no. 100). There is no other evidence for the cult in the Piraeus.

Nymphs

There is a reference to a Nymphaion in an inscription of the *orgeônes* of Bendis dated 261/0 (no. 101; cf. Edwards 1986, no. 34).

Paralos

The Attic hero Paralos was reputed by Hegesias of Magnesia (*FGrH* 142 F 21 ap. Pl. *NH* 7.56.207) to have been the son of Poseidon and inventor of the warship. He was worshipped by a group calling itself the Paraloi, who are to be identified with the crew of the sacred trireme Paralos (Dain 1931, 299). An inscription (no. 102) dating to around the middle of the fourth century indicates that the crew made a thank-offering, probably annually, at the end of their period of service with each trierarch. Two other inscriptions of similar date (nos. 103-4) recording honorific decrees passed by the Paraloi have been discovered in connection with the Mahdia shipwreck off the coast of Tunisia in 86. The fact that other items on board had been looted from the Piraeus makes it certain that the Paralion or shrine of Paralos which is referred to in the inscriptions was located in the port.

The worship of Paralos appears to have been state-controlled, as is indicated by the fact that its *tamias* was appointed by a vote of the Athenian assembly. Demosthenes (21.171), doubtless with forensic hyperbole, ranked it alongside the post of cavalry commander (*hipparchos*) and supervisor of the Mysteries as one of the chief liturgical appointments of the state. That the *tamias* was the effective head of this association is demonstrated by the fact that he is eponymous in its decrees. A festival known as the Paralia was held in the hero's honour.

Poseidon

It is somewhat surprising to note that the earliest reference to the worship of the sea-god Poseidon only dates to *c.* 330 when Lykourgos, a member of the genos of the Eteoboutadai for whom was reserved the priesthood of Poseidon-Erechtheus (Ps.-Plu. *Mor.* 842a), instituted a contest or *agôn* in the god's honour in the Piraeus comprising 'at least three cyclic choruses'. There is no evidence for a temple of Poseidon in the port, though the law on silver coinage dated 375/4 alludes to a *stêlê* which stood in the Emporion (no. 106).

Sabazios

A cult of the Thrako-Phrygian god Sabazios existed either in the Asty or the Piraeus from the late fifth century onwards. The god, whose name is perhaps derived from the ritual cry 'saboi', had much in common with Dionysos. His initiates, known as Saboi, worshipped him with nocturnal rites which included ecstatic dances to the accompaniment of flute and kettledrum.

Public hostility to the new god was at first intense. From 422 onwards there are uncomplimentary references to him in no fewer than four Aristophanic comedies, including one in which Sabazios and other foreign deities were expelled from the state (Cic. *de Leg.* 2.37). The god's reputation and that of his worshippers did not immediately improve in the next century: as a means of blackening his opponent's character, Demosthenes (18.259-60) evoked a picture of Aischines' mother performing unsavoury rites which were in part devoted to the worship of Sabazios. According to the Scholiast on this passage, it was around this period (i.e. *c.* 350) that the Athenians received an oracle on whose recommendation they desisted from persecuting the god. Theophrastos' 'Superstitious

Man' and 'Late Learner' were both devotees of Sabazios (*Char.* 16.4 and 27.8). The Sabaziastai appear to have been an extremely cosmopolitan association: a list of 51 members dated 102/1 reveals that 36 were Athenians and 12 were metics (no. 109). As noted above, they do not, however, appear to have included women. It is conceivable that the three Sabaziastai whose place of origin is not given were slaves. The priest himself was a metic from Antioch.

Sarapis

The earliest evidence for the worship of Sarapis in Attike dates to 215/4, when a group of self-styled Sarapiastai issued a decree bestowing honours on officials of their cult (no. 110). The find-spot of the decree is given as 'either Athens or the Piraeus'. The establishment of the cult may well be connected with the development of close diplomatic links between Athens and Egypt in the third century.

'Sarapis' and 'Osorapis' are Greek corruptions of Osiris-Hapi, that is, Osiris in his Apis form as sacred bull. The cult originated at Memphis in Egypt where the bodies of deceased Apis bulls were stored in underground chambers. The worship of the hellenized Sarapis began just before 300 in the reign of Ptolemy I, who appears to have sought to make the god an imperial deity in order to provide the Greek population living in Egypt with a focus for devotion. According to tradition, his aim was accomplished with the assistance of two Athenians, Demetrios of Phaleron and a certain Timotheos of the genos of the Eumolpidai. Sarapis was a syncretic deity, combining the attributes of Osiris with those of a number of Hellenic deities including Asklepios, Dionysos, Plouton and Zeus. As such he healed the sick, worked miracles, protected navigation and presided over the underworld.

The Piraeic and/or Athenian Sarapiastai were headed by an official known as a *proeranistria* whose rank was equivalent to that of priestess. Since no demotics are supplied with the surviving list of members (no. 110), it is probable that the cult was confined to metics and slaves. In the second century a dedication was made in the Asty jointly to Sarapis and Isis (no. 111). Interestingly this later inscription is dated by the year of incumbency of a male priest, which lends some weight to the possibility that there was a separate Piraeus cult.

Sarapieia existed throughout the Greek world, from the Euxine to the shores of the Atlantic. In Egypt alone 42 temples to the god were known. The cult was particularly popular among the merchants of Delos who erected no fewer than three sanctuaries to the god.

Zeus Ammon

Zeus Ammon, whose cult reached Athens from Egypt in the first half of the fourth century, was the first Egyptian god to be officially received in Athens. Ammon was chiefly famed for his oracle at the oasis of Siwa in the Libyan desert, which ultimately came to rival those of Delphi and Dodona. The inventories of the treasurers of Athene after *c.* 375 onwards contain references to a silver *phialê* belonging to Zeus Ammon, which suggests that the god acquired a public cult. Its establishment should probably be seen as a reflection of the suspension in oracular business at Delphi from 373 onwards following the destruction of the sanctuary by an earthquake. Some time before 333/2, and perhaps as early as 363/2, a *hieron* was set up, probably in the Piraeus. The cult did not attract much state support: a *stêlê* recording the proceeds from the sale of skins of sacrificial animals records that the sacrifice performed by the strategoi on the deity's behalf in 333/2 raised a paltry 44 dr., as compared with 457 dr. from the Bendideia and 853 dr. from the City Dionysia. Since the sacrifice is not referred to under any other year of the quadrennium covered by the *stêlê*, Woodward (1962, 7) has ingeniously proposed that it may have coincided with the completion of a new fountain house attached to Ammon's shrine. Evidence of the god's importance in the 320s is provided by the fact that the sacred trireme known as the Salaminia was replaced by another known as the Ammonias (Ps.-Arist. *AP* 61.7). The vessel may have been used to convey theoric missions to Cyrene en route to the oracle at Siwa. The last reference to the cult dates to 262/1, when an annexe (*prosoikodomia*) was attached to the already existing shrine (no. 4).

Zeus Labraundos

To the beginning of the second century dates a decree passed by the *thiasôtai* of Zeus Labraundos regarding the construction of a temple to their god (no. 115). Zeus Labraundos (or Labraundeus), whose other epithets include Stratios, Karios and Chrysaoreus, was the chief deity of Mylasa in Karia. His cult name derives from the neighbouring village of Labraunda. The god owed his promotion to the Hekatomnid dynasty, particularly to the satrap Mausollos and his brother Idrieus. On Karian coins Zeus Labraundos is represented as holding a double-axe (*labrus*) and spear. His warlike aspect was well-suited to a militaristic people who frequently hired themselves out as mercenaries.

Zeus Meilichios

The significance of the cult epithet 'Meilichios' is not fully understood, but most likely derives from *meilissô* ('soothe, make mild or treat kindly'). In the majority of votive offerings (nos. 116-23) found in the Piraeus, all dated to the fourth century, the god is depicted reclining at a symposium or seated on a throne, holding either a sceptre or a horn of plenty. Alternatively he is represented in the form of an erect and bearded snake, indicating that he was a chthonic deity connected with the cult of the dead.

The cult seems to have had something of a rustic flavour. Thukydides (1.126.6) states that there existed 'a very great *heortê*' to the god called the Diasia which was celebrated outside the Asty and at which 'all the demes collectively (*pandêmei*) make offerings of local produce (*thumata epichôria*) instead of sacrifices (*hiereia*)'. As Jameson (1965, 165; cf. Mikalson 1977, 429f.) suggests, '*pandêmei*' seems to indicate that demes sent representatives with offerings to the chief sanctuary of Zeus Meilichios at Agrai in Athens, though celebrations may well have also taken place at local sanctuaries like the one in the Piraeus. Thukydides indicates that the festival was of considerable antiquity, its foundation preceding the conspiracy of Kylon, conventionally dated to *c.* 632. According to Hesychios (s.v. *Diasia*), it was celebrated with some repugnance.

Foucart (1883, 513) ingeniously proposed that Zeus Meilichios was a Greek transcription of the Phoenician god Ba'al Milik or Moloch. As Harrison (1922, 18) pointed out, however, there is no evidence that Milik was ever worshipped as a snake. Moreover, the fact that the god was well-established elsewhere in Attike makes it very unlikely that there would have existed an eccentric local aberration in the Piraeus. The key to the god's identity surely lies in his dual portrayal as both Olympian and chthonic deity (cf. Harrison, pp. 19-21).

Evidence for the worship of Zeus Meilichios has also been found on the northern slope of the Hill of the Nymphs and beside the bed of the Ilisos River.

Zeus Philios

Zeus Philios, a god of friendship, who is likewise sometimes represented in the form of a snake (cf. Fig. 25), seems also to have combined the attributes of both Olympian and chthonic deity. The most elaborate of the series of fourth-century reliefs from the Piraeus (nos. 124-8) depicts him reclining at a symposium, holding a horn of plenty and a shallow dish or *phialê* for making libations. His wife Agathe Tyche sits next to him. A wine-pourer attends the couple and three diminutive worshippers approach from the left, raising their right arms in salutation. Literary and iconographical evidence alike indicates that he was associated with feasting. A fragment of the New Comedy poet Diodoros of Sinope (*CAF* II, fr. 2 p. 420 ap. Ath. *Deipn.* 6.239b) states how the god:

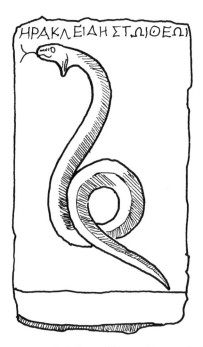

Fig. 25. Fourth-century relief from Mounychia, probably found in the sanctuary of Zeus Philios.

enters into homes without distinguishing between rich and poor, and wherever he sees a couch beautifully laid with a table beside it, piled with everything necessary, he reclines in state with the others, and after feasting his fill and drinking, he goes back home without making any contribution.

Zeus Philios was also worshipped on the northern slope of the Hill of the Nymphs where a *stêlê* was found set up by a group of *eranistai*. In the period of Augustus his priest enjoyed a seat of honour (*proedria*) in the theatre of Dionysos in Athens.

Zeus Soter and Athene Soteira

The date of the inception of the cult in honour of Zeus Soter and Athene Soteira at the Piraeus is not known, but in view of its evident importance, it is very probably contemporary with the port's foundation. An approporiate occasion would have been 480, immediately after the victory at Salamis. Pausanias' (1.1.3) description of the Diisoterion in the Piraeus indicates that the cult was associated with success in war since the bronze statue of Zeus which stood in the *temenos* depicted the god holding a Nike, the personification of victory. In addition, portraits of military heroes were displayed there. Significantly, too, ephebes participated in the Diisoteria held in their honour down in the Piraeus, and at Rhamnous inscriptions have come to light referring to sacrifices to the deities made by strategoi. Finally, the name of Zeus Soter is probably to be restored in a catalogue listing soldiers who made a dedication to a deity in the Piraeus (no. 139). The fact that every ship upon safe completion of a voyage was required to pay 1 dr. to the saviour gods suggests that they were also regarded as protectors of navigation, and for many inhabitants of the Piraeus this was perhaps their chief sphere of competence (no. 129).

Though not mentioned in the fifth century, the cult of Zeus Soter was extremely important in the fourth (cf. nos. 129-33). His priest in Aristophanes' *Wealth* (1173ff.), which was produced in 388, objects that ever since the god Ploutos has regained his sight, his services have not been required. Consequently he is starving 'even though I am the priest of Zeus Soter'. It is part of Aristophanes' comic fantasy that the joke should be at the expense of one of the most important gods of the day. Further testimony to the cult's importance is provided by an inscription dated to the middle of the fourth century regarding major construction work carried out on the Diisoterion (no. 130).

The Diisoteria took place in Skirophorion, the final month of the Attic year. It included a procession through the streets of the Piraeus and a banquet (*strôsis*) in honour of the gods. Its popularity and size are indicated by an inscription (no. 131) dated 334/3 found in Athens recording that the sale of hides after the sacrifice of oxen to Zeus Soter in that year produced 1,005 dr. out of a total revenue of 5,099 dr. raised from all the sacrifices to the Other Gods (i.e. excluding Athene). It is variously alleged (Ps.-Plu. *Mor.* 846d; Plu. *Dem.* 28.6) that the sum laid aside for the sacrifice in 323 was either 30 or 50 talents, though these figures are likely to be inflated, since Demosthenes, who was put in charge of the sacrifice for that year, was expected in addition to pay the bulk of an outstanding fine from the money allocated to him. Further funding of the cult seems to have come from the tax of 1 dr. alluded to above. The festival was celebrated down until 86 B.C. In the late period it included a naval race from the Grand Harbour to Mounychia Port, similar to that conducted at the Mounychia (no. 135).

The Soteres can be fairly described as foremost among all the deities worshipped in the Piraeus. Their continuing importance in the first century B.C. is indicated by the inscription regarding the restoration of sanctuaries in Attike which states that one copy of the decree is to be lodged in the shrine of Athene Polias on the Acropolis and another in the Diisoterion in the Piraeus (no. 138).

Zeus Xenios

A single inscription (no. 140) dated 112/1, not certainly attributable to the Piraeus, refers to the existence of a *sunodos* of *nauk[lê]roi* and *emporoi* who worshipped Zeus Xenios, aptly described by Farnell (1896, I p. 73f.) as 'the god to whom any stranger is consecrated'.

4. Topography

The Piraeus is particularly niggardly of testimonia from the archaeological point of view because the Hippodamian city has been inhabited continuously and among changing vicissitudes in the course of time. Though the first excavations carried out during the nineteenth century ... were able to reveal some significant details regarding its layout in antiquity, it is today inconceivable that there should be any further investigation of a site that has been completely covered over by the modern city and vastly developed in the course of the last hundred years.

B. Falciai (1982, 157)

This judgement is depressingly all too accurate. Our understanding of the topography of the Piraeus will never be more than fragmentary. We can only hazard a guess as to the exact location of such major architectural features as the sanctuary of Zeus Soter, the arsenal of Philon, and large stretches of the Themistoklean Wall. The existence of a number of important buildings is known only from archaeological reports dating to the 1870s and 1880s, when the Customs House and other modern harbour facilities were under construction. Changes in the shape of the Grand Harbour, which cut deeper into the shoreline on its southern side in antiquity, further compound the difficulties. Inevitably most finds now come from rescue excavations, since the modern port is a densely populated and highly commercialised urban area.

The chief obstacle to an accurate reconstruction of the appearance of the ancient harbour in its heyday is, however, its destruction by Sulla. What recovery it staged subsequently is still open to question, but Strabo's assertion (*Geog.* 9.1.15) that in the time of Augustus the fortifications of Mounychia were in ruins and the Piraeus merely 'a small settlement (*katoikia*) around the harbours and the shrine of Zeus Soter' is unlikely to be very far wide of the mark. The fact that Pausanias' description of the port is perfunctory in the extreme may also be taken as evidence of its sad decline.

It follows that to a very large extent we are reliant for our understanding of its topography first upon ancient literary sources, many of them of very late date, and secondly upon the accounts of eighteenth- and nineteenth-century travellers to Greece. Of the latter the most useful are Leake (1841), Dodwell (1819), Ulrichs (1843), Hirschfeld (1878), Milchhöfer (1881) and Judeich (1905; 2nd ed. 1931).

The most significant existing remains are as follows: (1) the so-called Aphrodision Gate on Eetioneia to which adjoins a short stretch of wall; (2) large sections of the circuit wall which skirts the edge of Akte peninsula; (3) the supposed grave of Themistokles, now in restricted territory; (4) a small section of the Themistoklean Wall enclosed within the Nautical Museum in Zea Port and a further section a short distance to the east under the modern flyover; (5) the foundations for some of the shipsheds in Zea Port; (6) Zea Theatre; (7) a fraction of the mole attaching to the east peninsula of Mounychia Port; and, finally, (8) the bottom courses of the so-called Asty Gate. Finds from excavations undertaken in the Piraeus and its environs are on display in the Piraeus Museum which was re-opened in June 1981. Others are kept in the National Museum of Athens.

The Piraeus *horoi*

The principal archaeological evidence for Hippodamos' work is the series of boundary stones or *horoi*, at present 24 in number as listed in Appendix I. The two most interesting (nos. 14 and 15) are those which state, 'Up to this road here the Asty has been cut up (*nenemêtai*)' (cf. above p.2) and 'Up to this road here is the cutting up (*nemêsis*) of Mounychia', since they are consistent with Aristotle's claim that this was the technique of land-division invented by Hippodamos. One *horos*, which exists in four copies (nos. 8-11), indicates that buildings, as well as areas, were allocated limited space. Whether the whole series is to be connected with Hippodamos is doubtful. Certainly those which have to do with shipping arrangements are likely to belong to the Themistoklean period (cf. nos. 5-7).

Broadly speaking, the *horoi* mark four progressive kinds of division (cf. McCredie 1971, 97):

(a) between public and private land (nos. 12 and 13)

(b) between separate sectors of the city (nos. 14, 15 and probably 16)

(c) around specified public areas such as the Emporion, the public anchorage and the Agora (nos. 2, 3, 5-7 and 17)

(d) around individual public structures such as the Leschai and Propylon (nos. 4, 8-11).

The stages of the planning process may thus be analysed as follows:

(1) the division of the city into separate sectors
(2) the application of a grid-plan to each sector, its orientation reflecting the configurations of the land
(3) the designation of broadly defined functions within each sector such as the Agora and the Emporion
(4) a further sub-division of space so as to define the boundaries of individual public structures.

The Hippodamian Agora

The heart of the Piraeus was its agora, known variously as the Hippodameia, the Hippodamian Agora, the Agora in the Piraeus or the Agora of the Demesmen. Bounded on all sides by *horoi*, it was treated as sacred space from which the ritually impure were excluded. It occupied an area directly west of Mounychia Hill and north of Zea, its centre lying approximately at the intersection between modern Odhoi Vasilias Sophias and Tsamadou. Being orthogonal, it must have differed markedly in appearance from the Agora in Athens.

The Hippodameia served as a focus for the life of the town as both deme and urban centre. It was also the most likely site for the 'old council chamber (*archaion bouleutêrion*)' mentioned in the first-century B.C. inscription regarding the repair of buildings, where 'old' presumably signifies that it no longer retained its original function. Few archaeological finds have come to light in the area identified as the Agora, and the only shrine known to have existed here is that of the goddess Hestia (above p. 75), which served for the display of deme decrees. In the Athenian Agora, Hestia's shrine was incorporated within the *prutaneion*, but the possibility that a similar arrangement existed in the Piraeus is generally thought to be precluded by Thukydides' assertion (2.15; cf. Plu. *Thes.* 24.3) that Theseus established a single *prutaneion* and a single *bouleutêrion* for the whole of Attike (cf. Giangiulio 1982, 951; Miller 1978, 15 n. 23). Since the Piraeus ultimately came to acquire its own *bouleutêrion*, however, it is not inconceivable that it also acquired premises for the prytaneis as well, particularly since regular meetings of the boule and ekklesia were held here (above p. 81f.).

By the first half of the fourth century at least one side of the Agora may have been bounded by private residences (above p. 42). In general, however, it was probably an impressive complex, not least in view of the fact that it possessed a monumental entrance (below p. 158). The fact that the Agora was named after Hippodamos is grounds for suspecting that here at least the town-planner did more than merely allocate an open space and align it in relationship to the road system. As Burns (1976, 420) points out, however, the naming of the Hippodameia may in effect have been little more than a mark of appreciation for the urbanist's overall contribution to the town-plan, particularly since no ancient source alludes to any individual buildings which he designed.

Housing

Many prosperous Athenians and metics owned residences in the Piraeus including the rich merchant Diodotos, the property-owner Euktemon, the 'industrialists' Komon and Polemarchos, the dramatist Menander, the banker Pasion, the sophist Proklos, the strategos Timotheos and the urbanist Hippodamos. Some wealthy Athenians owned houses in both the Piraeus and the Asty, as did the aristocrat Kallias and the orator Demosthenes.

As in the case of Olynthos, houses probably had to conform to set specifications regarding size, plan and location, in accordance with the grid-iron pattern of the town as a whole. A large fourth-century house-plot recently discovered at the junction formed by Odhoi Karaoli, Dimitriou and Theatrou, northwest of Mounychia Hill, incorporated several substantial houses, including two which possessed men's quarters or *andrônes* that were decorated with mosaic floors. A marked deterioration in building standards in the Hellenistic period is indicated by a recent excavation on Odhos Hypselantou near the Asty Gate. The original Classical house, which had been arranged around an open court about 9m square, was substantially built of isodomic poros blocks and incorporated a pebble floor thought to belong to an *andrôn*. Its later Hellenistic walls were thinner and poorly constructed out of small, irregularly-shaped stones. Well-preserved traces of houses have also come to light on Akte peninsula, where a long street pierced by cross-streets at intervals of approximately 60m was excavated in the 1870s. Each block so formed seems to have enclosed on average only two house-plots.

Multiple dwellings

Spacious and luxurious dwellings evidently existed for those who could afford them. The majority, however, had to be content with much less. Given the size of the population of the port, there must have been a large number of multiple dwellings or *sunoikiai*, the ancient equivalent of the modern slum. No trace of any such building has, to my knowledge, been identified, but there is literary evidence for their existence both in the Piraeus and elsewhere. In addition, Finley (1951, 65) has plausibly suggested that three *horoi* found in the Piraeus, which estimate the values of hypothecated dwellings, may refer to *sunoikiai* in view of the very large sums involved which range from 1,000-3,000 dr.

Brothels

One such *sunoikia* was the property of Euktemon of Kephisia, a client of Isaios (6.19) who is not embarrassed to admit to a jury that he rented his property out as a brothel (*porneion*). Probably the majority of such establishments, of which there were no doubt many in the ancient port as in the modern, lay on the outskirts of the town, as was the case in the Asty where some have been discovered beside the Dipylon Gate.

Hostelries

In view of the large number of visitors to the Piraeus, it would be reasonable to assume that the port was amply provided with inns and hostelries. The literary evidence suggests, however, that it was deficient in facilities of this kind – or at any rate that their standards were deplorably low. Aristophanes (*Frogs* 112-5) certainly implies that the inns known to his audience had a reputation for discomfort, prostitution and bedbugs. In mitigation of this bleak picture, I would suggest that some of the numerous shrines that existed in the Piraeus may have provided lodgings for short-stay visitors who could demonstrate bona fide attachment to a cult. By the middle of the fourth century the lack of decent accommodation led Xenophon (*Por.* 3.12) to recommend 'the construction of more hotels (*katagôgia*) for shipowners (*nauklêroi*) around the harbours ... as well as public hostels (*dêmosia katagôgia*) for visitors'. After the sack of Sulla, the situation deteriorated still further. When Servius Sulpicius, the friend of Cicero, went to collect the body of Marcus Marcellus who had died in the Piraeus at the hands of assassins in 45 B.C., he found his friend stretched out on a bier in the tent which he had pitched in the port, evidently because he had been unable to find accommodation in the port (Cic. *ad Fam.* 4.12.3).

The road system

The most obvious difference between the road system of the Asty and that of the Piraeus is that whereas the former reflected the needs of a gradually expanding population, the latter possessed an inner coherence from the start.

Horoi nos. 8-11 reveal the existence of a major thoroughfare or *plateia* which led south from the Hippodamian Agora towards Zea Port, skirting the deme theatre to the west. A second *plateia* (nos. 2 and 3), situated on the western side of the isthmus, ran parallel to the outer wall of the Emporion, almost exactly along modern Odhos Notara. Between these two outer thoroughfares were two inner ones: one to the east (no. 15) which skirted Mounychia, and another to the west which bordered the *hieron* of the Dionysiastai. A road of uncertain location is referred to in *horoi* nos. 12 and 13.

Thus at least four *plateiai* ran diagonally down the central part of the peninsula, the westernmost bordering the back wall of the Emporion and the easternmost bordering the back wall (?) of the Zea shipsheds, adjacent to Philon's Arsenal and the Hippodamian Agora. The axial orientation of the street plan was thus practically identical to that of the modern city, being dictated by the outline of the Grand Harbour and the angle of incline on southeast Akte. In the centre of the isthmus the *plateiai* were aligned along a north-northeast by south-southwest axis, whereas on Akte their axis slewed through a slight angle to become almost exactly northeast by southwest. Major thoroughfares were periodically re-surfaced at the expense of the state, particularly in preparation for major festivals.

Plateiai were intersected at frequent intervals by narrower, transverse streets known as *stenôpoi*. At least one *stenôpos* was about 40m broad, however, namely that mentioned by Xenophon (*Hell.* 2.4.11) which led eastwards out of the Hippodamian Agora and enabled the Thirty and their supporters to advance along it in hoplite formation 'not less than fifty shields in depth'.

The Piraeus was connected to the Asty by the Hamaxitos or Cart

Road which, as its name indicates, was used by wheeled traffic. This left the Asty on the west side of the city via the Dipylon Gate and entered the Piraeus via the Asty Gate (Fig. 7). A road also ran the entire length of the Long Walls: in times of siege it was the only connecting link between the two communities.

The water system

Geologically the Piraeus peninsula consists of a limestone bedrock with a clay overmantle. Water can be found either by digging down to the seam between the limestone and the impervious clay or by following the seam along to the point where it surfaces. Excavations conducted in the Piraeus are constantly bringing to light cisterns, reservoirs, tanks, bell-shaped wells, pipelines and channels which testify to the existence of a highly complex system of storing and conducting water. Indeed it was probably its very complexity which led to the rumour in 430 that the Peloponnesians had put poison into the cisterns (Thuk. 2.48.2).

Though no remains have come to light, Thukydides' statement that in 430 there were as yet no fountains (*krênai*) in the Piraeus clearly intimates that some were constructed before his death. Conceivably their design was the work of the Athenian engineer Meton, who is credited by Phrynichos with laying out fountain houses before 414, though there is no explicit testimony to this effect.

The lack of a public water supply in the port until the last decades of the fifth century throws a startling light upon the priorities of the state in respect of its civic amenities. As Panessa (1985, 368) suggests, however, the deficiency may partly have been alleviated by the sale of water from sanctuaries and shrines, many of which for cult-purposes would have been situated close to a stream. This theory is supported by a fourth-century sacral decree of the citizen *orgeônes* of Bendis which regulates that proceeds from the sale of water in the Bendideion are to be set aside for building projects in the sanctuary (Appendix III no. 39).

The principal water conduit in the Piraeus ran in a north-northwest by south-southeast direction, in exact alignment with the ancient road system and slightly to the east of the Emporion. A typical-size reservoir measuring 4m square and 3m in depth recently came to light on the northwest coast of Akte at the intersection between Odhoi Sachtoure and Kolokotrone. A stream called Tzirloneri which perhaps rose in central Akte close to the district known as the Mills and which debouches into an inlet on the west side of Zea no doubt served as a source of water in antiquity as it does today. Finally, there is evidence to suggest that in Classical times water was diverted to the Piraeus from the Ilisos River.

The *hieron* of the Dionysiastai

The *hieron* of the Dionysiastai, which lies a short distance due west of modern Plateia Korais, close to the intersection of two ancient roads, is one of the most impressive buildings to come to light in the Piraeus. It possessed a courtyard surrounded by a colonnaded hall over 21m in breadth with eight columns down one side and an unknown number down the other. On the eastern side of the courtyard lay a rectangular building (40m by 23m) which was divided into a large number of very small rooms. The sanctuary's wealth and importance are further indicated by what has been described as the most remarkable window ever discovered in the Greek world (Lawrence-Tomlinson 1983, 330). Its long rectangular frame was intersected by Ionic columns which were surmounted by an architrave and crowned by a Doric entablature. The *hieron*, which was probably constructed at the beginning of the second century, remained in use until the sack of Sulla as is indicated by a hoard of bronze coins dated 87-86 found among its foundations.

Metroon

A number of inscriptions, found immediately southeast of Zea Theatre on the northeast edge of Akte, testify to the existence of a shrine of the Mother of the Gods. It was sufficiently large to possess its own kitchen and remained in use until the second century A.D.

The Roman Forum (?)

In a block to the south of the Metroon and west of Zea Theatre, on the site designated for the new Hall of Justice, remains of a public building of Roman date have recently been discovered. If, as has been suggested, the building belongs to a Roman Forum, its eventual publication will shed important light upon the harbour in the Roman imperial period.

Akte

Akte, the plateau which forms the southwest extremity of the Piraeus peninsula, may have been largely uninhabited in antiquity except in its northeast sector, where a large number of well-preserved buildings were found inside the line of the so-called Themistoklean crosswall (below p. 164). A reference to a district called Hippasiai suggests that in later times a riding course existed here. Akte was the chief supplier of Piraeic poros or *Aktêtês lithos*, as is indicated by extensive remains of ancient quarries on its slopes. This stone was widely used both in the Piraeus and in the Asty. It is a grey or yellowish grey limestone of varying hardness, some of it so soft that in the course of a winter's night some Syracusan prisoners of war who had been put to work in the quarries made their escape by digging through it (Xen. *Hell.* 1. 2. 14). Inscriptions found 'at the Mills' on Akte prove that there were a number of foreign shrines here, including those of Aphrodite Ourania, Bendis and the Mother of the Gods. On the north coast of Akte, overlooking the entrance of the Grand Harbour, once stood a giant marble lion which probably served as a grave monument. The sculpture, which was removed to Venice by Morosini in 1687, gave to the Grand Harbour its alternative modern Greek name of Drako, which in recent times has dropped out of use.

The tomb of Themistokles

According to Diodoros the Topographer, 'a sort of elbow juts out from the promontory of Alkimos beside the Grand Harbour of Piraeus, and when you have rounded this elbow on the inner side where the sea is calm, there is a large foundation on which stands an altar-shaped tomb erected to Themistokles.' The promontory of Alkimos cannot be certainly identified and there are two ancient structures on opposite sides of the Grand Harbour which have been claimed for the tomb of Themistokles. Both are now in restricted territory belonging to the Greek Naval Command.

The preferred candidate is situated a few metres outside the circuit wall on the westernmost tip of Akte, along the northern shoreline of the inlet known as Ormos Aphrodites or Kanelopoulou. Such a site would certainly have provided a fitting setting for the commemoration of the architect of the victory of Salamis, being 'the

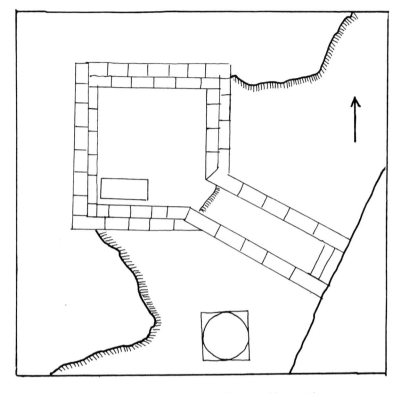

Fig. 26. The so-called Tomb of Themistokles on Akte.

first point on the south which could be regarded as part of the mouth
of the Piraeus as one enters the port' (Wallace 1972, 451). The
remains, which are now submerged (above p. 9), were restored in
1952. They consist of a square peribolos enclosing one or more
sarcophagi and an unfluted Ionic capital (Fig. 26).

A less likely location for the tomb is on the north side of the
entrance to the Grand Harbour, on the promontory called Kavos
Krakari in the region of Drapetsona, where Dragatsis excavated two
column drums and a circular foundation pierced by a central
depression which contained a marble cinerary urn.

As Lenardon (1978, 206) has aptly remarked, an appropriate
moment to rehabilitate the memory of Themistokles by means of a
prominently-placed public memorial would have been in *c.* 395
when the decision was taken to rebuild the Piraeus fortifications
(above p. 37).

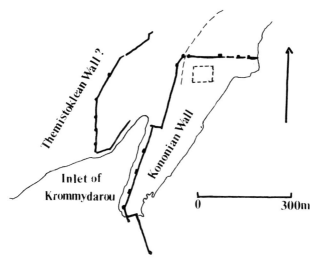

Fig. 27. Plan of remains of walls on Eetioneia.

Eetioneia

Projecting from the northwest shore of the Grand Harbour is the long promontory of Eetioneia, aptly described by Thukydides (8.90.4) as 'a mole (*chêlê*) of Piraeus'. Here in 411 the Council of Four Hundred built a wall 'with the express object ... of admitting the enemy whenever they should wish' (8.90.3). From Thukydides' account it seems that this wall was built on the eastern side of Eetioneia, and faced inwards towards the harbour rather than outwards towards the Saronic Gulf (Fig. 27; cf. Gomme, Andrewes and Dover, *HCT* V p. 305). No traces of it, however, have come to light. The remains of a wall built of conglomerate ashlar which was provided with two circular towers facing outwards towards the sea almost certainly belong to the Kononian circuit. The eastern coastline of the peninsula may have been the site of the Athenian dockyards known as Telegoneia (sc. *naupêgia*). Here, too, was probably the berth for the sacred ships which conveyed the embassy (*theôria*) to Delos and which were used in races from the peninsula to Mounychia Port. A number of cults existed on Eetioneia, including those of a deity known only as Soter, the Phoenician god Sakon or Sochen, a Sidonian deity who is probably Baal, Hermes, the hero Eetion(?) and Athene Eetioneia.

The Aphrodision

The existence of a sanctuary of Aphrodite on the neck of the promontory of Eetioneia is known from an inscription dated 394/3 which was discovered in the conglomerate wall referred to in the previous section. It records that a Boeotian named Demosthenes had been contracted to provide stones for rebuilding a portion of the wall which extended 'from the mark (*sêmeion*) to the front (*metôpon*) of the gate at the Aphrodision, on the right as you go out'.

There are three testimonia for the state worship of Aphrodite in the Piraeus: first Ammonios (*Rhet. gr.* VI, p. 393 ed. Walz), who states that Themistokles dedicated a shrine to Aphrodite after the battle of Salamis; secondly Pausanias (1.1.3), who reports that a sanctuary to Aphrodite Euploia was built by Konon after his victory off Knidos in 393; and thirdly an inscription found in Plateia Vasilias Amalias, near the modern Customs House, which records a dedication to Aphrodite Euploia by a strategos of the Piraeus in *c.* 97/6 B.C. This evidence is usually interpreted to mean that there existed two Aphrodisia in the Piraeus, one on Eetioneia, dedicated by Themistokles, and another at the southern end of the series of stoas aligning the eastern shoreline of the Grand Harbour, dedicated by Konon. It is perfectly feasible, however, as Culley (1973, 163) has proposed, that the shrine put up by Themistokles was identical with the one associated with Konon and that the inscription found near the Customs House has wandered from its original home. If this supposition is correct, then Konon should merely be credited with having enlarged the previously existing structure.

Thieves' Cove or *Phôrôn Limên*

Demosthenes (35.28) refers to a feature designated Thieves' Cove which is identified as a small inlet situated 'outside the signs marking your Emporion'. The expression 'To anchor in the Thieves' Cove,' Demosthenes goes on to explain, 'is the same as if you were to anchor in Aegina or Megara, for anyone can sail out of that harbour to any place he wishes and at any moment he wishes'. The exact location of the cove in question is not known, but it probably lies some distance to the west of Eetioneia where a number of such features are to be found.

The Grand Harbour or *Megas Limên*

The Grand Harbour served as the centre of the Athenian naval command whenever a fleet was due to set sail. Its southern shoreline was reserved exclusively for shipsheds, of which there were 96 by the middle of the fourth century. As today, it was the only port which handled passengers and freight, all commercial trade being confined to its northern and eastern shoreline. A recent press report refers to the discovery of a section of ancient breakwater attaching to Akte Miaouli on Akte peninsula.

It was probably in the waters of the Grand Harbour that initiates bathed their piacular pigs during the celebration of the Greater Mysteries. The ritual was not without its hazards. The story is told by Plutarch (*Phok.* 28.3) that while one initiate was scrubbing his pig shortly after the Macedonian garrison had been installed on Mounychia in 322, a shark seized hold of him and devoured him up to the waist , an occurrence which was interpreted as signifying that the Athenians would soon lose control of the Piraeus.

A feature called the Still Harbour or *Kôphos Limên,* to which Xenophon (*Hell.* 2.4.31) alludes in his description of the events of 403, is almost certainly to be identified with the bight attaching to the northern side of the Grand Harbour. This designation, which suggests that the harbour was not troubled by waves, does not occur in any other author and may well have been a descriptive term of Xenophon's own invention. The harbour so identified was excluded by the circuit wall of Konon, known at this juncture as the *Dia mesou chôma* (below p. 166). Though serviceable in an emergency, the Kophos Limen was probably of little value to shipping in antiquity, being considerably smaller then than it is today.

The Jetty or *Chôma*

The *Chôma* is referred to in a number of sources. It is possibly to be identified with the short mole which projects westwards from Plateia Karaiskakis. It was the place where dockyard supervisors distributed ships and equipment, and where trierarchs annually presented their triremes for inspection in the month of Mounychion. Here, too, sessions of the boule took place whenever naval matters were under urgent discussion. Probably the trittyes markers listed in Appendix I a-e refer to the disposition of the fleet in relation to the *Chôma,* though their precise significance is unclear.

The Diisoterion or Shrine of Zeus Soter and Athene Soteira

Pausanias (1.1.3) considered the Diisoterion to be the most notable sight in the Piraeus, though since it happened to be one of the few buildings to escape the Sullan destruction this judgement is of limited value. Despite its good fortune in antiquity, however, its location none the less remains a matter for conjecture. Clerc (1893, 136) identified it with traces of a building in the southern part of the Piraeus where six large altars were found with dedications to Zeus Soter. Others, notably Milchhöfer (1881, 41f.), situate it at the northeast corner of the Grand Harbour and to the west of the *hieron* of the Dionysiastai, where remains of large Doric capitals have come to light. The sanctuary was repaired in the second half of the fourth century.

In the Diisoterion or within its sanctuary precinct paintings and sculptures were displayed. Among the former was a portrait by Arkesilaus of the strategos Leosthenes who was killed at the siege of Lamia in 322. The most notable sculpture was a bronze Athene which is probably to be identified with the 'mirabilis Minerva' of the Piraeus, alleged by Pliny (*HN* 34.74) to have been the work of a certain Kephisodoros. As no Greek sculptor of this name is otherwise known, however, Pliny's text is usually emended to read 'Kephisodotos', the father of Praxiteles. Pausanias also reports seeing a statue of Zeus and Demos 'behind the stoa near the sea' which was apparently connected with the Diisoterion.

The Emporion

The Emporion, described by Pausanias (1.1.3) as 'an agora for those beside the sea', occupied the northern and eastern shoreline of the Grand Harbour. Within this area there were also moorings for ferry-boats (*porthmeia*), as is indicated by two *horoi* (nos. 6 and 7) which were dredged up out of the harbour. *Horoi* nos. 2 and 3, which both bear the inscription 'Boundary of the Emporion and of the road', suggest that the rear of the Emporion was surrounded by a wall.

Its major buildings were 'the five stoas round about the harbour' to which the Scholiast on Aristophanes' *Peace* (l.145) refers. The Alphitopolis Stoa, said to have been erected by Perikles, should probably be included among their number. It may well be identical to the Makra Stoa from which loaves and barley were distributed in times of famine (Dem. 34.37; cf. Paus. 1.1.3). A probable location for the Alphitopolis Stoa is on the peninsula separating the Grand Harbour from the Still Harbour, since in his account of the events of 411-410 Thukydides (8.90.5) states that the Council of Four Hundred, while building their fortification on Eetioneia, 'walled off (*dioikodomêsan*) a stoa as well, one that was very large and immediately adjoining this wall', which they then used as a storehouse for corn. If this supposition is correct, then the four remaining stoas probably extended the length of the eastern shoreline of the Grand Harbour. Remains of what may well be one of them came to light in 1886, just south of the modern Customs House. The stoa was 15.5m in depth, had a single colonnade, and was divided approximately down the centre by a wall. Behind this wall, which was excavated for a length of only 12m, lay two small rooms (about 6m by 5m), both with an off-centre doorway. They presumably formed part of a series that extended the full length of the stoa. The date of the stoa is uncertain, but pottery associated with the excavation suggests that it was constructed in the late fifth or early fourth century. It was oriented on a northwest-southeast axis, facing the harbour and with its back towards the town. Remains of another stoa with similar orientation have come to light on Odhos Iasonos. This second stoa, thought to be the southernmost of the series, was 9.6m wide and similarly faced towards the sea. Traces of burning and fragments of iron indicate that it was later used as an iron foundry. Nearby, close to the modern Town Hall, a cache of bronze and marble statues came to light (above p. 56).

The Emporion contained statues set up to public benefactors. One such was erected to Spartakos, king of the Bosporos, who was awarded this honour in 289/8 for supplying Athens with subsidised corn. It also possessed a *stêlê* of Poseidon, where the *agoranomoi* sat beside laws regulating market activity. Here, too, in all likelihood were kept the Piraeus set of weights and measures (*metra kai stathma*). Other features of the Emporion included the *stratêgion* and the office of the harbour supervisor (*epimelêtês tou limenos*).

Xenophon's recommendation (*Por.* 3.12) that 'suitable places of exchange for merchants' should be constructed in the port area to encourage traders was probably based on a study of the Emporion and implies that by the 350s its facilities were in need of refurbishment.

The Deigma

The Deigma or Sample was a building or area devoted to the display (*deiknumi*) of wares for sale inside the Emporion. It must have been situated alongside the quayside because when Teleutias and Alexander of Pherai raided the port, their men were able to leap directly onto (or into?) it. The inscription dated to the first century B.C. regarding the repair of sacred monuments which refers to the 'Deigma erected by Magnus' should probably be associated with its repair by Cn. Pompeius Magnus following its destruction by Sulla. An edict sent out by the Emperor Hadrian ordering the diversion of fish sales from the Piraeus to Eleusis contained the provision that it should be displayed in front of the Deigma. The inscription was found approximately in the centre of the Emporion which, as Judeich (1931, 448) suggests, probably marks the actual site of the Deigma.

The Diazeugma

The Diazeugma or Pier was the place where Theophrastos' 'Boastful Man' stands and 'tells strangers that he has made a lot of money at sea' (*Char.* 23.2). It was located within the boundaries of the Emporion.

Sanctuary of Aphrodite Euploia

The Scholiast on Aristophanes' *Peace* (l. 145) refers to a sanctuary of Aphrodite situated 'between the docks and the five stoas'. If the *hieron* built by Konon in honour of Aphrodite is not to be identified with the Aphrodision which stood beside the reconstructed circuit wall as suggested above (p. 150), then the most likely site for it is in Plateia Vasilias Amalias, where the dedicatory inscription to Aphrodite Euploia came to light.

Zea Port

Zea, the second largest harbour of the Piraeus, was reserved for the Athenian navy (Fig. 28). Its development may possibly antedate that of the other two harbours, since it provides the best natural shelter for shipping.

Fig. 28. Zea Port looking east towards Mounychia Hill.

Fig. 29. Remains of shipsheds in Zea Port with obtuse-angled retaining wall on right.

The naval zone was marked off from the rest of the town by an enclosure wall of ashlar masonry in the shape of an obtuse-angled polygonal wall which ran about 50m from the water's edge and served as the back wall of the shipsheds (Fig. 29). Traces of the fourth-century shipsheds, 196 in number, are still visible. Several were excavated at the end of the last century and one is preserved under cover close to the Maritime Museum on the west side of the port. Their foundations were cut directly out of the bedrock and their walls, too, were constructed of Piraeic limestone. The stone slipway onto which each ship's keel was hauled was about 3m wide and sloped into the sea at a gradient of 1 in 9. The dry length of the slip (the part clear of the water) was 37m, the exact length of a trireme. Rows of unfluted stone columns, alternately high and low, spaced 6m apart, supported a pitched roof of wood and tiles. Partition walls probably divided the sheds into units of four for protection against fire. The sheds also housed the wooden gear (*skeuê xulina*, viz. oars, ladders, yards, masts and poles) with which each trireme was provided.

The first-century B.C. inscription relating to the repair of sacred monuments contains an obscure reference to 'the *psuchtrai* near the dockyards (*neôria*) of Zea Port, beside the keys (*kleithra*)'. Most scholars derive *psuchtrai* from *psugmos* meaning 'a drying place', which they take to be a stretch of shoreline allocated to the drying-out and re-calking of waterlogged triremes; others connect it with '*psuchtêr*', meaning 'a cool, shady place'.

The Arsenal of Philon

The Arsenal of Philon (Fig. 30) was one of the most admired buildings in the ancient world, inviting comparison, in Pliny's eyes (*NH* 7.37.125), with the temple of Artemis at Ephesos. 'Arsenal' is in fact a misnomer since the building was not an ammunition store but a *skeuothêkê* or warehouse for storage of hanging gear (*skeuê kremasta*, viz. rigging, sails and rope) which was removed when triremes were berthed. An earlier *skeuothêkê* is epigraphically attested for *c.* 370, though whether it remained in use after the new building had been completed is not known.

Philon's Arsenal was so completely destroyed in 86 that no traces of it have ever come to light. Its specifications (*sungraphai*), however, are preserved in an inscription dated 347/6 inviting tenders from contractors. This provides us with so much detailed information that

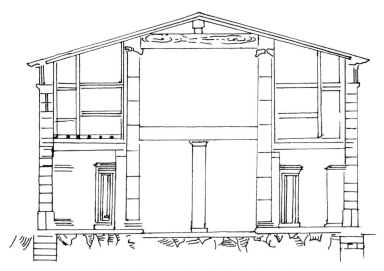

Fig. 30. Cross-section of Philon's Arsenal.

in the words of Dinsmoor (1950, 241): 'We know more about its construction than if its actual remains, rather than the description had been found.' The inscription states that the *skeuothêkê* was to be built at Zea 'beginning from the *propulaion* that leads from the Agora, as you come from behind the shipsheds which are roofed in together.' The most probable location is therefore in the space between the southern extremity of the Hippodamian Agora and the northern (back) wall of the shipsheds, on a northeast-southwest alignment.

The Arsenal was approximately 400 Attic feet long, 50 feet broad and stood 30 feet high. It was mainly constructed out of Piraeic limestone, though highlighted features, such as doorframes, capitals and ceiling, were executed in Hymettic or Pentelic marble. Two rows of columns, 35 apiece, ran the entire length of the interior, thus creating a central gangway 20 feet in width and two side aisles each 15 feet in width. It was in these side aisles on wooden shelves that the hanging gear was stored. The central gangway was left clear and served as a public thoroughfare. By modern standards the lighting inside the building would have been judged quite inadequate because the windows, set between each intercolumniation and above the doors, were small and high up. The outside walls terminated in a Doric frieze and cornice. The low-pitched roof was protected by Corinthian terracotta tiles. The architectural sophistication of the building is indicated by the concluding specification which regulated that 'Gaps should be left in certain of the joints between the blocks wherever the architect instructed so that there should be fresh air in the *skeuothêkê*', an essential provision to prevent the *skeuê kremasta* from mouldering in an airless atmosphere. The Arsenal was completed in *c.* 330.

The Public Gateway or Demosion Propylon

Four identical *horoi* (nos. 8-11), inscribed 'Boundary of the Demosion Propylon', allude to an ornamental gateway which led from Zea into the Hippodamian Agora. It perhaps took its name from the fact that the area outside the Agora, which was not subject to market controls, was designated simply '*dêmosios*'. No remains of the gateway have been discovered.

Zea Theatre

On the southwest side of Zea Port, some 150m from the modern shoreline, are the well-preserved remains of a Hellenistic theatre which was constructed in *c.* 150. The theatre remained in use until the Roman imperial period, without undergoing any noticeable alterations. The auditorium, which faces the port, has a diameter of 67m and is divided into thirteen wedges. A central gangway (*diazôma*), which separated the upper tiers from the lower ones, probably lies behind the tenth or eleventh row. The design and dimensions are identical to those of the theatre of Dionysos in the Asty, with the important exception that its stage was included in the original plan. It is believed to have been the last Greek theatre to have been constructed with side buildings (*paraskênia*).

Phreatto

In the vicinity of Zea was Phreatto, the lawcourt in which persons charged with homicide who were already in exile for an identical offence were tried (above p. 81). Judeich (1931, 436) has suggested that a number of circular depressions cut into the rock found 2m from the sea, close to the eastern side of the harbour mouth, may have served as seats for the jury. It is unclear whether the court at Phreatto is identical to the *dikastêrion* in the Piraeus for which there is epigraphical evidence. Phreatto evidently takes its name from the large number of wells (*phreata*) found in the region.

The Serangeion

Close to the shore and about halfway between Zea and Mounychia, two circular rooms were discovered in the last century which were hewn out of the living rock and connected to each other by a hollowed-out passageway. *Horos* no. 20, inscribed '*hêrôöu horos*', was found close by. The complex has been identified as a bathing house dedicated to the hero Serangos, whose name is derived from *sêranx* meaning 'a hollow rock'. The Serangeion, a privately-owned establishment whose existence is known from a number of literary sources, is first mentioned in Aristophanes' lost play the *Geôrgoi* which was produced in 422 (*CAF* I, p. 421 fr. 122). It was sold by Euktemon of Kephisia for 3,000 dr., probably soon after 376 (Is. 6.33).

The larger of the two circular rooms, whose diameter is 6.6m, has 26 rock-cut depressions around the wall which were perhaps intended for bathers' clothing and strigils. The second, smaller rotunda was probably reserved for women, as seems to have been the case with similar establishments found elsewhere. Two auxiliary rooms of rectangular shape lay off to the side. The floor of one is decorated with a well-preserved pebble mosaic depicting a galloping quadriga dated to the fourth century (Donaldson 1965). Plans of the original excavation reveal that the floor of another room was paved with a mosaic of Skylla, but this has since been covered over. The presence of a damaged poros altar of Hellenistic date dedicated to Apollo Apotropaios indicates that Serangos did not receive exclusive worship in the caves.

The Shrines of Zeus Meilichios and Zeus Philios

A grotto was discovered in the last century in the foothills between Zea and Mounychia, approximately 400m northwest of the island of Stalida. It contained a recess lined with red stucco and framed by pilasters which supported an architrave. The decoration is believed to belong to the fourth century. A number of niches carved in the rock were reported 90m to the west. Epigraphical data indicate that Zeus Meilichios, Zeus Philios and Agathe Tyche were all worshipped in this region.

The Asklepieion

The remains of an Asklepieion were discovered on the southwest slope of Mounychia Hill in 1888. Though only preliminary reports of the excavation were published, it seems that the foundations of the temple and a considerable portion of the temenos wall were uncovered. Since a number of *sunnaoi theoi* (above p. 115) had to be accommodated inside the sanctuary, it is highly probable that the complex was both extensive and elaborate. The first century B.C. inscription concerning the restoration of sacred monuments refers to '*psila* (open areas?)' belonging to the Asklepieion. The sanctuary also owned a quarry whose income helped to finance certain sacrifices. Furtwängler (1897, 407) believed that it incorporated the shrines of Zeus Meilichios and Zeus Philios, but there is no evidence to support this view.

Mounychia

Mounychia, modern Kastella, is described by Strabo (*Geog.* 9.1.15) as 'a hill which forms a peninsula, hollowed out and considerably undermined, both naturally and artificially, so that it provides dwelling-places, with an entrance in the shape of a small mouth' (Fig. 10). Though what Strabo observed was almost certainly the remains of quarries, the discovery in situ of *horos* no. 15 at the northwest corner of Mounychia Hill, which refers to the *nemêsis* of Mounychia 'as far as this road', confirms the view that its lower slopes were indeed inhabited. Its tiny port, which is situated at the southeastern foot of Mounychia Hill, was reserved exclusively for the navy (Fig. 31).

Mounychia played an important and indeed fateful role on a number of occasions in Athenian history, as Epimenides allegedly warned. The first was in *c.* 510 when the tyrant Hippias set about fortifying it after the murder of his brother Hipparchos: a short stretch of walling in quarry-faced Lesbian masonry discovered on the southwest flank of Mounychia Hill possibly dates to this period. In the fourth century it was garrisoned by ephebes and put under the control of the strategos of Mounychia. After Athens' defeat in the Lamian War in 322 its fortification constituted the Macedonians' preferred method of exacting obedience from Athens. It was again briefly occupied in 86.

Fig. 31. Mounychia Port from Mounychia Hill, looking west. In the background is Koumoundourou promontory.

The Theatre of Dionysos

The theatre of Dionysos lay about halfway up the northwest flank of Mounychia Hill. Its auditorium faced northwest, affording a superb view of the Grand Harbour and the Saronic Gulf beyond. Very probably its construction was contemporary with the Hippodamian commission. Its full title seems to have been 'the Dionysiac Theatre at Mounychia', but after the construction of Zea Theatre it is referred to simply as 'the old theatre'. In 324/3 the theatre was leased out to a syndicate of four Athenians who agreed to pay the deme 330 dr. per annum and to maintain it 'in good repair *(ortha kai hestêkota)*'. It was excavated in 1888 and has since been covered over. Political rallies as well as dramatic festivals and deme assemblies were occasionally held in the theatre, notably in 411 and 404.

The Dionysion

The exact site of the sanctuary of Dionysos or Dionysion is not known, but it was probably situated in close proximity to the theatre mentioned above, an arrangement found commonly elsewhere. The hero Akrapotes (Drinker of Unmixed Wine) also had a sanctuary on Mounychia, possibly within the Dionysion.

Shrines on Mounychia Hill

The *hieron* of Mounychian Artemis and the Bendideion both lay alongside the road which led eastwards out of the Hippodamian Agora. The former is generally thought to be situated on the small hill known as Koumoundourou at the neck of the west peninsula of Mounychia Port, on the site now occupied by the Yacht Club (Fig. 31). Excavation here in 1935 by Threpsiades brought to light the remains of a rectangular building with dimensions 24.9m by 10.2m, together with an inscription stating '*N[aos] Artemidos*'. Recently, however, a private dedication 'to gracious Artemis' (Appendix III no. 25) has come to light in the course of an excavation conducted by Papachristodoulou (1973) on the summit of Mounychia. The location of Artemis' shrine thus remains problematical. Literary evidence indicates that it contained an altar which frequently served as a place of asylum (Lys. 13.24; Dem. 18.107). On or near the hill were also located an altar to Phosphoros, a *hieron* to the hero Munichos, a Nymphaion and a cult of the Moirai.

A Bendideion was erected on the southwest slope of Mounychia Hill, where the inscription establishing the public cult came to light. The *hieron* belonging to the citizen *orgeônes* possessed a house which was let for profit and a spring whose water was sold (above p. 145). From the fact that two other inscriptions, one incontrovertibly belonging to the Thracian *orgeônes*, were found on the site of the Zanneion Hospital on the west side of Zea Port, it is conceivable that the goddess occupied separate premises on Akte where evidence for other foreign associations has come to light (above p. 119).

The Theseion and Thesmophorion

A Theseion and Thesmophorion are both referred to in a deme lease dated 321/0. This Theseion is perhaps identical with the one where those living inside the Long Walls were ordered to muster during the crisis brought on by the mutilation of the herms in 415 (Andok. 1.45). It is possible that the foundations of a large rectangular building (56m by 60m) built of ashlar masonry which were discovered on a spur north of Mounychia quite close to the Southern Long Wall should be identified with it. As Milchhöfer (1881, 37f.)

has pointed out, its elevated situation would have served admirably for the exchange of fire signals with the Asty during the crisis of 415. No other evidence supports the identification, however, and it is conceivable, as Judeich (1931, 456) suggests, that these remains may belong to the Thesmophorion which has not otherwise been located.

Shrine set up by Themistokles

The inscription referring to the repair of sacred buildings contains a cryptic and mutilated reference to '(the shrine of) ... -*kanes* which Themistokles set up before the battle of Salamis'. Neither the identity nor the location of this *hieron* has been established. Foucart (1907, 183-6) restored the inscription to read '*Artemidos* (or *theas*) *Hurkanês*', a Persian goddess who, according to his interpretation, was co-opted by Themistokles before the battle of Salamis in a panicky attempt to appropriate the goodwill of the enemy's gods. Culley (1973, 154) has since proposed '*Athenas* (or *Artemidos*) *Herkanês* (Of the Fenced Enclosure)', an otherwise unknown deity whose cult, he suggests, was established by Themistokles to commemorate the fortification of the Piraeus. While accepting Culley's restoration, I would suggest that the fenced enclosure in question is none other than the wooden walls in which the Athenians were urged to put their trust (Hdt. 7.141-2).

The Themistoklean circuit

Thukydides (1.93.5) alleges that Themistokles built the circuit wall around the Piraeus in such a manner that:

> Two waggons going in opposite directions (*enantiai allêlais*) brought along the stones, and the space inside (i.e. between the outer faces) was not filled with rubble or clay, but large stones cut into square blocks were laid together, fastened to one another on the outside with iron clamps and lead.

The purpose in building such a strong wall was, he explains, to economise on manpower, though in the event it was only completed to half its intended height. Thukydides (2.13.7) later informs us that at the outbreak of the Peloponnesian War the length of the entire circuit around the Piraeus including Mounychia was 60 stades.

Archaeological evidence can contribute little to our knowledge of the first circuit. In the last century a section of ancient fortification,

some 200m in extent, was visible in the southwest region of Akte
peninsula near the church of Aghios Vasileios. Though he later
recanted, in the first edition of his *Topographie von Athen* (1905) Judeich
conjectured that this crosswall belonged to the Themistoklean circuit
which traversed Akte diagonally from northwest to southeast, cutting
off the southwest segment of the peninsula (Fig. 1). Likewise Noack
(1908, 36f.) claimed to have observed traces of 'an older
(Themistoklean?) polygonal wall' near the coast in the southeast part
of the peninsula, apparently following much the same course as its
Kononian successor. It is just conceivable that this belonged to the
circuit commenced in the year of Themistokles' archonship, and that
when work was resumed in *c.* 479, the previous line was abandoned
and the circuit extended to encompass the entire peninsula. All traces
of the wall have since disappeared.

A further stretch of polygonal wall which may also be
Themistoklean ran across the ridge to the northwest of Eetioneia,
enclosing the inlet known as Krommydarou (Fig. 27). Its course to
the east is pure conjecture. Judeich believed that it bent northwards to
enclose the northern bight of the Grand Harbour; others have
suggested that it proceeded due east to join up with the fourth-century
wall at the so-called Aphrodision Gate.

Also probably Themistoklean are the remains of two oval towers
built of solid ashlar masonry flanking the Asty Gate (see below) which
have sections of wall on either side; and a square tower adjoining
some 50m of preserved wall in Zea Port discovered in 1967 which now
lies under the modern flyover (Fig. 5). Finally, Leake (1841, 411)
reported seeing walls in Mounychia Port preserved to a height of three
or four courses 'constructed, throughout the whole thickness, of large
stones, either quadrangular or irregularly-sided, but fitted together
without cement, and the exterior stones cramped together with
metal', which he plausibly attributed to the fifth-century circuit.

What was the size of the garrison that defended the Piraeus at the
time of the Peloponnesian War? According to Thukydides (2.13.6),
the total manpower available for defending the forts and mounting
the ramparts (*hoi par'epalxin*) of Attike in 431 was 16,000. If we assume
that at least two-thirds of this force was available in emergency
for defending the entire fortificatory system, I estimate that about
2,000 were reserved for the defence of the Piraeus, split into two
watches of 1,000 men apiece, since only half its circuit was actually
patrolled.

There is no report of any rebuilding or repair work being carried out on the Piraeus circuit between its completion in *c.* 479 and its destruction in 404, other than the closing up of all three ports by means of moles (*chêlai*) terminating in fortified towers (above p. 29).

The Kononian circuit

Both Xenophon (*Hell.* 4.8.9) and Diodoros Siculus (14.85) give credit for the early fourth-century reconstruction to Konon who utilised the booty from his victory over the Spartans off Knidos in August 394, supplemented by funds provided by the Persian satrap Pharnabazos. Inscriptions found in the wall adjoining the Aphrodision Gate on Eetioneia reveal, however, that the project was actually commenced before the naval battle and that Konon's return merely gave the labour added impetus (Tod *GHI*, II p. 23). Further accounts relating to the same project indicate that the work was not completed before 391.

Both Nepos (*Timoth.* 4.1) and Xenophon (*Por.* 6.1) intimate that some repairs may have been carried out before the middle of the fourth century, and Demosthenes (19.125) suggests that there was a public debate concerning the Piraeus fortifications in *c.* 346. A later decree dated 337/6 refers to repairs on fortifications at both Eetioneia and Mounychia. Further refurbishment took place in 307/6 and *c.* 228.

Most of the surviving fortifications in the Piraeus, being manifestly not in the style described by Thukydides, are generally attributed to the Kononian rebuilding. They are best represented in the well-preserved remains of the circuit which winds around the coastline of Akte, skirting the shore at an average distance of 20-40m from the sea, and in places considerably closer (Fig. 9). Its thickness varies from 3-3.6m. The outer faces are built of carefully cut blocks of ashlar masonry, the core being composed of rubble and earth. Part at least of the upper courses was constructed of crude baked brick. The curtain is interrupted at intervals of 50-60m by projecting towers, many of them recently reconstructed, approximately 6m in length. The stone utilised throughout is Piraeic poros and evidence of quarrying is visible at many points both in front of and behind the wall. It is not improbable that this wall adopts more or less the same course as its Themistoklean predecessor, perhaps even incorporating portions that escaped destruction in 404. However, the regularly-spaced towers, more a feature of fourth- than fifth-century architecture, are unlikely to pre-date Konon.

Beginning from the northern side of the entrance to the Grand Harbour, the course of the Kononian Circuit was as follows: it ran along the western coast of the rocky promontory of Eetioneia for a distance of some 500m, turning due eastward at its neck, apparently cutting straight across the mouth of the Still Harbour along an artificial dam known as the *Dia mesou chôma*. On the northeast side of the Piraeus peninsula, in the area between the Grand Harbour and Mounychia Hill, where the terrain is relatively flat and the risk of attack accordingly greatest, the wall is built of solid ashlar with a thickness of 8m and apparently merges with its Themistoklean predecessor. It was further safeguarded at this point by means of a ditch some 10m in width, traces of which have been found at the intersection between Odhoi Navarinou and Gounari, just in front of the gate near the Makra Stoa. Further traces of a ditch have been discovered outside the Aphrodision Gate at the north end of Eetioneia.

On the southern peninsula of Mounychia Port, just to the north of the rectangular building which Threpsiades identified as the *hieron* of Mounychian Artemis (above p. 162), a wall of ashlar masonry incorporating a curved tower has come to light. This, too, should probably be connected with the circuit wall of Konon.

Gates

At least six gates are known to have existed on the landward side of the fourth-century wall. The principal gate, known today as the Asty Gate or Asteos Pyle, lies about 150m west of the Northern Long Wall. It is situated along Odhos Pyles within the block formed by Odhoi Philonos and Kolokotrone (Fig. 32). As noted above, most of the wheeled traffic passing between Athens and the Piraeus probably entered and left via this gate. Though only partially excavated, it is believed to have been similar in form to the great Dipylon Gate in Athens, consisting of a narrow gatecourt (estimated width 15m) with square towers at each of its four corners. Only the foundations of the two northern towers are now visible, their internal width being 6.75m. The oval bases of the gate's forward projections almost certainly belong to the Themistoklean period and were later remodelled on a square plan. The Asty Gate is the most likely location for the statue of the so-called 'Hermes at the Gate (*pros têi pulidi*)', set up by the nine archons in 394/3.

Approximately 170m to the east of the Asty Gate stood a gate

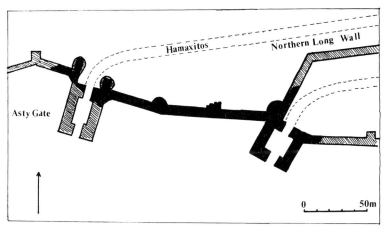

Fig. 32. The Asty Gate and the Gate beside the Northern Long Wall.

within the Long Walls, at the juncture between the Northern Long Wall and the Piraeus circuit (Fig. 32). This, too, resembled the Dipylon, having a square gatecourt with an internal width of 19m. A third gate lay just to the south of the juncture with the Southern Long Wall, close to a small postern situated inside the same wall. Traces of a possible fourth gate at the eastern edge of the circuit wall were observed by Leake (1841, 401) in the northeast angle of Mounychia. No remains of any of these gates are now visible.

At least two other gates lay to the west of the Asty Gate: one, near the Makra Stoa, of which no traces remain, and another, still visible, at the north end of Eetioneia. The latter, known as the Aphrodision Gate because of the discovery of an inscription associating it with the *hieron* of Aphrodite, is flanked by two round towers over 10m in diameter (Fig. 33).

The Long Walls

Thukydides (2.13.9) alleges that the Northern and Southern Long Walls, which according to Strabo (*Geog.* 9.1.24) were designated 'the Legs (*ta Skelê*)', were each 40 stades (i.e. 8km) in length (Fig. 7). It has now been established, however, that their combined length was only 13.6km and that the Southern Long Wall was approximately 1km shorter than the Northern. They began in the circuit wall of the Piraeus about 450m apart, converged to within a distance of 184m, ran parallel for most of their length, and then diverged again as they

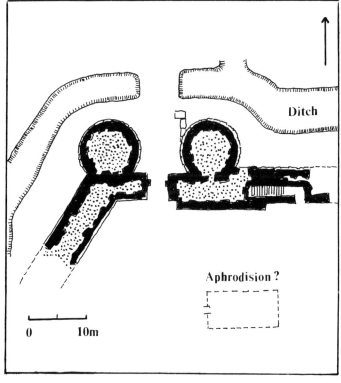

Fig. 33. The so-called Aphrodision gate on Eetioneia.

approached Athens. In the last century Leake (1841, 417f.) was able to trace the foundations of the Northern Long Wall for a distance of about 2.5km. The wall proceeded towards the Asty in a northeast direction with the same orientation as modern Odhos Peiraios. Its southern partner, which is less easy to trace, took the same course as the modern electric railway which links Athens to the Piraeus.

Both Long Walls appear to have had a minimum thickness of 3.9m and were built of isodomic masonry on a stone sockle surmounted by mudbrick. A well-preserved section of the Southern Long Wall recently came to light close to the railway station at Moschato. Its lowest course was 5.3m in width and subsequent courses 4.5m. Until the decay of the Phaleric Wall the Southern Long Wall was not usually manned (Thuk. 2.13.7). Square towers interrupted the curtain walls at regular intervals. One such tower, which has been excavated in the Southern Long Wall, measures over 9m along its front and 10.2m down its side. These walls were pierced by several gates, with an additional outlet for the Kephisos River (Str. *Geog.* 9.1.24). Remains of what is perhaps a *proteichisma* or advance wall have been discovered just south of Moschato Station.

Both the Long Walls and the Phaleric Wall were intact in 431. Before Athens' final defeat, however, the Phaleric Wall had evidently either fallen into decay or been destroyed because the Spartan peace proposal of 404 demanded only that the two Long Walls should be destroyed for a distance of 10 stades (Xen. *Hell.* 2.2.15; Lys. 13.8). In the event they were destroyed in their entirety, as was the circuit wall around the Piraeus (Plu. *Lys.* 14; D.S. 13.107.4). The Long Walls were almost certainly included in the restoration work undertaken on the Piraeus fortifications in the 390s, but it is unclear whether they were repaired in 337/6 when the walls of Eetioneia and Mounychia were refurbished. They were apparently still functioning in 322 when Antipatros established his garrison at Mounychia (Paus. 1.25.5), and are mentioned in the law regarding the general review of Athens' fortifications passed in 307/6. Thereafter their fate is difficult to determine. When Athens accepted a garrison in 322 they probably fell into decay, but it is certain that they were not completely destroyed. Though Livy (31.26.8) describes them as being half-ruined when Philip VI attacked Athens in 200, evidence for their use in the Roman period is provided by a superstructure of rubble and mortar which was discovered along a section of the Northern Long Wall some 200m northwest of Kallithea Station.

Cemeteries

Only isolated burials have come to light in the Piraeus in this century, but many were visible at the beginning of the last. Dodwell (1819, I p. 430) describes excavating an extensive cemetery which lay to the north outside the Asty Gate (cf. *horos* no. 23). Probably the roads outside the other gates of the Piraeus were also lined with tombs, as was the case with those leading out of the Asty.

The Tropaion

Ephebic inscriptions dated *c.* 120 onwards refer to a feature called the Tropaion or Trophy to which ephebes sailed and made an annual sacrifice in honour of Zeus Tropaios as the giver of victories. It is almost certainly to be identified with one of the two trophies erected after the battle of Salamis, one of which stood on Salamis itself (Pl. *Menex.* 245a; Paus. 1.36.1) and the other on the island of Psyttaleia (Plu. *Arist.* 9). Their precise location has not been fixed with certainty but Wallace (1969, 299-303) has convincingly suggested that the one on Salamis stood at the tip of the cape known today as Kynosoura and that Psyttaleia is best identified with the island of Leipsokoutali situated between Salamis and the Piraeus.

Chronology of the Piraeus

c. 510	Mounychia Hill fortified by Hippias
493	Work on the Piraeus fortifications begun in the year of Themistokles' archonship
483/2	New silver strike made at Lavrion
482	Athenian ekklesia votes to use revenue from silver mines to build a fleet of 100 (or possibly 200) ships
479	Resumption of Piraeus project
477(?)	Piraeus fortifications completed
c. 467	Kimon modifies trireme design and lays foundations for Long Walls(?)
458-7	Construction of the Long Walls
c. 455	Middle Long Wall begun
c. 450(?)	Hippodamos 'divides up' the Piraeus
430	Plague attacks the Piraeus
c. 429/8	Bendideion established
429	The Piraeus is converted into a closed port (*kleistos limên*) following an abortive Spartan raid
415	Launching of Sicilian Expedition
411	The oligarchs begin building a wall on Eetioneia peninsula
405	The sacred trireme Paralos sails into the Piraeus with news of Athens' defeat at Aigospotamoi
404	Athens surrenders to Sparta on terms that include the loss of all but 12 triremes along with the destruction of the Piraeus circuit and Long Walls. The Thirty assume power and appoint the Ten as their deputies to rule the Piraeus
404 or 403	The Pnyx auditorium is altered so as to face away from the sea. 5,000 citizens expelled from the Asty to the Piraeus. Demolition of the Piraeus shipsheds
403	The democrats defeat the Thirty in the battle of

	Mounychia Hill. Following the expulsion of the Piraeus Ten, the democrats take control of the Piraeus and form themselves into a separate polity. In Aug./Sept. the Piraeus is re-absorbed into the Athenian state
401/0(?)	Ekklesia bestows honours 'on all those [sc. metics] who had joined in the return from the Piraeus'
394-1	Reconstruction of Piraeus circuit and Long Walls. Aphrodision established (or enlarged) in honour of Konon's naval victory off Knidos. Tomb of Themistokles constructed on Akte peninsula(?)
391	Athens passes a decree to rebuild her navy(?)
387	The Spartan Teleutias makes a successful raid on the Piraeus
387/6	In accordance with the terms of the King's Peace, Athens agrees to leave the Piraeus ungated(?)
378	Sphodrias plans an abortive land attack on the Piraeus
377	Earliest surviving naval inventory
361	Alexander of Pherai makes a successful raid on the Piraeus
355/4	Xenophon (*Por.*) puts forward recommendations concerning the refurbishment of the Piraeus
354-*c.* 346	Euboulos undertakes the building of new shipsheds and construction of naval arsenal in Zea
353/2	Naval inventory records 349 triremes in the Athenian fleet
after 350	Repair work carried out on the Diisoterion
346	Philip II suborns Antiphon to set fire to the Piraeus shipsheds
337/6	Repair work carried out on walls of Eetioneia and Mounychia
333	*Enktêsis gês* granted to merchants of Kition in order to establish a shrine to Aphrodite
c. 330	Completion of Philon's Arsenal in Zea
322	Naval defeat off Amorgos puts an end to

Athenian naval power. Macedonian garrison established on Mounychia Hill by Antipatros. Menyllos appointed as its first *phrourarchos*

319 On death of Antipater, Kassandros replaces Menyllos with Nikanor as *phrourarchos*. Nikanor seizes control of the Piraeus fortifications and harbour walls. Second separation of the Piraeus from the Asty. The Piraeus comes totally under the control of Nikanor

317 Athens comes to terms with Kassandros and accepts the principle of a Macedonian garrison 'as long as the war between the kings lasts' (D.S. 18.74.3). Demetrios of Phaleron is appointed *epimelêtês* of Athens. The Piraeus is re-united with the Asty

307 Demetrios Poliorketes sails into the Piraeus and liberates Athens, completely destroying the garrison on Mounychia Hill. Re-building of Piraeus circuit and Long Walls

305 or 303-1 Olympiodoros thwarts an attempt by Kassandros to recover the Piraeus

295/4 Revolt of the Peiraikoi from the tyranny of Lachares brings about the third separation of the Piraeus from the Asty

294 With the support of the Piraeus, Demetrios Poliorketes starves the Asty into surrender. The Macedonian garrison is re-installed on Mounychia Hill. The Piraeus is re-united with the Asty

287 or 286 Athens successfully revolts from Demetrios Poliorketes, leaving the Piraeus in Macedonian control. Fourth separation of the Piraeus from the Asty

286-1 The Athenians make an abortive attempt to recover the Piraeus

281(?) Possible removal of Macedonian garrison and re-unification of the Piraeus with the Asty

c. 261 Defeat of Athens in the Chremonidean War leads to the establishment of Macedonian garrisons throughout Attike and to the reunification of the Asty with the Piraeus

240	Aratos of Sikyon makes an unsuccessful attempt to capture the Piraeus
229	Departure of the Macedonian *phrourarchos* Diogenes and evacuation of all forts in Attike
c. 229-8	Piraeus circuit repaired but Long Walls left out of the refurbishment. Henceforth the Asty and the Piraeus exist as two separate cities
200	Long Walls described as 'half-ruined' (Li. 31.26.8)
200-197	The Piraeus serves as a base for Roman naval operations during the Second Macedonian War. Athens' fleet now comprises a total of three open ships
192	Flamininus establishes a garrison of 500 auxiliaries in the Piraeus
192-88	The Piraeus serves as a base for Roman naval operations during the Syrian War
171-68	The Piraeus serves as a base for Roman naval operations during the Third Macedonian War
166	Delos is ceded to Athens as a free port
c. 150	Theatre constructed in Zea Port
c. 120	Revival of festivals including the Mounychia, the Diisoteria and the Piraeus Dionysia
86	Destruction of the Piraeus by Sulla

Notes

1. HISTORY

7 **Etymology of Piraeus.** Cf. also Pl. *NH* 2.87.201 and Sud. s.v. *Embaros eimi*. For modern discussion, see Schmidt s.v. Peiraieus in *RE* XIX (1938) col. 100 no. 2.

Geological formation. See Judeich (1931, 425f.), Milchhöfer (1881, 23f.), Négris (1904, 348ff.), Papachatses (1974, 98) and Travlos (1960, 12f.). Ulrichs (1843) reported that in the mid-nineteenth century the water was so deep in Halipedon that it came up to his horse's knees and that in the winter the region was impassable. Harp. s.v. *Halipedon* states that Halipedon was an alternative name for the Piraeus.

9 **Natural advantages of the Piraeus as a port.** Cf. Thuk. 1.93.3; Isok. 15.307 (*T*).

Designation of Piraeic harbours. Cf. Sch. Ar. *Peace* 145; Hsch. s.v. *Zea*; Paus. 1.1.2 and 4. The varied apportionment of names bestowed upon the three ports by eighteenth- and nineteenth-century topographers have been exhaustively collated by Panagos (1968, 255-57). For early maps, see Day (1927, 44f.).

Change in sea-level. See Négris (1904, 352), Travlos (1960, 12), Eliot (1962, 26 n.4), Pritchett (1965, 97-100) and Wallace (1969, 295). Carpenter (1966, 24f.) exaggeratedly postulates a uniform rise of about 3m throughout the Mediterranean around the turn of the modern era. Other regions where submerged structures have been found include the island of Keos and the southern coast of Turkey.

10 **Mycenaean remains in the Piraeus.** LH IIIb burial at Charavgi: Simpson (1981, cat. B5 p. 44). There are also unconfirmed reports of the discovery of Mycenaean sherds from Koumoundourou, the hill to the southwest of Mounychia Port (Simpson, loc. cit.). LH IIIb-c cemetery at Porto Rafti: Simpson (1981, cat. B30 p. 49). Myth of Erysichthon: Apollod. 3.14.2; Paus. 1.31.2. Mycenaean remains from Palaio Phaleron, etc.: Simpson (1981, cat. B4 p. 43); Stubbings (1947, 8). The earliest reference to the existence of an Athenian navy is in the so-called Catalogue of Ships, where it is stated that Athens contributed fifty ships under the command of Menestheus to the Greek expedition to Troy (Hom. *Il.* 2.556). For the problems concerning this entry, see Simpson and Lazenby (1970, 56). A cult of Mnesitheos (Menestheus?) *nauklēros* in the Piraeus is referred to in Luk. *JTr* 15.

11 **Middle Geometric I cemetery at Palaia Kokkinia.** Theochares (1951, 119ff.); and Coldstream (1968, 344; 1977, 78). The graves include cists, a pithos-burial and urn-cremations.

Late Geometric cemetery at Phaleron. See Pelekides (1916, 13-64) and Young (1942, 23-57). The cemetery lies close to the end of Leophoros Syngrou, to which it runs adjacent, probably following the course of an ancient road. Many different methods of interment were employed, including pit- and cist-burials, pithos burials, urn- and pit-cremations and sarcophagi. Further testimony to the impoverishment of the eastern coastal region in the LG period is provided by the cemetery at Anavysos (Coldstream 1977, 134f.). Among the finds from graves of all periods are 17 so-called SOS amphorai, the largest concentration of this type of vase which has been found in Attike outside Athens. Since the SOS amphora was used chiefly for storing olive oil, it is possible that Phaleron served as a centre for its export.

Athens' maritime backwardness *c.* 750-600. Some memory of Athens' lack of interest in the sea in the early period seems to be preserved in Plu. *Thes.* 17.6 in which it is stated that in the time of Theseus 'the Athenians had not yet turned their attention to the sea'.

Seizure of Sigeion. Hdt. 5.94.1; D.L. 1.74; Str. *Geog.* 13.1.38; Steph. Byz. s.v. *Sigeion.* For discussion see Bengston (1939, 216), Legon (1981, 125), Jeffery (1976, 89f.) and Boardman (1980, 264). Page (1955, 152-8) doubts whether Athens had the means to undertake any large enterprise at the turn of the sixth cent. in view of the fact that she was undergoing severe economic hardship at the time and found the recapture of Salamis a hazardous undertaking (see next note). Cf. also Beloch (1890, 467). Page's objections have been countered by Frost (1984) who suggests that it was 'probably a colonial foundation' established for the purpose of distributing land to poor Athenians, including *hektêmoroi.* Frost is surely right to suggest that the settlement of Sigeion was not a naval venture, since it only required cargo ships to transport the settlers. The date of the enterprise is much disputed, but it probably belongs to the final years of the seventh century. The earliest archaeological evidence appears to be an aryballos from the Troad with Athenian graffito dated by Jeffery (1961, 72) to 'the first quarter of the sixth century'. See also Cirio (1980, 108-12).

Recovery of Salamis. For the tradition of an Athenian naval defeat at the hands of the Megarians, see Paus. 1.40.5. For the recovery of the island, see Ps.-Arist. *AP* 17.2; Plu. *Solon* 8-9 and *Comp. Sol. et Publ.* 4; Solon fr. 3 *OCT* (ed. West); Polyain. *Strat.* 1.20.2. The motives behind the struggle are hard to ascertain, though Legon's claim that 'possession of the island ... was primarily an emotional, patriotic issue for both sides' is an over-statement in view of the fact that Salamis does have undoubted strategic advantages (cf. French 1957, 238-46). Haas' view (1985, 42) that it was essentially a border conflict between Athens and Megara, success in which 'would ensure dominance over the bay of Eleusis and would lay open to attack wide tracts of land within each polis' may not be wide of the mark. As Frost (1984, 289) points out, the claim that the final assault was launched with only a single triakontor gains credibility from Plu. *Solon* 9.4, where there is a reference to a religious ceremony (identified merely as *ta drômena*) which 'confirmed' the historical tradition.

Phaleron Port. The exact location of the ancient settlement of Phaleron has not been established, but it is thought to have been situated near the church of Aghios Georgios in Palaio Phaleron on the east side of the bay (cf. Eliot, *PECS* p. 698 and Kalogeropoulou *AD* 24 [1969] A, p. 211 with n. 1). Its antiquity is indicated by the fact that it contained a number of ancient sanctuaries and shrines to both gods and heroes (Paus. 1.1.4). The cults of Nausithoös and Phaiax (cf. Plu. *Thes.* 17.6) may in reality not be any older than the fifth cent., given the fact that the elevation of their father Theseus to national hero postdates 508 (see p. 22). This anachronism, however, far from weakening the case for the antiquity of Phaleron as an *epineion*, actually confirms it, since it demonstrates that the area was clearly perceived as an appropriate setting for legends relating to the distant past. Phaleron's importance and size in the late sixth cent. are suggested by its 'Kleisthenic' bouleutic quota of 9 (Traill 1975).

3   **Piratical raids on Attike.** Hdt. 6.138.1 refers to a raid by Lemnians which led to the abduction of Athenian women who were celebrating the festival of Artemis at Brauron. He connects it with the legendary expulsion of the Pelasgians, but the reference to the Brauronia, combined with the implication that Brauron was at this date dependent on Athens, suggests a date in the seventh or sixth cent.

Naukraries. The testimonia on this subject are assembled and discussed in exhaustive detail by Jordan (1975, 9-16). The earliest reference is in Hdt. 5.71.2 where 'the presidents (*prutaneis*) of the *naukraroi*' are described as ruling Athens at the time of the Kylonian conspiracy. Since the existence of an Athenian navy in *c.* 636-24 (cf. Wright *HSCP* 3 [1892] 1-74) is problematic, Jordan proposes that this board might originally have been in charge of the sacred ships which conveyed *theôriai* to festivals around Greece. Allusions to naukraries in connection with naval administration are confined to two late, lexicographical references (viz. Poll. 8.108; *Anecd. Bekk.* I, 283.20), and any extrapolation based on suspect etymology (viz. *naukraros* = a person in charge of a ship) should be rejected.

4   **Tetrakomoi.** Lewis (1963, 33) suggests that Tetrakomoi might be the missing name after Tetrapolis in Str. *Geog.* 9.1.20 (citing Philochoros *FGrH* 328 F 94) where the list (described by Lewis as one which 'certainly reflects some truth about early Attike') is quoted. See also Solders (1931, 107f.). For the components of the Tetrakomoi, see Poll. 4.105. Roughly speaking, Thymaitadai lies to the northwest of the Piraeus, Xypete to the northeast and Phaleron to the east. For the site of the sanctuary of Herakles Tetrakomos, cf. Stanton (1984, 37). For evidence of the religious activity of the Tetrakomoi in the fourth cent., see Appendix III no. 113.

Archaic grave monuments. A sphinx dated to the middle of the sixth cent. is also said to have been found at Phaleron (Richter 1961, no. 18 with figs. 60-1, 63). For other Archaic grave monuments from the western coastal region, see Jeffery (1962, 135f.). I would point out that the so-called Piraeus Amphora (NM V. 353), a funerary marker dated *c.* 630 in the Protoattic style, is in fact of uncertain provenance.

Hippias' fortification of Mounychia. The only reference to this incident is in Ps.-Arist. *AP.* For the date of Hippias' expulsion, see Rhodes (1981, 197 and 233). It is just conceivable that Hippias had in mind the establishment of harbour fortifications in the Piraeus, but if so Ps.-Arist. knew nothing of this.

15   **Athenian naval contribution to the Ionian revolt.** It is not clear whether the Athenian contingent consisted of triremes or old-fashioned pentekontors. Charon of Lampsakos (*FGrH* 262 F 10 ap. Plu. *Mor.* 861 cd) states categorically that they were triremes, but Hdt. 5.99 seems to contrast the *nêes* (ships) of the Athenians with the triremes of the Eretrians. Since Hdt. is generally more reliable than Charon, his version is therefore to be preferred (cf. Jacoby, comment. ad loc.). Not much credence need be attached to the admonitory anecdote told in Plu. *Them.* 2.6 of Themistokles' father Neokles warning his son of the hazards of a political career by pointing out to him old and cast-off triremes lying rotting on the seashore.

Archonship of Themistokles. The eponymous archonship of Themistokles is placed by D.H. 6.34.1 in Olympiad 71.4 (i.e. 493). Fornara's arguments (1971, 534ff.) for challenging the orthodox interpretation of Thuk.'s reference to it (viz., *epi tês ekeinou archês hês kat' eniauton Athenaiois êrxe*) and for suggesting that the words refer instead to some undefined magistracy which he held continously from year to year 'in connection with the establishment of a secure harbour for the fleet' (p. 540) are rightly rejected by Dickie (1973) and Lewis (1973). That aside, it has to be admitted that the syntax of the Thukydidean passage is problematic. Everything depends on punctuation, and I have adopted here the reading of the *OCT*, which most commentators prefer. The other possibility (favoured by Shreiner 1969) is to link the participle '*nomizôn* (in the belief)' with the clause preceding it, and to render 'The project was begun during his archonship in the belief that the Piraeus, etc.'

The foundation of the Piraeus and beginnings of Athenian sea power. Cf. Andok. 3.5; Aristodem. *FGrH* 104 F 1.5.4; Ar. *Knights* 815; Ps.-Arist. *AP* 22.7; D.S. 11.41-3; Hdt. 7.144, cf. 6.89 and 132; Lib. *Or.* 9.38; Nep. *Them.* 6.1; Paus. 1.1.2; Pl. *Gorg.* 455e; Plu. *Them.* 4.1-3 and 19; Polyain. *Strat.* 1.30.6; Sud. s.v. *Themistokles*; Thuk. 1.14.3 and 1.93. Shreiner (1969, 24) is surely right to point out that it would have been remarkable if the Athenians had begun to fortify the Piraeus without at the same time taking limited steps to expand their navy. Likewise Garlan (1974, 47) believes that the construction of the Piraeus fortifications and the development of Athenian naval power derive from one and the same strategic project.

18   **Athenian supremacy as the goal of Themistoklean policy.** Intimations of this intention may be detected in Thuk. 1.93.4, Plu. *Them.* 20.1 and D.S. 11.41.3.

Political implications of the Themistoklean project. Some slight indication that Themistokles did in fact comprehend the political – and hence revolutionary – nature of his proposal is provided by Thuk. 1.93.6-7, where it is implied that he intended to reduce the hoplite force and concentrate manpower in the navy. However, I agree with Frost (1968, 120) that we are wrong to seek 'any purposeful and partisan strengthening of the *thêtes* ... as a political force' and that Themistokles' intentions were 'strictly strategic and extramural'.

19   **Opposition to Themistokles' project.** Stesimbrotos of Thasos (*FGrH* 107 F 2 ap. Plu. *Them.* 4.5) states that Themistokles forced through his naval act against opposition from Miltiades. For the return of Miltiades from the

Chersonese, see Hdt. 6.40-1 and 104. Gruen (1970, 97) suggests that Miltiades might have been opposed to Themistokles' scheme because of his desire to recover his overseas property as soon as possible, whereas the latter looked forward to a long-term settlement. Gruen further credits Miltiades with having the imagination 'to foresee the political and social consequences of a turn to the sea'. This I doubt. Jacoby (loc. cit., p. 283) would substitute Aristeides' name for that of Miltiades as the opponent of Themistokles in the Stesimbrotos passage. Likewise, Meister (1978, 283) believes that if Stesimbrotos is alluding to Themistokles' naval law of 483/2, rather than to the Piraeus fortification plan of 493/2, then Aristeides and not Miltiades must be meant. Evidence of hostility between Themistokles and Aristeides in the 480s is inconclusive, however.

New silver strike at Lavrion. Cf. Hdt. 7.144 and Ps.-Arist. *AP* 22.7. Judging by fourth-cent. evidence, the state obtained revenue from silver mines by the sale of leases farmed out to contractors, but these were extremely cheap and it is by no means clear how a surplus of 100 talents could have been obtained by this method, unless there was also a tax on production.

Themistokles' proposal. Hdt. 7.144 states that 200 triremes were built, whereas Ps.-Arist. *AP* 22.7 and Plu. *Them.* 4.2 both put the number at 100. According to Nep. *Them.* 2.2 and 8, there were two building phases of 100 triremes each. Since the estimated cost of building a trireme is put at one talent, the lower figure is more likely to be correct (cf. Rhodes 1981, 278). Labarbe (1957, 21-51) has tried unconvincingly to reconcile the divergent traditions by suggesting that Themistokles passed two naval bills, the first reserving the income from the silver mines at Maroneia, the second that from Lavrion, each of which yielded 100 talents for 100 ships. As Bengston (1954, 458f.) notes, Themistokles' proposal was not without precedent in the Greek world. Between 494/3 and 491/0 the Thasians had dedicated their import revenues, largely derived from mines, to the construction of triremes and to the building of a city wall (Hdt. 6.46-8). To what extent their decision acted as an inspiration to Themistokles cannot be known but it doubtless added weight to his arguments. Plu. *Them.* 4.2 alleges that Themistokles exploited Athenian anger and rivalry against the Aeginetans as 'the Persians ... were a long way off and presented no firm fear that they would attack'. For relations between the two states throughout the decade 490-80, see Podlecki (1976, 403-8). Other instances in the ancient world of a sudden build-up of naval forces by a hitherto continental power include Persia in *c.* 525 and Rome in 260 (cf. Thiel [1954] and Wallinga [1984, 406]). Cf. also the dramatic increase in the size of the Corinthian fleet, from 30 to 90 triremes in the two years leading up to the outbreak of the Peloponnesian War (Thuk. 1.27.2; 1.46.1), for which see Meiggs (1982, 492 n. 50).

The origins of Athens' naval establishment. The first surviving mention of supervisors of the docks (*epimelomenoi to neorio*) is in an inscription (*IG* I² 73.19 = *IG* I³ 153) found in the Piraeus dated by Jordan (1975, 20) to between 450 and 435.

Availability of timber in Attike. Meiggs (1982, ch. 7) is of the view that Attike was not as bereft of serviceable timber as is sometimes alleged but points out that its poor quality, combined with the difficulty of transporting it to the coast from either Mount Parnes or Mount Kithairon, ruled it out as a major source of shipbuilding supply.

21   **The abandonment of the Asty as the logical goal of Themistoklean policy.** That Themistokles himself seems to have recognised the logic behind such a move in time of crisis is perhaps indicated by his urging the Athenians to 'go down to the Piraeus if ever they found themselves hard-pressed by land'. This is not, of course, the same as urging upon them a permanent abandonment of the Asty – for which see Plu. *Them.* 11.3-5 (n.b. not in connection with a migration to the Piraeus).

22   **Promotion of the cults of Theseus and Poseidon.** Bacch. *Dith.* 17, a paean written for a Kean choir on Delos dated before *c.* 475, contains the earliest surviving mention of Theseus' visit to the depths of the sea in defence of his claim to be the son of Poseidon. From *c.* 500 onwards date also the earliest vase depictions of Theseus at the court of Poseidon and Amphitrite (Boardman 1975, 229 with fig. 223.1: red-figure vase in Paris [Louvre G 104] from Cerveteri). Theseus' connections with sea-power are alluded to by Plu. *Them.* 19.5 where it is alleged that he built a fleet with which he defeated the Cretans. The cult of Poseidon Erechtheus on the Acropolis may not have been founded much before *c.* 470-60. Judith Binder has pointed out to me by letter that one reason for the god's promotion was to enable the Athenians as head of the Delian Confederacy to 'match' Poseidon Helikonios, whose cult was a focus for panionic sentiment among the Ionian cities of Asia Minor (cf. Farnell 1907, IV p. 10f.). For the interpretation offered here regarding the motives behind the fundamental religious readjustment that took place in this period in line with Athens' new maritime role I am greatly indebted to Judith Binder. The joint promotion of hero and god would appear to be a clear instance of that co-operative spirit which, more often than we have the means to detect, may well underlie the reception of new cults into Attike.

     The Delian League from 478-*c.* 466. The events of this period are briefly summarised in Thuk. 1.108. An exact chronology is impossible to establish.

23   **The Long Walls.** For the problems in Thuk.'s narrative, see Walker (1957, 35). That the tradition reported by Plu. is not necessarily to be dismissed as an invention is also the view of Gomme (*HCT,* I p. 311) who suggests that Kimon might have effected repairs to the walls following his return from ostracism. The earliest known Long Walls were those constructed by the Athenians at Megara in 459 in order to enable them to control the city with seaborne troops in the eventuality of the Megarid being occupied by the enemy (Thuk. 1.103.4). Later examples include Corinth in *c.* 450, Amphipolis in 424, Patrai in 420 and Argos in 417. See Lawrence (1979, 155-7). The year 458/7 was important for Athenian democracy in a number of other ways. It also saw the production of Aeschylus' *Oresteia* (described by Forrest [1966, 214] as 'the radicals' justification of their reforms') and the admission of the *zeugitai* to the archonship.

24   **Athenian disaster in Egypt.** For the reliability of Thuk.'s assessment of the scale of the disaster, which has been seriously challenged in recent years, see Westlake (1969), Meiggs (1972, 104-8), Blackman (1969, 198), and

Salmon (1965, 151-8). For the consequences of the disaster, see Meiggs (1972, 109-24) and the bibliography cited in Barron (1983, 11 n. 38).

Athenian corn-shortage in the mid-fifth century. Cf. Meiggs (1972, 95) who cites Plu. *Per.* 37.4; Schol. on Ar. *Wasps* 718; and *IG* I² 31.6 = *SEG* X 32.

5 **The Middle Wall.** Pl. *Gorg.* 455de with Schol.; Harp. s.v. *dia mesou teichos.* Perikles ridiculed in Comedy: Plu. *Per.* 13.7-8 and *Mor.* 351a (quoting Kratinos in *CAF* I fr. 300 p. 100). Meiggs (1972, 188) suggests that after the conclusion of peace with Sparta the Athenian assembly would have needed some convincing that 'defence against the threat from the Peloponnese was still needed', but I do not myself believe that the assembly would have been so naive. Although the Phaleric Wall was rendered strategically obsolete by the building of the Middle Wall, it none the less continued to function as a line of first defence. Perikles evidently seems to have envisaged defending it at the outbreak of the Peloponnesian War since the Middle Wall was initially left unguarded (Thuk. 2.13.7). Athens' hubristic confidence in her walls was a consequence of the inefficiency of fifth-cent. siegecraft.

5 **Planning commission.** For the colony at Brea, see *IG* I³ 46.10-12 = *IG* I² 45 = *ML* 49 = *GHI* I 44: 'Ten *gêonomoi* shall be elected, one from each tribe (*phylê*); these will allocate (*nemantôn*) the land.' Regarding the appointment of planning commissions, see Martin (1951, 363; 1974, 55f.), Meritt (1935, 357-97), Robert (1936, 158f.) and Boersma (1970, 49). At Sounion a commission of three was appointed to determine the boundaries of the new agora (*IG* II² 1180 = *SIG*³ 913). The appointment of a commission to survey the Piraeus may be compared with the appointment of Pierre l'Enfant at the turn of the nineteenth century to survey the site of the future capital of the United States. In both cases there was a need to anticipate the future growth of an urban settlement commensurate with its projected importance.

Expropriation. A third-cent. decree from Tanagra in Boeotia regarding the transfer of a sanctuary of Demeter and Kore from outside the walls to the interior of the city sets out the procedure for expropriation as follows (*DHR* II no. 36 pp. 354ff. = Reinach, *REG* 12 [1899] p. 71):

> After the decree (sc. to expropriate) will have become law, the people shall elect a commission (*archê*) for three years composed of three citizens not less than thirty years old. The elected commission shall erect the sanctuary in the city in consultation with the polemarchs and the architects. If they have need of anyone's land or anyone's house in order to erect the sanctuary, the polemarchs, having summoned the people, shall appoint eleven valuers (*timatai*) according to the law common to the Boeotians (ll. 11-17).

For other laws regarding the expropriation of private property by the state, see Reinach (op. cit. 87).

Sacred land retains its sacredness. Cf. *IG* I³ 46.13-15 ('The *temenoi* which are reserved are to remain exactly as they are and no others are to be established'); and Pl. *Laws* 12.955e ('No one shall consecrate a second time what is already sacred to the gods'). For the concept, see Malkin (1984).

Hippodamos of Miletos. The only other testimonia for his work in the Piraeus are Hsch. and Phot. s.v. *Hippodamou nemêsis*; and Schol. on Ar. *Kts.* 327. There is no mention of Hippodamos in Thukydides. *Diaresis* is a synonym for '*nemêsis*', which appears on *horoi* found in the Piraeus (Appendix I nos. 14 and 15). As Burns (1976, 423f.) notes, there is no ancient evidence to support the commonly held view that Hippodamos was responsible for the rebuilding of his home town of Miletos in 479. We have absolutely no knowledge of his career before he came to Athens and can only speculate as to why he was selected for such a major undertaking.

27 **Rhodes.** Strabo's claim that Hippodamos was responsible for the layout of Rhodes has received support from air-photography and archaeological work carried out over the last thirty years. Cf. Kondis (1958, 148), Bradford (1956, 57-69) and *AD* 20 (1965) B3 p. 602.

The dating of Hippodamos' commission. In our present state of knowledge, any year between *c.* 470 and *c.* 445 is theoretically possible as the date of Hippodamos' arrival in Athens. Unlike Falciai (1982, 83-5), I do not place much weight upon the testimony of the Schol. on Ar. who may well be confusing the Themistoklean initiative with the subsequent development of the residential and commercial areas.

Financial decree of Kallias. *IG* I² 91, 92 A 30f. = *IG* I³ 52 = *SEG* X 45 = *ML* 58. Meiggs (1972, 519-23) and, most recently, Lewis (in *IG* I³) assign the decree to 434/3; Mattingly (1968, 450-85) to 422/1; and Fornara (1970, 185-96) to 418/7.

28 ***Hellespontophulakes.*** *IG* I² 57.34-41 = *IG* I³ 61 = *ML* 65. Meiggs-Lewis see the introduction of these officials as 'possibly ... a war measure' (p. 65). As Finley (1978, 119) points out, however, this view ignores the fact that 'very few years since 478 were not "wartime" years'. MacDonald's (1982, 119 n. 56) suggestion that the term merely refers to the military forces stationed in the region is improbable.

Megarian Decree. Thuk. 1.67.4, 1.139.1 and 1.144.2. Cf. Ar. *Ach.* 524-39 and *Peace* 605-11; Plu. *Per.* 29-30. De Ste. Croix's claim (1972, 287) that 'the harbours of the empire' ought not to include the Piraeus on the grounds that *archê* properly means 'rule beyond one's own proper boundaries', linguistically impeccable though it may be, is unconvincing. As Gauthier (1975, 500) has pointed out, it would surely be patently absurd to permit or deny the use of ports where one has *archê*, without at the same time permitting or denying the use of one's own.

Periklean strategy. Thuk. 1.143.3-144.1; 2.13.2, 62 and 65.7. The merits of Periklean strategy continue to arouse mixed feelings, just as they did in antiquity. Sealey (1967, 94) comments that it was 'the best that could be attempted in untoward circumstances'; Ober (1985, 52) that it was 'startlingly original and well thought out'. It is insufficiently appreciated by scholars that the possibility of having to abandon the Attic countryside as a means of survival had been envisaged as long ago as *c.* 457 when the Long Walls were first built. What was radical about Periklean strategy in 431 was simply the fact that Athens should accept a state of siege even before hostilities had begun. Even so, from 445 onwards, Athens' increasing concentration upon sea-power had inexorably been depriving her of any alternative response.

29 **The Piraeus converted into a closed port.** Cf. Thuk. 8.90.4; *IG* II² 1035.44-6; Schol. on Ar. *Peace* 145. Other examples include: Chios in the first half of the fourth cent. (Aen. *Comm. Poliork.* 11.3 *T*); Tyre in 322 (Ar.

An. 2.24.1); and Carthage in the mid-second cent. (App. *Pun.* 14.96). See Garlan (1974, 388), Jameson (1969, 335f.), and Lehmann-Hartleben (1923, 65-74).

Fortification of Rhamnous, Sounion and Thorikos. For Rhamnous, see Pouilloux (1954, 58f.). Its importance on the northeast Attic coast is indicated by the very impressive series of *peribolos* tombs currently being excavated and reconstructed by Vasileios Petrakos. See Petrakos (*PAE* 1975, 5-35; 1976, 5-60; 1977, 3-19; 1978, 1-16; 1979, 17-22; and 1982, 154-8). For the fortification of Sounion in 413/2, see Thuk. 8.4 with Mussche (1964, 423ff.); for that of Thorikos in 409, see Xen. *Hell.* 1.2.1 with Mussche (1961, 176ff.).

Imposition of the *eikostê*. The fact that Athens manifestly anticipated increasing her revenue by this measure permits an approximate notion of the amount of trade handled by the allied ports. Aegina, for instance, whose pre-war assessment was the largest of all the allies (30 talents), must have handled goods whose total value exceeded 600 talents in order to make the imposition beneficial to Athens' coffers. See further Figueira (1981, 124).

Trade during the Peloponnesian War. See MacDonald (1982) who argues from the presence of Attic pottery in Corinth during the late fifth cent. that the two states went on trading throughout the war. Since Corinth was possibly the most anatagonistic of all the Peloponnesians towards Athens during the war, a fortiori it is unlikely that economic links between Athens and any other hostile state were fully severed. I would point out that what makes Ar. *Ach.* even less trustworthy as evidence of a general import ban is the fact that at l. 918 the sycophant denounces the Boeotian for importing lamp wicks on the grounds that they could be used to set fire to the Piraeus dockyard.

The Piraeus Ten. Cf. Ps.-Arist. *AP* 35.1; Pl. *Ep.* 7.324c 3-5; Xen. *Hell.* 2.4.19; Plu. *Lys.* 15.1; Androtion *FGrH* 324 F 11. Charmides was the cousin of Kritias, one of the leading members of the Thirty, and uncle of Plato (Davies 1971, 330f.). Whitehead (1986, 394) rightly observes that the appointment of the Piraeus Ten by the Thirty is evidence of 'a well-founded apprehension that Piraeus would be the focal point for radical opposition to their regime, and called for special controls as such'. For their role and powers, see Krentz (1982, 58f.) and Rhodes (1981, 438f.).

Second assembly place of the Pnyx. Ceramic evidence supports a date for the remodelling around the turn of the fourth cent. Some scholars (e.g. Moysey 1981) have rejected the tradition that it was the Thirty who were responsible for the project and have suggested on a priori grounds that it is more likely to have been accomplished by the restored democracy. But as Krentz (1984, 230) points out: 'The fact that the anecdote does not fit the traditional picture of the "Thirty Tyrants" is a strong argument against the hypothesis that it is fictitious.' For political symbolism behind the reversal, cf. Krentz (1984, 230). Thompson (1982, 140) is more cautious. My discussion of the remodelling owes much to Judith Binder who suggests to me that the remodelling may have been due to a desire to control the entrances.

Motivation behind the Thirty's programme of reforms. My interpretation is a modification of Krentz's view (1982) that the Thirty sought to remodel the Athenian state along Spartan lines. I fully agree with Whitehead (1982-3, 105) that it was 'not so much the Athenian constitution as Athenian society at large' which they sought to revolutionise.

Expulsions to the Piraeus. Cf. Isok. 7.67; Lys. 12.92 and 13.47; D.S. 14.32.4; Ps.-Arist. *AP* 36.1; Xen. *Hell.* 2.4.1. According to Xen., many of those who fled to the Piraeus were subsequently evicted to Megara and Thebes. See Cloché (1911).

Arrest and execution of metics. The number of metics seized is variously reported: Lys. 12.6-7 puts it at ten, Xen. *Hell.* 2.3.21 at thirty, and D.S. 14.5.6 at sixty. Since Lysias had no reason to minimise the brutality and rapacity of the Thirty, ten is the most likely figure. Krentz (1982, 80) comments: 'Lysias' poignant account has made the execution of certain metics one of the best-known atrocities committed by the Thirty.' Though confined to only a handful of victims, the atrocity would none the less have sent a clear signal to Athens' metic community, in much the same way as terrorist attacks have done to westerners living in the Middle East. Whitehead (1982-3, 130) rightly equates the Thirty's action with Sparta's policy of *xenêlasia*, its intention being 'to purge Attike of its dangerously cosmopolitan immigrant population'.

Revoking of proxenies. See Walbank (1978, nos. 26, 61, 63, 72 and 79). The five surviving documents may represent only a small fraction of the total number.

Demolition of dockyards. Lys. 12.99 and 13.46; Isok. 7.66. Possibly the money thus raised was used to pay the Spartan garrison. The emotive value attaching to the Athenian dockyards is indicated by Lys. 12.99 where this act of vandalism is put in the same category of offences as appropriating temple treasures and assassinating one's opponents. The work of demolition may not have been completed when the Thirty fell from power, since Lys. 30.22 in 399 speaks of the dockyards as 'falling into decay (*perikatarrheonta*)'.

Resistance to the Thirty. *IG* II² 10 (discussed below p. 37) proves the extent to which Thrasyboulos' resistance movement was aided and abetted by metics. According to Lys. 31.29 their contribution went 'beyond the call of duty', though his own personal involvement with the events of this period makes his judgement admittedly partial. Middleton (1982, 299f.) plausibly argues for the presence of 'a notable number of Thracians' among the resistance.

36   **Separation of the Piraeus from Athens.** The exact period covered by the separation is disputed. According to Lenschau (s.v. 'Peiraieus' in *RE*) it was from Feb. to Aug.; according to Fuks (1953) from Apr. to Sept. It extended from the day of the battle of Mounychia to the restoration of democracy.

The men of the Piraeus. Cf. Lys. 12.53, 55, 59, etc., and 25.28; Xen. *Hell.* 2.4.23, 26, etc.; Ps.-Arist. *AP* 38.3. In Xen.'s account the term 'men of the Asty' first appears in his description of the battle of Mounychia (2.4.11) where they are contrasted with 'the men from Phyle'. The term 'men of the Piraeus' is only used in relation to events subsequent to the battle.

Examination of the Piraeus Ten. Ps.-Arist. *AP* 39.6. See Amit (1965, 93), Cloché (1915, 268-72), Rhodes (1981, 470f.) and Munro (1938).

The democrats' return to Athens. It is noteworthy that in the speech ascribed to him in Xen. *Hell.* 2.4.40, Thrasyboulos interprets the conflict between the men of the Piraeus and the men of the Asty as a class struggle (a fact oddly overlooked by de Ste. Croix [1981]).

Decree honouring 1,000 non-Athenians. The decree (*IG* II² 10 + Addendum p. 665 = *SEG* XII 84 = *GHI* II 100) is notoriously controversial and contains numerous difficulties. Recent discussion includes Rhodes (1981, 476f.), Osborne (1981, I cat. no. D6), Krentz (1980) and Whitehead (1984). One of the major problems is whether the decree specified differentiated honours for different groups (cf. the references to 'those who came down from Phyle' (l. 4), 'those who fought at Mounychia' (l. 7) and 'those who remained with the Demos in the Piraeus' (l. 8, as restored by Osborne). Whitehead is emphatic that all the honorands were enfranchised, though he concedes that the idea of granting citizenship to 1,000 foreigners at a stroke 'may seem bewildering, even grotesque'. Conceivably, it could have been anxiety about the return of her metic population in 401/0 that prompted Athens' signally uncharacteristically generous gesture. In an article forthcoming in *ZPE*, however, Peter Krentz continues to argue that the decree merely confined itself to upgrading the legal rights of the honorands.

Athenian desire for the restoration of supremacy. Cf. the inscription on the *stêlê* erected to Konon which states that 'Konon freed the allies of Athens' (Dem. 20.69) with Seager (1967, 99-101). Seager (p. 115) writes of the period between 403 to 386: 'The constant determining factor ... is the refusal of the mass of Athenians to accept the fact that the empire had been lost and their desire to attempt to recreate it in fact as soon as or even before the time was ripe.'

Restoration of the Piraeus circuit and Long Walls. Xen.'s claim (*Hell.* 4.8.10) that some Boeotian volunteers assisted in the rebuilding finds confirmation in a reference to the transporting and laying of stones by a Boeotian contractor called Demosthenes (*IG* II² 1657 = *GHI* II 107 B = Maier, I no. 2). For building accounts relating to the same project, cf. *IG* II² 1656-64 = Maier, I nos. 1-9. See also D.S. 14.84.3-5 and 85.2-4.

Rehabilitation of Themistokles' reputation. The earliest indications of this wind of change date to the outbreak of the Peloponnesian War when the embassy to Sparta delivered a brief eulogy in Themistokles' honour (Thuk. 1.74.1). The alleged request to the Magnesians for the return of his bones 'at a time when the Athenians were suffering from the plague' (in 430/29 according to Podlecki 1971, 143) is, if historically trustworthy, further evidence of the same tendency (cf. Schol. on Ar. *Knights* 84).

Athens' decision to rebuild her navy. Cawkwell (1976) believes that the proposal originated with Thrasyboulos who also took the first steps in reconstituting the Athenian empire. Cf. Lys. 28.4 and 14.

Re-imposition of the *eikostê*. Cf. *IG* II² 24.7f. = *GHI* I 114, dated 387: decree exempting the Klazomenians from all impositions except the 5 per cent tax.

The Piraeus gates. As Cawkwell (1973, 54) remarks, it seems very improbable that the Piraeus was not actually fitted with gates at the time of the rebuilding in 394-1, particularly since Athens was then engaged in the

Corinthian War. Sinclair's alternative suggestion (1978, 32) that the work 'may well have languished after the arrest of Konon and the discontinuation of Persian finance in 392' is unconvincing.

Raid of Sphodrias. See MacDonald (1972) for the problems concerning the two versions of this event.

42   **Athens' land defence system in the fourth century.** Ober (1985, 213) dates the forts at Gyphtokastro and Phyle to after 378, along with a number of watch towers and relay stations throughout Attike. He claims that the land defence system was not brought to final completion until the late 340s. For criticism and rejection of Perikles' defence strategy by fourth-cent. writers, see Garlan (1974, 66f.) and Ober (pp. 52-66).

Formation of the Second Athenian Confederacy. This interpretation of the order of events, which accords with the chronology of Diodoros, is the view proposed by Cawkwell (1973) who identifies two distinct phases in its evolution: the first dating to the aftermath of the King's Peace in 387/6; and the second to Sphodrias' raid, which resulted in the declaration that peace had been broken. Others see the formation of the Confederacy as a reaction to the raid of Sphodrias, rather than a consequence of it. The earliest epigraphical indications are to be found in an inscription dated 379/8 referring to an alliance between Athens and a state whose name is not preserved (Pritchett 1972, 164-9).

Athenian naval build-up. See especially *IG* II² 1605 (after 377/6); 1611.5-9 (dated 357/6); 1613.302 (dated 353/2). The rate of Athens' naval re-armament in the fourth cent. is discussed below p. 97.

43   **Athens at the end of the Social War.** See Cawkwell (1963, 61-3; 1981, 54f.). For a contemporary view of Athens in 355, cf. Isok. *On the Peace*.

Euboulos. The evidence for Euboulos' building activity in the Piraeus is provided by Dein. 1.96 where it is contrasted with Demosthenes' inertia. In view of its political overtones, however, the passage must be treated with caution.

44   **Hypereides' proposal.** Cf. Hyp. frr. 32-43 *T*; Aristogeit. fr. 3 *T*; Ps.-Plu. *Mor.* 849a.

Lykourgos. For a general critique of Lykourgos' activities, see Mitchel (1970) and Humphreys (1985). Lykourgos is known to have been the proposer of the decree permitting Cypriots to set up a shrine to Aphrodite (Appendix III no. 6). That he may also have assisted the Egyptians in establishing their shrine to Isis is suggested by the fact that his grandfather was mocked in Ar. *Birds* 1296 for his sympathy towards Egyptian cults.

45   **Battle of Amorgos.** Ashton (1977, 9) proposes a date for the battle 'three or four days before the close of the year 323/2' on the grounds that the naval inventory for the year 323/2 (*IG* II² 1631.171-4), according to his restoration, reflects no depletion in the size of the fleet in the light of a crushing naval defeat. It has often been remarked that the defeat at Amorgos is in antithetical relationship to the victory at Salamis. Will (1966, I p. 28; cf. *CAH*² VII.2 p. 32), for instance, writes:

> Salamis had established Athens' naval power. This battle extinguished it for ever in the waters of Amorgos, so much so that the history of Classical Athens is, so to speak, framed by these two engagements undertaken for the liberty of Greece, with very different results (quoted by Ashton, p. 2).

A Panathenaic amphora (Louvre Inv. N. 3164 MN 705 = *CVA*, France fasc. 8, Louvre fasc. 5, III Hg, pl. 6, 4-7 and 11) depicting two Nike figures holding stern ornaments (*aphlasta*) as trophies and dated to the archonship of Archippos is taken by Hauben (1974, 64) as evidence of a subsequent Athenian victory at sea and thus of 'a rehabilitation – meagre, to be sure – of the Athenian navy after the terrible setbacks of 322'. Hauben believes that this battle occurred in 321/0 (i.e. in the year of Archippos' second archonship) and involved a flotilla of ten Athenian ships which were assisting Antigonos Monophthalmos in Asia Minor (loc. cit. for references). For the interpretation of *aphlasta* on vases, see Casson (1971, 86 n. 49).

Mounychia under Macedonian domination. Cf. also the warning sent to Athens from the oracle at Dodona 'to guard the heights of (Mounychian) Artemis'; and the devouring of the lower part of the body of an Eleusinian initiate in the Grand Harbour, interpreted as a sign that Athens 'would lose the lower, coastal part of her city but preserve the upper part' (Plu. *Phok.* 28; below p. 160). The importance of Mounychia under Macedonian domination was well summarised by Leake (1841, 403):

> Secured by an Acropolis, Mounychia was admirably adapted to be the citadel of a maritime city, which generally had the command of the sea, but was sometimes inferior to its enemies by land; for on this side (i.e. the land side) it was surrounded by other well fortified quarters of the city, and could only be approached through them. Thus Mounychia became the citadel not only of the maritime town, but of Athens itself; and the Macedonians, during their occupation of it, were generally content to leave the Asty, and even the ports and their claustra in possession of the Athenians.

Macedonian garrisons were also established at Rhamnous, Sounion and Salamis at an unknown date. A decree dated *c.* 252 honouring Herakleitos 'appointed by the king (viz. Antigonos Gonatas) as *stratêgos epi tou Peiraieôs* and the places administered along with the Piraeus' may possibly contain a reference to these garrisons, as Gabbert (1983, 130) proposes. The garrisoning of strong points was the primary means by which the Macedonian kings kept the mainland in check for 150 years, other fortresses being established at Acrocorinth, Chalkis, Eretria, Megara and elsewhere (Plu. *Demetr.* 43; D.L. 2.12.7, 141-4; Trog. *Prologue* 26). The main concentration of Antigonid troops was at Demetrias in southern Thessaly, founded *c.* 293.

Decentralisation of Attike. Cf. *IG* II² 1244-8 and Ferguson (1911, 230f.)

Chronology of the period of the Macedonian occupation. Precisely when during this 93-year stretch the Piraeus was free of a Macedonian presence is, as Habicht (1979, 96) rightly emphasises, 'fundamental to our understanding of Athenian history and politics during the early Hellenistic era'. The periods during which a Macedonian garrison is known to have been present on Mounychia Hill are the following: 322-307, 294-287, and 262/1-229. The interval between 287 and 262/1 is particularly problematical (see below).

Restored unity in 317. Gauthier (1979, 354) sees a reference to this event in *SIG*³ 318 = *IG* II² 1201.9: 'Demetrios [*epanêga*]*gen eis to auto*'.

Repair of fortifications in 307/6. Cf. *IG* II² 463 + *Hesperia* 9 (1940)

66-72. Particularly interesting is the stated purpose for the rebuilding (l. 2f.), viz. that the fortifications should last 'for all time *(eis ton hapanta chronon)'*.

Macedonian attempt to recover the Piraeus in *c.* 305. The sole evidence for this postulated event derives from Paus. 1.26.3 who refers to Olympiodoros as *'Peiraia kai Mounychian anasôsamenos'*. The passage has been much discussed, notably by de Sanctis *(RFIC* 55 [1927] 495f.), who rejected it as fallacious. Habicht (1979, 102-107) ingeniously takes *anasôsamenos* to mean not 'recovered', as it is usually translated, but 'preserved from loss' ('vor dem Verlust retten'). He thus concludes that Olympiodoros' achievement, which he dates to 305 or 303-1, was to rescue the Piraeus when it was in danger of falling into the hands of the Macedonians. For a contrary view, scc Bultrighini (1984, 54-62).

Lachares' tyranny. See *P. Oxy.* 17.2082 = *FGrH* 257a (Phlegon of Tralles, late second cent. A.D.). Cf. also Paus. 1.25.7 and 29.10; Plu. *Demetr.* 33; Polyain. 4.7.5. For the date, see Shear (1978, 52 n. 144), Habicht (1979, 8-13) and Osborne (1982, 273).

50   **Establishment of oligarchy in 294.** See Shear (1978, 53-5) and Habicht (1979, ch. 2). Judith Binder informs me that when the Colonels took over Greece on 21 April 1967, the only place in Athens occupied by the military was Mouseion Hill.

Olympiodoros' capture of the Mouseion. See Plu. *Demetr.* 46.1-2; Paus. 1.26.1-2; *IG* II² 666 and 667 (decree honouring Strombichos). Shear (1978) dates the uprising to the last months of 286. Osborne (1979, 186), however, has cogently argued for the summer of 287 on the basis of a reference to the successful gathering in of the harvest of that year in a decree honouring Phaidros of Sphettos *(IG* II² 682.35f.).

Decree honouring Kallias of Sphettos. Shear (1978), Habicht (1979, 45-67) and Osborne (1979, 181-94); *SEG* XXVIII 60 and XXXII 112. The peace negotiations in the Piraeus are referred to at ll. 32ff.

51   **References to the Piraeus in Attic decrees dated 286-1.** Cf. *IG* II² 654 + Addendum p. 662.30ff. (285/4); *IG* II² 655 (285/4); *IG* II² 657 + Addendum p. 662.34ff. (283/2); *SEG* XXV 89 (282/1).

The failed attempt to recapture Mounychia. Cf. *IG* II² Addendum 5227a = Kyparisses and Peek *(AM* 57 [1932] p. 146 no. 2): epitaph on one of the dead who gave his life 'beneath the walls of Mounychia, striving to rescue his country from slavery'. Shear (1978, 82f.) and Gauthier (1979, 356 n. 20) date this abortive attack to 286/5, whereas Osborne (1979, 193f.) puts it as late as 281.

Possible expulsion of the Macedonian garrison in the 280s. Shear's view is based largely on Paus. 1.26.3, whose interpretation, as noted above, is open to doubt. In support of his theory that the Macedonians were bribed to depart, Gauthier (1979, 357) cites a decree dated 281 honouring the ex-archon Euthios (Meritt, *Hesperia* 7 [1938] 100 no. 18, lines 28-31), which contains the words 'when the Piraeus and the Asty are re-united', proof in his view that 'reunification was close or at least that the Athenians had every reason to believe that it was close.' Osborne, who does not consider the possibility of bribery, rejects Shear's theory of a second successful assault on the grounds that 'references to the need to win back the Piraeus are uniformly "routine" and colourless throughout the 280s and this seems rather surprising if there has been a disastrously abortive attempt at the expense of no less than 420 lives soon after the revolt.'

Chremonidean War. Decree containing Chremonides' proposal of alliance with Sparta: *SIG*³ 434-5 = *SVA* 476. It is described by Tarn (1913, 296) as 'a noble document, a fitting prelude to the last great struggle entered on by Athens for the liberties of herself and Greece'. The mention in an inscription of the '[*pro*]*schôseis* [*tôn l*]*imenôn* (banking-up of harbours)' undertaken about the time of the Chremonidean War (see Oikonomidou, *Neon Athênaion* 1 [1955] 9-14, lines 3f.) may, as Garlan (1974, 391) has suggested, refer to repair work on the quayside rather than to an attempt to block access to the port. There is also a reference to the Macedonian garrison in the Piraeus (*hoi tetagmenoi en toi Peiraiei*) for whom supplies have had to be requisitioned in a deme decree of Rhamnous dated 263/2 (*IG* II² 1217 = Pouilloux 1954, no. 118). The main base for Patroklos' fleet was probably on Kea, as Gabbert (1983, 135 n. 20) proposes. Habicht (1979, 108-12), rightly in my estimation, regards the ejection of the garrison as the foremost object of Athenian policy since 322. Both Ferguson (1911, 182-7) and Tarn (1913, 307-10) paint an excessively bleak picture of Athens' condition after the war. It is important to balance the political consequences of defeat (admittedly dire) alongside the social consequences (perhaps quite positive). On Athens' overall performance in the post-war period Fraser (1981, 242) comments: 'We are left wondering what, in addition to the political consequences of the occupation of the Piraeus, went so wrong; what psychological factors, what failure of individual and collective will, caused Athens to sink to the role of a minor power ...'. The answer, quite simply, is that the occupation of the Piraeus had itself a profoundly damaging impact upon Athenian morale, quite sufficient to produce just such a failure of will.

Diogenes *phrourarchos.* For Diogenes' withdrawal, cf. *IG* II² 834 = *SIG*³ 497. See Will (1966, I p. 329) for the date. For the cult, cf. *IG* II² 1011.14f. For his heroic status, see Oikonomides' discussion (1982) of a dipinto found in the Athenian agora containing a reference to Diogenes' *hierothutês*. The Diogeneion seems to have been situated near the church of Demetrios Katephores in Athens where a number of inscriptions have come to light (see Wycherley 1978, 232). It continued in use until the third cent. A.D. See further Pélékides (1962, 252 and 264ff.), Will (1966, I p. 329), Stewart (1977, 517f.), Habicht (1982, 83f. and 105-17) and Gauthier (1985, 63-6).

Athens' increased attachment to the hinterland from 228 onwards. As Mossé (1973) points out, the predominance of landowning interests over trading interests in this period is perhaps indicated by the fact that from the first half of the third cent. *enktêsis gês* was no longer granted unrestrictedly but carried an upper limit of 1000 dr. for a house and 2 talents for land. See Pečírka (1966, 96ff.).

Economic condition of the Piraeus. Ferguson (1911, 237-47) argued that the presence of the Macedonian garrison over such a long period led to a degree of economic prostration in the Piraeus which was not experienced to the same degree anywhere else in Attike. Antony Spawforth, however, has pointed out to me by letter (12/3/1986) that: 'In Rome's northwestern provinces garrisons are normally seen as generators of local wealth by virtue of their spending power', though he is careful to add that the analogy may not necessarily apply to the Piraeus.

Repair of fortifications. Cf. *IG* II² 786.7, 834.14 = *SIG*³ 497 and 835.9f.

The Piraeus described as a polis. See the five inscriptions covering the period 204/3-165/4 as listed in Gauthier (1982, 275-90).

Relations with Macedon and Egypt. See Pritchett *AJA* 63 (1942) 413ff., Meritt (*Hesperia* 38 [1969] 441) and Traill (1975, 29f.). Probably the Ptolemaia, or festival in honour of Ptolemy, was established in Athens in *c.* 224/3 (cf. Volkmann, s.v. Ptolemaia in *PW* XXIII.2 [1959] col. 1585). It is often remarked that the Athenians did not suppress the two 'Macedonian' tribes Antigonis and Demetrias which had been created in 307/6 until the outbreak of the Second Macedonian War in 200.

54   **Athens' fleet in 200.** For the term *navis aperta*, see further Torr (1964, 51f. with n. 121) and Briscoe (1973, 117). There is a reference to Athenian *aphraktoi*, perhaps identical to the ones mentioned by Livy, in an inscription from Delos (*SIG*³ 582.9) dated 200-197. Li. 31.15.5 reports that four Athenian *naves longae* were captured by the Macedonians in 200 and subsequently returned to them by the Rhodians. Nothing further is heard of these ships.

The Piraeus as a base for the Roman and allied fleets. As Ferguson (1911, 278f.) points out, this must have resulted in the presence of thousands of foreign sailors in the Asty and the Piraeus during the winter months of the year when the fleets were laid up.

Delos as a free port. For the shift in east-west trade routes, see Day (1942, 82). Casson (1984, 74 and 78f.) emphasises that Delos was important as an *emporion* both for slaves (cf. Str. *Geog.* 14.5.2) as well as the transshipment of goods from Arabia, India and the Far East, but not for corn, for which Rhodes remained the dominant distributor. Cf. also Rostovtzeff (1941, 744), who sees Delos as exercising a virtual monopoly on transit trade between Asia Minor, Syria, Egypt and Italy, but having very little impact on trade between the Greek states themselves.

56   **Destruction of the Piraeus.** Cf. App. *Mith.* 30-2, 34, 36-7 and 40. As Sherwin-White (1984, 138 n. 22) observes, Plu. *Sulla* says little about the assault on the Piraeus, concentrating instead 'out of historical sentiment' on the siege of Athens. It is ironic, in view of its past history, that Mounychia served as the final Athenian stronghold against the invader.

Works of art lost at the time of Sulla's sack. Dontas (1982, 33) believes that these statues all formed part of the sacred treasure which Aristion, under orders from Archelaos, brought with him from Delos to the Piraeus (App. *Mith.* 28) 'where they were deposited in the warehouses, apparently near to the port until their final fate had been decided'. The Apollo, dated *c.* 520-10, is the oldest surviving colossal bronze statue found in Greece. In the marble statue of Artemis, Jucker (1982, 133ff.) recognises a version of Artemis Kindyas of southeast Asia Minor. For the Athene-type, see Schefold (1971). A silver bracelet of unknown provenance inscribed 'in the Piraeus [vacat] Archelaos *stratopedarchês*' was perhaps given by Archelaos to one of his soldiers during the siege (*SEG* XXXI 1590). For the Mahdia shipwreck, see Merlin (1930, 408-11) and Fuchs (1963). Plentiful numismatic evidence relates to the siege, in the form of hoards of coins which were buried by Piraeans in the hope that they would not fall into Roman hands. The largest is a hoard of 1716 Athenian bronze coins which came to light in 1926. These indicate that a new, heavier-leaded bronze issue was struck during this period, possibly as Kleiner (1973, 181) has tentatively suggested, in response to the very high rate of inflation which allegedly caused the price of wheat to rise to 1,000 dr. per *medimnos* (Plu. *Sull.* 13.2). Another hoard of 210 bronze coins (191 Athenian, 8 Pontic) was discovered in 1973 (Oeconomides-Caramessini 1976, 220-3; below p. 146). In both instances the Athenian coins are badly struck, evidently indicating that they were minted in great haste. A third hoard of 13 Athenian silver tetradrachms and 2 Pontic tetradrachms were dug up in 1937 (Schwabacher 1937, 162-6).

2. POPULATION, TRADE AND COMMERCE

Death-rate. For evidence of much lower-than-average age of death in cities with poor accommodation and inadequate drainage as compared with rural areas, see Girouard (1985, 268).

Size of the population of the deme of Piraeus. Though the Piraeus' bouleutic quota is based on the deme's representation after 307/6 when the quotas were altered and a general reapportionment took place, Traill (1975, 58) points out that the occasion was not in fact used 'to remedy abuses in the ratio of representation to population which had crept into the system over a period of two centuries', and estimates that the Piraeus may have acquired only one more representative in 307/6. I would also note that 235 Peiraieis are listed in Kirchner's *Prosopographia Attica* (1901-03), thereby giving the Piraeus the tenth highest demotic rating of all Attic demes (see Gomme 1933, 63). It is not known what change, if any, occurred in the deme's bouleutic quota at the time of the reapportionment which took place in 224/3.

Population movement within Attike. For movement of population to Asty-Piraeus during the fourth and third centuries, see Gomme's study of funerary inscriptions (1933, Tables A and B on p. 44f.) with Whitehead's comments (1986, 353) on the reliability of his material. Another Attic deme which attracted a large number of non-*demôtai* was Acharnai which, as Burn (1966) suggests, might have witnessed a sizeable migration of professional charcoal-burners in line with the expansion of Athens.

Sepulchral inscriptions commemorating Peiraieis buried in the Piraeus. *IG* II² 7150, 7152, 7170, 7171/2, 7174, 7189, 7192 and 7195. The high incidence of gravestones found in the Piraeus commemorating non-Peiraieis contrasts strikingly with the situation, say, in the deme of Rhamnous where the overwhelming majority commemorate Rhamnousioi. See Petrakos (*PAE* 1975, 5-35; 1976, 5-60; 1977, 3-19; 1978, 1-16; 1979, 17-22; and 1982, 154-8). Mention may also be made here in passing of a gravestone (*c.* 400-390) found in the Piraeus commemorating a certain Littias, who lived to be a hundred (Tsirivakos 1969, 23-7).

Metics resident in the Piraeus. For earlier discussions, see Clerc (1893, 450f.), Wilamowitz-Moellendorff (1887), Gerhardt (1933, 15-17) and Diller (1937, 120f.).

Overall metic total in 431. Gomme (1933, 26) estimates that in 431 the entire population of Attike numbered around 315,000, of whom 28,500 were metics. Finley (1951, 64) also puts the metic population at this date at 30,000. Duncan-Jones (1980, 102) calculates that metics may have accounted for 43 per cent of the total hoplite force available for service in 431, while 'lower down the social scale the metic element could be larger'. My own suspicion, however, is that metic males outnumbered metic females quite considerably and that projections regarding their overall total based on numbers available for military service should be treated with caution. In time of war probably many metics served on garrison duty around the Piraeus circuit.

62   **Parepidêmoi, parepidêmountes.** For the legal distinction between metics and *parepidêmoi*, see Ar. Byz. fr. 38 (Nauck) and Harp. s.v. *metoikion*. No source is earlier than the fourth cent. See Whitehead (1977, 7-9). Cf. also *IG* II² 141.30-36 = *GHI* II 139 (discussed below).

Fourth-century decrees honouring metics. Decree honouring the metics Nikandros and Polyzelos: *IG* II² 505.7-41 = Maier I, no. 13. For commentary, see Pečírka (1966, 8f.; 1967, 25). Other decrees honouring metics include *IG* II² 276, 351 (= *GHI* II 198), 360, 373, 421, 483, 505, 551, 554, 715, 768, 786 and 835.

Grants of enktêsis. Pečírka (1967, 25; cf. 1966, passim) points out that from a total of nearly 60 grants of *enktêsis* known from Attic inscriptions, 35-39 date to the fourth cent. The majority of these belong to the years following the conclusion of the Social War (i.e. after 354), thereby lending limited support to Cawkwell's contention (1963, 64) that something was done for metics at this time along the lines proposed by Xen. *Por.* 2.6, including permission to erect houses on vacant sites (for a contrary view, see Whitehead 1977, 128f.). The clause '*kata ton nomon*', used regularly in connection with such grants in the last third of the fourth cent., may refer to the passing of a law laying down general regulations for grants of *enktêsis* (cf. Pritchett 1946, 159f.; and Pečírka 1966, 140-2).

Dikai emporikai. Cf. Dem. 21.176, 32.1 and 34.42; Ps.-Dem. 33.1; Ps.-Arist. *AP* 59.5. Xen.'s recommendation (*Por.* 3.3) that the settlement of disputes in commercial courts should be expedited in order to attract more foreigners to the Piraeus precedes by half a decade the introduction of the new procedure. Though the precise jurisdiction of *dikai emporikai* is unclear, we can be certain that they only covered disputes which: (1) involved either an *emporos* or a *nauklêros*; (2) resulted from a commercial voyage either to or from Athens; and (3) arose out of a written contract (cf. Millett 1983, 40). See further Cohen (1973, 100-14), Gauthier (1972, 1-6), Gernet (1955, 173ff.), Isager and Hansen (1975, 86), MacDowell (1978, 231-4) and Rhodes (1981, 664f.). The court may possibly have been located in the Piraeus (see below p. 81).

Metic tomb in Kallithea. The tomb, which is in the Piraeus Museum, awaits full publication. For a preliminary report, see Tsirivakos (1968, 35f.). It is listed as L2 in Garland (1982).

Lykourgos' involvement with metics. *Enktêsis* to *emporoi* of Kition: below p. 108. Xenokrates and the *metoikion*: Plu. *Flam.* 12.4; Ps.-Plu. *Mor.* 842b. For other versions of this incident (e.g. D.L. 4.14, Plu. *Phok.* 29.6, etc.), see Whitehead (1981, 235-8) who none the less inclines towards the version reported here. Eudemos honoured: *IG* II² 351.

4   **Metics from Lydia, Syria and Phrygia.** Isager and Hansen (1975, 69) point out that these are precisely the regions from which Athens recruited her slaves, but in my view this does not necessarily signify that Xen. is 'undoubtedly thinking of those who were granted freedom': there is no evidence to suggest that Athens ever manumitted slaves on the scale that Xen. apparently has in mind.

5   **Metic tombstones.** For the usefulness or otherwise of this evidence for assessing the size of foreign communities in Attike, see Clerc (1893, 381-3), Hommel (*RE* XV.2 [1932] col. 1442), Gerhardt (1933, 13-15), Isager and Hansen (1975, 70, 217-19 and 223), Gauthier (1972, 123f.) and Whitehead (1977, 110). For fourth-cent. metics, see Isager and Hansen (1975, 217-9). For Hellenistic Athens, see Davies (*CAH²* VII.1, p. 267). Excavations in the Athenian Agora have yielded 300 gravestones commemorating metics of whom the best-represented are the Milesians, the Herakleians and the Antiochenes (Bradeen 1974, nos. 386-685). For tombstones commemorating Kitians, see *IG* II² 9031-6.

6   **Thracians.** Possibly fifth-cent. in date is *IG* II² 11688 = *SEG* XVIII 327. Thracian ethnicity is the subject of a forthcoming monograph by Sterling Dow.

     Decline in population after 86 B.C. Sepulchral inscriptions of Roman date commemorating Peiraieis but found outside the Piraeus: *IG* II² 7154-61, 7163-5, 7167-8, 7175-6, 7178, 7185, 7187, 7190 and 7201-3. Those found in the Piraeus: 7150 and 7174.

7   **Phoenicians.** Sidonians enjoyed a privileged status in Attike which may not have been extended to any other group of metics. (For a possible instance of a similar grant made to some Cretans in the mid-fourth cent., see *Hesperia* 26 [1957] 229-31, cited by Whitehead 1977, 23 n. 59). An honorific decree (*IG* II² 141.30-6 = *GHI* II 139, dated 364 by Moysey 1976, 184) passed in favour of Strato, basileus of Sidon, carries the following rider:

> All Sidonians resident in Sidon and exercising political rights in that city who visit Athens (*epidêmôsi*) on business (*kat' emporian*) are exempt from the metic tax (*metoikion*), from liability for having to pay for a dramatic performance (*chorêgia*), and from the special war tax (*eisphora*).

The earliest evidence for Sidonians in the Piraeus is *IG* II² 2946 (Graeco-Phoenician bilingual dedication, late third cent.).

Jews. *Acts* 17.17, which refers to Paul's visit to a synagogue in Athens, has often been adduced as evidence of a sizeable Jewish community in Attike. Sepulchral inscriptions allegedly commemorating Jews are assembled by Urdahl (1968), but J. and L. Robert (*REG* 82 [1969] 453f. no. 206) have demonstrated that the onomastic criteria used for making the identification are almost invariably suspect.

     Contributions by metics to repair of Piraeus fortifications. See Day (1942, 16 with n. 92). In addition to Maier I, no. 13., cf. also *IG* II² 786 which refers to metics' contributions to the repair of the harbours after 228.

8   **Bankers and accountants.** For the activities and careers of individual

bankers, see Bogaert (1968, 61-94), where may also be found a summary of the career of Pasion (pp. 63-70), the most important Athenian banker in the Classical era. Gravestone of Charion (mid-fourth cent.): Clairmont (1970, 58 with pls. 26-7). Cf. also Ath. *Deipn.* 12.554e (referred to below).

Manufacturing businesses. For the *aspidopêgeion* of Pasion, cf. Dem. 36.4. The claim frequently made on the strength of Lys. 12.19 that Polemarchos employed 120 slaves in his *aspidopêgeion* ignores the likelihood that some proportion of his workforce may have been domestics (cf. Davies 1971, 589). For the *ergastêria* of Demosthenes, cf. Dem. 27.9. For the association of all three with the Piraeus, see below p. 142.

Quarrying. Fourth-cent. lease for a quarry in the Piraeus: Meritt (1936, 401: no. 10 lines 138-40). The only other recorded fee for leasing an Attic quarry is 100 dr. per annum (Coumanoudis and Gofas, *REG* 91 [1978] 289-306 = *SEG* XXVIII 103). Certain sacrifices performed in the Piraeus Asklepieion were paid for out of the income from a *lithotomeion* which may well have been located within the sanctuary on Mounychia Hill (cf. *IG* II² 47.30 = Appendix III no. 27). For quarry leases in Attike, see Ampolo (1982) and Osborne (1985, 103-7). In Skirophorion 394, day-teams who were employed in reconstructing the fortifications around the Piraeus were paid 160 dr. (*IG* II² 1656 = Maier I, no. 1).

69   **Farming and fishing.** See p. 95. Phaleric cabbages: Arist. *H. Anim.* 5.19; Hsch. s.v. *Phalêrikai*. For a lexicographical note on the variant Attic form *raphinos*, see Renehan (1975, 175). Phaleric *aphuê*: Ar. *Ach.* 901 and *Birds* 76; Arist. *H.Anim.* 6.15; Poll. 6.63.

Wealthy Peiraieis. Osborne (1985, Table 2a) records five wealthy demesmen on the basis of their performance of military and festival liturgies but there were in fact at least six. His wealth index of Piraeus *dêmotai* should therefore be revised upwards to 0.86 per cent (though in view of the large numbers of non-Peiraieis among the population, this is a wholly unreliable indicator of the region's prosperity). The six as recorded by Davies (1971) are : (1) Bathyllos (2817), a syntrierarch between 356 and 346/5 (*IG* II² 1622.763); (2) ---lou (A 116), a choregos in mid-fourth cent.; (3) Diokles (4046), a syntrierarch between 355 and 346/5 (*IG* II² 1622.593); (4) Olympiodoros (11407), a syntrierarch in 322 (*IG* II² 1632.317); (5) Phormion, son of Ktesiphon (11672, XI), a principal trierarch before 334/3 (*IG* II² 1623.245; cf. Dem. 21.157); and (6) Archippos, son of Phormion (12672, IX), son of the above, a syntrierarch between 336 and 334/3 (*IG* II² 1623.300-1) and choregos in 331/0 (*IG* II² 2318.335-6). For the metic Kephisodoros, cf. *IG* I² 329 = *IG* I³ 421 = *ML* 79A (lines 33-49) = Fornara 147. It may also be noted that out of a total of 46 proposers of decrees during the years 352/1-319/8 only one was a demesman of the Piraeus; and that out of a sample of 107 fifth- and fourth-cent. strategoi not one demesman occurs (Osborne 1985, Maps 5 and 6 p. 70f.). For Peiraieis named in deme decrees or otherwise known to have been active in deme politics, see Whitehead (1986, nos. 302-7).

73   **The tribe Hippothontis.** Prytany decrees honouring Hippothontis vary considerably in the number of prytaneis representing the deme Piraeus and cannot therefore be used to calculate size of population. See Dow (1937, no. 64) and Pritchett (1940, nos. 24 and 25). For other prytany decrees

recording the names of possible Peiraieis, see Raubitschek (1943, no. 14) and Pritchett (1946, no. 11).

Demarch of the Piraeus. For eligibility and election, see Whitehead (1986, 395f.) who points out that an appointment open to all Athenians 'would have been a major departure from, indeed violation of, traditional practice'. For Phrynion, see Whitehead (1986, no. 37). Ps.-Arist.'s text does not expressly state who conducted the election, but the nearest subject is the Demos (54.5) and there is no justification in concluding with Osborne (1985, 77) that it was the boule. Osborne (75-80, 87f.) believes that the demarch of Eleusis was also elected in the Asty, though not by the boule. Epigraphical evidence regarding the Piraeus demarch is contained in Appendix II nos. 1-3, 6. For demarchs as collectors of state taxes, etc., see Davies (1981, 146f.). For the *enktêtikon*, see *IG* II² 1214.26, no. 6.29 and Dem. 50.8. The only securely dated decree of the deme Piraeus (Appendix II no. 4) describes the year according to both the eponymous archon and the demarch. On this official, see further Rhodes (1981, 611), Hornblower (1983, 111) and Whitehead (1982, 37; 1986, 395f.).

The deme Piraeus. For the *kêrux* and *tamias*, see Appendix II no. 6.7, 8 and 18. Only thirteen demes are known to have appointed *tamiai* (Whitehead 1986, 144). The majority, whose financial affairs were less complex, may have been content to let the demarch administer their finances unaided. For the *epitimêtai*, see Appendix II no. 2.23f. and Whitehead (1986, 146). For the *horistai*, see Appendix II no. 1.21-4 where they are charged, along with the demarch, with the task of inscribing the decree on stone and setting it up in the Thesmophorion. Though the evidence for these last-named officers only dates to the fourth cent., it is possible that they were involved with the Hippodamian commission and subsequently empowered to ensure that its provisions were upheld. There is no reference to either a deme *euthunos* or *hieropoioi*, such as are attested elsewhere.

Taxes. As a reward for his services to the deme, Kallidamas of Cholleidai is permitted 'to pay the same taxes in the deme as do the Peiraieis, and the demarch is not to collect the *enktêtikon* from him'. It is not clear from this whether Kallidamas is being excused payment merely of the *enktêtikon* or of the *enktêtikon* plus an additional tax on non-demesmen. For a tenant's liability to pay the *eisphora* on deme property, see Finley (1951, 93) and Whitehead (1986, 155f.). Isager (quoted by Whitehead p. 157) attractively suggests that the stipulation in the lease that tenants whose annual rent exceeded 10 dr. must put up a security (*apotimêma*) may have been intended to prevent metics 'from leasing the choicest of the deme's *temenê*'.

Astunomoi. Invaluable discussion of the *astunomoi*, along with all the other official boards represented in the Piraeus which are mentioned in Ps.-Arist., is contained in Rhodes (1981, 573-9). For the *koprologoi*, see Owens (1983) who concludes that these were private contractors (or slaves thereof), possibly engaged on an occasional basis by the Athenian state.

Agoranomoi. Law transferring responsibilities from *astunomoi* to *agoranomoi*: *IG* II² 380 = *SIG*³ 313 = *SEG* XXI 307 = *SEG* XXVI 84. As Owens (1983, 45f.) points out, the main concern of the law may have been with the route taken by processions at festival time (below p. 144), rather than with hygiene and cleanliness as such. In addition to Ar. and Ps.-Arist., the literary evidence for *agoranomoi* includes Aes. *Septem* 272 (*agoras episkopoi*) and Kratinos in *CAF* I fr. 115 p. 50 ap. Poll. 10.177. As Busolt-Swoboda (1920, I p. 491) note, boards of *agoranomoi* are epigraphically attested in no fewer than 120 Greek states.

Pentêkostologoi. Dem. 21.133 credits these officials with the power to confiscate illegal imports. In Dem. 34.6 it is indicated that they kept records of imports and exports. The quotation is from a law of Delos dated *c.* 250-200 (*SIG*³ 975 = *Inscr. Délos* 509 = Austin 1981, no. 109). The tax which they collected is discussed below p. 88.

Metronomoi. Vanderpool (1968, 75) plausibly suggests that *IG* II² 1710 and 1711, both discovered in the Piraeus, may be lists of either *metronomoi* or *agoranomoi* serving in the port.

Sitophulakes. The Athenian currency law of 375/4 has aroused considerable scholarly interest and controversy. See Stroud (1974, 157-88): *SEG* XXVI 72, XXIX 87, XXX 59 and XXXI 63 = Austin and Vidal-Naquet (1977, no. 102) = Harding (1985, no. 45). See Giovanni (1975), Bogaert (1976), Buttrey (1979) and Mørkholm (1982, 293-5). Further bibliography is cited by Harding (loc. cit.). For discussion of the duties of the *sitophulakes*, see Rhodes (1981, 579) and Seager (1966, 173f.).

78 **Dokimastês em Peiraiei.** The new appointment is referred to in the currency law of 375/4 (see note above) lines 3-17. The task of this official was to test three different types of coins: genuine Attic silver coins (lines 3f.), good quality foreign silver coins of Athenian appearance (lines 9f.) and counterfeits (lines 10f.).

Epimelêtês tôn krênôn. For the decree honouring Pytheas, see *IG* II² 338 (cf. also *IG* II² 215).

Control of the naval port by the boule. Not only Ps.-Arist. but also Ps.-Xen. (*AP* 3.2) allude to the boule's control of naval affairs. For discussion, see Jordan (1975, 25) and Rhodes (1972, 115-22). For council sessions on the Choma, see below p. 82. The evidence for the ekklesia as the supreme decision-making body in all naval matters (as discussed by Jordan 1975, 21-4) includes: Hdt. 7.144; Ar. *Knights* 1350-4; Ps.-Arist. *AP* 46.1; D.S. 11.43; *IG* I² 91.30f. = *IG* I³ 52; and *IG* I² 98.16-22 = *ML* 78 = *IG* I³ 93.

79 **Dockyard supervisors.** Fifth-cent. evidence: *IG* I² 73.19 = *IG* I³ 153 ([*hoi epime*]*lomenoi to neôrio*), dated 440-25; *IG* I² 74.15,24 = *IG* I³ 154 with *SEG* X 41 (*neôroi*), dated 435-20; *IG* II² 1.30 = *ML* 94 (*neôroi*), dated 405. For evidence that *epimelomenoi*, *epimelêtai* and *neôroi* were not only concurrently used titles but also merely 'different titles for one and the same board', cf. Jordan (1975, 35). Fourth-cent. refs. to naval supervisors: *IG* II² 1607.1f. and 1623.1ff. See Blackman (1968, 189), Jordan (1975, 30ff.) and Rhodes (1972, 117f.).

Diagrammata. The two earliest *diagrammata* are *IG* II² 1604 and 1604a (Addendum p. 811), republished as *SEG* X 355 = Robinson (1937). They are merely dated to the second half of the fifth cent. See Blackman (1969, 207). For the fourth cent. naval lists, see *IG* II² 1605-32. Additional fragments have been published by Schweigert (1939, 17-25; 1940, 343-5). The fourth-cent. series covers the period from *c.* 377/6 to 323/2 but with a gap between *c.* 370/69 and 357/6. They include a list of all the ships in the Athenian navy, whether in the Piraeus shipsheds or on the high seas (*hupaithrioi*). Ships are listed by category, according to the harbour in which they were berthed, followed by their equipment. See also the bibliography cited in *SEG* XXVIII 138-40. The exact find-spot of the *diagrammata* has not been properly recorded but it may have been close to the site later occupied by Philon's Arsenal. One (*IG* II² 1610) was found 'near the ancient theatre of Zea', two others come 'from west of the harbour of Koumoundouros' (Robinson 1937, 292-4). In some, if not all cases an identical copy was displayed in Athens (Schweigert 1939, 21).

Signalling network relating to the Piraeus. For the role of Boudoron in relation to the Piraeus, see Eliot (1962, 131f.). The suggestion that the forts at Anagyrous and Atene were part of a signalling network was first made by Eliot (op. cit., 41f. and 133-5). See further McCredie (1966, 25-9) and Whitehead (1986, 400f.).

Strategoi. For the strategos of the Piraeus, see Reinmuth (1971, nos. 7, [*c*. 334] and 9 col. ii.9 [333/2]). For the strategos of the Piraeus mentioned alongside the strategos of Akte, see ibid. no. 15 r.h.s. (324/3). As Rhodes (1981, 679) points out, the title 'strategos of Mounychia' occurs only once, apparently as an alternative title for the strategos of the Piraeus. It is used with reference to Philokles, strategos in 324, who was accused of taking bribes from Harpalos and hence of betraying 'Akte and the harbours and the *neôria*' (Dein. 3.13). Three strategoi: *SIG*³ 719 (dated 95/4). For the old *stratêgion*, see below p. 218f.

Ephebic training in the Piraeus. The 20 surviving ephebic inscriptions dating to the fourth cent. are assembled by Reinmuth (1971, 1ff.).

The court in Phreatto. Cf. also Arist. *Pol.* 1300 b 29; Ps.-Arist. *AP* 57.3; Thphr. in Harp. s.v. For further references and discussion, see Boegehold (1976, 14-6) and Latte s.v. 'Phreattys' in *RE* 20.1 cols. 759-60. There is no recorded example of any trial taking place in this court during the historical period. See further Harrison (1971, 37), Bonner and Smith (1938, 105, 110, etc.) and MacDowell (1963, 82-4). For the site see below p. 158. Parker (1983, 119) suggests that as well as protecting the land from pollution, the regulations may also have been intended to protect the exile himself, who, had he stepped ashore, would have been liable to a revenge-killing. A *dikastêrion* in the Piraeus, which may or may not be identical with the court in Phreatto, is referred to in *IG* II² 244.36 and 1669.18, 21 and 38.

Ballot tokens from Piraeus well. These are listed in Boegehold (1976, cat. nos. 1-10 = *SEG* XXVI 161). They are wheel-shaped and all, with one exception, pierced in the centre. Boegehold (p. 8) reports that notations on their NM catalogue cards indicate that they were found at a well 'near the sea, west of Kastella on Mounychia'.

Meetings of the ekklesia in the Piraeus. For the period from 208/7 onwards, see McDonald (1943, Table II). The following prytany inscriptions listed in Meritt and Traill (1974) contain references to such meetings: 165.3 (197/6); 171.4 (190/89); 174.4 (188/7); 199.3 (175/4); 200.4 (175/4); 208.4 (172/1); 219.4 (164/3); 220.5 (164/3). Ekklesia in the Piraeus transferred to the theatre: ibid. 246.3f. The restoration of *IG* I² 98.16f. so as to include a reference to an assembly being held in the *neôrion* at the time of the despatch of the Sicilian Expedition is now generally rejected (cf. *ML* 78; *IG* I³ 93).

82   **Meetings of the boule in the Piraeus.** Cf. *IG* I² 57.53f. = *ML* 65 = *IG* I³
61, dated 426/5; Dow (1937, 94 no. 44.3) = Meritt and Traill (1974, no.
161.3), beginning of second cent.; *IG* II² 783.4, dated 163/2 by Meritt in
Hesperia 3 (1934) 28 no. 20. See McDonald (1943, 142 n. 63). Boule in the
Phosphorion: Meritt and Traill (1974, no. 240.39) and Meritt (1948, 20).
After Chaironeia Hypereides proposed that the boule should go down to the
Piraeus under arms and debate what measures should be adopted for
defence (Lykourg. 1.37).

83   ***Epimelêtês tou limenos.*** *IG* II² 1013.47f. with *Hesperia* 7 (1938) 127 no. 27.
Cf. also *IG* II² 1012 dated 112/1: decree authorising the setting up of a
picture of a certain Diodoros in the *archeion* of the *epimelêtês tou limenos.* The
only other reference to this officer belonging to the pre-Sullan period known
to me is in an inscription recording contributions to the Delian Pythaid
between 103/2 and 97/6 (*IG* II² 2336 + 2454). See Geagan (1967, 119).

         Emporion. There is no adequate translation of *emporion* other than 'the
place where *emporoi* do business'. Poleis with *emporia* include Tartessos (Hdt.
4.15.23), Pantikapaion (Dem. 20.31) and Corinth (Str. *Geog.* 7.6.20). Cf.
Ps.-Arist. *Oik.* 1346 a 17 (p.161). Polanyi's term 'port of trade', which he
used to describe an institution set up to facilitate a type of exchange
determined by embedded non-material 'equivalences' rather than simple
supply and demand, is problematic and of marginal applicability to the
Piraeus. For a critique, see Figueira (1984).

84   **Entry of goods into Attike overland.** Cf. Thuk. 7.28.1 who states that
after the Spartan occupation of Dekeleia in 413:

> The transporting of goods from Euboia, which had previously been more
> expeditious (*thassôn*) overland from Oropos through Dekeleia, now became
> expensive (*polutelês*), coming by sea around Sounion.

See further Finley (1973, 126f.). The Piraeus was not the only Attic port
handling merchandise in the late Classical and Hellenistic periods.
Rhamnous, Thorikos and Sounion also served as ports of entry, especially
for merchandise from Boeotia, Euboia and the islands close to the east Attic
coast. The port at Thorikos presumably handled food and other essentials
destined for the slave workforce at Lavrion (Mussche, *BCH* 85 [1961] 178).

85   **Segregation of the commercial zone.** Other *emporia* which were
segregated from the rest of the town include Alexandria (Str. *Geog.* 17.1.9)
and Chalkis (Dikaiarch. fr. 59.29). For discussion, see Hasebroek (1933,
160).

         The Greek sailing season. Hesiod (*Erg.* 663-5) pronounces that it was
only safe to begin sailing fifty days after the summer solstice (cf. Snider 1978
for the correct interpretation of this passage), but his was a cautious view
expressed on behalf of mariners who are first and foremost farmers. Dem.'s
observation (33.23) that maritime suits could only be initiated during the
months from Mounychion (Apr./May) to Boedromion (Sept./Oct.) is a
more accurate guide to the length of the sailing season.

86   **Methods of unloading.** For harbour-craft, see Casson (1971, 335-7) and
Rougé (1966, 158-60). *Hupêretikai skaphai*: Str. *Geog.* 5.3.5. For a
swing-beam, see Sparkes (1975, pl. XIVe): Attic black-figure *pelikê*. For

literary references., see Ar. fr. 679 and Men. *Dysk.* 536f. The earliest evidence for the use of cranes is dated *c.* 515 (cf. Coulton 1974, 16). For pulleys, see *IG* II² 1672.156 (329/8) and Shaw (1967). Attic black-figure vase in Basle depicting an amphora being transported on a pole held by two men: Hopper (1979, pl. 23).

Capacity of merchant ships. Thasian decree: *IG* XII Suppl. p. 151 no. 348 + *SEG* XVII 417. See Casson (1956, 234; 1971, 171 n. 23); Hansen (1975, 58). Cf. also Thuk. 4.118 where a ship with a load of 500 talents is described as 'small'. The commonest size for shiploads of grain to the Piraeus in the fourth cent. appears to have been around 3,000 *medimnoi* (1 *medimnos* = 40kg.). See the inscriptions cited in Casson (1971, 183f.). The largest merchantman built in antiquity was the Syrakousia, whose capacity was around 1,940 tons (Athen. *Deipn.* 5.206d-209; cf. Casson 1971,186). It may well have berthed in the Piraeus from time to time. Cf. also the description provided by Luk. *Navig.* 5-6 of the Isis, a Roman grain ship which Lukian saw in the Piraeus, estimated to have had a capacity of 1,200-1,300 tons (Casson 1950, 51-6). The majority of merchantmen which docked in the Piraeus were probably no larger than the Kyrenia, which sank off the north coast of Cyprus during the last decade of the fourth cent. (Fig. 16) carrying a mixed cargo which included 400 *amphorai* (Katzev 1969, 55-9; 1970, 6-14; Steffy 1985). For further discussion of the size of merchant ships, see Hasebroek (1933, 95f.), Knorringa (1926, 61), Casson (1956; 1971, 172), Wallinga (1964, 1-40) and Hansen (1975, 58f.).

87 **Decree permitting Methone to import grain from Byzantion.** *IG* I² 57 = *SIG*³ 75 = *ML* 65.34-40 = Fornara 128. The special concession was probably due to Methone's 'usefulness as a base, military and diplomatic, in an area that was dominated by Macedon' (*ML* p. 179).

The Greek economy. For a clear summary of the contribution made by Weber, Hasebroek and Polanyi to the present understanding of the Greek economy, see Austin and Vidal-Naquet (1977, 3-11). Thanks to their work it is now an established fact that the subject cannot be treated independently of the social and political conditions of the ancient city in the way that the study of modern economics is treated as an autonomous category. For a recent assessment of the Weber-Hasebroek analysis, with particular reference to the Archaic period, see Cartledge (1983, 4).

88 **Harbour dues in the Piraeus.** Cf. Lykourg. 1.58; And. 1.133; Dem. 21.133, 24.120, 34.7, 35.29-30 and 59.27; *Et. Mag.* s.v. *pentêkostê.* Lewis (1959, 244f.) rightly cautions against assuming that all references to the *pentêkostê* necessarily belong under the single heading of import and export tax. A 2 per cent tax was imposed by a large number of trading communities in the Greek world including Atarneus, Erythrai, Kyparissiai, Delos, Epidavros, Halikarnassos and Troezen. See Busolt-Swoboda (1920, I p. 614 n. 4). Reference to *hekatostas* in a decree dated *c.* 420-414: Walbank (1976, p. 291 II 9-10). Sale of collection of taxes: Ps.-Arist. *AP* 47.2. Grain levy collected separately: Dem. 59.27. It is not clear whether Andok.'s figure includes the 2 per cent duty levied on grain. Hansen (1975, 52) estimates that if it does not, 'a minimum of 500 talents must be added ... so that total foreign trade comes to 2,300 talents per annum'.

89   **Athenian imports.** Erxleben (1975, 393) divides Athenian imports into
three main categories: (1) corn and fish for general consumption; (2) raw
materials used in manufacture, especially in the shipbuilding industry; and
(3) a few exotic foodstuffs and luxury items for a relatively small market of
consumers. Finley (1973, 133) judges Athens to have been self-sufficient
'only in honey, olive-oil, ordinary wine, silver, building stone (including
marble), potting clay and fuel'.

    Sitônai. The earliest known appointment of *sitônai* was after the defeat at
Chaironeia in 338 (Dem. 18.248), though it is possible that Kallisthenes was
a *sitônês* as early as 357 (cf. Dem. 20.33). Other references include: *IG* II²
479.11, 584.4, 670.11, 744.8, 792.5, 906.5 and 1272.9f. (305/4 to *c.* 175/4).
See also Thalheim s.v. *Sitônai* in *RE* III.A (1929) cols. 396-7 and Finley
(1973, 170).

    Athenian anxiety regarding her corn supply. See Bravo (1983), Gernet
(1909), Hasebroek (1933, 146-50), Hansen (1975, 19-29), Jameson (1983),
Jardé (1925) and Noonan (1973, 231-42). Garnsey (1985, 73) believes that
in a normal year Attike was able to support 'perhaps 120,000-150,000 of its
residents', i.e. about half its total population, whereas in a bad year (rather
more than one in twenty) her import of foreign grain must have been
'enormous'. Foxhall and Forbes (1982) suggest that grain contributed about
70-75 per cent of the calories in the 'average classical diet' and probably
more in the case of those of very low income. For Athens' corn supply as an
essential topic of debate on the ekklesia agenda, see Ps.-Arist. *AP* 43.4. Cf.
also Xen. *Mem.* 3.6.3 (a subject of debate which budding politicians must
master); and Dem. 18.301 (it is the duty of every politician to ensure that
grain-shipments reach the Piraeus). Athenian legislation concerning corn:
Dem. 34.37, 35.51, 56.6.11; Ps.-Arist. *AP* 51.4; Lykourg. 1.27. Gauthier
(1981) has proposed that Ps.-Arist. *AP* 51.4 should be interpreted to mean
that all grain entering the Piraeus had to be sold in Athenian markets,
two-thirds being conveyed to the Asty and one-third remaining in the
Piraeus. Naval escort for grain ships: D.S. 15.34.3 (dated 376); *IG* II²
1628.37-42 (326/5) and 1629.165-271. Athens was by no means alone in
being heavily dependent on imports of foreign corn. Salmon (1984, 131)
calculates that about half of the total cereal consumption in the Corinthia
had to be imported. Corinth herself was perhaps the second largest importer
of foreign corn. As MacDonald (1982, 119) notes, attempts by Athens and
Sparta to interfere with the grain trade during the Peloponnesian War do
not appear to have met with any success. Cf. Thuk. 3.86.4; 2.69.1; 8.35.2-3;
Xen. *Hell.* 2.1.17.

    Sitopôlai. Cf. esp. Lys. 22.14: 'They make their largest profits when they
sell their corn at a high price upon news of a disaster reaching Athens. They
are so delighted to witness your afflictions that they either get news of them
in advance of anyone else or make up stories themselves.' One of the
accusations levelled against them is of buying up more than the fixed upper
limit of fifty measures (*phormoi*) of corn from the Emporion (22.6). For the
difficulties in this passage, see Seager (1966). For the unpopularity
attaching to *sitopôlai* as a group, see Parker (1983, 262).

    Provision of corn for Athens by the Spartokids. Dem.'s claim (20.30)
that Leukon and his sons were made Athenian citizens is confirmed by a

decree dated 347/6 bestowing on Spartokos II and Pairisades I the same privileges as had been granted to their predecessors Satyros I and Leukon (*IG* II² 212.20ff. = Athens NM 1471). The decree was found near the Grand Harbour and probably stood in the Emporion. Here in 285/4 was erected a statue of Spartokos III who had sent a gift of 15,000 *medimnoi* of corn to the Athenian people (*IG* II² 653.8ff. = *SIG³* 370).

Stockpiling of grain. The suggestion that Byzantion may have served as a storage centre under Athenian control for reserve stocks of grain is made by Meiggs-Lewis in their commentary on the Methone Decree (*ML* 65 = *IG* I³ 61). See also MacDonald (1982, 119 n. 56).

90   **Athenian grain-crises in the fourth century.** Years of hardship (as listed by Hansen 1975, 201 n. 8) include: 386 (Lys. 22), 362 (Dem. 50.6), 357 (Dem. 20.33) and 355 (Dem. 34.38). The inscription from Cyrene regarding the supply of grain to 41 Greek states during the prolonged crisis in the 320s reveals that Athens' apportionment was twice as high as that of any other community and represented 13 per cent of the overall total (*GHI* II 196). For the price of corn in the fourth cent., see Heichelheim s.v. Sitos in *RE* Supp. VI (1935) cols. 887-8 and Pritchett (1956, 197).

Decrees honouring metics for gifts of grain, etc. As listed by Hansen (1975, 207 n. 55) these include: *IG* II² 342, 360, 398, 400, 401, 407, 408, 409, 416, *SEG* XXI 298 and *Hesperia* 9 (1940) 332f. The majority of these shiploads were between 3,000 and 4,000 *medimnoi* in capacity .

Elaiônai. See Robert (1969, 24-30) with ref. to *IG* II² 3680.11f. (Athens, third cent.). Gauthier (1982, 287) tentatively restores '*elaiônai*' in *IG* II² 903.13f. (discussed below).

Import of timber. Cf. Ps.-Xen. *AP* 2.12; Ar. *Frogs* 362-5 and *Lys.* 421; And. 2.11; Dem. 19.265; Ps.-Dem. 49.26 and 36; *SIG³* 248 N7 135. A variety of evidence indicates that fir was the preferred choice of ship timber (e.g. *GHI* II no. 111.10-15; Thphr. *HP* 5.1.7), though pine occasionally served (cf. Ar. *Knights* 1307-10). See further Meiggs (1982, 118f.). The export of timber from Macedon appears to have been personally supervised by the king, certainly during the period 440-380, and probably both earlier and later as well (cf. Wallace 1970, 200 n. 13). The earliest explicit testimony for the existence of an undertaking on the part of Macedon to sell timber to Athens is dated 417-413? (*IG* I³ 89.31). For Athens' difficulty in obtaining timber when she broke off relations with Macedon, cf. Ps.-Dem. 17.28. with Meiggs (1982, 132).

Import of ruddle. Cf. *IG* II² 1128 = *GHI* II 162 = Austin and Vidal-Naquet 1977, no. 86 (fourth cent. treaty with Keos). For the painting of triremes, see Torr (1964, 35f.).

Import of slaves. The absence of evidence regarding the slave trade in both Greek and Latin sources proves nothing about the scale of the enterprise, as Finley (1981, 168) points out. It was simply not a subject which drew much comment. Athens' needs for imported slaves in the fifth and fourth centuries included 300-1,200 state-owned Scythian slaves (Plassart 1913; Vos 1963, 68) and perhaps as many as 30,000 privately-owned non-Greek slaves working in the silver mines at Lavrion, of whom 'most came from Asia Minor and other eastern countries, with a high proportion from countries having their own mines, such as Thrace and

Paphlagonia' (Lauffer, quoted in Finley, p. 169). See also the fragmentary auction accounts of the Hermokopidai (*IG* I³ 421-2), which list 32 slaves whose nationality can be identified including 13 Thracians and 7 Carians. In all, 70 per cent were non-Greek and only 7.5 per cent homebred. See Pritchett (1956, 276ff.) supplemented by *Hesperia* 30 (1961) 23-9.

Decree honouring a merchant. *IG* II² 903 = *SIG*³ 640 = *SEG* XXXII 132. I adopt the restoration and interpretation proposed by Gauthier (1982, 278-90). For '*en tais polesi*' (l. 9) to be taken as 'in the Asty and the Piraeus', see above p. 53. For parepidemic status, see above p. 62.

91   **Export of silver.** For the (potential) importance of the export of Attic silver coins and bullion, see Xen. *Por.* 3.2. Dem. 8.45 alleges that Philip of Macedon was covetous of 'the Athenian harbours and dockyards and triremes and silver-mines'. See Montgomery (1984, 128-31). It should be noted that the so-called Athenian Coinage Decree, which imposed the use of Athenian coins, weights and measures on all the subject states within the Athenian empire (*ML* 45 = Fornara no. 97 = Austin and Vidal-Naquet 1977, no. 101) did not necessarily boost the export of Attic silver because: (1) Athens never exercised a monopoly over the sale of silver within her empire; and (2) the allies were free to have their own coinage re-struck.

Export of agricultural products. Honey: *P. Cair. Zen.* 59012, 59426; *P. Mich. Zen.* 3 (all third cent.). Olive oil: *IG* II² 1100, dated *c.* A.D. 125 (revised by J. H. Oliver *TAPhS* 43 (1953) pt. 4, pp. 960-3). Finley (1973, 133) rightly attaches little importance to these exports.

Export of Athenian pottery. The significance of the export of Attic pottery for the Athenian economy is sometimes dismissed out of hand, since the industry accounted for only a small fraction of the labour force. This view is unnecessarily cautious, as Johnston (1979, 51) observes. See ibid., pp. 49-52 for the stages by which vases destined for export left the Kerameikos and reached their ultimate destination. Vases probably formed only a relatively insignificant part of any cargo.

95   **Decline of the commercial importance of the Piraeus.** For economic interchange in the Hellenistic world, see Davies (*CAH*² VII.1 pp. 270-85). Davies (p. 285) makes the important point that by the 420s Athens was already 'importing goods to an extent and from a radius very little different from anything the Hellenistic world can show'. The Piraeus' contracting role after 323 was affected by (1) a shift in the pattern of trading throughout the eastern Mediterranean generally, and (2) a decline in the quantity of imported goods, principally raw materials for shipbuilding and luxury items. Rostovtzeff's theory (1941, I pp. 74-125) that the Greek world began to experience an economic decline as early as the end of the fifth cent. onwards has recently been challenged, notably by Hansen and Isager (1975, 53f.) who point out that it is based exclusively on the evidence of vase finds and that these indicate very little about the extent of Athenian foreign commerce; and by de Ste. Croix (1981, 294), who writes:

> I certainly know of no single passage in any Greek literary source which gives the slightest hint that any of the Greeks realised that the market for Greek goods was contracting against them, or which betrays any awareness of a need to increase exports.

Rhodian commerce in the fourth century. See the evidence collected by Berthold (1980, 49 n. 65) which indicates that already by 323 Rhodes had established itself as an important emporion. Lykourgos' description of the Rhodians in 330 as 'men who sail the entire world for trade' is ominous for the Piraeus (*Or.* 15). Geographically the island was well-situated both as an importer (from the Crimea and Egypt) and as an exporter (to the islands of the Cyclades and the cities of Asia Minor). For further discussion of Rhodes as a centre for the international grain trade, see Casson (1984, 70-95).

Number of shipsheds. Cf. *IG* II² 1627.398-405 (330/29), 1628.552-9 (326/5) and 1629.1030-6 (325/4). The three naval ports are designated Mounychia, Zea and Limen Kantharou.

96 **Mustering of the allied fleet at the Piraeus.** The Andokides passage, which is the only evidence for this arrangement, probably refers to 454 but may possibly refer to 477 (see Blackman 1969, 194). If there was a different mustering place in the League's earlier history, then it was surely at Delos. Allied contingents of naval expeditions to the eastern Mediterranean probably mustered in Ionia (Blackman, loc. cit.).

Shipsheds. For naval installations dating to the time of Themistokles, cf. Pl. *Gorg.* 455e with 517c and 519a; Poll. 10.10 with reference to Aes. *Psychagôgoi* fr. 274 *TGF*. The figure of 1,000 talents as the cost of the Periklean shipsheds should be treated with caution since it suits Isokrates' rhetorical purpose to exaggerate. It is, however, unlikely to be wildly inaccurate, since the building accounts of the *neôsoikoi* would have been open to public scrutiny. There is possibly a reference to fifth-cent. *neôsoikoi* in *IG* I² 90.30f. Probable influence of Euboulos in the building of shipsheds: cf. Dein. 1.96; Aischin. 3.25. Possibly from as early as 357/6 onwards, and certainly from 347/6 until 323/2, the cost was met from a special tax (*eisphora*) levied on citizens compulsorily and metics voluntarily, cf. *IG* II² 505.12 (inscription dated 302/1 honouring metics for contributions received between 347/6 and 323/2). Ps.-Plu. *Mor.* 851d states that the fourth-cent. *neôsoikoi* were completed under Lykourgos.

97 **Size of crew serving on a trireme.** For 200 as the total number serving on a trireme, see Morrison (1984, 55). Of these 200, 170 were oarsmen, as is indicated by naval lists in which the number of oars is regularly given as 170 (distributed from top to bottom among the three banks in the ratio 62: 54: 54), supplemented by 30 spares. The remaining 30 crew members were probably the *huperesia*, a body of specialists 'over and above the oar-crew' (loc. cit.).

Composition of Athenian crews. It is evident from Ps.-Xen. *AP* 1.2 that Athenian citizens constituted a large proportion of the *nautikos ochlos*. Thuk. 1.143.1-2 indicates that mercenaries were also an important element in the Athenian navy. For metics, cf. Nikias' speech before the last sea battle in the Great Harbour at Syracuse where it is suggested that they constituted the majority (7.63.3-4). Slaves were only used in emergencies. As Meiggs (1972, 441) notes, though there was often ample warning before expeditions set sail, occasionally a fleet would be dispatched immediately following the decree, in which case it might be advantageous for sailors to be resident in the Piraeus. For further discussion see Amit (1965, 30-49) and Meiggs (1972, 439-41).

Training and pay. See the evidence collected by Jordan (1975, 103-6 and 111-16).

Size of Athens' navy in the fifth and fourth centuries. For further details see Amit (1965, 18-27), to whose account this summary is much indebted.

Athenian fleet built in Macedonia. The evidence for the theory that the new fleet was not built in the Piraeus is based on a fragmentary decree (*IG* I² 105 = *ML* 91) honouring Archelaos of Macedon, apparently for allowing Athenian shipwrights to proceed to the source of supply. As Meiggs (1982, 128) suggests, this departure from normal practice was presumably due to the fact that Athens no longer had the capability to protect convoys carrying timber from enemy action. An equally spectacular shipbuilding feat was achieved by the Romans in the First Punic War when a fleet of 220 ships was built in the space of 45 days (Pl. *HN* 16.192).

98   *Tetrêreis* and *pentêreis.* For discussion of their design, see Meiggs (1982, 137). They do not appear to have been used in naval battles fought before the age of Alexander. *Tetrêreis* perhaps had two banks with two men per oar, *pentêreis* two banks with three men per oar.

Shipbuilding specialists. See Poll. 1.84 and 7.160-1.

The dockyard in the Piraeus. References to the Athenian *naupêgion* include *IG* I² 122 = *SEG* X 131; *IG* II² 1611.133; Ar. *Birds* 1157. Shipyards leave little trace in the archaeological record, as Blackman (1969, 203 n. 72) notes, since their only features are wooden slipways and stocks. The phases of shipbuilding are described in Ar. *Thesm.* 52ff., where the tragic poet Agathon uses shipyard analogies to describe his peculiarly laboured method of poetic composition. For a modern account, see Torr (1964, 31-8).

Lifespan of triremes. For estimates of the average lifespan of an Athenian trireme, see Kolbe (1901, 386-407), Miltner s.v. 'Seewesen' in *RE* Supp. 5 (1931) col. 923, Labarbe (1957, 127 and n. 4), Amit (1965, 27) and Blackman (1969, 214f.). The longest-lived trireme known was in service for 26 years (Kolbe, 388f.). Casson (1971, 90) observes that Athenian triremes must have been built with extreme care to last 20 years, since Venetian ships 'normally ... lasted 13 years, and poorly built ones less than half that.' For the operational limitations on triremes in an extended campaign, see Gomme (1937, 194) who writes: 'A Greek fleet of triremes had every day, so to speak, to have a base of some kind within easy reach.' During the Sicilian Expedition the deteriorating condition of waterlogged triremes became a cause of acute concern (Thuk. 7.12.3).

99   **Special shipbuilding programmes in *c.* 451 and 431/0.** See the detailed discussion of the relevant literary and epigraphical evidence in Blackman (1969, 203-12).

Dearth of naval equipment in the fourth century. As Cawkwell notes (1984, 334), the most valuable document for assessing the efficiency of Athens' naval establishment in this period is Ps.-Dem. 50. See also the discussion of the naval inventories in Meiggs (1982, 131). The full equipment of a trireme comprised 200 oars, two steering oars, a main mast with yard and two supporting stays, three ladders and three poles.

Symmories. Isok. 15.145; Dem. 14.16. For discussion, see Poland s.v. '*Symmoria*' and '*Symmoriarchês*' in *RE* IV.A (1932) cols. 1161-8; and Rhodes

(1981, 679-82). With the exception of the syntrierarchy (i.e. joint trierarchy), which was probably introduced during the final years of the Peloponnesian War (Lys. 32.24), no other certain reforms took place in the naval system between 415 and 357.

Demosthenes' reform of the trierarchy. Cf. Dem. 18.102-9; Aischin. 3.222; Dein. 1.42 and Hyp. fr. 134 (Sauppe).

00   **Efficiency of Athens' naval administration in the fourth century.** Cawkwell (1984, 342) takes the view that throughout the fourth cent. Athens' naval system was 'perfectly adequate for the calls made on it' and argues, 'If the naval system was gravely in need of reform, it is remarkable how limited in scope were the two reforms of which we are informed'. However, it was improved by measures additional to the reform of the trierarchic system, notably by the building of Philon's Arsenal.

3. RELIGION

01   **Siting of sanctuaries.** Mounychia Hill, the only acropolis in the region, was hardly comparable to the one in Athens in terms of religious aura, despite the fact that several cults clustered around its slopes (e.g. Artemis Mounychia, Asklepios, Bendis, Phosphoros, the Moirai and the Nymphs). We crucially lack information about the cults that were located in the Hippodamian Agora, which, like any agora, would have been a centre for religious devotion (below p. 141).

03   **Non-Piraeic cults with a festival venue in the Piraeus.** Panathenaic boat-race: *SIG*³ 1055 (dated *c.* 400-350). The Schol. on Pl. *Rep.* 1.327a alleges that the Lesser Panathenaia took place in the Piraeus, but as Solders (1931, 10) suggests, the author has probably confused the Lesser Panathenaia with the Plynteria.

Monthly festivals. The eighth day of the month, being sacred to Poseidon and probably also his son Theseus (cf. Mikalson 1975, 19f.), would fittingly have been observed as an important holy day in the Piraeus.

04   **Multiplicity of deities affording protection to the sea-faring community.** The festival calendar of Thorikos also reveals a plurality of cults connected with seafaring deities (see Daux 1983). These include Poseidon at Sounion (l. 19), Poseidon 'at the salt [works]' (l. 23), the Anakes (l. 37), Artemis Mounychia (l. 40) and Sosineos (l. 50). Seafaring engendered an extremely acute fear of the unknown in ancient Greece, requiring stringent rituals of aversion. See Wachsmuth (1967, passim).

Seafaring rituals. *Embatêria*: Phil. *VA* 5.43; Hld. 5.15 and 4.16. *Apobatêria*: St. Byz. s.v. *Bouthrôtos*; Poll. 2.200. 'Apobaterios' is known as a cult title of both Zeus (cf. Ar. *Ann.* 1.11.7) and Artemis (cf. *IGRom* 4.1539, Erythrai). See Burkert (1985, 266f.).

05   **Introduction of foreign cults.** Associations of traders are prevalent both at Delos and Rhodes, as well as at Athens. They are not, however, found at lesser *emporia* such as Demetrias, Ephesos or Miletos, probably, as Davies (*CAH*² VII.1 p. 283) suggests, because they are 'diagnostic of major long-term routes of exchange'. In her study of the introduction of foreign cults into Attike in the fifth and fourth cents., Rhonda Simms (1985) rightly emphasises the prominent part played by economic and diplomatic considerations. See further s.v. Bendis (below p. 118).

Laws of cult associations. Nock (1972, 415) describes the law of the Egyptian guild of Zeus Hypsistos as 'in the nature of a contract by which members bound themselves', and cites an occasion when the Pharaoh intervened to compel the *thiasos* to honour its obligations to a deceased member. Though there is no evidence that the Athenian state ever intervened in this way, obviously it was in its best interests that religious law should be upheld.

107   **Funerary aspect of Piraeic *thiasoi*.** The unknown *thiasos* at Phaleron enjoined upon its members compulsory attendance at the funeral (*ekphora*) of any of their number (Appendix III no. 143); and the *thiasôtai* of the Mother of the Gods contributed towards a burial fund for deceased members (Appendix III no. 90). Poland (1909), however, was undoubtedly right to emphasise that this funerary aspect was not as prominent in Greek clubs as in Roman *collegia funeratica*, where the overriding purpose seems to have been to provide members with a decent burial.

Membership of religious associations. Unknown association with 93 members: *IG* II² 2358, dated *c.* 150. For the size of Greek associations see Poland (1909, 282ff.), who puts the average membership at 'approximately two to three dozen'. Evidence for membership of 100 plus is confined to the late Hellenistic and Roman periods. The prominence of women in Attic associations is not matched elsewhere in the Greek world, as Tod (1932, 84) observes. For the statutes of the Iobacchoi (*IG* II² 1368), indisputably the most informative document regarding the organisation, rules and procedural practices of Greek associations, see Tod (1929, 1-4; 1932, 86-93).

108   **Leases of sacred properties.** See Walbank (1983, IV Table 1) for the *editio princeps* of five *stêlai* which list no fewer than 86 sacred properties leased out by the Athenian state. For references to *temenê* 'on the right hand as you go to Mounychia', see ibid. II, p. 179: *stêlê* 2B, IIa lines 6f. and 23f. There is a good possibility that three other leases on the same *stêlê* also refer to sacred properties in the area (ibid. II, p. 185); so, too, may a lease on another *stêlê* (ibid. I, p. 108: *stêlê* 1, III c line 1), which was purchased by a metic who was resident in the Piraeus.

Athenian *philoxenia* towards foreign cults. It was Strabo (*Geog.* 10.3.18) who observed that the Athenians were ridiculed in Comedy because of their hospitality (*philoxenia*) towards foreign cults. The evidence for this view may be based on a lost play by Aristophanes in which 'Sabazios and certain other foreign gods' were put on trial and exiled from the state (Cic. *de Leg.* 2.37). Rather than providing evidence of *philoxenia*, however, this seems to suggest that the Athenians regarded foreign gods not only as a fit target for derision (an attitude hardly distinct from that which they commonly adopted in Comedy towards Olympian deities, notably Dionysos), but also, more revealingly, as tiresome and unwelcome. Other Comedies which treated of foreign deities include Eupolis' *Dippers* (*Baptai*), in which the rites of the Thracian goddess Kotyto were satirised (Schol. on Juv. *Sat.* 2.91); Apollophanes' *Cretans*, in which foreign gods were attacked (*CAF* I, p. 799 fr. 7 ap. Hsch. s.v. *theoi xenikoi*); and Plato Comicus' *Adonis* (*CAF* I, p. 600f. frr. 1-8).

09 **Bilingual inscriptions in Phoenician and Greek.** The decree of the *koinon* of the Sidonians records the decision of the *gav* (i.e. *koinon*) taken at the *ma'assefat* (*agora*) to reward the *nassi* (*epimelêtês*) Shama'baal with a gold crown because of his *mesharet* (*eusebeia*) 'so that the Sidonians may be seen to be rewarding those who have rendered *mesharet* on their behalf'. Other bilingual Greek-Phoenician inscriptions from the Piraeus include Cooke (1903) nos. 32, 34 and 35. Another has been found at Athens (Gibson 1982, no. 40) and three more at Rhodes (Fraser 1970, 31). For Phoenician ethnicity, see Millar (1983, 60f.).

Deme cults. Sacrificial calendars of Thorikos and Ercheia: Daux (1983; 1963). Other Attic demes for which sacral calendars are preserved at least in part are Eleusis, Marathon, Agrileza and Teithras. See *SEG* XXVI 136-8, XXVII 6, XXVIII 111 and XXXI 124. See the extensive discussion in Whitehead (1986, 185-208). The decree honouring Kallidamas of Cholleidai (Appendix II no. 6) indicates that for religious (and possibly secular) purposes the demesmen of the Piraeus were divided up into groups of thirty known as *triakades*. Cf. Poll. 8.111 with Schoeffer, s.v. '*Dêmoi*' in *RE* V (1905) col. 24. Kallidamas is privileged in being permitted 'to assign himself to whichever *triakas* he wishes' (ll.18f.).

10 **Introduction of new cults after 228.** See Stewart (1977, 517f.), who notes that no new civic temples are attested for the period *c*. 325-229. Immediately subsequent to the departure of the Macedonian garrison, shrines of Diogenes (*SIG³* 497, after 228), Demos and the Charites (*SIG³* 536, in 209/8) and Asklepios at Sounion (*IG* II² 1302, in 222/1) were established.

11 **Religious revival or revivalism.** As further evidence of this trend, Stewart (1977, 527) instances the renewal in 138/7 of the dispatch to Delphi from Athens of the sacred delegation known as the Pythais (*SIG³* 696-99) and of a similar Pythais to Delos established on a nine-year cycle commencing in 96/5 (*SIG³* 728); a new interest in the Eleusinian Mysteries and its officials from *c*. 100 onwards; and a large number of decrees honouring ephebes and *ergastinai*, the girls who wove the peplos for Athene (*IG* II² 1034, 1036 + 1060, 1942, 1943). Cf. also *IG* II² 1035, which refers to the restoration of holy places in Attike, now dated by von Freeden (1983, 174) to 'the period between 74/3-65/4'.

12 **Aphrodite on Eetioneia.** Cf. Schol. on Hermogenes, *Rhet. Gr.* VI p. 393 (ed. Walz).

Aphrodite Ourania. The fact that the boule is not mentioned in the actual decree probably indicates that it did not issue a *probouleuma* recommending that the request be granted, but merely referred the matter to the demos (cf. Tod, *GHI* II, p. 251; Rhodes 1972, 67f.). See Foucart (1873, 61-3), Deubner (1932, 220-2), Atallah (1966) and Burkert (1985, 176f.). References in Comedy: Ar. *Lys.* 387-98, Diphilos fr. 43.38ff. in *CAF* II, p. 554) and Men. *Sam.* 39-46. Cf. also Theokr. *Id.* 15 (*Adoniazousai*). The Schol. on Ar. *Lys.* 389 writes: 'Women celebrate the orgiastic rites in honour of the deities (i.e. Sabazios and Adonis) which are neither public nor prescribed'. At Kition itself (modern Larnaka) the importance of the worship of Aphrodite is indicated by the fact that her sanctuary was situated on the Acropolis adjacent to that of Herakles-Melkart, the chief tutelary god of the city. From the discovery of Greek and

Phoenician dedications in the sanctuary it seems that she was identified
with the Phoenician goddess Astarte (Nicolaou 1976, 105f.).

113   **Artemis Mounychia.** Testimonia for the worship of Artemis Mounychia
are collected by Solders (1931, 22-4). See Frazer (1898, II p. 32), Mommsen
(1898, 452ff.), Nilsson (1967, I p. 485), Deubner (1932, 204-7), Parke (1977,
137-9) and Osborne (1985, 154-72). For the *aition*, cf. also Eust. on Hom. *Il.*
2.732, p. 331.26; Hsch. s.v. *Embaros eimi*; Becker, *Anecdota* I p. 444; *Paroem.
gr.* I, p. 402. The structures of the Brauronian and Mounychian versions of
the myth are discussed in Henrichs (1981). I do not agree with Osborne
(1985, 163) that the difference in the aetiologies associated with the two
sanctuaries 'implies that the two stories were independent to a late stage'.
As Osborne himself points out, the details of the Piraeus myth are in
themselves not entirely consistent: in some versions the bear is killed by
Athenians and in others by 'certain young men'; again in some versions
plague ensues, in others famine. *Krateriskoi* have also been found at Halai
Araphenides (modern Loutsa), the shrine of Artemis Aristoboule close to
the Agora, the cave of Pan and the Nymphs at Eleusis, and in the Agora
itself close to the Stoa of Zeus (Kahil 1965). On the vase from Mounychia
(pl. 9.12, 13 and 14 in Kahil) there are no actual figures, but a palm tree and
altar indicate that a sanctuary of Artemis is intended. For the origins of the
Arkteia, see Schol. on Ar. *Lys.* 645; Sud. s.v. *Arktos ê Braurôniois*. For the
question as to whether the ritual was performed both at Brauron and
Mounychia, see Deubner (1932, 206) who is against the hypothesis, and
Mommsen (1898, 454) and Nilsson (1967, 485 with n. 6) who both support
it. More recent discussions are less dogmatic (cf. Kahil 1965, 26; Osborne
1985, 162). The deme calendar of Thorikos refers to the sacrifice to Artemis
Mounychia in the month Mounychion (Daux 1983, line 40). Other
sacrifices to the goddess may well have taken place at other Attic demes,
particularly those on the coast.

114   **Artemis Nana.** Cf. Jos. *AJ* 12.354 and Macr. *Sat.* 2.1.1. For discussion,
see Clerc (1893, 142) and Stewart (1977, 524).

115   **Asklepios.** Arrival in Zea and the Asty: *IG* II^2 4960.2 and 12f. For the
establishment of new cults as a response to plague, see Parker (1983, 275f.).
Burford's suggestion (1969, 20 n. 7) that Asklepios may have arrived in the
Piraeus as early as 430 (i.e. ten years before his arrival in Athens) does not
allow for the difficulties in establishing a new and alien deity on Attic soil,
which must surely have taken place under guidance and instruction from
the Epidaurian priesthood. Walton's claim (1935, 186f.) to identify
'non-Epidaurian influence' in the Piraeus cult on the basis of the deities
mentioned in Appendix III no. 26 is not compelling. For the siting of
Asklepieia generally, see Plu. *Mor.* 286d. For the healing ritual see Burkert
(1985, 267-8). As noted above, certain sacrifices performed at the shrine
were paid for out of the income from a quarry, presumably on Mounychia
Hill. Stewart (1979) bases his dating of the colossal statue partly on the fact
that it was made in at least six separate pieces and that the torso manifests
extreme déhanchement. Among the votive offerings to Asklepios found are
two terracotta representations of female breasts (cf. van Straten in Versnel
[1981, 120 no. 10.3]: Piraeus Museum nos. 107-8). Others include Athens
NM 1429 and 3304. The dogs and their handlers have been much discussed.

Some scholars believe that they were *daimones* or spirits, others that they were sacred dogs placed under the protection of the sanctuary. See Judeich (1931, 441-2 n. 4), Wilamowitz-Moellendorff (1932, II p. 226-7), Sokolowski (*LSG* no. 21 n. 2) and Walton (1935, 182-7). Dogs credited with healing powers appear to have been kept at the Asklepieion in Epidavros. Cf. *SIG*³ 1169.36-8 where it is alleged that an Aeginetan boy suffering from a tumour in the neck was cured when one of the temple dogs licked him. For the *sunnaoi* of Asklepios, cf. also *IG* II² 4388 (Athens) and *IAGIL* 10 (Ampurias). Their identity varied from place to place (cf. Oikonomides [*AncW* 1978] 115-18). At Pergamon they included Hygieia, Telesphoros (son), Koronis (wife), Apollo Kalliteknos and Artemis. As Ohlemutz (1940, 158-65) points out, the existence here of so large a circle of deities implies a sizeable body of religious personnel. The same was surely true of the Zea sanctuary.

18   **Bendis.** For the identity of Bendis, see Nilsson (1967, 833f.); Fol and Marazov (1977, 22-4). The earliest reference to Bendis in Athenian literature is in Kratinos (*CAF* I, fr. 80 p. 37 ap. Hsch. s.v. *dilonkon*), dated by Edmonds (*FAC*, I p. 45) to 442. For the cult, see Deubner (1932, 219f.), Ferguson (1944, 96-107; 1949, 131-63), Hartwig (1897), Roussel (1943, 177ff.), Nilsson (1951, 45-8), Parke (1977, 149-52) and Wilhelm (1902, 132-4). The absence of demotics (and in some cases patronymics) in Appendix III nos. 42-4 and 46 suggests that these were resolutions of the Thracian *orgeônes*, whereas nos. 39-40 were passed by the citizen *orgeônes*. As Ferguson (1944, 98) suggests, it was certainly on Deloptes' account that the cult had a priest as well as priestess. Ferguson (p. 134) believed that 'the dominating motive' which led the majority of Athenians to accept the introduction of the new cult in 430 was 'their disposition to do anything and everything that might stop the plague', whose outbreak, he postulates, might have been interpreted as punishment for the goddess' previous neglect at their hands. However, there are no firm grounds for assuming that Bendis was a healing goddess. For close relations between Athens and Thrace towards the end of the fifth cent., cf. Thuk. 7.27; *IG* I² 208 = *ML* 89; and *IG* I² 301.114-20. For Thrace's importance to Athens after Aigospotamoi, see Middleton (1982, 302). Bendis was also worshipped in Attike by Salaminian *thiasôtai*, whose membership may have been confined to slaves, cf. *IG* II² 1317 and *SEG* II 10. There was possibly also a cult at Lavrion where Thracians supervised mining activities. Cf. Hartwig (1897, 17) and Simms (1985, fig. 6) with Xen. *Por.* 4.14. My translation of Appendix III no. 43.29ff. owes much to helpful criticism I received from Albert Henrichs in reply to a paper which I gave at Harvard in April 1986.

22   **Demeter.** It is conceivable that the Thesmophorion referred to in Appendix III no. 48 was the same as the Eleusinion at Phaleron known from an inscription found at Eleusis (*SEG* X 24.27, dated after 450). The law specifically prohibited unauthorised persons from manumitting slaves, holding religious gatherings, setting up dedications (*hiera*), carrying out purifications (*katharmoi*), entering the megaron unaccompanied by the priestess, or taking wood from the sanctuary. Votive offerings from the Thesmophorion include Athens NM nos. 176 and 1403 (both dated *c.* 420), and 1461 (dated to second half of fourth cent.).

124   **Dionysiastai.** See Poland (1909, 197) and Ziebarth (1896, 37, 39 and 45-8; *RE* 5 [1905] col. 882). For the *technitai* of Dionysos, see Pickard-Cambridge (1968, ch. 7).

   Dionysos. See Deubner (1932, 137), Mikalson (1975, 97), Parke (1977, 103), Pickard-Cambridge (1968, 46f.) and Rhodes (1981, 611). For cults of Dionysos in other demes, see Whitehead (1986, 221). For the votive relief of Dionysos and Paideia, see Bieber (1961, 32 with figs. 113a-b). Colossal bronze mask: see above p. 56. To the first cent. A.D. dates a large head of Dionysos which was found in the Piraeus (NM 3478).

126   **Hermes.** The dedication states that the herm was made by Euphron of Paros. See Harrison (1965, 121). Hermes Hegemonios is referred to in Ar. *Plout.* 1159. Related cult titles include 'Hodios' and 'Agetor'. See Nilsson (1967, 507f.).

   Isis. The earliest evidence for Isis in the Asty does not predate the mid-first cent. B.C. For the Ploiaphesia, see the lengthy description of the *navigium Isidis* in Apul. *Metam.* 11.16. For Attic grave-reliefs commemorating women in Isis dress, see Conze (nos. 1954-72), Brady (1938, 294-304) and Walters (1985).

128   **Men.** Some 14 inscriptions, sculptural reliefs etc., relating to the Attic cult of Men are known (Lane 1964, 6-10).

129   **Mêtêr theôn.** See Burkert (1985, 177-9) and Garland (1984, 95f., where I erroneously equate the goddess with Kybele, to which she is closely allied). The cult spread to mainland Greece through northern Ionia, in particular Kyzikos (Hdt. 4.76). Cosi (1980-1) dates the goddess's entry into Athens to the time of the Peloponnesian War, when feelings ran high and state religion was under attack. He is of the opinion that the Mother of the Gods never achieved full state recognition at Athens, as is demonstrated by the fact that her temple could be put to use as a repository for state archives. Attis first receives mention in Athens in a fragment of the comic poet Theopompos (*CAF* I, fr. 27 p. 740), probably dated to the end of the fifth cent. Stewart (1977, 518) plausibly suggests that the second of the two goddesses referred to in Appendix III no. 92 may have been Syrian Aphrodite. The reference to 'both the Attideia' in no. 89 is obscure: it would appear that either there were two separate festivals or else, as Deubner (1932, 222) suggested, that the one festival lasted two days. For the *agermos*, which is a characteristic of unofficial sects, see Burkert (1985, 101f.). For gravestones of 'priestesses' of the Mother of the Gods, see nos. 81-2. See also *BCH* (1972, 611 with fig. 68): seated statue found at Moschato, dated *c.* 400.

131   **Paralos.** For the Paraloi, see Schol. Ar. *Frogs* 1071; Ar. *Lys.* 58; Lenschau s.v. 'Paraloi' in *RE* XVIII.3 (1949) col. 1208. As Jordan (1975, 173) remarks, Thuk.'s account (8.73-4; 86.8-9) of their conduct in 411 after the democratic coup on Samos, during which they exhibited strong democratic leanings, proves that they 'were held together in an organisation with ties stronger than those which spring from common political sympathies or from loyalty to shipmates.' On the analogy of the Salaminioi, Jordan goes so far as to suggest that they were a genos. This is disproved by the fact that the *tamias* was an elected official of the Athenian state. For the inscriptions, see Dain (1931, 292-302).

132   **Sabazios.** References to Sabazios in Ar.: *Wasps* 9; *Birds* 873 with Schol.;

Lys. 388; *CAF* I, fr. 566 p. 535f. The play referred to by Cicero was probably the *Hôrai*, a fragment of which contains a reference to Sabazios. Though Demosthenes does not specify by name the rites practised by Aischines' mother, Strabo (*Geog.* 10.3.18) asserts categorically that they were those in honour of Sabazios and the Mother of the Gods. See MacDowell (1971, 128f.), Dodds (1940, 171-5) and Foucart (1873, 71-83).

33 **Sarapis.** See Dow (1937, 192ff.), Fraser (1960; 1972, 246ff.), Clerc (1893, 140), Tarn and Griffith (1952, 356). Stewart (1977, 518f.) notes that the cult never achieved front-rank status at Athens. There was a Sarapieion in the Asty, as well as in the Piraeus, which Pausanias (1.18.4) saw. Dow (1937, 199) believes that the priest of the Athenian Sarapieion was an Athenian citizen and that this circumstance indicated that the cult was official, but the inscription is too fragmentary to permit this deduction. Fraser (1960, 19) is right to dismiss the fanciful theory that Ptolemy I set up the cult in order to unite both his Greek and Egyptian subjects in common worship. He also rejects the belief that Sarapis-worship was actively propagated by the Ptolemies outside Egypt as a mark of Ptolemaic sovereignty (pp. 20ff.). 'Sarapion' as a theophoric name first appears in Athens in *c.* 250 (Dow 1937, 221ff.). Meiggs (1960, 387) suggests that the cult of Sarapis at Ostia was 'probably inspired by the close association of the Alexandrian corn fleet with the imperial harbours in the second cent. A.D.' The same may well have been true for Athens in the third cent. B.C. For Sarapieia in Egypt, cf. Aristeid. *Eis ton Sarapin* I p. 96 ed. Dindorf.

34 **Zeus Ammon.** The earliest consultation of Zeus Ammon by an Athenian was in *c.* 450 when Kimon made a secret enquiry of the god (Plu. *Kim.* 18.7). The oracle was again consulted before the sailing of the Sicilian Expedition in 415 and unhelpfully responded by declaring that the Athenians would capture all the Syracusans (Plu. *Nik.* 13.1). See Vidman (1970). For the silver phiale, see Woodward (1962, 5f.). For the sacrifice by the strategoi in 333/2, see *IG* II² 1496 a 96f. Since there was a *stratêgion* in the Piraeus as well as in the Athenian Agora, it cannot be assumed that Ammon had a second shrine in the Asty. For the new fountain house, see *IG* II² 338.13f. For honours paid to a priest of Ammon, see *IG* II² 410.19.

Zeus Labraundos. Hdt. 5.119 alleges: 'Only the Karians sacrifice to Zeus Labraundos' (but cf. 5.66). For an explanation of the epithet Labraundos, see Plu. *Mor.* 302a, who derives it from '*labrus*'. For discussion of the god's identity, see Laumonier (1958, 62-101). Despite the nomenclature, there is no evidence of assimilation between the Greek Zeus and the Karian god.

35 **Zeus Meilichios.** See Nilsson (1967, 412-14); Cook (1925, II pp. 1104-14), Harrison (1922, 12-28) and Burkert (1985, 201). Both 'Milichios' and 'Meilichios' occur in the dedications found in the Piraeus (Appendix III nos. 116-23). The god is regularly connected with purification (e.g. Paus. 1.37.4; Plu. *Thes.* 12). Cf. also Hsch. and Sud. s.v. *Dios kôdiou.* For the Diasia, see Parke (1977, 120-2), Deubner (1932, 155-7), Jameson (1965, 159-66), Harrison (1922, 12-15, 22f.) and Mikalson (1975, 117). Cook (op. cit., pp. 111-12) implausibly explains the duality of Zeus Meilichios in terms of a local king 'reverenced during his life-time as Zeus incarnate' and 'after his death worshipped as an anguiform soul'. The chthonic aspect of the god is further indicated by the fact that one of the reliefs depicts a pig being led

forward for sacrifice (fig. 943). The series of reliefs from the region are reproduced in Harrison (figs. 1-4) and Cook (figs. 942-6). They are listed in Foucart (1883, 507-15). Hsch.'s reference to the 'repugnance' surrounding the Diasia seems to imply that the festival combined both gloomy and joyful elements (cf. Mikalson 1982, 220).

136   **Zeus Philios.** See in general Cook (1925, II pp. 1160-210), Poland (1909, 177f.), Farnell (1896, I p. 74) and Harrison (1922, 354-8). The series of reliefs found in the Piraeus are discussed in Mitropoulou (1977, 97-112 with figs. 40-2). Relief depicting the god in the company of Agathe Tyche: Ny Carlsberg Glyptothek 1558 (reproduced as fig. 42 on p. 102 in Mitropoulou and as fig. 970 on p. 1162 in Cook).

137   **Zeus Soter and Athene Soteira.** See Deubner (1932, 174-6), Parke (1977, 167-9), Pélékides (1962, 249), Mikalson (1975, 180), Rhodes (1981, 628), Farnell (1896, I p. 60f.) and Clerc (1893, 136). The testimonia relating to the cult are collected by Solders (1931, 2f.). Poll. 6.15 relates that it was customary at a symposium to pour a libation from the third mixing-bowl to Zeus Soter, though this rite may have had little if anything to do with the deity worshipped in the Piraeus. The sacrifice known as the *eisitêtêria*, which was performed in the Asty on the last day of Skirophorion to mark the new year, was in honour of the Soteres, cf. *IG* II² 689 and 690 (dated 262/1). See also Mikalson (1975, 180). Offerings to Zeus Soter on safe completion of a voyage: Ar. *Ploutos* 1189f. Sacrifice by strategoi: Pouilloux (1954, no. 23). For Zeus Soter's association with military success, see Launey (1950, II pp. 914-16) and Robert (1969, 21). It is indicative of the god's importance for the Piraeus that when Deinarchos (3.15) is accusing Philokles of having betrayed the public trust invested in him as strategos of the Piraeus, it is Zeus Soter whom he invokes as his witness. The cult of Zeus Soter was extremely widespread throughout the eastern Mediterranean, cf. Schwabl s.v. 'Zeus' in *RE* X.A (1922) cols. 362-4. According to Fraser (1972, 194), Zeus Soter was 'the most popular cult of Zeus in Egypt'. His role as a protector of navigation at Alexandria is indicated by the fact that a statue of the god crowned the Pharos. The joint cult of Zeus Soter and Athene Soteira is only occasionally attested outside the Piraeus (cf. *ID* 372.73f., dated *c.* 200). Copies of a decree of Roman date to be set up on the Acropolis and in the Diisoterion: *IG* II² 1035.15f.

4. TOPOGRAPHY

139   **Pausanias' description of the Piraeus.** All that Paus. 1.2.1-4 reports seeing are the docks (revealingly described as 'being in existence even in my day'), Themistokles' tomb, the sanctuary of Zeus and Athene, the Makra Stoa, and the shrine of Aphrodite. For his route, see Papachatses (1974, fig. 54). It is evident that even in its heyday, however, the Piraeus would not have attracted a tourist's attention as much as the Asty.

140   **The Piraeus *horoi*.** The 24 *horoi* comprise 16 different texts and include 8 duplicates. All, except *horos* no. 13, were found in the Piraeus. Since they all use the three-barred sigma, they are thought to pre-date *c.* 445 (cf. *ML* p. 81), which is consistent with my proposed date of Hippodamos' planning

activity. The theory that two distinct periods are reflected in the series was advanced by Hill (1932) and later endorsed by Wycherley (1964, 138). That certain *horoi* belong to the Themistoklean period while others are more recent was also the view of Foucart (1907) and Martin (1951, 359f.). For further discussion, see McCredie (1971, 97) Martin (1974, 53f.) and Slidat (1980).

Hippodamian Agora. For its various titles, see Xen. *Hell.* 2.4.11; Andok. 1.45; Harp., Phot. and Sud. s.v.; Ps.-Dem. 49.22; *IG* II² 380.9, 36f. and 39 + *SIG*³ 313 = *SEG* XXI 307; *IG* II² 1668.5 = *SIG*³ 969; Appendix II no. 2.20. Every Attic deme possessed its own agora. Cf. *IG* II² 1180 = *SIG*³ 913: a decree passed by the deme of Sounion making provision for the establishment of a new agora, as the existing one had become built over (dated before 330). Old *bouleutêrion* : *IG* II² 1035.43f. See further Gurlitt (1890, 210 and 241f.), Judeich (1931, 455) and Rhodes (1972, 120). Shrine of Hestia: Appendix II no. 4.37. For the publication of deme decrees, see Appendix II no. 2.18-20 and von Schöffer s.v. *Dêmos* in *RE* V.I (1903) col. 14.

Orthogonal planning. The Piraeus, Thourioi and Rhodes, the three cities on whose plan Hippodamos allegedly worked, all adopted the grid-plan system. Hippodamos was not, however, the inventor of orthogonal planning as is commonly alleged. Megara Hyblaia, founded *c.* 728, may have had a grid-plan, and likewise Selinous, founded a century later (cf. Rykwert 1976, 88). A grid-plan is also attested for the Archaic city of Miletos destroyed by the Persians (Kleiner 1968, 25). The system was thus one with which Hippodamos, as a Milesian, was entirely familiar. Regarding Kasmenai in Sicily, Métraux (1978, 208) observes: 'The long straight streets crossing the city were intended more as divisions between roughly equal amounts of property than as a planning method for making the city viable for circulation and intramural contact and communication.' The same is likely to have been true of the Piraeus.

Houses. Lys. 32.8; Dem. 48.12 and 27; Schol. on Ar. *Knights* 327; Alkiphr. 4.18.4; 4.19.17; Deinarch. *c. Dem.* 69 (*T.*); Ps.-Dem. 49.22; Philostr. *VS* 2.21.2; Xen. *Symp.* 1.2; Antiph. 1.14-7. Euktemon of Kephisia (see below) owned a house in both the Asty and the Piraeus, a *sunoikia* in both the Kerameikos and the Piraeus, a bath house in the Piraeus, and land in Athmonon (Is. 6.19, 20 and 33). Wachsmuth's (1890, II p. 150) proposition that 'very frequently' wealthy Athenians owned a second house in the Piraeus where they passed the summer months 'in order to enjoy the fresh sea breeze' is fanciful. For houses in Olynthos, see Robinson and Graham (1938, 12 and 29); and Martin (1974, 110-13). Building plot northwest of Mounychia Hill: Catling (1984-5, 10); *Kathemerini* 26.6.1984. The excavation is under the direction of G. Steinhauer. Classical complex on Odhos Hypselantou: Alexandri (1973-74, 153-6 with plan 37). Housing complexes on Akte: Jones (1975, 98). Remains of Classical houses from recent excavations in the Piraeus are reported at the following sites: Odhoi Kountouriotou 67 and Evangelistrias; Odhos Phrangiadon 81; Odhos Kantharou 42; Odhoi Karageorge tes Servias, Pavsilipou and Papadiamante; Odhoi Hypselantou and Soteros Dios; and Odhos Salaminomachon. See Liankouras (1972, 171) and Alexandri (1973-74,

101-3 and 151-3). Density of population was likely to have ensured that houses fetched high prices. Bury-Meiggs (1975, 363) claim that in the fourth cent. the Piraeus became more densely populated than Athens, but I believe that this development occurred earlier. For a house dating to the Roman period, cf. Alexandri (1976, 49f.).

143   **Sunoikiai.** The earliest reference to a *sunoikia* is Thuk. 3.74.2, but they probably existed much earlier (cf. Davies 1981, 51 with n. 25). Hypothecated *sunoikiai*(?): Finley (1951, 64f. with nos. 73, 78 and 70 = *IG* II² 2732, 2736 and 2743). Very likely the *sunoikiai* owned by the banker Pasion were situated in the Piraeus, where he owned a house and a shield factory (Dem. 36.5). Another *sunoikia*, which belonged to Meixidemos of Myrrhinous, lay just below Mounychia Hill 'south of the house of Euthykles of Myrrhinous, north of the house of Protarchos of the Piraeus, west of the road to the Asty and east of the house of Euthymachos of Myrrhinous' (Meritt 1936, no. 10 ll. 119-22, dated 341). An '*oikêsis*' (possibly here a synonym for *sunoikia*, cf. Xen. *Por.* 3.12) is included among the property referred to in a lease found in the Piraeus dated after the mid-fourth cent. The terms of the lease indicate that a return of approximately 8 per cent was expected on the money invested by the lessee (*IG* II² 2496 = *SIG*³ 1216).

Porneia. Cf. Ar. *Peace* 164f. and Ps.-Plu. *Mor.* 849f = Ath. *Deipn.* 13.590d. We should not envisage the red-light district of the Piraeus as necessarily comparable in dereliction and unwholesomeness to modern Soho. Solon is alleged to have established state-run brothels at the turn of the sixth cent. (Ath. *Deipn.* 13.569de) and a prostitution tax was farmed out to contractors by the boule (Aischin. 1.119). For brothels in the Kerameikos, cf. Wycherley (1957, 222f.) and Williams (1983, 97).

Hostelries. Cf. Ziebarth (1935) who plausibly suggests that Xen.'s proposal was borne out of his experiences travelling abroad in Asia Minor and the Pontic region. Cf. also Hug s.v. *katagôgion* in *RE* X.2 (1919) cols. 2459-61 and ibid. s.v. *pandocheion* in *RE* XVIII.3 (1949) cols. 520-9, esp. 522. For the two kinds of hostelries mentioned by Xen., see Gauthier (1976, 105f.).

144   **Road system.** See in general Judeich (1931, 431f.); Martin (1974, 107f.); and Falciai (1982, 158f.). The contrast between the broad, straight thoroughfares of the Piraeus and the narrow, winding lanes of Athens was perhaps in Aristotle's mind when he recommended (*Pol.* 7.11 1330 b 21ff.) a mixture of the old and new methods of building for his ideal city, on the grounds that streets laid out in the Hippodamian manner were 'more attractive and convenient for general purposes', whereas those that were crooked 'made it difficult for foreign troops to enter and difficult for aggressors to find their way about'. Evidence of a ritual or religious significance behind the layout of Greek street systems is slender, though a few (e.g. Herakleia under Latmos in Karia, Rhodes, Perge in Pamphylia, etc.) were oriented according to the cardinal points of the compass. As Martin (1974, 44) observes:

> Considerations of a practical and topographical nature were, it seems, predominant: the shape of the land, the appearance of the site, communications with the port in the case of maritime cities, the line of the coast, and the direction of the prevailing winds, all had a real importance.

The fact that the *agoranomoi* were instructed to 'make the *plateiai* level' (*IG* II²
380.19ff., 34ff. = *SIG*³ 313 = *SEG* XXI 307) would further seem to indicate
that all roads in the Piraeus, like most Greek roads, were unpaved. Very
possibly as Martin (p. 256) further suggests with reference to the road out of
the Hippodamian Agora, we should think not in terms of a properly made
up road in the modern sense, but of a 'zone of public land, marked out by
crude boundary stones'. Road between the Long Walls: Thompson and
Scranton (1943, 315f. with fig. 27).

15   **Water system.** For the archaeological evidence for water-courses in the
Piraeus, see *AM* 25 (1900) 455; Judeich (1931, 432 and plan III C2); and
Milchhöfer (1881, 45f., 48 and 56). For recent reports of the discovery of
water installations in the Piraeus, see Alexandri (1973-74, 98-103 and
144-56; 1976, 44, 47f. and 50); Catling (1984-5, 10); and Liankouras (1972,
168-79). Cf. also Dodwell (1819, I p. 426) who reported:

> Amongst the ruins of Mounychia are a great quantity of wells, cisterns, and
> subterranean chambers cut in the rock. The mouths of these are generally
> circular, but the chambers are of varying forms and dimensions. Some are
> bell-shaped, and others square: several of them appear spacious. Their
> number renders it dangerous to walk about the ruins.

Dora Crouch points out to me that the advantage of bell-shaped cisterns
with narrow necks over rectangular cisterns is that below 6ft water remains
at a constant temperature of 55 degrees throughout the year. Meton: Schol.
on Ar. *Birds* 997; Phrynichos in *CAF* I, fr. 21 p. 376. For the theory that he
was responsible for the construction of fountain houses in the Piraeus
shortly before 414 (the date of Phrynichos' *Monotropos* where the allusion to
Meton's work occurs), cf. Ullrich (1846, 85-7), Wachsmuth (1890, I p. 572
n. 2) and Herbst (*Philologus* 38 [1879] 528). It is disputed by Gomme (*HCT*
II, p. 148). Water diverted from the Ilisos: Judeich (1931, 202f.). A detailed
investigation of the Piraeus water supply summarising the results of
archaeological findings in the region is very much needed, its value to our
understanding of the urban development of the Piraeus being potentially
immense. I entirely concur with the judgement of Crouch (1984, 364) who
writes: 'As signifiers of social networks, water systems have a kind of value
to the urban historian that art objects or buildings have to other
investigators.' Her own case-study of the Hellenistic water supply system
and drainage of Morgantina in Sicily provides an excellent model for future
research at other sites. For a catalogue of pottery found in a third-cent.
cistern, see Metzger (1971, 41-94).

16   **Hieron of the Dionysiastai.** See Dörpfeld (1884, 279-87 with fig. 13);
Judeich (1931, 431 and 451); and Rider (1965, 222f. with fig. 38). For more
recent excavation of the colonnaded hall, see Papachristodoulou (1971, 35-7
with fig. 1). The *hieron* now lies beneath the modern Demotikon Theatre, at
the intersection between Odhos Kolokotrone and Leophoros Vasileos
Georgiou I. Alexandri (1973-4, 146-9 with figs. 32 and 33) reports the
discovery of a large number of rooms which are evidently to be connected
with the *hieron*. Among the foundations was found an altar dedicated to
Mithras and Helios which had been used as filling material (Appendix III

no. 67). For the coin hoard, see Oeconomides-Caramessini (1976, 220-3).

Metroon. The inscriptions found in this area include *IG* II² 1273, 1301, 1314-16 and 1327-9. Chalioris (*Pir. Chron.* 2nd fasc. 15.3.45) states that the 'Metroon was constructed in the Doric style with Piraeic stone on the incline now occupied by the Zanneion Hospital', i.e. southeast of Zea Theatre.

Roman Forum. *Mesemvrini* 18.3.1981; *Augi* 20.6.1981; *Nea* 6.12.1981. The site is in the block formed by Odhoi Philhellenon, Skouze and Leosthenous, and Leophoros Vasileos Konstantinou.

147   **Akte Peninsula.** Str. *Geog.* 9.1.3 reports that Akte (and Aktike) were once ancient names for Attike. Cf. Harp. and Sud. s.v. *Akte* who state: 'Some derive the name from a certain king called Aktaion, others from the fact that most of the land is coastal (i.e. constitutes a promontory)'. Akte was incorrectly designated Mounychia by Leake (1841). *Hippasiai* on Akte: *IG* II² 1035.42. *LSJ*⁹ render 'riding, horse-exercise, horsemanship' with the secondary meaning 'cavalry'. 'Riding course', which is Gurlitt's suggestion (1890, 242 n. 17), remains the most plausible interpretation.

Piraeic poros. Piraeic poros was used for the Piraeus circuit, for the substructures of the Parthenon, the Propylaia, the Erechtheion and the Propylaia, and for the walls of Philon's Arsenal and the Stoa of Attalos. It was also used in the modern rebuilding of the Stoa by the American School of Classical Studies in 1953-56. It is not clear whether the expression 'stone from Akte (*Aktêtês lithos*)' denotes all Piraeic limestone or merely that quarried on Akte itself. For the epigraphical references, see Wachsmuth (1890, II p. 167 n. 1). Cf. also Harp. and Sud. s.v.; Ps.-Dem. 53.17. Many of the quarries on Akte are now submerged 2 or 3m below sea-level. For Attic quarries generally, see Osborne (1985, 93-7).

Marble lion. See Panagos (1968, ch. 11) who notes (p. 24) that a large number of life-size lions were recovered in the course of excavations carried out in the Piraeus 'some years ago'. I have not been able to trace the excavation report. One lion is currently on display in the entrance lobby of the Piraeus Museum. Cf. also Judeich (1931, 449), Leake (1841, 370f.), Milchhöfer (1881, 53f.), and Wheler (1682, 418).

Tomb of Themistokles. Plu. *Them.* 32.5 citing Diodoros Periegetes (*FGrH* 372 F 35). In support of his assertion, Diodoros quotes Plato Comicus (*CAF* I, fr.183 p. 651):

> Fair is the place where your tomb is heaped up for it has a welcome for merchants everywhere. It shall behold seamen sailing in and out, and gaze down whenever there is a ship race.

Plutarch is highly sceptical of the tomb's identity on the grounds that Diodoros' account conflicts with the report that Themistokles was buried in the Agora in Magnesia. He regards the tradition of his bones being brought home and buried secretly in Attike (cf. Andok. fr. 3 *T*; Thuk. 1.138.6 and Nep. *Them.* 10.5) as mere propaganda, intended to incite the oligarchs against the democrats. However, even if Themistokles' bones were not recovered, there was nothing to prevent the Athenians from erecting a cenotaph to him at a time when he was no longer thought of as an exile and traitor. The view that Themistokles had a monument in the Piraeus is further supported by Paus. 1.1.2 who locates it 'near the largest harbour'. The appropriateness of Akte as the site of a *mnêma* to Themistokles is remarked upon by Dodwell (1819, I p. 423) who wrote: 'What locality could be more appropriate ... than the same shore which had witnessed his triumph, and which still overlooked the Psytalian and the Salaminian rocks, and the whole extent of the Saronic gulph?' Although in restricted territory, the monument on Akte is visible today as one sails in or out of the Grand Harbour. It is listed as L10 in Garland (1982).

Eetioneia. Philochoros (*FGrH* 328 F 72 ap. Harp. s.v. *Eetiôneia*) derives the name from 'a certain Eetion who gained possession of the land'. See Jacoby in his note ad loc. Wall of the Four Hundred: Boersma (1970, cat. 1 p. 150), Judeich (1931, 82); and Scranton (1941, pp. 116 and 120). As Gomme, Andrewes and Dover (*HCT* V, p. 304) rightly point out, the walls and counterwalls which were constructed at the time of the siege of Syracuse in 414-3 have left no trace and there is no reason to suppose that this one would have done so either. Xen.'s description of it (*Hell.* 2.3.46) as an '*epi tôi chômati eruma* (wall on the peninsula)' is confused and inaccurate. Telegoneia: *IG* II² 1611.132f. (dated 357/6). See also Judeich (1931, 449 with n. 4) and Culley (1973, 119). Sacred ships at Eetioneia: *IG* II² 1035.36. See Hirst and Hirst (1927, 113f.), Meyer s.v. Prasiai in *RE* XXII.2 (1954) cols. 1695-6; and Culley (1973, 121).

Cults of Eetioneia. See Judeich (1931, 450) and Day (1927, 443f.). Cf. Appendix III nos. 34, 36, 63 and 69. Near the dedication to Hermes, a Roman herm was also found. Cf. Harrison (1965, 121).

Aphrodision. Inscription dated 394/3: *IG* II² 1657 = *GHI* II 107, with Foucart *BCH* 11 (1887) 131ff. The argument against the identification of the Aphrodision on Eetioneia with Konon's *hieron* was first advanced by Frazer (1898, II p. 31). His case rests on the fact that (1) Konon did not return to Athens until the summer of 393 (Xen. *Hell.* 4.8.7-10), whereas the inscription in the wall is dated to the year July 394-July 393, and (2) Paus. situated Konon's sanctuary 'near the sea', whereas this one is about 200m from the water's edge. Neither objection is particularly compelling.

The Grand Harbour. For the name *Megas Limên*, see Plu. *Them.* 32.4 and Paus. 1.1.2 (where, however, it is referred to as the *megistos limên*). 'Kantharos, (Goblet) or 'Kantharou limen' also probably designated the whole harbour or, less likely, its northern bight. Cf. Hsch. s.v. *Kantharou limên*; Plu. *Phok.* 2.8.3. The Schol. on Ar. *Peace* (l.145) derives Kantharos from an eponymous local hero of that name. See further Judeich (1931, 443 n. 3) and Angelopoulos (1898, nos. 151-5). For the ancient breakwater, see Catling (1984-85, 10); and *Kathemerini* 3.5.1984. Discussion of the shipsheds is reserved for their best-preserved remains in Zea Port. For their discovery in the Grand Harbour, see Alexandri (1973-74, 144f.).

The *Kophos Limên*. See Day (1927, 441-9). Though the northern bight of the Grand Harbour has changed its outline since Classical antiquity, von Gerkan's hypothesis (1924, 55f.) that this bay is an entirely modern harbour produced by dredging is invalidated by its inclusion in Stuart and Revett's map of the Piraeus (1827, III pl. III). Another harbour called Kophos existed in Torone in Chalkidike. It was proverbially noted for its tranquillity (Zen. 4.68; cf. Sud. s.v. *kôphoteros tou Tôronaiou limenos*).

Chôma. Cf. *IG* II² 1629 b 247-51 (dated 325/4). Xen. *Hell.* 2.3.46 appears to confuse the *Chôma* with Eetioneia. Trittyes markers: Raubitschek (1956, 280-2); Hill (1932, 257 n. 9); Wade-Gery (1932, 883-7); Göhler s.v. Trittyes in *RE* VII.A.I (1939) cols. 361-2, no. 3; and Lenschau s.v. Peiraieus in *RE* XIX (1938) col. 92.39-46. They are listed in Appendix I a-e. Siewert (1982, 10-16) believes that this and other groups of trittyes markers refer to the divisions of the citizen body into trittyes at meetings of the ekklesia. His view is refuted by Hansen (1985, 247-50).

Diisoterion. It is not clear why Sulla chose to spare this temple. The site proposed by Milchhöfer is just to the east of Aghia Triada church. Waywell (1971, 379) has suggested that the colossal bronze statue of Athene which was discovered in a warehouse (see below) may perhaps be the original Athene Soteira of Kephisodotos, set up in *c.* 375 and lost in 86.

Emporion. For a list of references, see Angelopoulos (1898, nos. 163-85). Isok. 4.42 eloquently describes the Piraeus as 'an *emporion* set in the centre of Greece'. Cf. also Dem. 35.28, which refers to *horoi* (described in the passage as *sêmeia*) marking the limits of the Emporion.

Ferry-boats. Pl. *Gorg.* 511d indicates that the usual fare for a ferry-ride from the Piraeus to Aegina for a whole family in the 380s was just two obols. By the second century A.D. the cost had apparently risen to four obols per person (Luk. *Navig.* 15). See Dodds (1959, 347).

Stoas. I assume that the stoas were used chiefly for storage (cf. Ar. *Ach.* 548), though John Camp has suggested to me that some of the back rooms might have served as dining-rooms (*hestiatoria*) in view of the fact that they have characteristic off-centre doorways for the arranging of couches around the walls. For the stoa found south of the Customs House, see Dragatsis (1886, 17f.) and Coulton (1976, 44 and 277, with fig. 24). On the basis of its style of masonry, Coulton (p. 86) favours a late-fifth cent. construction-date. For the stoa on Odhos Iasonos, see Alexandri (1976, 45f. with pl. 42a). Praxagora in Ar. *Ekk.* 686 designates the Alphitopolis Stoa as the place where in the communist state persons whose names begin with the letter kappa will assemble in order to dine at state expense. For further discussion of the siting of buildings in the Emporion, see Boersma (1970, cat. no. 87), Panagos (1968, 210f.), Papachatses (1974, 113f.) and Frazer (1898, II p. 24f.). Both Judeich (1931, 448) and Lenschau s.v. Peiraieus in *RE* XIX (1938) col. 94.36-40 believe the Makra Stoa and Alphitopolis Stoa to have been identical. The warehouse containing bronze and marble statues lay on the south side of Odhos Vasileos Georgiou, at the intersection with Odhos Philon and near the Town Hall (cf. Vanderpool 1960, 265). Statue of Spartokos: *IG* II² 653.8ff. = *SIG*³ 370. Cf. Dem. 20.36. For other statues of Athenian benefactors in the Emporion, see Judeich (1931, 449) and Lolling (1881, 309-11). *Stêlê* of Poseidon: Appendix III no. 106. Set of weights and measures: *IG* II² 1013.56f. Other sets were kept in the Tholos, on the Acropolis and at Eleusis. *IG* II² 1035.47 contains an obscure reference to certain objects referred to as *tupoi* which appear to have been located close to the Deigma. Roux (1961, 13) believes that *tupoi* were used to check the size of roof-tiles, etc. It is possible, therefore, that weights, measures and standards were all displayed beside the Deigma under the supervision of the *metronomoi*, as Culley (1973, 169) has proposed. *Stratêgion*: *Hesperia* 53 (1984)

371 no. 3 ('*pro tou stratêgou* (sic) *tou en tôi empori*[*ôi*]'); *IG* II² 1035.44 ('the old *stratêgeion*').

Deigma. Tim. *Lex. Pl.*, Harp., Sud. and *Et. Mag.* s.v. *Deigma* state: 'Primarily that which is put on display by any tradesman. It is also an area (*topos*) in the Emporion at Athens to which items on display (*deigmata*) are brought, which is how it gets its name.' The Schol. on Ar. *Knights* (l.979) writes: 'It was where many strangers and citizens congregated and made deals (*elogopoioun*)'. Cf. also Dem. 35.29 and 50.24. See Panagos (1968, 209f.), Culley (1973, 164-8), Judeich (1931, 448 n. 3), Szanto s.v. Deigma in *RE* IV (1901) cols. 2383-4, and Gurlitt (1890, 236ff.). 'Deigma erected by Magnus': *IG* II² 1035.47. Regarding the probable identification of 'Magnus' with Cn. Pompeius, Culley (1973, 166, quoting Graindor) points out that the omission of *praenomen, nomen* and *cognomen* in an Athenian inscription honouring a Roman 'would be surprising if one was dealing with an obscure person'. Hadrianic rescript: *IG* II² 1103 (after A.D. 124/5).

Sanctuary of Aphrodite Euploia. Both Frazer (1898, II p. 29f.) and Papachatses (1974, fig. 25) locate the sanctuary in Plateia Vasilias Amalias. Leake (1841, 381 with plan IV), however, situated it at Plateia Karaiskake.

Zea. Hsch. s.v. *Zea* writes: 'A name for Hekate in Athens. Also one of the harbours in the Piraeus, so named from the growing of wheat (*zeia*)'. Cf. also Tim. *Lex. Pl.* s.v. *Mounychia*. See Judeich (1931, 437 n. 1). For references, see Angelopoulos (1898, nos. 156-62). Shipsheds: Graser (*Philologus* 1872, 1ff.), Frazer (1898, II pp. 14-17), Wachsmuth (1890, II pp. 59-74), Blackman (1968, 181-92) and Alexandri (1973-74, 99 and 151f.). The remains of two shipsheds, probably Macedonian in date, are also visible on the promontory of Sounion. Since these have an extremely steep gradient (1 in 3.5), they could not have accommodated full-size triremes (see Kenny 1947, 194ff.). *Psuchtrai*: *IG* II² 1035.43. Culley (1973, 139-43) translates *psuchtrai* as 'parks', following Gurlitt (1890, 242 n. 16) who rendered 'shady walks and avenues'.

Philon's Arsenal. For the inscription see *IG* II² 1668 = *SIG*³ 969. An Attic foot is 14 per cent longer than the modern measure, but as Lawrence-Tomlinson rightly state conversion obscures the simplicity of the proportions. For partial text, translation and commentary, see Bundgaard (1957, 117-32). The carpentry techniques are discussed by Martin (1967). Timber was used very sparingly for the roof, as Meiggs (1982, 213f.) emphasises. Philon was assisted in his task by a certain Euthydemos, but in what capacity is unknown. He was also responsible for the façade of the Telesterion at Eleusis (Vitr. 7 *praef.* 12; cf. Lawrence-Tomlinson 1983, 339 with fig. 328). Literary references to the Arsenal include Str. *Geog.* 9.1.15; Cic. *de Or.* 1.62; Val. Max. 8.12.2. Earlier *skeuothêkê*: *IG* II² 1610.6 and 1627.396. For descriptions and reconstructions of the Arsenal, see Dörpfeld (1883, 147-64), Frazer (1898, II p. 18-20), Judeich (1931, 441), Dinsmoor (1950, 241f.), Amit (1965, 78f.), Jeppesen (1961, 221-3), Lorinzen (1964), Panagos (1968, 226f.), Papachatses (1974, 109 and fig. 36) and Lawrence-Tomlinson (1983, 341f. with fig. 333). Despite their detail, the *sungraphai* none the less omit a number of crucial details, including the arrangement of the Doric frieze and the spacing of the columns, as Coulton points out (1977, 54). On Kolonos Agoraios north of the Hephaisteion remains of a Hellenistic building have recently been discovered 'whose ground plan was doubtless inspired by that of the Naval Arsenal in the Piraeus' (Pounder 1983, 249). This was apparently used as an arsenal for military equipment. Ceramic evidence suggests a date of construction in the 270s or 260s.

158   **Demosion Propylon.** Mention of 'a great building (*oikêma*) beside the gates (*pulai*)' in *IG* II² 1627b.280 (dated 330/29) was plausibly interpreted by Hill (1932, 257) as a reference to Philon's Arsenal and the Demosion Propylon, which, she postulated, lay opposite one another on the eastern side of Zea Port. Hill further proposed that it was here that there stood the statue of 'Hermes at the Gate', for which see above p. 126.

     Zea Theatre. See Philios (1880, 47-61); Judeich (1931, 442 with n. 1); Fiechter (1950, 35-41 with pl. 6); and Bieber (1961, 122 with fig. 463). The theatre lies directly in front of the Piraeus Museum, at the intersection between Odhoi Alkibiadou and Kountouriotou. Points of identity with the theatre of Dionysos in Athens include the division of the auditorium into thirteen wedges, the size of the radius of the orchestra (9.12m), and the distance between the *proskênion* and the orchestra (11.50m). An inscription dated *c*.150 (*IG* II² 2334), which was found 'on the isthmus which joins the harbours of Kantharos and Zea', lists the names of those who made financial contributions towards the construction of the theatre.

     Phreatto. Cf. Dem. 23.77, 78; Arist. *Pol.* 1300 b 29; Harp. s.v.; Poll. 8.120. Paus. 1.28.11 gives the alternative form 'Phreattys'. Papachatses (1974, 129) notes that wells (*phreata*) have been found on both sides of the entrance to Zea Port. Judeich's identification of the court must, therefore, be regarded with caution. *Dikastêrion* in Piraeus: *IG* II² 244.36; 1669.18, 21 and 38; see above p. 81.

159   **Serangeion.** See Dragatsis (1925-6, 1-8; 1928); Ginouvès (1962, 195f. and pls. 57-8); Judeich (1931, 436); and Papachatses (1974, 128). Phot. s.v. *Sêrangeion* writes: 'A place in the Piraeus founded by Serangos; there is also a *hêrôön* there'. Cf. also Harp. and Hsch. s.v. For the dating of Euktemon's sale of the bathing-house, see Wyse (1904, 484) and Donaldson (1965, 78 n. 8). Donaldson draws particular attention to the artist's skill in handling perspective and rendering emotion. Altar of Apollo Apotropaios: Dragatses (1897, 16) and Appendix III no. 15. The Serangeion now serves as a wine-cellar for a restaurant.

     Shrines of Zeus Meilichios, etc. See Papachatses (1974, 124); Curtius and Kaupert (1881, 35 and pl. 12.1); Cook (1925, II.2 p. 1104); Furtwängler (*SB Academie München* 1897, 406ff.); Judeich (1931, 435); and Culley (1973, 146f.). The fact that the *temenos* of Agathe Tyche is listed separately in *IG* II² 1035.44 indicates that she had a separate precinct. Another *temenos* of the goddess lay in the vicinity of the Long Walls (*IG* II² 1035.48).

160   **Asklepieion.** See Dragatsis (*AD* 1888, 132ff.); Judeich (1931, 441); Wolters (1892, 10ff.); Culley (1973, 127-9) and Papachatses (1974, 123f.). For the stone quarry, see above p. 147. It was probably in this Asklepieion that Ploutos in Ar. *Plout.* (653-7) spent the night in the hope of regaining his sight, in view of the fact that before entering the sanctuary he first purified himself in the sea.

     Mounychia. Hellanikos (ap. Schol. on Dem. p. 148 Reiske), D.S. fr. 7, and Harp. and Sud. s.v. *Mounychia* all derive the name from a certain Mounychos, son of Panteukles, who was king of Athens. In Attic inscriptions the alternative spelling 'Mounichia' is almost invariably used (e.g. *IG* I² 310.27; *IG* II² 1604.72, 98). For houses on Mounychia, see also Meritt (1936, no. 10), as discussed above p. 214. For stone quarrying, see Alexandri (1973-4, 149) and above note. Hippias' fortification: Judeich (1931, 67 and 163); Scranton (1941, 42, 119, 161 and A4.9); and Boersma (1970, cat. 2, p. 150). Macedonian fortification: Tsirivakos (1968, 114f.). Literary references to Mounychia are assembled in Angelopoulos (1898, nos. 119-150).

Theatre of Dionysos. See Dragatsis (*Parnassos* 3 [1879] 577ff.); Leake (1841, 329); Milchhöfer (1881, I p. 63); Hirschfeld (1878, 20ff.); Judeich (1931, 451); Frazer (1898, II p. 32); and Rhodes (1981, 611). References to the theatre include Thuk. 8.93.1 ('the Dionysiac theatre at Mounychia'); and *IG* II² 1035.44 ('the old theatre'). For the lease, see Appendix II no. 2 with Finley (1951, 216 n. 68). A decree appended to the lease (Appendix II no. 3) honours a certain Theaios 'who made the theatre fetch 300 dr. more'. The source of the additional income is not disclosed. See above p. 76.

Dionysion. Other proposals regarding the location of this shrine include Wachsmuth (1890, II p. 136), who suggested a site on the western slope of Mounychia Hill; Milchhöfer (1881, 39), who placed it 200m south of the north gate; and Culley (1973, 136), who located it close to the *hieron* of the Dionysiastai in Plataia Korais. *Horos*-marker of the *hieron*: Appendix I no. 1. Hero Akrapotes: Athen. *Deipn.* 2.39c.

Shrines on Mounychia Hill. Excavation on Koumoundourou Hill: Threpsiades (1935, 172ff.). Excavation on Mounychia Hill: Papachristodoulou (1973, 46-8). Papachristodoulou (p. 48) states categorically: 'The location of the *hieron* of Artemis Mounychia ... on the Koumoundourou promontory cannot be disputed, as a result of Threpsiades' excavations.' Judeich (1931, 162f.), writing before Threpsiades' excavations, believed that the cult of Artemis was situated on Mounychia itself, which seems intrinsically to be a more natural home for such a venerable cult. As Osborne (1985, 157) notes, Attic shrines of Artemis are either coastal (Mounychia, Vouliagmeni and Loutsa) or fluvial (Ilisos and Oinoe). For other cults on Mounychia, see Judeich (1931, 452f.). Walbank (1983, II p. 183) points out that although the nymphs had many sanctuaries in Attike, only those in Athens, Mounychia and (possibly) Phyle seem to have been accorded the title Nymphaion (Appendix III no. 101). Altar of Phosphoros: Clem. Al. *Strom.* 1.163; above p. 36. *Hieron* of the hero Munichos or Mounychos: Appendix III no. 99 with Phot. s.v. *Mounychia* and *Mounychion*. Moirai: Appendix III no. 79. For the various theories concerning the site of the Bendideion, see Papachatses (1974, 122f.).

Theseion and Thesmophorion. Lease: Appendix II no. 4. For the excavation of the building within the Long Walls, see Milchhöfer (1881, 37f.), Judeich (1931, 456), Papachatses (1974, 127f.) and Culley (1973, 172-4). A brief account of the alarm in 415 is given in Thuk. 6.61.2. The Piraeus Theseion was probably one of the four Attic Theseia mentioned by Philochoros (*FGrH* 328 F 18 ap. Plu. *Thes.* 35.2). Theseia are included among the sacred monuments listed for restoration in *IG* II² 1035.47f.

163 **Shrine set up by Themistokles.** Frazer (1898, II p. 30) and Judeich (1931, 73 n. 5) both identify this shrine with the sanctuary of Aphrodite referred to in a fragment of Ammonios (*Rhet. gr.* VI, p. 393 ed. Walz), though the latter categorically states that this was dedicated *after* the victory, presumably as a thank-offering or memorial. 'Herkane' is coined by Culley from *herkos* (enclosure) on the analogy of Athene's epithet 'Ergane (the Worker)', derived from *ergon* (work).

Fortifications. See Foucart (1887, 129ff.); Lechat (1888, 337ff.); Hirschfeld (1878); Wachsmuth (1890, II pp. 1-50); Frazer (1898, II p. 8-10); Judeich (1931, 144-54); Noack (1908, 33-8); Lenschau s.v. Peiraieus (Mauern) in *RE* XIX (1938) cols. 83-8; Gomme (*HCT* II, p. 261-70); Scranton (1941, 114-9); Panagos (1968, 230-6); Liankouras (1972, 168ff.); Alexandri (1973-4, 150); Podlecki (1975, 179); and Lenardon (1978, 96).

Themistoklean circuit. The expression 'two waggons going in opposite directions' is ambiguous. Widmann (1923, 215f.) suggests that the waggons drove up to the wall at right angles to it, whereas Powell (1936, 8) proposed that the size of the stones was so great that the waggons had to be placed end-to-end. As Gomme (*HCT* I, 263) emphasises, however, the purpose of the passage is not to explain how the stones were brought to the wall, but the wall's thickness. Cf. the comment made by a traveller to China in the first half of the sixteenth cent. that the wall of Peking was 'so wide that twelve horses could gallop abreast on it at full speed without colliding' (quoted by Braudel 1981, 492). More problematic is the fact that Thuk.'s figure of 60 stades for 'the whole circuit of the Piraeus including Mounychia' does not correspond to any known circuit around the Piraeus. If it is correct, the Themistoklean wall must have been considerably shorter than its fourth-cent. successor, estimated by Gomme (*HCT* II, p. 40) to have been approximately 78 stades in length. It is partly on the strength of this anomaly that some scholars postulate the existence of the crosswall. The only other estimate is that of D. Chr. 25.4 who puts it at over 90 stades. For its course east of Eetioneia, see Judeich (1931, 146), Hirschfeld (1878, fig. 6), von Alten (1881, 21) and Gomme, Andrewes and Dover (*HCT* V, 304). Portion of wall beneath the modern flyover: *AR* 1968-9 (Suppl. to *JHS* 89 [1969] 6). Some five courses are preserved.

165 **Chêlai.** The Schol. on Thuk. 7.90 describes a *chêlê* as 'a line of stones jutting out from the wall facing the sea to prevent the force of the waves from damaging the wall'. The word literally means a 'hoof' or 'claw of a crab'. For the Piraeus *chêlai*, see von Alten (1881, 10-15), Frazer (1898, II p. 9) and Judeich (1931, 434). Von Alten (1881, 13) describes the *chêlai* of Mounychia Port as 'the most magnificent surviving examples of ancient Greek fortification architecture'. The chains strung between the towers were probably coated in tar to prevent them from rusting (Vitr. 5.12.1; Aen. *Comm. Poliork.* 11).

Kononian circuit. Accounts relating to Kononian circuit built into Aphrodision Gate: *IG* II² 1656 and 1657 = *GHI* II 107 = Maier I, nos. 1 and 2. See Xen. *Hell.* 2.2.19; 6.5.35; Isok. 14.31; D.S. 14.85. For further accounts see *IG* II² 1658-64 = Maier I, nos. 3-9. Repairs in 337/6 (?): *IG* II² 244 = Maier I, no. 10. An appendix to the decree states that the work is to be carried out at Mounychia. The generally accepted date of 337/6 is disputed by Cawkwell (1963, 66 with n. 109) who assigns it 'to the period of Euboulos' (i.e. 354- *c.* 346). Repairs in 307/6: *IG* II² 463 = Maier I, no. 11. Repairs in *c.* 228: *IG* II² 834.14f. = Maier I, no. 15. Towers: see Frazer (1898, II p. 8), Noack (1908, 33-8); Judeich (1931, 148) and Papachatses (1974, 104). On Stranz's plan in Curtius (1868), some 40 are marked. App. *Mith.* 30 alleges that the height of the Piraeus fortifications at the time of the Sullan sack was 'about 40 cubits'.

6   **Dia mesou chôma.** Alexandri (1973-4, 150) records the recent discovery of a wall 1.1m thick built of facing poros blocks with a rubble core along Odhos Kapodistriou, which belongs to this section of the wall. See also *AE* 1900, p. 93 1.13. Ditch behind Plateia Karaiskake: Liankouras (1972, 168-71 with pl. 113 and fig. 14). See also Leake (1841, 400), Judeich (1931, 151) and Papachatses (1974, 114). Curved tower: Threpsiades (1935, 159ff.); and Papachatses (1974, figs. 48 and 49).

Gates. See Papachatses (1974, 114-18). Of particular interest are the 19th-cent. photographs depicting the Aphrodision Gate in op. cit., figs. 42-4.

'Hermes at the Gate'. Philochoros (*FGrH* 328 F 40 ap. Harp. s.v. *pros têi pulidi Hermês* and *Hermês pros têi pulidi*); Dem. 47.26. The epigram has caused considerable controversy. Judeich (1931, 153), Gomme (*HCT* I, p. 262) and Lenschau s.v. Peiraieus in *RE* XIX (1938) cols. 87-8 associated it with Themistokles. Jacoby (comment. ad loc.), who first identified it as a quotation from Philochoros' *Atthis*, correctly placed it in 395/4. For the practice of dedicating herms, cf. Harrison (1965, 117).

7   **Long Walls.** See Leake (1841, 417f.); Frazer (1898, II pp. 38-41); Lenschau s.v. Peiraieus in *RE* XIX (1938) cols. 88-9; Lehmann-Hartleben (1923, 79f.); Ferguson (1938, 26); Judeich (1931, 155-60, 428f.); Day (1932, 1ff.); Scranton (1938, 525-36); Threpsiades (1950, 100); Gomme (*HCT*, I p. 312 and II p. 39f.); Travlos (1960, 48-50); Verdeles and Davaras (1966, 92-5); Liankouras and Papachristodoulou (1972, 339-46); Boersma (1970, 4); and Schilardis (1975, 66-149). For the photographed remains of a section of the Northern Long Wall at Neo Phaleron, see Papachatses (1974, fig. 61). For the section of the Southern Long Wall found at Moschato, see Alexandri (1976, 52 with figs. 9 and 10; pl. 46a); Catling (1984-85, 10 with fig. 10). References to Long Walls in a decree dated 307/6: *IG* II² 463.7, 37 = Maier I, no. 11. Repair in Roman period: Vanderpool (1959, 280 with pl. 75 fig. 8).

9   **Cemeteries.** *Horos* no. 23 is inscribed (uniquely to my knowledge) '*horos mnêmatôn*', though the singular frequently denotes the boundary of an individual grave (cf. Tillyard 1904-5, 67f.). Dodwell's description of the contents of the tombs is supplemented by a fascinating description of his archaeological methods. Entry to a sepulchre, he informs us, may be gained 'by first breaking the *trapeza*, or cover, with a large hammer, and then overturning it with a strong pole, as a lever.' With a team of ten men he was able in this way to open 30 tombs in one day – a considerable achievement, as he proudly boasts, in view of the fact that the normal expectation was 'that two men can open four in a day'. Dodwell does not state how long he remained in the Piraeus thus engaged, but even if it was for only a few days, he probably succeeded in destroying more evidence about the material culture of the Piraeus than anyone else except Sulla. A more scientific excavation of the cemetery to the northwest of the Piraeus was undertaken by the Greek archaeologist K.S. Pittakis in the years 1836-41. Grave-*stêlai* from this region as listed in Conze include the following: 40/19, 115/24, 121/42, 129, 139/43, 205/62, 241/61, 264, 274/63, 314/77, 386, 400/92, 410/97, 439/100, 449/105, 501, 519, 538, 581/117, 624/120, 695c and 697/133. As Judith Binder points out to me, it was the discoveries made here 'which gave the first overwhelming impression of Attic grave reliefs', not as is generally assumed, those made in the Kerameikos which were not actually excavated until the 1860s. Cf. *Archaeologische Zeitung* 1849, Archäologischer Anzeiger 4/5 (April-May 1849) col. 50. A few graves have also come to light along the southern shore of Akte peninsula, near the supposed tomb of Themistokles, cf. Conze 91 and 201/54. For a recently discovered grave-relief on Odhos Philippoupoleos , see *AD* 29 p. 103. *AD* 1888 (p. 35) records the discovery of a tomb outside the Asty Gate.

Tropaion. Cf. *IG* II² 1006.28, 1008.17 and 1028.27. For Zeus Tropaios, see S. *Ant.* 143, *Trach.* 303 and Eur. *Herakl.* 867. The cult and shrine are discussed by Culley (1977, 294f.).

Appendix I
The Piraeus boundary markers

The Horoi

1   *IG* I² 868; *ADelt* 1888, 67.   'Boundary of the Dionysion'
From Piraeus.

2, 3   *IG* I² 887a and 887b; Hill   'Boundary of the Emporion
1932, 256.   and of the road'
From Grand Harbour. One copy
was found in situ beside the
church of Aghios Nikolaos.

4   *IG* I² 888 = *SEG* X 377 = Schwyzer   'Boundary of the public
1960, 384 no. 9.4; Hill, 1932, 256   *leschai*'
adn. 3.
Discovered in situ 'approx. 50m in
front of the gate of the Naval School'
and 'at the top of Akte'.

5   *IG* I² 889 = *SEG* X 378.   'Boundary of the public
From 'the hospital in Piraeus'.   anchorage (*hormos*)'

6, 7   *IG* I² 890a and 890b = *SEG* X 378.   'Boundary of the anchorage of
Both found in the Grand Harbour   ferry-boats (*porthmeia*)'
quite near to the shore. One dredged
up near the Customs House, the other
not far from the Railway Station.

8-11   *IG* I² 891 = *SEG* X 379; Hill 1932,   'Boundary of the Demosion
255f.   Propylon'
From the eastern side of Zea Port.

12,13   *IG* I² 892 = *SEG* X 380; Hill 1932,   'From this road, that which
254f.   lies in the direction of the
One copy was found in the Piraeus,   harbour is all public
the other on the northwest slope of   (*dêmosios*)'
the Acropolis.*

14   *IG* I² 893 = *SEG* X 381; Hill 1932,   'Up to this road here the Asty
256 adn. 3.   has been cut up (*nenemetai*)'
From Odhos Makras Stoas in Piraeus.

15   *IG* I² 894 = *SEG* X 382 = Schwyzer   'Up to this road here is the
1960, 384 no. 9.2; Hill 1932, 256f.   cutting up (*nemêsis*) of
adn. 3.   Mounychia'
Found in situ on the northwest side
of Mounychia Hill between the
Long Walls.

---

* See A.N. Oikonomides, *Acta of the 5th Epigraphic Congress* (GB 1967), pp. 22-5, for a restoration of the Acropolis *horos* connecting it with a street leading to the 'Piraeus gates' of the city wall.

16	*IG* I² 895.	'Up to this road ...'
	From Piraeus.	Fragmentary *horos* apparently identical to no. 15.
17	*IG* I² 896 = *SEG* X 383; Hill 1932. Discovered on the western side of Zea Port.	'Boundary of the Agora'
18	*SEG* X 384; Hill 1932, 258f. From Piraeus.	'Boundary of the ropes (*schoinoi*)
19	Hill 1932, 259. Found at southwest corner of Leophoros Sokratous and Odhos Char. Trikoupi in the Piraeus.	'Road'
20	*IG* I² 855. Found between Zea and Mounychia.	'Boundary of the *hêrôön*'
21	*IG* I² 867. From the Serangeion.	'Boundary of *hieron*'
22	*IG* I² 858. from the southern slope of Mounychia Hill. Probably from the Asklepieion.	'Boundary of the *hieron*'
23	Dodwell 1819, I p. 430.	'Boundary of the tombs (*mnêmata*)'. From a hill to the north of Piraeus.
24	*IG* II² 2623.	Referred to below p. 227.

The Trittyes Markers

a	*IG* I² 897. From the harbour area of Piraeus.	'Here the trittys of the Eleusinioi ends, and the trittys of the Peraioi begins'
b	*IG* I² 898 = *SEG* X 385 = Schwyzer 1960, 384 no. 9.1. From the harbour area of Piraeus.	'Here the trittys of the Paianioi ends, and the trittys of the Myrrhinosioi begins'
c	*IG* I² 899 = *SEG* X 386; Wade-Gery 1932, 884-6. From the eastern side of Zea Port.	'Here the trittys of the [Epak]reis ends, and the trittys of the Thriasioi begins'. Wade-Gery reads 'Pedieis' for 'Epakreis'.
d	*IG* I² 900 = *SEG* X 387. From the harbour area of Piraeus.	'Here the tribe Aiantis ends and its trittys Tetrapolis, and the tribe Akamantis begins and its trittys Cholargeis'
e	*IG* I² 901 = *SEG* X 388; Wade-Gery 1932, 886f. From the harbour area of Piraeus.	Largely illegible *horos* delimiting the tribes Hippothontis(?) and (?).

See also *SEG* XXXII 18.

Appendix II
Decrees of the deme Piraeus

1   *IG* II² 1177 = *SEG* XXI 517 and XXV 143 = *LSG* 36. Decree dated *c.* 350 instructing the demarch and priestess of Demeter to maintain order in the Thesmophorion.

2 & 3   *IG* II² 1176 = *SIG³* 915 = *Hesperia* 29 (1960) p. 1 no. 1 = Stroud, *CSCA* 7(1974) p. 290-8. Line numbers are cited according to Stroud. Two decrees on a fragmentary *stêlê* dated 324/3. The first is a leasing agreement between the demesmen of Piraeus and contractors for the management of the theatre (*hoi priamenoi to theatron*) of Dionysos. The agreement concerns both its refurbishment and administration during festival times. The second decree honours the outgoing *priamenoi to theatron*.

4   *IG* II² 2498 = *SIG³* 965 = *SEG* XXXII 226. Lease drawn up in 321/0 by the demesmen of Piraeus relating to the renting out of the 'Paralia, Halmyris, the Theseion and all the other *temenê*'. Ll. 3-6 state that those whose annual rent exceeded 10 dr. were to put up security (*apotimêma*) equivalent in value to the rent, while those leasing for under 10 dr. were to supply a guarantor (*enguêtês*). Payment was due twice yearly. The rental period was for ten years.

5   Meritt, *Hesperia* 3 (1934) 44-6 no. 33. Fragmentary decree apparently containing a reference to 'the financing of some public work of construction'. Early third cent. From the Athenian Agora.

6   *IG* II² 1214 = *SIG³* 912. Decree in honour of Kallidamas of the deme of Cholleidai, granting him the right to participate in all demotic *hiera* that are common to all (*koina*) and assigning him a seat of honour (*proedria*) in the deme theatre. As Gauthier (1979, 394-6) suggests, a probable date for the decree is soon after the reunification of the Asty with the Piraeus, i.e. after *c.* 261 in my view, because of the reference in l. 3f. to 'the Demos of the Peiraieis and the Demos of the Athenians'. For the honorand, see Whitehead (1986, no. 150).

Cf. also *IG* II² 2623: a *horos*-marker of the territory (*chôrai*) of the Piraieis. Fourth cent. or later. No find-spot recorded.

Deme decrees of the Piraeus are listed in Whitehead (1986, nos. 85-9).

Appendix III
Epigraphical testimonia for religious activity*

Adrasteia	1	The existence of a cult of Adrasteia is suggested by a reference to the goddess in association with Bendis (no. 37; Solders 1931, 82).
Agathe Tyche	2	*IG* II² 1035.44. Decree concerning repair of sacred monuments including a *temenos* of Agathe Tyche in the Piraeus. Dated by von Freeden (1983, 174) to 74/3-65/4. From the Acropolis.
Akratopotes Hero	3	Athen. *Deipn.* 2.39c.
Ammon	4	*IG* II² 1282 = *SIG*³ 1105. Decree honouring an *épimelêtês* and others who built an annexe (*prosoikodomia*) to the temple of Ammon. Dated 262/1.
Aphrodite Euploia	5	*IG* II² 2872. Dedication to Aphrodite Euploia by Argeios, strategos of the Piraeus. Dated *c.* 97/6.
Aphrodite Ourania	6	*IG* II² 337 = *SIRIS* 1 = *GHI* II 189 = *SIG*³ 280 = *LSG* 34 = Pečírka (1966, 59-61). Decree of Athenian demos dated 333/2 granting merchants of Kition the right to own a plot of land on which to establish a *hieron* to Aphrodite 'just as the Egyptians have built the temple to Isis'.
	7	*IG* II² 4636. Dedication by a Kitian to Aphrodite Ourania dated to 4th cent. From south part of Piraeus pensinsula.
	8	*IG* II² 4637. Dedication to Aphrodite Ourania (?). Dated to 4th cent. From same find-spot as no. 7.

*Testimonia are arranged chronologically. Unless otherwise stated, the find-spot is simply 'the Piraeus'. In the absence of epigraphical testimonia, a literary reference is supplied instead.

9   *IG* II² 1261 = *SIG*³ 1098. Three decrees of the *thiasôtai* or *koinon* of Aphrodite dated 302/1, 301/0 and 300/299, honouring Stephanos, a breastplate manufacturer, who served first as *epimelêtês* and then as *hieropoios*. He is particularly praised for organising the *pompê* of the Adoneia and for making a dedication to Demeter Homonoia. The third decree (ll. 44-55) is inscribed by a different hand from the first two. From Odhos Alkibiadou 'near the ruins of the temple of Aphrodite'.

10   *IG* II² 1290. Decree of the Salaminians of Cyprus dated to mid-third cent. concerning the worship of Aphrodite and celebration of Adoneia.

11   *IG* II² 1337. Decree of *orgeônes* of Syrian Aphrodite dated 95/4. For identification, see Ferguson (1944, 119).

12   *IG* II² 4586. Dedication to Aphrodite dated to mid-fourth cent. From 'east of the public reservoir'.

13   *IG* II² 4616. Dedication to Aphrodite dated to end of fourth cent. From same find-spot as no.12.

Apollo Delios(?)

14   *IG* I³ 130 = *IG* I² 128. Found between Zea and Mounychia, but probably originating from Phaleron. See Lewis (1960). Public decree establishing a *hieron* and imposing a levy (*eparchê*) on *nauklêroi*. Dated *c.* 432.

Apollo Apotropaios

15   *IG* II² 5009. Altar to Apollo Apotropaios 'from the Serangeion'.

Artemis Horaia

16   *IG* II² 4632. Inscribed altar dedicated to Artemis Horaia dated to fourth cent. See Mitsos (1949, 75).

Artemis Mounychia

17   *IG* II² 1006. Ephebic decree dated 122/1. Lines 29f. refer to ship race performed by ephebes from Megas Limen(?) to Mounychia Port at the Mounychia and the Diisoteria.

18   *IG* II² 1011. Ephebic decree dated 106/5. Line 16 refers to a race to Mounychia 'in sacred ships'.

19   *IG* II² 1028. Ephebic decree dated 106/5. Line 21 refers to a race to Mounychia and sacrifice to 'the goddess'.

20   *IG* II² 1029. Ephebic decree dated 94/3.
      Line 13 refers to *pompê* 'in honour of
      Artemis Mounychia'.

21   *IG* II² 2130. Ephebic catalogue dated
      A.D.192/3 . L. 49 refers to a staged sea
      battle (*naumachia*) at the Mounychia.

22   Undated inscription stating '*N*[*aos*]
      Artemidos', found on Koumoundourou
      headland (Megaw 1936, 142).

Artemis Nana   23   *IG* II² 4696. Dedication to Artemis Nana
      dated to second or first cent.

Artemis   24   *IG* II² 4970 = *LSG* 23. Sacral law
      referring to offerings of cakes to Artemis
      dated to middle of fourth-cent. As
      Sokolowski (*LSG* ad loc.) notes, the fact
      that Artemis' name occurs in genitive
      case 'seems to indicate that the
      dedication belonged to an altar or shrine
      of Artemis'. It was allegedly found in the
      sanctuary of Asklepios, though this is
      disputed.

25   *SEG* XXVI 267 = Papachristodoulou
      (*AD* 28 [1973] B p. 48). Dedication to
      'gracious Artemis' dated to first half of
      fourth cent. In the same find-spot on
      Mounychia Hill a sacred law referring
      to the worship of Moirai (Fates) was
      found (unpublished).

Asklepios   26   *IG* II² 4962 = *SIG*³ 1040 =*LSG* 21.
      Marble block carved on four sides
      containing a decree prescribing pre-
      paratory offerings (*prothumata*) in the
      form of cakes (*popana*) to Asklepios and
      'the gods sharing the sanctuary (*sunnaoi
      theoi*)', viz. Maleatas, Apollo, Hermes,
      Iaso, Akeso, Panakeia, the Kynegetai
      and the dogs. Dated to beginning of
      fourth-cent. Subjoined to the decree is a
      later dedication by Euthydemos, priest
      of Asklepios, who first made an offering
      in the manner ordained. A yet later
      inscription on the other two sides
      contains references to Helios and
      Mnemosyne. Found along east shore of
      Zea.

27   *IG* II² 47. Decree passed by the demos at
      the instigation of the priest Euthydemos
      dated to beginning of fourth-cent.
      regarding *prothumata* to Asklepios which
      are to be paid for out of the income from

a *lithotomeion*. It is preceded by a survey of medical instruments in the Asklepieion.

28   *IG* II² 4453. Dedication to Asklepios and Hygieia. From south slope of Mounychia Hill.

29   Ionic column base inscribed '*Askle [piou]*'. See Gurlitt (1890, 210 n.14).

30   *IG* II² 4529. Dedication to 'Mounychian Asklepios and Hygieia' dated to second or third cent. A.D.

31   *IG* II² 4527. Dedication to 'Asklepios Epekoos' dated to second or third cent. A.D.

32   *IG* II² 2963 = *SIG*³ 1110. Decree of thanks by Paianistai of Mounychian Asklepios dated A.D. 212/3

33   *IG* II² 4537. Dedication to 'Asklepios(?) and Hygieia(?)'. Undated. Found east of Zea.

Athene Eetioneia   34   *IG* II² 5120. Possible reference to '*Athenas Ee[tioneias]*'. Found in Athens.

Athene Skiras   35   *IG* II² 1177.10. Reference to Skira festival.

Baal or Bel(?)   36   *IG* II² 2946 = Cooke (1903, no. 33) = Gibson (1982, no. 41) = Renan (1888, 5). A bilingual inscription (upper part Phoenician, lower part Greek) erected by a *koinon* of Sidonians to an unknown deity who is most probably Baal. The Phoenician text states that it was erected 'in the 14th year of the people of Sidon', which should be 96 B.C. The Greek text, however, is dated by letter-forms to the late third or early second cent. B.C., and it may be, as Gibson has suggested, that there was an earlier era of Sidon of which we have no record. The Phoenician text, which is more extensive than the Greek, states that the vestibule of the temple was erected by a certain Shama'abaal. It is probable that the inscription was set into the temple wall. It was found just to the west of Eetioneia.

Bendis   37   *IG* I³ 383.143 = I² 310.208. Treasury Accounts of the Other Gods for the year 429/8.

38   *IG* I³ 136 = *SEG* X 64 = *LSGS* 6 = Ferguson (1949,134f.) = Bingen (1959,

31ff.). Decree of Athenian boule and ekklesia regarding public worship of Bendis. Dated by Bingen and Lewis to 413/2, but it may have been passed any time between 431 and 411. It makes provision (29f.) for a priest(?) to be elected *[ex Athena]iôn hapantôn*. The public cult of Bendis was probably served by both a priest and priestess, as was the case in the private cult. There is an isolated reference (l. 27) to a night festival (*pannuchis*). From Mounychia Hill.

39   *IG* II² 1361 = *SEG* XXV 167 = *LSG* 45. Decree of citizen *orgeônes* of Bendis levying a fee of 2 dr. on each member 'for the sacrifice'. Dated to fourth cent. That the decree refers to worship of Bendis has to be inferred from a reference to 16 Thargelion, three days before celebration of Bendideia. It indicates that membership was originally hereditary (l. 2), but will henceforth be open to all on payment of the requisite fee (20ff.). There is reference to the repair of the *hieron* and of a house attached thereto.

40   *IG* II² 1255. Decree of citizen *orgeônes* of Bendis honouring their *hieropoioi*, dated 337/6.

41   *IG* II² 1496 = *Hesperia* 9 (328ff.) = *SIG³* 1029 = *SEG* XII 98. Treasury Accounts regarding money accruing from sale of sacrificial pelfs. Ll. 86f. and 117 refer to Bendideia. Dated 334/3-331/0.

42   *IG* II² 1256 = *SIG³* 1095. Decree of Thracian *orgeônes* of Bendis honouring their *epimelêtai*, dated 329/8. The *stêlê* carries a representation of Bendis and Deloptes.

43   *IG* II² 1283 = *SEG* XXV 99 = *SEG* XXIX 136 = *LSG* 46. See Gauthier (1979, 396f.). Decree of Thracian *orgeônes* of Bendis resident in the Piraeus dated to 261/0. It lays down procedures for celebration of the *pompê* jointly with Thracian *orgeônes* in the Asty and for reception of latter in Piraeus. The *orgeônes* in the Asty will henceforth enjoy reciprocal rights of membership (ll.

29ff.). There is also a reference to a grant of *enktêsis* given exclusively to the Thracian *ethnos* by the demos (4ff.). From the Zanneion.

44 *IG* II² 1284. Decrees of Thracian *orgeônes* of Bendis honouring their officers. Since the proposer of one of the decrees, Sosias son of Hipokratos, was the proposer of no. 43, these, too, should be dated *c.* 261/0.

45 *IG* II² 1317. Decree of *thiasôtai* of Bendis honouring their treasurer, *epimelêtai* and secretary. Found on Salamis.

46 *IG* II² 1324. Decree of Thracian *orgeônes* of Bendis and Deloptes honouring Stephanos as *epimelêtês*. Dated late fourth or early third cent. (Dow, *HThR* 37 p. 197 n. 54). From the Zanneion.

Charites 47 Votive relief dated *c.* 500. See Mitropoulou (1977a, no. 18 with fig. 36), Furtwängler (*AM* 3 [1878] 189) and Farnell (1909, V p. 430).

Demeter 48 Appendix II no. 1. Decree of deme of Piraeus dated to end of 4th cent. ordering demarch and priestess to ensure that unauthorised *thiasoi* do not carry out illegal sacrifices, cause pollution, etc., in the Thesmophorion.

Dionysos 49 Athens NM 1500. Votive relief dedicated to Dionysos and Paideia dated to end of fifth cent. (Fig. 23)

50 *IG* II² 1496 = *SEG* XII 98 = *SIG*³ 1029 = *Hesperia* 9 (328ff.). Treasury Accounts dated 334/3 to 331/0 regarding money accruing from sale of sacrificial pelfs. Ll. 70f., 136(?) and 144f. refer to 'the Dionysia in the Piraeus'.

51 *IG* II² 1672. Accounts of *epistatai* of Eleusinian Mysteries, dated 329/8, recording that they have contributed to a sacrifice at the Dionysia in the Piraeus.

52 *IG* II² 380 = *SIG*³ 313 = *SEG* XXI 307 = Oikonomides, *Platon* 8 (1956) 117f. no. 12. Public decree concerning the *agoranomoi*, dated 320/19. Ll. 20f. contain references to *pompê* 'in honour of Zeus Soter and Dionysos'.

53 *IG* II² 456. Decree honouring

Kolophonian ambassadors, dated 307/6. Ll. 32f. refer to 'the Piraeic Dionysia'.

54   *IG* II² 1008.13f. Ephebic decree dated 118/7 referring to ephebes sacrificing a bull at temple of Dionysos in the Piraeus.

55   *Hesperia* 16, p. 171. Ephebic decree dated 116/5 referring to ephebes escorting a statue of Dionysos to theatre of Dionysos in the Piraeus and performing a sacrifice there.

56   *IG* II² 1011.12f. Ephebic decree dated 107/6 referring to ephebes dedicating a *phialê* costing 100 dr. at temple of Dionysos in the Piraeus.

57   *IG* II² 1028.16f. Ephebic decree dated 100/99 referring to ephebes sacrificing a bull at temple of Dionysos in the Piraeus.

58   *IG* II² 1029.11f. Ephebic decree dated 94/93 referring to ephebes sacrificing a bull at temple of Dionysos in the Piraeus.

59   *IG* II² 1039.54f. Ephebic decree dated 83-73 referring to ephebes sacrificing at the Dionysia.

Dionysiastai   60   *IG* II² 1325 = *SIG*³ 1100. Two decrees of *orgeônes* of Dionysos in honour of their treasurer and priest Dionysios and another official, dated *c.* 185/4. One of the decrees is prefaced by a list of 15 members. Found between Grand Harbour and Zea.

61   *IG* II² 1326 = *LSG* 49 = *SEG* XXV 160 = Ferguson (1944, 115-19) = *SIG*³ 1101. Decree of *orgeônes* of Dionysos passed on death of Dionysios in *c.* 176/5 conferring priesthood on his eldest surviving son, Agathokles. There is a reference to heroisation (*aphierôsis*) of Dionysios (line 46). Found between Grand Harbour and Zea.

62   *IG* II² 2948. Poem dated to beg. of second cent. in honour of Dionysios who had erected a temple (*naon*), shrine (*temenos*) and statues (*xoana*) to god Dionysos. Dionysios is invoked as protector of the *thiasos*. Found between Grand Harbour and Zea.

Eetion Hero(?)	63	*SEG* X 330. Cf. Andrewes (*JHS* 81 [1961] 11). Dedication by '*thiasos* of Etionidai', dated *c.* 450. Found between Moschaton and Piraeus.
Eurymedon Hero	64	*IG* II² 4567. Dedication to Eurymedon Hero. Dated to first half of fourth cent. See *RE* s.v.
Hekate	65	Hsch. s.v. *Zea* suggests that there might have been a cult of Hekate in the Piraeus.
Helios	66	See no. 26.
Helios & Mithras	67	*SEG* XXIX 197. Dedication on poros altar to Helios and Mithras.
Herakles	68	*SEG* XXVIII 232. Votive relief depicting Herakles Alexikakos and Hermes beside a small shrine, dated *c.* 350.
Hermes	69	*IG* I² 826. Fifth cent. votive offering to Hermes. Found to west of Eetioneia in Krommydarou Bay.
	70	See no. 26.
	71	*SIG*³ 719. Dedication by three '*stratêgoi hoi epi ton Peiraia*' to Hermes Hegemonios, 95/4.
Hermes & Nymphs	72	NM 1447. Votive relief in the form of a cave depicting Hermes and the Nymphs, the head of Acheloos and an altar. Dated *c.* 300. Found on Mounychia.
Hestia	73	Appendix II no. 6.37f. Reference to the *hieron* of Hestia in a Piraeus deme decree dated after *c.* 261.
Isis	74	See no. 6.
Men	75	*IG* II² 4685 = Lane, *Berytus* 15 (1964) 8 no. 6. Dedication of *hieron* to Men by Dionysios and Babylia, dated third cent.
	76	*IG* II² 4687a = Lane, *Berytus* 15 (1964) 8 no. 7 = Robert, *BCH* 60 (1936) 206f. Dedication to Men, dated to late third cent. Attributed to Piraeus.
Mnemosyne	77	See no. 26.
Moirai	78	*IG* II² 4971 = *LSG* 22. Fragmentary law dated to 4th cent. regarding offerings of cakes to Moirai. Probably from Asklepieion in Piraeus. Cf. no. 25.
	79	See no. 25.
Mother of the Gods	80	*IG* II² 4563. Dedication to the Mother of the Gods, dated to first half of fourth cent. Possibly from Piraeus.
	81	*IG* II² 6288 = Conze 95/37 = Clairmont (1970, no. 26 pl. 13). Gravestone of

Chairestrate of Ikaria, described as 'attendant (*propolos*) and revered priestess (*geraira*) of the Mother who bears all things (*mêtros pantotechnou*)', dated 350-317. On her right stands a girl proffering a large circular object probably to be identified as a *tumpanon*.

82 Piraeus Museum no. 217 = Möbius 1968, pl. 24a. Gravestone of Nikomache shown as a seated woman clasping a giant *tumpanon*, dated 350/17.

83 *IG* II² 4609. Dedication dated to the end of fourth cent.

84 *IG* II² 4671. Dedication to Agdistis and Attis, dated to fourth or third cent.

85 *IG* II² 1316. Decree of votaries of 'the Goddess' in honour of their priestess and her husband, dated to mid-third cent. In text of decree, votaries call themselves *orgeônes*, whereas in crowns carved above and below they are referred to as *thiasôtai*.

86 *IG* II² 1273 = *SEG* XXVIII 108 = *SEG* XXX 96. Decree of *thiasôtai* of the Mother of the Gods in honour of their benefactors. Oikonomides (*ZPE* 32 [1978] 85f.) dates it 'most probably' to 222/1 . Cf. Habicht (*ZPE* 39 [1980] 1-5). From southern part of Piraeus peninsula.

87 *IG* II² 1301. Decree of votaries (*thiasôtai* or *orgeônes*) of 'the Goddess(?)' in honour of religious officials, dated *c.* 222/1. There is reference to a kitchen (*mageireion*) in need of repair (line 4f.).

88 *IG* II² 1314. Decree of *orgeônes* of 'the Goddess' in honour of their priestess, dated c. 213/2. From 'the Mills'.

89 *IG* II² 1315. Decree of *orgeônes* of 'the Goddess' in honour of their priestess and her husband(?), dated 211/0. They are commended for performing the *eisitêtêria*, the *strôsis* and 'both the Attideia'. The last-named expression is not fully understood, cf. Deubner (1932, 232) and Ferguson (1944, 140).

90 *IG* II² 1327. Decreee of *orgeônes* of 'the Gods' in honour of their treasurer, dated *c.* 178/7. There is reference to a burial fund (lines 10ff.) to which the treasurer

made a private contribution. From southern part of Piraeus peninsula.

91   *IG* II² 1328 = *LSG* 48. Decree of *orgeônes* of 'the Goddess' regarding economy measures to be introduced in order to release the priestess from supplementary expenses to which, up till now, she had been liable. A second decree concerns the appointment of a *zakoros* for life. The first is dated *c.* 183/2, the second *c.* 175/4.

92   *IG* II² 1329 = *SIG*³ 1102. Decree of *orgeônes* of 'the Goddesses' in honour of their secretary, dated 175/4. There is an interesting reference to his *philanthrôpa* to *hoi dêmotikoi* (l. 14).

93   *IG* II² 2950/1. Dedication dated 2nd cent.

94   *IG* II² 1334. Decree of *orgeônes* of 'the Goddess' in honour of their priestess, dated to end of second cent. Found on Melos, but carved in Piraeic stone.

95   *IG* II² 4703. Dedication dated before mid-first cent.

96   *IG* II² 4714. Dedication to 'the Mother of the Gods and the gracious midwife Aphrodite', dated to beginning of Augustan principate.

97   *IG* II² 4760. Dedication to 'the Mother of the Gods, gracious midwife', dated first or second cent. A.D.

98   *IG* II² 4579. Dedication to 'the Mother of the Gods, gracious midwife', dated to second cent. A.D.(?).

Mounychos Hero   99   *IG* II² 4590. Dedication to Mounychos, dated to mid-fourth cent. Found 'behind the church of Aghios Konstantinos'.

Nergal   100   Cooke (1903, no. 35). Bilingual funerary inscription (upper part Greek, lower part Phoenician), probably dated to third cent., erected by the chief priest of Nergal to commemorate his deceased daughter.

Nymphs   101   No. 43.18 contains a reference to a Nymphaion.

Paralos Hero   102   *IG* II² 2966. Dedication by Paraloi dated *c.* 350.

103   *IG* II² 1254. Honorific decree passed by Paraloi after *c.* 350. Found on Mahdia shipwreck.

	104	Dain (*REG* 44 [1931] 296-301). Honorific decree passed by Paraloi after *c*. 350.
Phreatos Hero	105	Harp. s.v. *en Phreattôi* alleges that Phreatos was the eponymous hero of Phreattys.
Poseidon	106	*SEG* XXVI 72.46f. Reference to a *stêlê* of Poseidon in the Piraeus, dated 375/4.
Proerosioi	107	Appendix II no. 1.7 contains a reference to the Plerosia festival, dated *c*. 350.
Sabazios	108	*IG* II² 2932. Dedication by *hieropoioi*, presumably of Sabaziastai, dated 342/1. From same find-spot as no. 109.
	109	*IG* II² 1335 = Lane (1985, 24-6 no. 51). Decree of Sabaziastai recording the names of their members (*eranistai*). 51 names appear in all, 12 of whom are foreigners. It is possible that those *eranistai* whose place of origin is not stated are slaves. Dated 102/1.
Sarapis	110	*IG* II² 1292 = *SIRIS* 2 = Dow (1937, 188f.). Decree of Sarapiastai in honour of their *tamias*, *grammateus*, *epimelêtês* and *proeranistria* (priestess?), dated 215/4. The decree ends with list of members (without patronymics or demotics). Either from Athens or Piraeus.
	111	*IG* II² 4692 = *SIRIS* 3. Joint dedication to Sarapis and Isis, dated to 2nd cent. From Athens.
Serangos Hero	112	Hsch. and Phot. s.v. *Sêrangeion* allege that Serangos was the eponymous hero of the Serangeion.
Tetrakomoi	113	*IG* II² 3103. Inscription recording victory by a team from the deme of Xypete in contest organised by Tetrakomoi (viz. Piraeus, Phaleron, Xypete and Thymaitadai). Dated 330/29.
Tyche	114	*IG* I² 827 in non-Attic (Chalkidikian?) lettering. Cf. no. 2. See further Solders (1931, 70).
Zeus Labraundos	115	*IG* II² 1271. Decreee of *thiasôtai* of Zeus Labraundos, honouring their *tamias* for supervising the addition of a portico (*prostôïon*) and pediment (*aetôma*) to the already existing *hieron* and for contributing to the expenses out of his own pocket.
Zeus Meilichios	116-123	*IG* II² 4617-22, 4569 and 4847. Dedications to Zeus Meilichios dated

		mainly to fourth cent. In some cases the god is represented in the form of an erect snake.
Zeus Philios	124-128	*IG* II² 4622-25 and 4845-6. Dedications to Zeus Philios dated mainly to fourth cent. In some cases the god is represented in the form of an erect snake.
Zeus Soter	129	*IG* I² 128. Public decree levying tax of 1dr. on every ship which docked in Piraeus, to be deposited by *nauklêroi* in sanctuary of Zeus Soter(?). Dated 428/7. Found 'almost in middle of isthmus between Zea and Piraeus'.
	130	*IG* II² 1669. Account of works carried out on temple, sanctuary and altar(?) of Zeus Soter, dated after middle of fourth cent.
	131	*IG* II² 1496 = *SIG*³ 1029 = *Hesperia* 9, 328f. = *SEG* XII 98. Treasury Accounts dated 334/3 to 331/0 regarding money accruing from sale of sacrificial pelfs. Ll. 88f. and 118f. refer to a sacrifice of bulls in honour of Zeus Soter.
	132	*IG* II² 4603. Dedication to Zeus Soter dated to end of fourth cent. From inlet of Krommydarou, west of Eetioneia.
	133	*IG* II² 4972. Dedication to Hermes and Zeus Soter, dated to end of fourth cent.
	134	*IG* II² 783. Bouleutic decree honouring 'the priest of Zeus Soter in the Piraeus and the *epimelêtai*' for sacrificing to Zeus Soter and Athene Soteira, Asklepios, Hygieia and the other gods. The inscription is dated by Meritt (*Hesperia* 3 [1934] 30) to 163/2.
	135	*IG* II² 1006. Ephebic decree dated 122/1. L. 30 refers to naval race by ephebes from Megas Limen to Mounychia Port performed at Diisoteria. This is the earliest reference to festival by name.
	136	*IG* II² 1008. Ephebic decree dated 118/7. Line 21 refers to ephebic participation in Diisoteria.
	137	*IG* II² 1030. Ephebic decree dated after 94/3. Line 23 refers to sacrifice of bull to Zeus Soter.
	138	See no. 2. Ll. 15ff. state that copy of inscription was to be deposited in sanctuary of Zeus Soter and Athene Soteira in Piraeus.

Zeus Xenios

Zeus

Unindentified thiasoi

Unidentified cults

139   *IG* II² 1954. Catalogue of soldiers. L. 2 is restored to contain a reference to Zeus Soter. Dated 306/5.

140   *IG* II² 1012. Bouleutic decree honouring treasurer of *sunodos* of *nauklêroi* and *emporoi* of Zeus Xenios. Dated 112/1. Possibly from Piraeus.

141   *IG* II² 4602 = *SIG*³ 1154. Dedication to Zeus dated to 4th cent.

142   *IG* II² 2945. Dedication to 'the Gods' by officers of *thiasos*(?), dated to 3rd or 2nd cent. Found 'beside the mill at top of peninsula'. Cf. no. 90.

143   *IG* II² 1275 = *LSGS* 126 = Tod (1906-1907, 328ff.). Thiasotic burial ordinance from Phaleron dated late 3rd or early 2nd cent.

144   *IG* II² 1262. Thiasotic decree honouring *epimelêtai* dated 301/0.

145   *IG* II² 1263. Thiasotic decree honouring *grammateus*, dated 300/299. Found 'at the mills'.

146   *IG* II² 1271. Thiasotic decree dated 298/7 honouring *tamias*. Probably from Piraeus.

147   *IG* II² 2943. Thiasotic decree honouring *epimelêtês* and *grammateus* dated third cent.

148   *IG* II² 1039.55. Reference to festival known as Peiraia.

149   *IG* II² 4589. Dedication dated to mid-fourth cent. possibly from Piraeus.

150   *IG* II² 4600. Dedication to 'the hero As...', dated after mid-fourth cent.

151   *IG* II² 2945. Dedication to 'gods', dated third or second cent. From 'beside the mill at the highest point of the peninsula'. Cf. no. 142.

152   *IG* II² 4935. Dedication to unknown goddess, dated second or first cent.

153   *IG* II² 4951. Dedication to 'Eu ...'. Found 'above the ancient Emporion'.

154   NM 1434. Dedication to 'the god' in the form of a snake by Herakleides.

155   *IG* II² 2952. Dedication by *emporoi* and *nauklêroi* in honour of an unknown deity on behalf of Argeios, strategos of the Piraeus. Cf. no. 5.

156-   Mitropoulou (1977, 211-6 and figs.
167   114-24) lists 12 votive reliefs from

Piraeus of an unidentified god or hero in the form of a snake.

168   *IG* I³ 242 = Papagiannopoulos-Palaios, *Polemon* 3 (1947-48) 17-19 = *SEG* XII 4. Sacred law dated 490-80. Cf. Whitehead (1986, no. 84).

From *IG* II² 1006.28f. and 71, 1008.17f. and 1028.27, it seems likely that there was a cult of Zeus Tropaios and the Megaloi Theoi in the Piraeus.

Bibliography

Alexandri 1973-4   O. Alexandri. 'Peiraieus', pp. 98-103 and 144-56 in *AD* 29 B1 (1973-4).

Alexandri 1975   O. Alexandri. 'Peiraias', pp. 29-35 in *AD* 30 B1 (1975).

Alexandri 1976   O. Alexandri. 'Peiraias', pp. 44-50 in *AD* 31 B1 (1976).

von Alten 1881   G. von Alten. 'Die Befestigungen der Hafenstadt Athens', pp. 10-22 in Curtius and Kaupert (1881).

Ampolo 1982   C. Ampolo. 'Le cave de pietra dell'Attici: problemi giuridici ed economici', pp. 251-60 in *OPUS* 1 (1982).

Andreiomenou 1961-2   A. Andreiomenou. 'Peiraieus', p. 43 in *AD* 17 B1 (1961-2).

Amit 1965   M. Amit. *Athens and the Sea: a Study in Athenian Sea-Power*. Brussels 1965.

Andrewes 1937   'Athens and Aegina 510-480 B.C.', pp. 1-7 in *BSA* 37 (1937).

Angelopoulos 1898   E. Angelopoulos. *Peri Peiraiôs limenôn autou kata tous archaious chronous*. Athens 1898.

Ashton 1977   N.G. Ashton. 'The naumachia near Amorgos in 322 B.C.', pp. 1-11 in *BSA* 72 (1977).

Atallah 1966   W. Atallah. *Adonis dans la littérature et l'art grec*. Paris 1966.

ATL   B.D. Meritt, H.T. Wade-Gery and M.F. McGregor. *The Athenian Tribute Lists*. 4 vols. Cambridge, Mass. 1939-53.

Austin 1981   M.M. Austin. *The Hellenistic World from Alexander to the Roman Conquest: a Selection of Ancient Sources in Translation*. Cambridge 1981.

Austin and Vidal-Naquet 1977   M.M. Austin and P. Vidal-Naquet. *Economic and Social History of Ancient Greece*. London 1977.

Baba   K. Baba. 'On Kerameikos Inv. I 388 (*SEG* XXII.79): a note on the formation of the Athenian metic-status', pp. 1-5 in *BSA* 79 (1984).

Barron 1983   J.P. Barron. 'The fifth-century *horoi* of Aegina', pp. 1-12 in *JHS* 103 (1983).

Barthes 1957   R. Barthes. *Mythologies*. First ed. 1957. Selected and translated by A. Lavers. London 1972.

Bass 1966   G.F. Bass. *Archaeology under Water*. London 1966.

Bauer 1881   A. Bauer. *Themistokles*. Merseburg 1881.

Behrend 1970   D. Behrend. *Attische Pachturkunden*. Munich 1970.

Beloch 1890   J. Beloch. 'Wann lebten Alkaeos und Sappho?', pp. 465-73 in *RM* 45 (1890).

Beloch 1925   K.J. Beloch. *Griechische Geschichte*. Berlin and Leipzig 1925.

Bengston 1939   H. Bengston. 'Einzelpersohnlichkeit und Athenische Stadt', pp. 216ff. in *Sitz. Bayr. Acad.* 1939.

Bengston 1954   H. Bengston. 'Thasos und Themistokles', pp. 485f. in *Historia* 2 (1954).

Berthold 1980   'Fourth-century Rhodes', pp. 32-49 in *Historia* 29 (1980).

Bieber 1961   M. Bieber. *The History of the Greek and Roman Theatre*. Princeton 1961.

Billheimer 1922   A. Billheimer. *Naturalization in Athenian Law and Practice*. Gettysburg 1922.

Bingen 1959   J. Bingen. 'Le décret *SEG* X 64 (Le Pirée, 413/2?)', pp. 31-44 in *RBPh* 37 (1959).

Blackman 1968   D.J. Blackman. 'The shipsheds', pp. 181-92 in Morrison and Williams (1968).

Blackman 1969   D.J. Blackman. 'The Athenian navy and allied naval contributions in the Pentekontaetia', pp. 179-216 in *GRBS* 10.3 (1969).

Boardman 1975   J. Boardman. *Athenian Red-figure Vases: the Archaic Period*. Thames and Hudson, London 1975.

Boardman 1980   J. Boardman. *The Greeks Overseas: their Early Colonies and Trade*. Thames and Hudson, London 1980.

Boeckh 1840   A. Boeckh. *Urkunden über das Seewesen des attischen Staates*. Berlin 1840.

Boegehold 1976   A.L. Boegehold. 'Ten distinctive ballots: the law court in Zea', pp. 7-19 in *CSCA* 9 (1976).

Boersma 1970   J.S. Boersma. *Athenian Building Policy from 561/0 to 405/4 B.C.* Groningen 1970.

Bogaert 1968   R. Bogaert. *Banques et banquiers dans les cités grecques*. Leyden 1968.

Bogaert 1976   R. Bogaert. 'L'essai des monnais dans l'antiquité', pp. 20-4 in *RBN* 1976.

Bonner and Smith 1938   R.J. Bonner and G. Smith. *The Administration of Justice from Homer to Aristotle*. Chicago 1938.

Bradeen 1974   D.W. Bradeen. *The Athenian Agora* vol. 17: 'Inscriptions: the Funerary Monuments'. Princeton 1974.

Bradford 1956   J. Bradford. 'Fieldwork on aerial discoveries in Attica and Rhodes: Part I, the town plan of classical Rhodes', pp. 57-69 in *AntJ* 36 (1956).

Brady 1935   T.A. Brady. 'The reception of the Egyptian cults by the Greeks (330-30 B.C.)': *Univ. Missouri Studies* 10. Columbia 1935.

Brady 1938   T.A. Brady. *Repertory of Statuary and Figured Monuments relating to the Cult of the Egyptian Gods*. Columbia 1938.

Braudel 1981   F. Braudel. *The Structures of Everyday Life*. Translated by S. Reynolds. London 1981.

Bravo 1983   B. Bravo. 'Le commerce des céréales', pp. 17-29 in *PCPhS* Supp. 8 (1983).

Briscoe 1973   J. Briscoe. *A Commentary on Livy Books XXXI-XXXIII*. Clarendon, Oxford 1973.

Briscoe 1978   J. Briscoe. 'The Antigonids and the Greek States', pp. 145-57 in Garnsey and Whittaker 1978.

Bruneau 1970   Ph. Bruneau. *Recherches sur les cultes de Délos à l'époque hellénistique et à l'époque impériale*. Paris 1970.

Brunt 1953-4   P.A. Brunt. 'The Hellenistic League against Persia', pp. 135-63 in *Historia* 2 (1953-4).

Bultrighini 1984   U. Bultrighini. 'Pausania 1.26.3 e la liberazione del Pireo', pp. 54-62, in *RivFC* 112 (1984).

Bundgaard 1957   J.A. Bundgaard. *Mnesicles: a Greek Architect at Work*. Copenhagen 1957.

Burford 1969   A. Burford. *The Greek Temple Builders at Epidauros*. Liverpool 1969.

Burkert 1985   W. Burkert. *Greek Religion: Archaic and Classical*. Translated by J. Raffan. Oxford 1985.

Burn 1966   A.R. Burn. 'Three thousand Acharnian hoplites', p. 376 in *Historia* 15 (1966).

Burns 1976   A. Burns. 'Hippodamus and the planned city', pp. 414-28 in *Historia* 25 (1976).

Bury-Meiggs 1975   J.B. Bury and R. Meiggs. *A History of Greece to the Death of Alexander the Great*. Fourth ed. London and Basingstoke 1975.

Busolt-Swoboda 1920-6   G. Busolt and H. Swoboda. *Griechische Staatskunde: Handbuch der Altertumswissenschaft* IV.1.1-2. 3rd ed. Munich 1920-6.

Buttrey 1979   T.V. Buttrey. 'The Athenian currency law of 375/4 B.C.', pp. 33-45 in *Greek Numismatics and Archaeology: Essays in honour of Margaret Thompson*. Wetteren 1979.

CAF   T. Kock (ed.). *Comicorum Atticorum Fragmenta*. 3 vols. Leipzig 1880-8.

CAH² VII.1 and 2   F.W. Walbank, A.E. Astin, M.W. Frederikson and R.M. Ogilvie (eds.). *Cambridge Ancient History*. 2nd ed. Cambridge 1984.

Camp 1979   J.M. Camp II. 'A drought in the late eighth century B.C.', pp. 397-411 in *Hesperia* 48 (1979).

Carpenter 1966   R. Carpenter. *Discontinuity in Greek Civilisation*. Cambridge 1966.

Cartledge 1983   P. Cartledge. '*Trade and Politics* revisited: Archaic Greece', pp. 1-15 in Garnsey, Hopkins and Whittaker 1983.

Cartledge and Harvey 1985   P. Cartledge and F.D. Harvey. *Crux: Essays presented to G.E.M. de Ste. Croix on his 75th Birthday*. Exeter 1985.

Caskey 1982   J.L. Caskey. 'Koroni and Keos', pp. 14-16 in *Hesperia* Supp. 19 (1982).

Casson 1950   L. Casson. 'The *Isis* and her voyage', pp. 43-56 in *TAPhA* 81 (1950).

Casson 1954   L. Casson. 'The grain trade of the Hellenistic world', pp. 168-87 in *TAPhA* 85 (1954).

Casson 1956   L. Casson. 'The size of ancient merchant ships', pp. 231-8 in *Studi in Onore di Aristide Calderini e Roberto Paribeni*. Milan 1956.

Casson 1971   L. Casson. *Ships and Seamanship in the Ancient World*. Princeton 1971.

Casson 1984   L. Casson. *Ancient Trade and Society*. Detroit 1984.

Castaglioni 1971   F. Castaglioni. *Orthogonal Town Planning in Antiquity*. Cambridge, Mass. and London 1971.

Catling 1984-5   H.W. Catling. 'Piraeus', p.9f. in *AR* 1984-5.

Cawkwell 1961   G.L. Cawkwell. 'The Common Peace of 366/5', pp. 80-6 in *CQ* n.s. 11 (1961).

Cawkwell 1962   G.L. Cawkwell. 'Notes on the Social War', pp. 38-49 in *C&M* 23 (1962).

Cawkwell 1963   G.L. Cawkwell. 'Eubulus', pp. 47-67 in *JHS* 83 (1963).

Cawkwell 1973   G.L. Cawkwell. 'The foundation of the Second Athenian Confederacy', pp. 47-60 in *CQ* n.s. 23 (1973).

Cawkwell 1976   G.L. Cawkwell. 'The imperialism of Thrasybulus', pp. 270-7 in *CQ* n.s. 26 (1976).

Cawkwell 1981   G.L. Cawkwell. 'Notes on the failure of the Second Athenian Confederacy', pp. 40-55 in *JHS* 101 (1981).

Cawkwell 1981a   G.L. Cawkwell. 'The King's Peace', pp. 69-83 in *CQ* n.s. 31 (1981).

Cawkwell 1984   G.L. Cawkwell. 'Athenian Naval Power in the Fourth Century', pp. 334-45 in *CQ* n.s. 34 (1984).

Cirio 1980   A. Cirio. 'Due iscrizioni del Sigeo e la cronologia dei poeti eolici', pp. 108-12 in *BollClass* 3.1 (1980).

Clairmont 1970   C.W. Clairmont. *Gravestone and Epigram*. Mainz-on-Rhine 1970.

Clerc 1893   M. Clerc. *Les métèques athéniens.* Paris 1893.

Clerc 1898   M. Clerc. 'De la condition des étrangers domiciliés dans les différentes cités grecques', *Revue des Universités du Midi* n.s. 4 (1898).

Clinton 1971   K. Clinton. 'Inscriptions from Eleusis', pp. 81-136 in *AE* 1971.

Cloché 1911   P. Cloché. 'Les expulsions en Attique avant la prise de Phylé', pp. 63-76 in *REG* 24 (1911).

Cloché 1915   P. Cloché. *La restauration démocratique à Athènes en 403 avant J.-C.* Paris 1915.

Cohen 1973   E.E. Cohen. *Ancient Athenian Maritime Courts.* Princeton 1973.

Coldstream 1968   J.N. Coldstream. *Greek Geometric Pottery.* London 1968.

Coldstream 1977   J.N. Coldstream. *Geometric Greece.* London 1977.

Cole 1984   S.G. Cole. *Theoi Megaloi: the Cult of the Great Gods at Samothrace.* Leiden 1984.

Conze no./pl.   A. Conze. *Die attischen Grabreliefs.* Berlin 1893-1922.

Cook 1925   A.B. Cook. *Zeus: a Study in Ancient Religion.* 2 vols. Cambridge 1925.

Cooke 1903   G.A. Cooke. *Textbook of North Semitic Inscriptions.* 1903.

Cosi 1980-1   D.M. Cosi. 'L'ingresso di Cibele ad Atene e Roma', pp. 81-91 in *Atti* 11 (1980-1).

Coulton 1974   J.J. Coulton. 'Lifting in early Greek architecture', pp. 1-19 in *JHS* 94 (1974).

Coulton 1976   J.J. Coulton. *The Architectural Development of the Greek Stoa.* Oxford, Clarendon 1976.

Coulton 1977   J.J. Coulton. *Greek Architects at Work: Problems of Structure and Design.* Cornell 1977.

Crawford 1972   M.H. Crawford. 'Solon's alleged reforms of weights and measures', pp. 5-8 in *Eirene* 10 (1972).

de Ste. Croix 1972   G.E.M. de Ste. Croix. *The Origins of the Peloponnesian War.* London 1972.

de Ste. Croix 1981   G.E.M. de Ste. Croix. *The Class Struggle in the Ancient Greek World.* London 1981.

Crouch 1984   D. Crouch. 'The Hellenistic water systems of Morgantina, Sicily: contributions to the history of urbanization', pp. 353-65 in *AJA* 88.3 (1984).

Culley 1973   G.R. Culley. *The Restoration of Sacred Monuments in Augustan Athens: IG II/III² 1035.* Ph.D dissertation, Univ. of N. Carolina. (A copy of this dissertation may be consulted in the library of the American School of Classical Studies at Athens).

Culley 1975   G.R. Culley. 'The restoration of sanctuaries in Attica', pp. 207-23 in *Hesperia* 44 (1975).

Culley 1977   G.R. Culley. 'The restoration of sanctuaries in Attica: part II', pp. 282-98 in *Hesperia* 46 (1977).

Curtius 1868   E. Curtius. *Sieben Karten zur Topographie von Athen.* Gotha 1868.

Curtius and Kaupert 1881   E. Curtius and J.A. Kaupert. *Karten von Attika* Heft I. Berlin 1881.

Dain 1931   A. Dain. 'Inscriptions attiques trouvées dans les fouilles sous-marines de Mahdia', pp. 290-303 in *REG* 44 (1931).

Dain 1933   A. Dain. *Inscriptions grecques du Musée du Bardo.* Paris 1933.

Daux 1960   G. Daux. 'Le Pirée: trouvailles fortuites', pp. 647-55 in *BCH* 84 (1960).

Daux 1963   G. Daux. 'La grande Démarchie: un nouveau calendrier sacrificiel d'Attique (Erchia)', pp. 603-34 in *BCH* 87 (1963).

Daux 1983　G. Daux. 'Le calendrier de Thorikos au Musée J. Paul Getty', pp. 150-74 in *L'Antiquité Classique* 52 (1983).

Davaras 1979　K. Davaras. *Sounion*. Athens 1979.

Davies 1969　J.K. Davies. 'The date of *IG* II² 1609', pp. 309-33 in *Historia* 18 (1969).

Davies 1971　J.K. Davies. *Athenian Propertied Families*. Clarendon, Oxford 1971.

Davies 1981　J.K. Davies. *Wealth and the Power of Wealth in Classical Athens*. New Hampshire 1981 (1984).

Day 1927　J. Day. 'The *Kôphos Limên* of the Piraeus', pp. 443-9 in *AJA* 31 (1927).

Day 1932　J. Day. 'Cape Colias, Phalerum and the Phaleric Wall', pp. 1-11 in *AJA* 36 (1932).

Day 1942　J. Day. *An Economic History of Athens under Roman Domination*. Columbia 1942.

Deubner 1932　L. Deubner. *Attische Feste*. Berlin 1932.

DHR　R. Dareste, B. Haussoulier and Th. Reinach. *Recueil des inscriptions juridiques grecques*. 2 vols. Rome 1965.

Dickie 1973　W.W. Dickie. 'Thucydides 1.93.3', pp. 758-9 in *Historia* 22 (1973).

Diepolder 1931　H. Diepolder. *Die attischen Grabreliefs des 5. und 4. Jahrhunderts v. Chr.* Berlin 1931.

Diller 1937　A. Diller. *Race Mixture among the Greeks before Alexander*. Illinois 1937.

Dinsmoor 1931　W.B. Dinsmoor. *The Archons of Athens in the Hellenistic Age*. Cambridge, Mass. 1931.

Dinsmoor 1950　W.B. Dinsmoor. *The Architecture of Ancient Greece*. 3rd ed. London 1950.

Dodds 1940　E.R. Dodds. 'Maenadism in the Bacchae', pp. 156-76 in *HThR* 33 (1940).

Dodds 1959　E.R. Dodds. *Commentary on Plato's Gorgias*. Oxford, Clarendon 1959.

Dodwell 1819　E. Dodwell. *A Classical Tour through Greece during the Years 1801, 1805 and 1806*. 2 vols. London 1819.

Donaldson 1965　M.K. Donaldson. 'A pebble mosaic in Peiraieus', pp. 77-88 in *Hesperia* 34 (1965).

Dontas 1982　G. Dontas. 'La grande Artémis du Pirée: une oeuvre d'Euphranor', pp. 15-34 in *AK* 25 (1982).

Dörpfeld 1883　W. Dörpfeld. 'Die Skeuothek des Philon', pp. 147-64 in *AM* 8 (1883).

Dörpfeld 1884　W. Dörpfeld. 'Ein antikes Bauwerk im Piräus', pp. 279-87 in *AM* 9 (1884).

Dow 1937　S. Dow 'Prytaneis': *Hesperia* Supp. 1 (1937).

Dow 1968　S. Dow. 'Six Athenian sacrificial calendars', pp. 170-86 in *BCH* 92 (1968).

Dow and Healey 1965　S. Dow and R.F. Healey. 'A sacred calendar of Eleusis', pp. 170-86 in *HThSt* 21 (1965).

Dragatsis 1886　I.Ch. Dragatsis. '*Anaskaphê en Peiraiei*', pp. 82-4 in *PAE* 1886.

Dragatsis 1897　I.Ch. Dragatsis. '*Anaskaphê en Peiraiei*', pp. 15f. in *PAE* 1897.

Dragatsis 1910　I.Ch. Dragatsis. *To Themistokleion*. Athens 1910.

Dragatsis 1925-6　I.Ch. Dragatsis. '*To en Peiraiei Sêrangeion*', pp. 1-8 in *AE* 1925-6.

Dragatsis 1928　I.Ch. Dragatsis. *To en Peiraiei Sêrangeion*. Athens 1928.

Dunbabin 1936-7　T.J. Dunbabin. '*Echthrê palaiê*', pp. 83-91 in *BSA* 37 (1936-7).

Duncan-Jones 1980　R.P. Duncan-Jones. 'Metic numbers in Periklean Athens', pp. 101-9 in *Chiron* 10 (1980).

Eadie and Ober 1985　J.W. Eadie and J. Ober. *The Craft of the Ancient Historian: Essays in Honour of Chester G. Starr*. New York and London 1985.

Edelstein 1945   E.J. and L. Edelstein. *Asclepius*. 2 vols. Baltimore 1945.

Edwards 1986   C. Edwards. *Greek Votive Reliefs to Pan and the Nymphs*. Ann Arbor 1986.

Efstratiades 1872   P. Efstratiades. *AE* 15 (1872) p. 400.

Eliot 1962   C.W.J. Eliot. 'Coastal demes of Attika: a study of the policy of Kleisthenes': *Phoenix* Supp. 5. Toronto 1962.

Erxleben 1975   E. Erxleben. 'Das Verhältnis des Handels zum Produktionsaufkommen in Attica im 5. und 4. Jahrhundert v.u. Z.', pp. 365-98 in *Klio* 57.2 (1975).

Fabricius 1882   E. Fabricius. 'Die Skeuothek des Philon', pp. 551-94 in *Hermes* 17 (1882).

FAC   J.M. Edmonds. *The Fragments of Attic Comedy*. 3 vols. Leiden 1959.

Falciai 1982   B. Falciai. *Ippodamo di Mileto*. Florence 1982.

Farnell 1896-1909   L.R. Farnell. *Cults of the Greek States*. 5 vols. London 1896-1909.

Ferguson 1911   W.S. Ferguson. *Hellenistic Athens*. London 1911.

Ferguson 1938   W.S. Ferguson. 'The Salaminioi of Heptaphylai and Sounion', pp. 1-76 in *Hesperia* 7 (1938).

Ferguson 1944   W.S. Ferguson. 'The Attic Orgeones', pp. 61-140 in *HThR* 37 (1944).

Ferguson 1949   W.S. Ferguson. 'Orgeonika', pp. 130-63 in *Hesperia* Supp. 8 (1949).

FGrH   F. Jacoby (ed.). *Die Fragmente der griechischen Historiker*. Leiden 1923-58.

Fiechter 1950   E.R. Fiechter. *Das Dionysos-theater in Athen*: vol. 4: 'Das Theater im Piraieus'. Stuttgart and Cologne 1950.

Figueira 1981   T.J. Figueira. *Aegina: Society and Politics*. New York 1981.

Figueira 1984   T.J. Figueira. 'Karl Polanyi and ancient Greek trade', pp. 15-30 in *AncW* 10 (1984).

Finley 1935   M.I. Finley. 'Emporos, naukleros and kapelos: prolegomena to the study of Athenian trade', pp. 320-36 in *CPh* 30 (1935).

Finley 1951   M.I. Finley. *Studies in Land and Credit in Ancient Athens, 500-200 B.C: the Horos Inscriptions*. New Jersey 1951.

Finley 1973   M.I. Finley. *The Ancient Economy*. London 1973.

Finley 1974   M.I. Finley (ed.). *Studies in Ancient Society*. London and Boston 1974.

Finley 1978   M.I. Finley. 'The fifth-century Athenian Empire: a balance sheet', pp. 103-26 in Garnsey and Whittaker (1978).

Finley 1981   M.I. Finley. *Economy and Society in Ancient Greece*. London 1981.

Fol and Marazov 1977   A. Fol and I. Marazov. *Thrace and the Thracians*. London 1977.

Fornara 1970   C.W. Fornara. 'The date of the Callias Decrees', pp. 85-96 in *GRBS* 11 (1970).

Fornara 1971   C.W. Fornara. 'Themistocles' archonship', pp. 534-40 in *Historia* 20 (1971).

Fornara   C.W. Fornara. *Archaic Times to the End of the Peloponnesian War*. Cambridge 1983.

Forrest 1966   W.G. Forrest. *The Emergence of Greek Democracy*. London 1966.

Foucart 1873   P. Foucart. *Des associations religieuses chez les Grecs*. Paris 1873.

Foucart 1883   P. Foucart. 'Bas-relief du Pirée: culte de Zeus Milichios', pp. 507-14 in *BCH* 7 (1883).

Foucart 1887   P. Foucart. 'Les fortifications du Pirée', pp. 129-44 in *BCH* 11 (1887).

Foucart 1907   P. Foucart. 'Constructions de Themistocle au Pirée et Salamine', pp. 177-86 in *Journal des Savants* 5 (1907).

Foxhall and Forbes 1982   L. Foxhall and H.A. Forbes. 'Sitometreia: the role of grain as a staple food in classical antiquity', pp. 41-90 in *Chiron* 12 (1982).

Fraser 1960   P.M. Fraser. 'Two studies on the cult of Sarapis in the Hellenistic world', pp. 1-54 in *OAth* 3 (1960).

Fraser 1970   P.M. Fraser. 'Greek-Phoenician bilingual inscriptions from Rhodes', pp. 31-6 in *BSA* 65 (1970).

Fraser 1972   P.M. Fraser. *Ptolemaic Alexandria*. 3 vols. Oxford, Clarendon 1972.

Fraser 1977   P.M. Fraser. *Rhodian Funerary Monuments*. Oxford, Clarendon 1977.

Fraser 1981   P.M. Fraser. Revue de C. Habicht *Untersuchungen zur politischen Geschichte im 3. Jahrhundert v. Chr.*, pp. 240-2 in *CR* 31 (1981).

Frazer 1898   J.G. Frazer. *Pausanias' Description of Greece*. 6 vols. London and New York 1898.

von Freeden 1983   J. von Freeden. *Oikia Kyrrêstou: Studien zum sogenannten Turm der Winde in Athen*. Rome 1983.

French 1957   A. French. 'Solon and the Megarian question', pp. 238-46 in *JHS* 77 (1957).

French 1964   A. French. *The Growth of the Athenian Economy*. London 1964.

Frost 1968   F.J. Frost. 'Themistocles' place in Athenian politics', pp. 105-24 in *CSCA* 1 (1968).

Frost 1984   F.J. Frost. 'The Athenian military before Cleisthenes', pp. 283-94 in *Historia* 33 (1984).

Fuchs 1959   W. Fuchs. *Die Vorbilder der neualtischer Reliefs*. Berlin 1959.

Fuchs 1963   W. Fuchs. *Der Schiffsfund von Mahdia*. Tübingen 1963.

Fuks 1953   A. Fuks. 'Notes on the Rule of the Ten at Athens in 403 B.C.', pp. 198-207 in *Mnemosyne* 4.4 (1953).

Gabbert 1983   J.J. Gabbert. 'The Grand Strategy of Gonatas and the Chremonidean War', pp. 129-36 in *AncW* 8 (1983).

Gardner 1881   P. Gardner. 'Boat-races among the Greeks', pp. 90-7 and 315-17 in *JHS* 2 (1881).

Garlan 1974   Y. Garlan. *Recherches de poliorcétique grecque*. Athens and Paris 1974.

Garlan 1975   Y. Garlan. *War in the Ancient World: a Social History*. London 1975.

Garland 1982   R.S.J. Garland. 'A first catalogue of Attic peribolos tombs', pp. 125-76 in *BSA* 77 (1982).

Garland 1984   R.S.J. Garland. 'Religious authority in archaic and classical Athens', pp. 75-123 in *BSA* 79 (1984).

Garnsey 1985   P.D.A. Garnsey. 'Grain for Athens', pp. 62-75 in Cartledge and Harvey 1985.

Garnsey, Hopkins and Whittaker 1983 P.D.A. Garnsey, K. Hopkins and C. Whittaker (eds.)   *Trade in the Ancient Economy*. Berkeley and Los Angeles 1983.

Garnsey and Whittaker 1978   P.D.A. Garnsey and C. Whittaker (eds.) *Imperialism in the Ancient World*. Cambridge 1978.

Garnsey and Whittaker 1983   P.D.A. Garnsey and C. Whittaker (eds.). 'Trade and famine in Classical Antiquity': *PCPhS* Supp. 8 (1983).

Gauthier 1971   P. Gauthier. 'Les xenoi dans les textes athéniens de la second moitié du 5ème siècle av. J.-C.', pp. 44-79 in *REG* 84 (1971).

Gauthier 1972   P. Gauthier. *Symbola: les étrangers et la justice dans les cités grecques*. Nancy 1972.

Gauthier 1975   P. Gauthier. 'Les ports de l'empire et l'agora athénienne: propos du Décret mégarien', pp. 498-503 in *Historia* 24 (1975).

Gauthier 1976   P. Gauthier. *Un commentaire historique des Poroi de Xénophon*. Geneva and Paris 1976.

Gauthier 1979   P. Gauthier. 'La réunification d'Athènes en 281 et les deux archontes Nicias', pp. 348-99 in *REG* 92 (1979).

Gauthier 1981   P. Gauthier. 'De Lysias à Aristote (Ath. pol. 51,4): le commerce du grain à Athènes et les fonctions des sitophylaques', pp. 5-28 in *RD* 59 (1981).

Gauthier 1982   P. Gauthier. 'Décret attique pour un commerçant', pp. 275-90 in *REG* 95 (1982).

Gauthier 1985   P. Gauthier. 'Les cités grecques et leurs bienfaiteurs (IVe-I^e siècle avant J.-C.)': *BCH* Supp. 12 (1985).

Geagan 1967   D.J. Geagan. 'The Athenian Constitution after Sulla', *Hesperia* Supp. 12 (1967).

Gerhardt 1933   P. Gerhardt. *Die attische Metoikie im vierten Jahrhundert*. Diss. Königsberg 1933.

von Gerkan 1924   A. von Gerkan. *Griechische Stadtanlage*. Berlin and Leipzig 1924.

Gernet 1909   L. Gernet. 'L'approvisionnement d'Athènes en blé au Ve et IVe siècles', pp. 271-391 in *Mélanges d'histoire ancienne*.

Gernet 1955   L. Gernet. 'Sur les actions commerciales en droit athénien', pp. 173-200 in *Droit et société dans la Grèce ancienne*. Paris 1955.

GHI   M.N. Tod. *Greek Historical Inscriptions*. 2 vols. Oxford, Clarendon 1946 and 1948.

Giangiulio 1982   L. Giangiulio. 'Edifici pubblici e culti', pp. 945-92 in *ASNS* 12.3 (1982).

Gibson 1982   J.C.L. Gibson. *Textbook of Syrian Semitic Inscriptions*. Vol. 3: 'Phoenician inscriptions'. Oxford, Clarendon 1982.

Ginouvès 1962   R. Ginouvès. *Balaneutike*. Paris 1962.

Giovanni 1975   A. Giovanni. 'Athenian currency in the late fifth and early fourth century B.C.', pp. 191-5 in *GRBS* 16 (1975).

Girouard 1985   M. Girouard. *Cities and People: a Social and Architectural History*. New Haven and London 1985.

Gomme, *HCT*   A.W. Gomme. *A Historical Commentary on Thucydides* Vols. I-III. Oxford 1956.

Gomme, Andrewes and Dover, *HCT*   A.W. Gomme, A. Andrewes and K.J. Dover. *A Historical Commentary on Thucydides*. Vols. IV-V. Oxford 1970 and 1981.

Gomme 1933   A.W. Gomme. *The Population of Athens in the Fifth and Fourth Centuries B.C.* Oxford 1933.

Gomme 1937   A.W. Gomme. *Essays in Greek History and Literature*. Oxford 1937.

Gruen 1970   E.S. Gruen. 'Stesimbrotus on Miltiades and Themistocles', pp. 91-8 in *CSCA* 3 (1970).

Gurlitt 1890   W. Gurlitt. *Über Pausanias*. Graz 1890.

Haas 1985   C.J. Haas. 'Athenian naval power before Themistocles', pp. 29-46 in *Historia* 34 (1985).

Habicht 1961   C. Habicht. 'Falsche Urkunden zur Geschichte Athens im Zeitalter der Perserkriege', pp. 1-35 in *Hermes* 89 (1961).

Habicht 1970   C. Habicht. *Gottmenschentum und griechische Städte*. 2nd ed. Munich 1970.

Habicht 1979   C. Habicht. *Untersuchungen zur politischen Geschichte Athens im 3. Jahrhundert v. Chr.* Munich 1979.

Habicht 1982   C. Habicht. *Studien zur Geschichte Athens in hellenistischer Zeit*. Göttingen 1982.

Habicht 1985   C. Habicht. *Pausanias' Guide to Ancient Greece*. California 1985.

Hackens 1969   T. Hackens. 'La circulation monétaire dans la Béotie hellénistique', pp. 701-29 in *BCH* 93 (1969).

Hammond 1955   N.G.L. Hammond. 'Studies in Greek chronology of the sixth and fifth centuries B.C.: the war between Athens and Aegina *c.* 505-481', pp. 409-11 in *Historia* 4 (1955).

Hammond 1967   N.G.L. Hammond. 'The origins and nature of the Athenian alliance of 478/7', pp. 41-61 in *JHS* 87 (1967).

Hammond 1982   N.G.L. Hammond. 'Herodotus VII and the Decree of Themistocles', pp. 75-93 in *JHS* 102 (1982).

Hansen 1975   M.H. Hansen *Aspects of Athenian Society in the Fourth Century B.C.* Odense 1975.

Hansen 1982   M.H. Hansen. 'Demographic reflections on the number of Athenian citizens: 451-309', pp. 172-89 in *AJAH* 7 (1982).

Hansen 1983   M.H. Hansen. *The Athenian Ecclesia: a Collection of Articles 1976-83.* Copenhagen 1983.

Hansen 1985   M.H. Hansen. 'Two notes on the Pnyx', pp. 241-50 in *GRBS* 26.3 (1985).

Hansen 1985a   M.H. Hansen. *Demography and Democracy: the number of Athenian citizens in the fourth century B.C.* Herning 1985 (1986).

Harding 1973   P. Harding. 'The purpose of Isokrates' *Archidamos* and *On the Peace*', pp. 137-49 in *CSCA* 6 (1973).

Harding 1985   P. Harding. *From the End of the Peloponnesian War to the Battle of Ipsus.* Cambridge 1985.

Harrison 1922   J. Harrison. *Prolegomena to the Study of Greek Religion.* 3rd ed. Cambridge 1922.

Harrison 1965   E.B. Harrison. *The Athenian Agora*: vol. XI: 'Archaic and Archaistic Sculpture'. Princeton 1965.

Harrison 1971   A.R.W. Harrison. *The Law of Athens* (vol. 2). Oxford 1971.

Hartwig 1897   P. Hartwig. *Bendis: eine archaeolögische Untersuchung.* Leipzig 1897.

Hasebroek 1933   J. Hasebroek. *Trade and Politics in Ancient Greece.* Trans. by L.M. Fraser and D.C. MacGregor. 1st ed. 1933. London 1965.

Hauben 1974   H. Hauben. 'An Athenian Naval Victory in 321 B.C.', pp. 61-4 in *ZPE* 13 (1974).

Hauben 1974a   H. Hauben. '*IG* II² and the siege of Athens in 304 B.C.', p. 10 in *ZPE* 14 (1974).

Haussoullier 1884   B. Haussouillier. *La vie municipale en Attique.* 1884.

Haverfield 1913   F. Haverfield. *Ancient Town Planning.* Oxford, Clarendon 1913.

Head and Poole 1888   B.V. Head and R.S. Poole. *A Catalogue of Greek Coins in the British Museum*: vol. II (Attica-Megaris-Aegina). London 1888.

Heinen 1972   H. Heinen. 'Untersuchungen zur hellenistischen Geschichte des 3. Jahrhunderts v. Chr.': *Historia* Einzelschriften 20. Wiesbaden 1972.

Henrichs 1981   A. Henrichs. 'Human sacrifice in Greek religion', pp. 195-235 in *Entr.Hardt* 27 (1981).

Henry 1984   A.S. Henry. 'Athenian financial officers after 303', pp. 49-92 in *Chiron* 14 (1984).

Herzog 1902   R. Herzog. 'Ein türkisches Werk über das ägäische Meer aus dem

Jahre 1520', pp. 417-30 in *AM* 27 (1902).

Higgins 1954   R.A. Higgins. *Catalogue of the Terracottas in the Department of Greek and Roman Antiquities in the British Museum.* London 1954.

Hill 1932   D.K. Hill. 'Some boundary stones from the Peiraieus', pp. 254-9 in *AJA* 36 (1932).

Hirschfeld 1878   G. Hirschfeld. *Topographischer Versuch über die Piraeusstadt.* Leipzig 1878.

Hirst and Hirst 1927   G.M. and M.E. Hirst. 'Prasiai or Phaleron', pp. 113-14 in *CR* 41 (1927).

Holladay 1977   A.J. Holladay. 'Sparta's role in the First Peloponnesian War', pp. 54-63 in *JHS* 97 (1977).

Holladay 1978   A.J. Holladay. 'Athenian strategy in the Archidamian War', pp. 399-427 in *Historia* 27 (1978).

Holland 1950   L.B. Holland. 'The Katastegasma of the walls of Athens', pp. 337-56 in *AJA* 54 (1950).

Hornblower 1982   S. Hornblower. *Mausolus.* Oxford, Clarendon 1982.

Hornblower 1983   S. Hornblower. *The Greek World 479-323 B.C.* London 1983.

Hopper 1979   R.J. Hopper. *Trade and Industry in Classical Greece.* Thames and Hudson, London 1979.

Humphreys 1985   S.C. Humphreys. 'Lycurgus of Butadae: an Athenian aristocrat', pp. 199-252 in Eadie and Ober 1985.

IAGIL   M. Almagro (ed.). *Las inscripciones Ampuritanas Griegas, Ibericas y Latinas.* Barcelona 1952.

ID   J. Coupry (ed.). *Inscriptions de Délos, période de l'amphyctyonie attico-délienne, actes administratifs, nos. 89-104.* Paris 1972.

IG   *Inscriptiones Graecae.*

Isager and Hansen 1975   S. Isager and M.H. Hansen. *Aspects of Athenian Society in the Fourth Century B.C.* Trans. by. J.H. Rosenmeier. Odense 1975.

Jacoby 1949   F. Jacoby. *Atthis.* Oxford, Clarendon 1949.

Jameson 1960   M.H. Jameson. 'A decree of Themistocles from Troizen', pp. 198-223 in *Hesperia* 29 (1960).

Jameson 1962   M.H. Jameson. 'Revised text of the decree of Themistokles from Troizen', pp. 310-15 in *Hesperia* 31 (1962).

Jameson 1965   M.H. Jameson. 'The sacrificial calendar from Erchia', pp. 154-72 in *BCH* 89 (1965).

Jameson 1969   M.H. Jameson. 'Excavations at Porto Cheli and vicinity', pp. 310-42 in *Hesperia* 38 (1969).

Jameson 1983   M.H. Jameson. 'Famine in the Greek world': *PCPhS* Supp. 8 (1983).

Jardé 1925   A. Jardé. *Les céréales dans l'antiquité grecque.* Paris 1925.

Jeffery 1961   L.H. Jeffery. *The Local Scripts of Archaic Greece.* Oxford, Clarendon 1961.

Jeffery 1962   L.H. Jeffery. 'The inscribed gravestones of Archaic Attica', pp. 115-53 in *BSA* 57 (1962).

Jeffery 1976   L.H. Jeffery. *Archaic Greece: the City States c. 700-500 B.C.* London and Tonbridge 1976.

Jeppesen 1961   K. Jeppesen. 'Arsenal von Piraeus', pp. 221-3 in *AArch* 32 (1961).

Johansen 1951   K.F. Johansen. *The Attic Grave Reliefs of the Classical Period.* Copenhagen 1951.

Johnston 1979   A.W. Johnston. *Trademarks on Greek Vases.* Warminster 1979.

Johnston and Jones 1978   A.W. Johnston and R.E. Jones. 'The 'SOS Amphora' ', pp. 103-41 in *BSA* 73 (1978).

Jones 1957 A.H.M. Jones. *Athenian Democracy*. Oxford 1957.

Jones 1975 J.E. Jones. 'Town and country houses of Attica in classical times', pp. 63-144 in H. Mussche (ed.), *Thorikos and the Laurion in Archaic and Classical Times*. Ghent 1975.

Jordan 1970 B. Jordan. 'Herodotos 5.71.2 and the naukraroi of Athens', pp. 153-75 in *CSCA* 3 (1970).

Jordan 1975 B. Jordan. 'The Athenian navy in the Classical Period': *Univ. of Calif. Public. in Class. Studies* 13 (1975).

Jucker 1967 I. Jucker. 'Artemis Kindyas in Gestalt und Geschichte' pp. 133ff. in *AK* Beiheft 4 (1967).

Judeich 1905,1931 W. Judeich. *Topographie von Athen*. Munich 1905 (1st ed.) and 1931 (2nd ed.).

Kahil 1965 L. Kahil. 'Autour de l'Artemis attique', pp. 20-33 in *AK* 8 (1965).

Kahil 1981 L. Kahil. 'Le cratérisque d'Artémis et le Brauronion de l'Acropole', pp. 253-63 in *Hesperia* 50 (1981).

Karavites 1977 P. Karavites. 'Realities and appearances, 490-80 B.C.', pp. 129-47 in *Historia* 26 (1977).

Karouzou 1957 Karouzou, S. '*Hê typhlê arktos*', pp. 68-83 in *AE* 1957.

Katzev 1969 M.L. Katzev. 'The Kyrenia shipwreck', pp. 55-9 in *Expedition* 11.2 (1969).

Katzev 1970 M.L. Katzev. 'A Greek ship is raised', pp. 6-14 in *Expedition* 12.4 (1970).

Kenny 1947 E.J.A. Kenny. 'The ancient docks on the promontory of Sunion', pp. 194-200 in *BSA* 43 (1947).

Kleiner 1968 G. Kleiner. *Die Ruinen von Milet*. Berlin 1968.

Kleiner 1973 F.S. Kleiner. 'The 1926 Piraeus Hoard and Athenian bronze coinage *c*. 86 B.C.', pp. 169-86 in *AD* 28 Mel. 1 (1973).

Knorringa 1926 H. Knorringa. *Emporos: Data on Trade and Traders in Greek Literature from Homer to Aristotle*. Amsterdam 1926.

Kolbe 1901 W. Kolbe. 'Zur attenischen Marineverwaltung', pp. 377-418 in *AM* 26 (1901).

Kondis 1958 J.D. Kondis. 'Stadtbauplan von Rhodos', pp. 146-58 in *AM* 73 (1958).

Krentz 1980 P. Krentz. 'Foreigners against the Thirty: *IG* II² 10 again', pp. 298-307 in *Phoenix* 34 (1980).

Krentz 1982 P. Krentz. *The Thirty at Athens*. Ithaca and London 1982.

Krentz 1984 P. Krentz. 'The Pnyx in 404/3 B.C.', pp. 230f. in *AJA* 88 (1984).

Kurtz and Boardman 1971 D.C. Kurtz and J. Boardman. *Greek Burial Customs*. London, Thames and Hudson 1971.

Labarbe 1957 Labarbe. *La loi navale de Thémistocle*. Paris 1957.

Lane 1964 E.N. Lane. 'A re-study of the God Men. Part I: the epigraphic and sculptural evidence', in *Berytus* 15 (1964).

Lane 1985 E.N. Lane. *Corpus Cultus Iovis Sabazii* vol. II. Leiden 1985.

Lang 1967 M. Lang. 'Revolution of the 400: chronology and constitutions', pp. 176-87 in *AJPh* 88 (1967).

Lange 1885 K. Lange. *Haus und Halle*. Leipzig 1885.

Laumonier 1958 A. Laumonier. *Les cultes indigènes en Carie*. Paris 1958.

Launey 1950 M. Launey. *Recherches sur les armées hellénistiques*. 2 vols. Paris 1950.

Lavedan and Hugueney 1966 P. Lavedan and J. Hugueney. *Histoire de l'urbanisme: antiquité*. Paris 1966.

Lawrence 1979   A.W. Lawrence. *Greek Aims in Fortification*. Oxford, Clarendon 1979.

Lawrence-Tomlinson 1983   A.W. Lawrence. *Greek Architecture*. 4th ed. rev. and with additions by R.A. Tomlinson. Harmondsworth, Middx. 1983.

Leake 1841   W. Leake. *The Topography of Athens with some Remarks on its Antiquities*. 2nd ed. London 1841.

Lechat 1887   H. Lechat. 'Fouilles au Pirée', pp. 201-11 in *BCH* 11 (1887).

Lechat 1888   H. Lechat. 'Fouilles au Pirée. Les fortifications antiques', pp. 337-54 in *BCH* 12 (1888).

Legon 1981   R.P. Legon. *Megara: the Political History of a Greek City-State to 336 B.C.* Ithaca and London 1981.

Lehmann-Hartleben 1923   K. Lehmann-Hartleben. 'Die antiken Hafenlagen des Mittelmeeres', pp. 79ff. in *Klio* Beiheft 14 (1923).

Lenardon 1978   R.L. Lenardon. *The Saga of Themistocles*. London, Thames and Hudson 1978.

Lévêque and Vidal-Naquet 1964 P. Lévêque and P. Vidal-Naquet. *Clisthène l'Athénien*. Paris 1964.

Levick 1971   B. Levick. 'The table of Mên', pp. 80-4 in *JHS* 91 (1971).

Lewis 1959   D.M. Lewis. 'Law on the Lesser Panathenaia', pp. 239-47 in *Hesperia* 28 (1959).

Lewis 1960   D.M. Lewis. 'Apollo Delios', pp. 190-4 in *BSA* 55 (1960).

Lewis 1963   D.M. Lewis. 'Cleisthenes and Attica', pp. 22-40 in *Historia* 12 (1963).

Lewis 1973   D.M. Lewis. 'Themistocles' archonship', p. 757-8 in *Historia* 22 (1973).

Liankouras 1972   A. Liankouras. 'Peiraieus', pp. 168-79 in *AD* 27 (1972) B1.

Liankouras and Papachristodoulou 1972   A. Liankouras and J. Papachristodoulou. '*Eidêseis peri tôn Makrôn Teichôn*', pp. 339-46 in *AAA* 5 (1972).

Linforth 1946   I.M. Linforth. 'The Corybantic Rites in Plato', pp. 121-62 in *Univ. Calif. Publications in Class. Phil.* 13 (1946).

Littman 1984   R.J. Littman. 'The plague at Syracuse: 396 B.C.', pp. 110-16 in *Mnemosyne* 37 (1984).

Lolling 1881   H.G. Lolling. 'Inschriften aus dem Peiraieus', pp. 309-11 in *AM* 6 (1881).

Lorinzen 1964   E. Lorinzen. *The Arsenal at Piraeus*. Copenhagen 1964.

Lloyd-Jones 1983   H. Lloyd-Jones. 'Artemis and Iphigeneia', pp. 87-102 in *JHS* 103 (1983).

LSG   F. Sokolowski. *Lois sacrées des cités grecques*. Paris 1969.

McCredie 1966   J.R. McCredie. 'Fortified military camps in Attica': *Hesperia* Supp. 11 (1966).

McCredie 1971   J.R. McCredie. 'Hippodamos of Miletos', pp. 95-100 in *Studies Presented to G.M.A. Hanfmann*. Mainz 1971.

MacDonald 1972   A. MacDonald. 'A note on the raid of Sphodrias', pp. 38-44 in *Historia* 21 (1972).

MacDonald 1982   B.R. Macdonald. 'The import of Attic pottery to Corinth and the question of trade during the Peloponnesian War', pp. 113-23 in *JHS* 102 (1982).

McDonald 1943   W.A. McDonald. *The Political Meeting Places of the Greeks*. Baltimore 1943.

MacDowell 1963   D.M. MacDowell. *Athenian Homicide Law in the Age of the Orators*. Manchester 1963.

MacDowell 1971   D.M. MacDowell. *Aristophanes' Wasps*. Oxford, Clarendon 1971.

MacDowell 1978   D.M. MacDowell. *The Law in Classical Athens*. London, Thames and

Hudson 1978.

Maier I   F.G. Maier. *Griechische Mauerbauinschriften* vol. I. Heidelberg 1959.

Malkin 1984   I. Malkin. 'What were the sacred precincts of Brea (*IG* I³ 46)?', pp. 43-8 in *Chiron* 14 (1984).

Martienssen 1964   R.D. Martienssen. *The Idea of Space in Greek Architecture.* Johannesburg 1964.

Martin 1951   R. Martin. *Recherches sur l'agora grecque.* Paris 1951.

Martin 1967   R. Martin. 'Note sur la charpenterie grecque', pp. 314-24 in *REG* 80 (1967).

Martin 1974   R. Martin. *L'urbanisme dans la Grèce antique.* 2nd ed. Paris 1974.

Masson 1969   O. Masson. 'Recherches sur les Phéniciens dans le monde hellénistique', pp. 679-700 in *BCH* 93 (1969).

Mattingly 1968   B. Mattingly. 'Athenian finance in the Peloponnesian War', pp. 450-85 in *BCH* 92 (1968).

Megaw 1936   H. Megaw. 'Archaeology in Greece', p. 142 in *JHS* 56 (1936).

Meiggs 1960   R. Meiggs. *Roman Ostia.* Oxford, Clarendon 1960.

Meiggs 1963   R. Meiggs. 'The crisis of Athenian imperialism', pp. 1-36 in *HSCPh* 67 (1963).

Meiggs 1972   R. Meiggs. *The Athenian Empire.* Oxford, Clarendon 1972.

Meiggs 1982   R. Meiggs. *Trees and Timber in the Ancient Mediterranean World.* Oxford, Clarendon 1982.

Meister 1978   K. Meister. 'Stesimbrotos' Schrift über die athenische Stadtsmänner', pp. 274-94 in *Historia* 27 (1978).

Meisternans and Schwyzer 1900   K. Meisterhans. Rev. by E. Schwyzer. *Grammatik der attischen Inscriften.* Berlin 1900.

Meritt 1928   B.D. Meritt. *Athenian Financial Documents of the Fifth Century.* Cambridge, Mass. 1928.

Meritt 1935   B.D. Meritt. 'Inscriptions of Colophon', pp. 357-97 in *AJPh* 56 (1935).

Meritt 1936   B.D. Meritt. 'Greek inscriptions', pp. 393-413 in *Hesperia* 5 (1936).

Meritt 1940   B.D. Meritt. 'Greek inscriptions', pp. 53-96 in *Hesperia* 9 (1940).

Meritt 1946   B.D. Meritt. 'Greek inscriptions', pp. 169-264 in *Hesperia* 15 (1946).

Meritt 1948   B.D. Meritt. 'Greek inscriptions', pp. 1-53 in *Hesperia* 17 (1948).

Meritt and Traill 1974   B.D. Meritt and J.S. Traill. *The Athenian Agora* vol. 15: 'Inscriptions: the Athenian Councillors.' Princeton 1974.

Merlin 1930   A. Merlin. 'Submarine discoveries in the Mediterranean', pp. 405-14 in *Antiquity* 4 (1930).

Métraux 1978   G.P.R. Métraux. *Western Greek Land-Use and City-Planning in the Archaic Period.* New York and London 1978.

Metzger 1971   I. Metzger. 'Piräus-Zisterne', pp. 41-94 in *AD* 26 A1 (1971).

Michel 1900   C. Michel. *Recueil d'inscriptions grecques.* Paris 1900.

Middleton 1982   D.F. Middleton. 'Thrasyboulos' Thracian support', pp. 298-303 in *CQ* 32 (1982).

Mikalson 1975   J.D. Mikalson. *The Sacred and Civil Calendar of the Athenian Year.* Princeton 1975.

Mikalson 1977   J.D. Mikalson. 'Religion in the Attic demes', pp. 424-35 in *AJPh* 98 (1977).

Mikalson 1982   J.D. Mikalson. 'The *Heorte* of Heortology', pp. 213-21 in *GRBS* 23 (1982).

Mikalson 1984   J. Mikalson. 'Religion and the Plague in Athens, 431-423 B.C.', pp.

217-25 in *Studies presented to Sterling Dow on his Eightieth Birthday*. North Carolina 1984.

Milchhöfer 1881   A. Milchhöfer. 'Der Peiraieus', pp. 23-71 in Curtius and Kaupert 1881.

Millar 1983   F.G.B. Millar. 'The Phoenician cities: a case-study of Hellenisation', pp. 55-71 in *PCPhS* n.s. 29 (1983).

Millett 1983   P. Millett. 'Maritime loans and the structure of credit in fourth-century Athens', pp. 36-52 in Garnsey, Hopkins and Whittaker 1983.

Miller 1978   S.G. Miller. *The Prytaneion: its Function and Architectural Form*. Berkeley and Los Angeles 1978.

Mitchel 1970   F.W. Mitchel. *Lykourgan Athens 338-322*: Lecture in honour of L.T. Semple. Cincinnati 1970.

Mitropoulou 1977   E. Mitropoulou. *Deities and Heroes in the Form of Snakes*. Athens 1977.

Mitropoulou 1977a   E. Mitropoulou. *Corpus I: Attic Votive Reliefs of the Sixth and Fifth Centuries B.C.* Athens 1977.

Mitsos 1949   M. Mitsos. 'Inscriptions of the eastern Peloponnesus', pp. 73-7 in *Hesperia* 18 (1949).

' *ML*   R. Meiggs and D. Lewis. *A Selection of Greek Historical Inscriptions to the End of the Fifth Century BC*. Oxford, Clarendon 1969.

Möbius 1968   H. Möbius. *Die Ornamente der griechischen Grabstelen: klassischer und nachklassischer Zeit*. Munich 1968.

Momigliano 1944   A. Momigliano. 'Sea power in Greek thought', pp. 1-7 in *CR* 58 (1944).

Mommsen 1898   A. Mommsen. *Feste der Stadt Athen*. Leipzig 1898.

Montgomery 1984   H. Montgomery. 'Siver, coins and the wealth of a city-state', pp. 123-33 in *OAth* 15 (1984).

Mørkholm 1982   O. Mørkholm. 'Some reflections on the production and use of coinage in Ancient Greece', pp. 290-305 in *Historia* 31 (1982).

Morrison 1984   J.S. Morrison. 'Hyperesia in naval contexts in the fifth and fourth centuries B.C.', pp. 48-59 in *JHS* 104 (1984).

Morrison and Williams 1968   J.S. Morrison and R.T. Williams. *Greek Oared Ships*. Cambridge 1968.

Mossé 1962   C. Mossé. *La fin de la démocratie athénienne: aspects sociaux et politiques du déclin de la cité grecque au IV* siècle avant J.-C.* Paris 1962.

Mossé 1973   C. Mossé. *Athens in Decline 404-86 B.C.* London and Boston 1973.

Mossé 1983   C. Mossé. 'The world of the Emporium in the private speeches of Demosthenes', pp. 53-63 in Garnsey, Hopkins and Whittaker 1983.

Mouterde 1951   R.P.R. Mouterede. 'Aperçu historique sur les ports anciens de la Mediterranée orientale', pp. 15-47 in Poidebarde and Lauffray 1951.

Moysey 1976   R.A. Moysey. 'The date of the Straton of Sidon decree', pp. 182-9 in *AJAH* 1 (1976).

Moysey 1981   R.A. Moysey. 'The Thirty and the Pnyx', pp. 31-7 in *AJA* 85 (1981).

Moysey 1982   R.A. Moysey. 'Isokrates' *On the Peace*: rhetorical exercise or political advice', pp. 118-27 in *AJAH* 7 (1982).

Munro 1937   J.A.R. Munro. 'The end of the Peloponnesian War', pp. 32-8 in *CQ* 31 (1937).

Munro 1938   J.A.R. Munro. 'Theramenes against Lysander', pp. 18-26 in *CQ* 32 (1938).

Murray 1980   O. Murray. *Early Greece*. Glasgow 1980.

Mumford 1961   L. Mumford. *The City in History*. Harmondsworth, Middx. 1961.

Mussche 1961   H.F. Mussche. 'La forteresse maritime de Thorikos', pp. 176-205 in *BCH* 85 (1961).

Mussche 1964   H.F. Mussche. 'Note sur les fortifications de Sounion', pp. 423-32 in *BCH* 88 (1964).

Musiolek 1981   P. Musiolek. 'Zur Bedeutung von *astu* und *polis* im archaïschen Griechenland', pp. 133-8 in *AAntHung* 29 (1981).

Mylonas 1961   G.E. Mylonas. *Eleusis and the Eleusinian Mysteries*. Princeton 1961.

Négris 1904   P. Négris. 'Vestiges antiques submergés', pp. 340-63 in *AM* 29 (1904).

Nicolaou 1976   K. Nicolaou. 'The historical topography of Kition': *Studies in Mediterranean Archaeology* 43 (1976).

Nilsson 1942   M.P. Nilsson. 'Bendis in Athens', pp. 169-88 in *From the Collections of Ny Carlesberg Glyptothek* 3 (1942).

Nilsson 1951   M.P. Nilsson. *Cults, Myths, Oracles and Politics in Ancient Greece*. Lund 1951.

Nilsson 1967   M.P. Nilsson. *Geschichte der griechischen Religion* (= *Handbuch der Altertumswissenschaft V.2.1)* 3rd ed. Munich 1967.

Noack 1908   F. Noack. 'Bemerkungen zu den Piraeusmauern,' pp. 33-8 in *AM* 33 (1908).

Nock 1972   A.D. Nock. Ed. by Z. Stewart. *Essays on Religion and the Ancient World*. 2 vols. Oxford, Clarendon 1972.

Noonan 1973   T.S. Noonan. 'The grain trade of the northern Black Sea in antiquity', pp. 231-42 in *AJP* 94 (1973).

Ober 1978   J. Ober. 'Views of sea power in the fourth-century Attic orators', pp. 119-30 in *AncW* 1 (1978).

Ober 1985   J. Ober. 'Fortress Attica: defence of the Athenian land frontier 404-322 B.C.', *Mnemosyne* 38 (1985).

Ober 1985a   J. Ober. 'Thucydides, Pericles, and the strategy of defence', pp. 171-97 in Eadie and Ober (1985).

OCT   Oxford Classical Text.

Ohlemutz 1940   E. Ohlemutz. *Die Kulte und Heiligtümer der Götter in Pergamon*. Diss. Giessen 1940. Darmstadt 1968.

Oeconomides-Caramessini 1976   M. Oeconomides-Caramessini. 'The 1973 Piraeus hoard of Athenian bronze coins', pp. 220-3 in *AAA* 9 (1976).

Oikonomides 1982   A.N. Oikonomides. 'The cult of Diogenes "Euergetes" in Ancient Athens', pp. 118-20 in *ZPE* 45 (1982).

Oikonomides 1984   A.N. Oikonomides. 'An Etruscan in fifth-century Athens (*IG* I² 923), pp. 127-8 in *AncW* 10 (1984).

Oliver 1935   J.H. Oliver. 'Greek inscriptions', pp. 1-70 in *Hesperia* 4 (1935).

Oliver 1960 J.H. Oliver. 'Reforms of Cleisthenes', pp. 503-7 in *Historia* 9 (1960).

Osborne 1979   M.J. Osborne. 'Kallias, Phaidros and the revolt of Athens in 287 B.C.', pp. 181-94 in *ZPE* 35 (1979).

Osborne 1981-2   M.J. Osborne. *Naturalization in Athens*. 2 vols. Brussels 1981 and 1982.

Osborne 1982   M.J. Osborne. Review of C. Habicht's *Untersuchungen zur politischen Geschichte Athens im 3. Jahrhundert v. Chr.*, pp. 272f. in *JHS* 102 (1982).

Osborne 1985   R. Osborne. *Demos: the discovery of Classical Attike*. Cambridge 1985.

Owens 1983   E.J. Owens. 'The koprologoi at Athens in the fifth and fourth centuries

B.C.', pp. 44-50 in *CQ* n.s. 33 (1983).

Page 1955   D.L. Page. *Sappho and Alcaeus*. Oxford, Clarendon 1955.

Panagos 1968   C. Panagos. *Le Pirée*. Translated by P. Gerardat. Athens 1968.

Panessa 1983   G. Panessa. 'Le risorse idriche dei santuarî greci', pp. 359-87 in *ASNP* 13.2 (1983).

Papachatses 1974   N. Papachatses. *Pausaniou Hellados Periêgêsis: Attike*. Athens 1974.

Papachristodoulou 1971   I. Papachristodoulou. 'Peiraieus', pp. 34-7 in *AD* 26 (1971) B1.

Papachristodoulou 1973   I. Papachristodoulou. 'Peiraieus', pp. 46-8 in *AD* 28 (1973) B1.

Papaghiannoupoulos-Palaios 1929   A.A. Papaghiannoupoulos-Palaios. '*Attikai epigraphai*', pp. 44-52 in *Polemon* 1 (1929).

Paraskevaidis 1961   M. Paraskevaidis. 'Zur Entdeckung der Statuen in Piräus', pp. 131-7 in *Das Altertum* 7 (1961)

Parke 1977   H.W. Parke. *Festivals of the Athenians*. London, Thames and Hudson 1977.

Parker 1983   R. Parker. *Miasma*. Oxford, Clarendon 1983.

Patterson 1981   C. Patterson. *Pericles' Citizenship Law of 451/50 B.C.* 1981.

PECS   R. Stillwell (ed.). *Princeton Encyclopaedia of Classical Sites*. Princeton 1976.

Pečírka 1966   J. Pečírka. *The Formula for the Grant of Enktesis in Attic Inscriptions*. Prague 1966.

Pečírka 1967   J. Pečírka. 'A note on Aristotle's conception of citizenship and the role of foreigners in fourth- century Athens', pp. 23-6 in *Eirene* 6 (1967).

Pečírka 1976   J. Pečírka. 'The crisis of the Athenian polis in the fourth century B.C.', pp. 5-29 in *Eirene* 14 (1976).

Peek 1941   W. Peek. 'Heilige Gesetze', pp. 171-217 in *AM* 66 (1941).

Pelekides 1916   S. Pelekides. '*Anaskaphê Phalerou*', pp. 13-64 in, *AD* 2 (1916).

Pélékides 1962   C. Pélékides. *Histoire de l'éphébie attique des origines à 31 avant J.-C.* Paris 1962.

Petrakos 1977   B. Petrakos. 'Peiraias', pp. 36-8 in *AD* 32 (1977) B1.

Philios 1880   D. Philios. '*Ekthesis peri tôn en Peiraiei anaskaphôn*', pp. 47-61 in *PAE* 1880.

Pickard-Cambridge 1968   A. Pickard-Cambridge. Rev. by J. Gould and D.M. Lewis. *The Dramatic Festivals of Athens*. Oxford, Clarendon 1968.

Plassart 1913   A. Plassart. 'Les archers d'Athènes', pp. 151-213 in *REG* 26 (1913).

Podlecki 1971   A.J. Podlecki. 'Cimon, Scyros and Theseus' bones', pp. 141-3 in *JHS* 91 (1971).

Podlecki 1975   A.J. Podlecki. *The Life of Themistocles: a Critical Survey of the Literary and Archaeological Evidence*. Montreal and London 1975.

Podlecki 1976   A.J. Podlecki. 'Athens and Aegina', pp. 396-413 in *Historia* 25 (1976).

Poland 1909   F. Poland. *Geschichte des griechischen Vereinswesens*. Leipzig 1909.

Polanyi 1968.   K. Polanyi. *Primitive, Archaic and Modern Economies: Essays of Karl Polanyi*. ed. G. Dalton. New York 1968.

Pope 1935   H. Pope. *Non-Athenians in Attic Inscriptions*. New York 1935.

Pouilloux 1954   J. Pouilloux. *La forteresse de Rhamnounte*. Paris 1954.

Pounder 1983   R.L. Pounder. 'A Hellenistic arsenal in Athens', pp. 233-56 in *Hesperia* 52 (1983).

Powell 1936   J.E. Powell. 'The Piraeus Wall of Themistocles', p. 8 in *PCPS* 153 (1930).

Préaux 1978   C. Préaux. *Le monde hellénistique: la Grèce et l'Orient 323-146 av. J.-C.* 2 vols. Paris 1978.

Pritchett 1940   W.K. Pritchett. 'Greek inscriptions', pp. 53-140 in *Hesperia* 9 (1940).

Pritchett 1946　W.K. Pritchett. 'Greek inscriptions', 138-68 in *Hesperia* 15 (1946).

Pritchett 1956　W.K. Pritchett. 'The Attic stelai', pp. 178-317 in *Hesperia* 25 (1956).

Pritchett 1965　W.K. Pritchett. 'Studies in Ancient Greek topography: part I': *Univ. Calif. Publications in Class. Studies* vol.1. Berkeley and Los Angeles 1965.

Pritchett 1972　W.K. Pritchett. 'Lucubrationes epigraphicae', pp. 153-81 in *CSCA* 5 (1972).

Pritchett 1980　W.K. Pritchett. 'Studies in Ancient Greek topography: part III (roads)': *Univ. Calif. Class. Publications in Studies* vol. 22. Berkeley and Los Angeles 1980.

Raubitschek 1943　A. Raubitschek. 'Greek inscriptions', pp. 73-7 in *Hesperia* 12 (1943).

Raubitschek 1956　A.E. Raubitschek. 'The Gates in the Agora', pp. 279-82 in *AJA* 60 (1956).

RE　G. Wissowa (ed.). *Paulys Real-Encyclopädie*. Stuttgart 1893-.

Reinmuth 1971　O.W. Reinmuth. 'The ephebic inscriptions of the fourth century B.C.', *Mnemosyne* Supp. 14. Leiden 1971.

Renan 1888　E. Renan. 'Inscription bilingue phénicienne et grecque du Pirée', pp. 5-7 in *RA* 12 (1888).

Renehan 1975　R. Renehan. 'Greek lexicographical notes: a critical supplement to the Greek-English Lexicon of Liddell-Scott-Jones': *Hypomnemata* 45. Göttingen 1975.

Rhodes 1972　P.J. Rhodes. *The Athenian Boule*. Oxford, Clarendon 1972.

Rhodes 1972a　P.J. Rhodes. 'The Five Thousand in the Athenian Revolutions of 411', pp. 115-27 in *JHS* 92 (1972).

Rhodes 1981　P.J. Rhodes. *A Commentary on the Aristotelian Athenaion Politeia*. Oxford, Clarendon 1981.

Richter 1954　G.M.A. Richter. *Catalogue of Greek Sculptures in the Metropolitan Museum of Art, New York*. Oxford, Clarendon 1954.

Richter 1961　G.M.A. Richter. *The Archaic Gravestones of Attica*. London 1961.

Rider 1965　B.C. Rider. *The Greek House*. Cambridge 1965.

Robert 1882　C. Robert. 'Relief im Peiraieus', pp. 389-95 in *AM* 7 (1882).

Robert 1931　F. Robert. 'Le "Plutus" d'Aristophane et l'Asclépiéion du Pirée', pp. 132-9 in *RevPh* 1931.

Robert 1936　L. Robert. 'Décrets de Kolophon', pp. 158f. in *RevPh* 10 (1936).

Robert 1962　J. and L. Robert. 'Trézène', pp. 152-8 in *REG* 75 (1962).

Robert 1969　L. Robert. 'Inscriptions d'Athènes et de la Grèce Centrale', pp. 1-58 in *AE* 1969.

Robert 1978　L. Robert. 'Malédictions funéraires grecques: une épitaphe métrique au Pirée', pp. 241-69 in *CRAI* 1978.

Robert 1981　L. Robert. 'Une épigramme d'Automédon', pp. 338-61 in *REG* 94 (1981).

Robertson 1927　D.S. Robertson. 'The duration of a trierarchy', pp. 114-16 in *CR* 41 (1927).

Robertson 1982　N. Robertson. 'The decree of Themistocles in its contemporary setting', pp. 1-44 in *Phoenix* 36 (1982).

Robinson 1937　D.M. Robinson. 'A new fragment of the fifth-century Athenian naval catalogues', pp. 292-9 in *AJA* 41 (1937).

Robinson and Graham 1938　D.M. Robinson and J.W. Graham. 'Excavations at Olynthos: part VIII: the Hellenic House', *Johns Hopkins Univ. Studies in*

Archaeology no. 25. Baltimore 1938.

Rost 1968   G.A. Rost. *Seewesen und Seehandel in der Antike.* Amsterdam 1968.

Rostovtzeff 1941 M. Rostovtzeff. *Social and Economic History of the Hellenistic World.* 3 vols. 1st ed. Oxford, Clarendon 1941.

Rostovtzeff 1953   M. Rostovtzeff. *Social and Economic History of the Hellenistic World.* 3 vols. 2nd ed. Oxford, Clarendon 1953.

Rougé 1966   J. Rougé. *Recherches sur l'organisation du commerce maritime en Mediterranée sous l'Empire Romain.* Paris 1966.

Roussel 1916   P. Roussel. *Délos, colonie athénienne.* Paris 1916.

Roussel 1930   P. Roussel. 'Un sanctuaire d'Agdistis à Rhamnonte', pp. 5-8 in *REA* 32 (1930).

Roussel 1930   P. Roussel. 'Un nouveau document relatif à la guerre Démétriaque', pp. 268-82 in *BCH* 54 (1930).

Roussel 1943   P. Roussel. 'A propos d'un décret attique relativ à la déesse Bendis', pp. 177-82 in *REA* 45 (1943).

Roux 1961   G. Roux. 'Le sens de *typos*', pp. 5-14 in *REA* 63 (1961).

Rykwert 1976   J. Rykwert. *The Idea of a Town: the Anthropology of Urban Form in Rome, Italy and the Ancient World.* London 1976.

Salmon 1965   P. Salmon. *La politique égyptienne d'Athènes.* Brussels 1965.

Salmon 1984   J.B. Salmon. *Wealthy Corinth: a History of the City to 338 B.C.* Oxford, Clarendon 1984.

Schefold 1971   K. Schefold. 'Die Athene des Piräus', pp. 37-40 in *AK* 14 (1971).

Schilardis 1975   D. Schilardis. *'Anaskaphê para ta Makra Teichê kai hê oinochoê tou Tavrou'*, pp. 66-149 in *AE* 1975.

Schwabacher 1939   W. Schwabacher. 'A find from the Piraeus', pp. 162-6 in *NC* 19 (1939).

Schweigert 1939   E. Schweigert. 'Greek inscriptions', pp. 1-47 in *Hesperia* 8 (1939).

Schweigert 1940   E. Schweigert. 'Greek inscriptions', pp. 309-57 in *Hesperia* 9 (1940).

Scranton 1938   R.L. Scranton. 'The fortifications of Athens at the opening of the Peloponnesian War', pp. 525-36 in *AJA* 42 (1938).

Scranton 1939   R.L. Scranton. 'The walls of Peiraieus', pp. 301f. in *AJA* 43 (1939).

Scranton 1941   R.L. Scranton. *Greek Walls.* Cambridge, Mass. 1941.

Schwyzer 1960   E. Schwyzer. *Dialectorum Graecarum Exempla Epigraphica Potiora.* 3rd ed. rev. by P. Cauer. Hildesheim 1960.

Seager 1966   R. Seager. 'Lysias against the Corndealers', pp. 172-84 in *Historia* 15 (1966).

Seager 1967   R. Seager. 'Thrasybulus, Conon and Athenian imperialism 396-386 B.C.', pp. 95-115 in *JHS* 87 (1967).

Sealey 1955   R. Sealey. 'Athens after the Social War', pp. 74-81 in *JHS* 75 (1955).

Sealey 1967   R. Sealey. *Essays in Greek Politics.* New York 1967.

Sealey 1970   R. Sealey. 'Notes on tribute-quota lists 5, 6 and 7 of the Athenian Empire', pp. 13-28 in *Phoenix* 24 (1970).

Sealey 1975   R. Sealey. 'Constitutional changes in Athens in 410 B.C.', pp. 271-95 in *CSCA* vol. 8 (1975).

SEG   Supplementum Epigraphicum Graecum.

Shaw 1967   J.W. Shaw. 'A double-sheaved pulley block from Kenchreai', pp. 389-401 in *Hesperia* 36 (1967).

Shear 1978   T.L. Shear. 'Kallias of Sphettos and the Revolt of Athens in 286 B.C.', *Hesperia* Supp. 17 (1978).

Sherwin-White 1978   S. Sherwin-White. *Ancient Cos: an Historical Study from the Dorian Settlement to the Imperial Period.* Göttingen 1978.

Sherwin-White 1984   A.N. Sherwin-White. *Roman Foreign Policy in the East: 168 B.C. to A.D. 1.* London 1984.

Shreiner 1969   J.H. Shreiner. 'Thucydides I.93 and Themistocles during the 490s', pp. 23-41 in *SO* 44 (1969).

*SIG*³   W. Dittenberger (ed.). *Sylloge Inscriptionum Graecarum.* 4 vols. 3rd ed. Leipzig 1915-24.

Siewert 1982   P. Siewert. 'Die Trittyen Attikas und die Heeresreform des Kleisthenes', pp. 154ff. in *Vestigia* 33 (1982).

Simms 1985   R.R. Simms. *Foreign Religious Cults in Athens in the Fifth and Fourth Centuries B.C.* Doctoral dissertation presented to the Univ. of Virginia in August 1985.

Simpson 1981   R. Hope Simpson. *Mycenaean Greece.* New Jersey 1981.

Simpson and Lazenby 1970   R. Hope Simpson and J.F. Lazenby. *The Catalogue of Ships in Homer's Iliad.* Oxford, Clarendon 1970.

Sinclair 1978   R.K. Sinclair. 'The King's Peace and the employment of military and naval forces 387-378', pp. 29-54 in *Chiron* 8 (1978).

SIRIS   L. Vidmann (ed.). *Sylloge Inscriptionum Religionis Isiacae et Sarapiacae.* Berlin 1969.

Slidat 1980   Slidat. 'Hippodamos von Milet: seine Rolle in Theorie und Praxis der griechischen Stadtplanung', pp. 31-44 in *BJ* 180 (1980).

Snider 1978   G.L. Snider. 'Hesiod's sailing season', pp. 129-35 in *AJAH* 3 (1978).

Snodgrass 1971   A. Snodgrass. *The Dark Age of Greece.* Edinburgh 1971.

Snodgrass 1980   A. Snodgrass. *Archaic Greece.* London 1980.

Solders 1931   S. Solders. *Die ausserstädtischen Kulte und die Einigung Attikas.* Lund 1931.

Solmsen 1979   F. Solmsen. *Isis among the Greeks and Romans.* Cambridge 1979.

Sommerstein 1981   A.H. Sommerstein. *Commentary on Aristophanes' Wasps.* Warminster 1981.

Sparkes 1975   B.A. Sparkes. 'Illustrating Aristophanes', pp. 122-35 in *JHS* 95 (1975).

Srebryny 1936   S. Srebryny. 'Kult der thrakischen Gottin Kotyto in Korinth und Sicilien', pp. 423-47 in *Mélanges Franz Cumont* I. Brussels 1936.

Stanton 1984   G.R. Stanton. 'The tribal reform of Kleisthenes the Alkmeonid', pp. 1-41 in *Chiron* 14 (1984).

Starr 1977   C.G. Starr. *Economic and Social Growth of Early Greece 800-500 B.C.* New York and Oxford 1977.

Steffy 1985   J.R. Steffy. 'The Kyrenia Ship: an interim report on its hull construction', pp. 71-101 in *AJA* 89.1 (1985).

Stewart 1977   Z. Stewart. 'La religione', pp. 503-616 in *Storia e civiltà dei Greci*: vol. 8 ('la società ellenistica: economia, diritto, religione'). Ed. by R.B. Bandinelli. Rome 1977.

Stewart 1979   A. Stewart. *Attika: Studies in Athenian Sculpture of the Hellenistic Age* (supp. paper no. 14 of the Soc. for the Promotion of Hellenic Studies). London 1979.

van Straten 1981   F.T. van Straten. 'Gifts for the Gods', pp. 65-151 in H.S. Versnel, *Faith, Hope and Worship: Aspects of Religious Mentality in the Ancient World.* Leiden 1981.

Stroud 1974   R.S. Stroud. 'An Athenian law on silver coinage', pp. 157-88 in *Hesperia* 43 (1974).

Stroud 1974a   R.S. Stroud. 'Three Attic decrees', pp. 279-98 in *CSCA* 7 (1974).

Stuart and Revett 1827   J. Stuart and N. Revett. *The Antiquities of Athens*. 3 vols. New ed.: London 1827.

Stubbings 1947   F.H. Stubbings. 'The Mycenaean pottery of Attica', pp. 1-75 in *BSA* 42 (1947).

SVA   Die Staatsverträge des Altertums. Ed. by H. Bengston (vol. II) and H.H. Schmittt (vol. III). Munich 1975 and 1969.

T   Teubner edition.

Tarn 1913   W.W. Tarn. *Antigonos Gonatas*. Oxford, Clarendon 1913.

Tarn 1934   W.W. Tarn. 'The new dating of the Chremonidean War', pp. 26-39 in *JHS* 54 (1934).

Tarn and Griffith 1952   W.W. Tarn and G.T. Griffith. *Hellenistic Civilisation*. 3rd ed. London 1952.

TGF   A. Nauck (ed.). Rev. by B. Snell. *Tragicorum Graecorum Fragmenta*. Hildesheim 1964.

Theochares 1951   D. Theochares. *Anaskaphê en Palaiai Kokkiniai Peiraiôs*, pp. 93-127 in *PAE* 1951.

Thiel 1954   J.H. Thiel. *A History of Roman Sea-power before the Second Punic War*. Amsterdam 1954.

Thönges-Stringaris   R.N. Thönges-Stringaris. 'Das griechische Totenmahl', pp. 1-98 in *AM* 80 (1965).

Thompson 1982   H. Thompson. 'The Pnyx in models', pp. 133-47 in *Hesperia* Supp. 19 (1982).

Thompson and Scranton 1943   H.A. Thompson and R.L. Scranton. 'Stoas and city walls on the Pnyx', pp. 269-383 in *Hesperia* 12 (1943).

Thompson and Wycherley 1972   H.A. Thompson and R.E. Wycherley. *The Athenian Agora*: vol. 14 'The Agora of Athens'. Princeton 1972.

Threpsiades 1935   I. Threpsiades. *Anaskaphikai erevnai en Kastella tou Peiraiôs*, pp. 159ff. in *PAE* 1950.

Threpsiades 1950   I. Threpsiades. *Anaskaphai notiôs tês Akropoleôs*, pp. 64-121 in *PAE* 1950.

Tillyard 1904-5   H.J.W. Tillyard. 'Boundary and mortgage stones', pp. 63-71 in *BSA* 11 (1904-5).

Tod 1906-7   M.N. Tod. 'Statute of an Attic thiasos', pp. 328-38 in *BSA* 13 (1906-7).

Tod 1929   M.N. Tod. 'The statutes of the Iobacchi', pp. 1-4 in *CQ* 23 (1929).

Tod 1932   M.N. Tod. *Sidelights on Greek History*. Oxford 1932.

Torr 1964   C. Torr. *Ancient Ships*. Ed. with intro. by A.J. Podlecki. Chicago 1964.

Traill 1975   J. Traill. 'The political organization of Attica', *Hesperia* Supp. 14 (1975).

Travlos 1960   J.N. Travlos. *Poleôdomikê Exelixis tôn Athênôn*. Athens 1960.

Travlos 1971   J.N. Travlos. *A Pictorial Dictionary of Athens*. London 1971.

Tsirivakos 1968   E.K. Tsirivakos. '*Eidêseis ek Peiraiôs*', pp. 113-16 in *AAA* 1 (1968).

Tsirivakos 1969   E.K. Tsirivakos. '*Epitumbia stêlê ek Peiraiôs*', pp. 23-7 in *AD* 24 Mel. A1 (1969).

Urdahl 1968   L.B. Urdahl. 'Jews in Attica', pp. 39-56 in *SO* 43 (1968).

Ullrich 1846   F.W. Ullrich. *Beiträge zur Erklärung des Thukydides*. Hamburg 1846.

Ulrichs 1843   H.N. Ulrichs. 'Topographie der Hafen von Athen', pp. 647ff. in *Abhandl. d. Bayer. Akad.* 3 (1843). Translated by E.P. Colquhoun. London 1847.

Ussher 1973   R.G. Ussher. *Aristophanes' Ecclesiazusae*. Oxford, Clarendon 1973.

Vanderpool 1959   E. Vanderpool. 'News letter from Greece', pp. 279-83 in *AJA* 63 (1959).

Vanderpool 1960   E. Vanderpool. 'News letter from Greece', pp. 265-7 in *AJA* 64 (1960).

Vanderpool 1968   E. Vanderpool. 'Metronomoi', pp. 73-6 in *Hesperia* 37 (1968).

Vatin 1970   C. Vatin. *Recherches sur le mariage et la condition de la femme mariée à l'époque hellénistique*. Paris 1970.

Vatin 1976   C. Vatin. 'Jardins et services de voirie', pp. 555-64 in *BCH* 100 (1976).

Verdeles and Davaras 1966   N. Verdeles and K. Davaras. '*Anaskaphê tmêmatos tou notiou makrou teichous*', pp. 92-5 in *AD* 21 B1 (1966).

Vermaseren 1966   M.J. Vermaseren. *The Legend of Attis in Greek and Roman Art*. Thames and Hudson, London 1966.

Vermeule 1964   E.T. Vermeule. *Greece in the Bronze Age*. Chicago and London 1964.

Vermeule 1977   E.T. Vermeule. *Greek Sculpture and Roman Taste*. Michigan 1977.

Vernant 1965   J.-P. Vernant. *Mythe et pensée chez les Grecs*. Paris 1965.

Versnel 1981   H.S. Versnel. *Faith, Hope and Worship: Aspects of Religious Mentality in the Ancient World*. Leiden 1981.

Vidman 1970   L. Vidman. *Isis und Sarapis bei den Griechen und Römern*. Berlin 1970.

Vos 1963   M.F. Vos. *Scythian Archers in Archaic Attic Vase-Painting*. Groningen 1963.

Wachsmuth 1890   C. Wachsmuth. *Die Stadt Athen im Alterthum*. 2 vols. Leipzig 1890.

Wachsmuth 1967   D. Wachsmuth. *Pompimos ho daimôn: Untersuchungen zu den antiken Sakralhandlungen bei Seereisen*. Diss. Berlin 1967.

Wade-Gery 1932   H.T. Wade-Gery. 'Horos', pp. 877-87 in *Mélanges Gustave Glotz*. Paris 1932.

Walbank 1933   F.W. Walbank. *Aratos of Sicyon*. Cambridge 1933.

Walbank 1940   F.W. Walbank. *Philip V of Macedon*. Cambridge 1940.

Walbank 1957-79   F.W. Walbank. *A Historical Commentary on Polybius*. 3 vols. Oxford, Clarendon 1957-79.

Walbank 1976   M.B. Walbank. 'Honours for Phanosthenes, Antiochides and associates', pp. 289-95 in *Hesperia* 45 (1976).

Walbank 1978   M.B. Walbank. *Athenian Proxenies of the Fifth Century B.C.* Toronto 1978.

Walbank 1982   M.B. Walbank. 'The confiscation and sale by the poletai in 402/1 B.C. of the property of the Thirty Tyrants', pp. 74-98 in *Hesperia* 51 (1982).

Walbank 1983   M.B. Walbank. 'Leases of sacred properties in Attica': Parts 1-4, pp. 100-35, 177-99, 200-6 and 207-31 in *Hesperia* 52 (1983).

Walker 1957   P.K. Walker. 'The "Pentekontaetia" in Thucydides, Book 1' pp. 27-38 in *CQ* n.s. 7 (1957).

Wallace 1970   M.B. Wallace. 'Early Greek proxenoi', pp. 189-208 in *Phoenix* 24 (1970).

Wallace 1969   P.W. Wallace. 'Psyttaleia and the trophies of the Battle of Salamis', pp. 293-303 in *AJA* 73 (1969).

Wallace 1972   P.W. Wallace. 'The tomb of Themistokles in the Peiraieus', pp. 451-62 in *Hesperia* 41 (1972).

Wallinga 1964   H.T. Wallinga. 'Nautika (I): the unit of capacity for ancient ships', pp. 1-40 in *Mnemosyne* 17 (1964).

Wallinga 1984   H.T. Wallinga. 'The Ionian Revolt', pp. 401-37 in *Mnemosyne* 37 (1984).

Walsh 1904-5   M.K. Walsh. 'Honorary statues in ancient Greece', pp. 32-49 in *BSA* 11 (1904-5).

Walters 1985   E.J. Walters. *Attic Grave Reliefs that Represent Women in the Dress of Isis.* Michigan 1985.

Walton 1935   F.R. Walton. 'A problem in the *Ichneutae* of Sophocles', pp. 167-89 in *HSCP* 46 (1935).

Waywell 1971   G.B. Waywell. 'Athena Mattei', pp. 373-82 in *BSA* 66 (1971).

Westlake 1969   H.D. Westlake. *Essays on the Greek Historians and Greek History.* Manchester 1969.

Wheler 1682   G. Wheler. *A Journey into Greece.* London 1682.

Whitehead 1977   D. Whitehead. 'The ideology of the Athenian metic', *CPhS Supp.* 4 (1977).

Whitehead 1981   D. Whitehead. 'Xenocrates the metic', pp. 223-44 in *RhM* 124 (1981).

Whitehead 1982   D. Whitehead. 'Notes on Athenian demarchs', pp. 37-42 in *ZPE* 47 (1982).

Whitehead 1982-3   D. Whitehead. 'Sparta and the Thirty Tyrants', pp. 105-30 in *AncSoc* 13/14 (1982-3).

Whitehead 1984   D. Whitehead. 'A thousand new Athenians', pp. 8-10 in *LCM* 9.1 (Jan. 1984).

Whitehead 1986   D. Whitehead. *The Demes of Attica.* Princeton 1986.

Widmann 1923   S.P. Widmann. 'Bericht über die Literatur zu Thukydides für die Jahre 1919-22', p. 215 in *Bursians Jahresbericht* 1923.

Wilhelm 1902   A. Wilhelm. 'Inschrift aus dem Peiraieus', pp. 132-4 in *JÖAI* 5 (1902).

Will 1966-7   E. Will. *Histoire politique du monde hellénistique.* 2 vols. 2nd ed. Nancy 1966 and 1967.

Wilamowitz-Moellendorff 1887   U. von Wilamowitz-Moellendorff. 'Demotika der attischen Metoeken', pp. 107-28, 211-59 in *Hermes* 22 (1887).

Wilamowitz-Moellendorff 1931-2   U. von Wilamowitz-Moellendorff. *Der Glaube der Hellenen.* 2 vols. Berlin 1931-2.

Williams 1983   D. Williams. 'Women on Athenian vases: problems of interpretation', pp. 92-106 in *Images of Women in Antiquity* (ed. A. Cameron and A. Kuhrt). London and Canberra 1983.

Winter 1971   F.E. Winter. *Greek Fortifications.* Toronto 1971.

Wolters 1892   P. Wolters. 'Darstellungen des Asklepios', pp. 1-15 in *AM* 17 (1892).

Woodward 1962   A.W. Woodward. 'Athens and the oracle of Ammon', pp. 5-13 in *BSA* 57 (1962).

Wycherley 1957   R.E. Wycherley. *The Athenian Agora*: vol. 3 'Literary and Epigraphical Testimonia'. Princeton 1957.

Wycherley 1964   R.E. Wycherley. 'Hippodamos and Rhodes', pp. 135-9 in *Historia* 13 (1964).

Wycherley 1978   R.E. Wycherley. *The Stones of Athens.* Princeton 1978.

Wyse 1904   W. Wyse. *The Speeches of Isaeus.* Cambridge 1904.

Yavis 1949   C.G. Yavis. *Greek Altars: Origins and Typology.* Missouri 1949.

Young 1939   R.S. Young. 'Late Geometric graves and a seventh-century well'. *Hesperia* Supp. 2 (1939).

Young 1942   R.S. Young. 'Graves from the Phaleron Cemetery', pp. 23-57 in *AJA* 46 (1942).

Ziebarth 1896   E. Ziebarth. *Das griechische Vereinswesen.* Leipzig 1896.

Ziebarth 1929   E. Ziebarth. *Beiträge zur Geschichte des Seeraubs und Seehandels im alten*

Griechenland. Berlin 1929.

Ziebarth 1935   E. Ziebarth. 'Gasthäuser im alten Griechenland', pp. 339-48 in *Eis mnêmên Spyr. Lambrou*. Athens 1935.

Index lapidum

References to numbers in the appendixes are given in *italic* type, e.g. *III 14* indicates Appendix III no.14. References to the pages of this book appear in **bold** type.

GHI
I 44, **181**
II 100, **185**
II 107, **217, 222**
II 111, **201**
II 114, **185**
II 123, **42**
II 139, **192, 193**
II 162, **201**
II 189, **228**
II 196, **201**
II 198, **192**
IAGIL
10, **209**
IG I²
31, **181**
45, **181**
57, **182, 198, 199**
73, **196**
74, **196**
79, **179**
90, **203**
91, **182, 196**
92, **182**
98, **196**
105, **204**
128, *III 14,* **128, 129, 137, 229, 239**
208, **209**
301, **209**
310, *III 37,* **231**
329, **194**
826, *III 69,* **126, 235**
827, *III 114,* **238**
855, *I 20,* **226**
858, *I 22,* **226**
867, *I 21,* **226**
868, *I 1,* **221, 225**
887 a and b, *I 2-3,* **140, 144, 225**
888, *I 4,* **140, 225**
889, *I 5,* **140, 225**

890 a and b, *I 6 and 7,* **140, 152, 225**
891, *I 8-11,* **140, 141, 144, 158, 225**
892, *I 12 and 13*
893, *I 14,* **140, 180, 225**
894, *I 15,* **140, 144, 182, 225**
895, *I 16,* **226**
896, *I 17,* **140, 226**
897, *Ia,* **226**
898, *Ib,* **226**
899, *Ic,* **226**
900, *Id,* **226**
901, *Ie,* **226**
IG I³
46, **181**
52, **182, 196**
61, **182, 198**
93, **196**
130, *III 14,* **104, 229**
136, *III 38,* **106, 118, 231**
153, **179**
154, **196**
242, *III 168,* **241**
383, *III 37,* **119, 231**
421, **194**
421-2, **202**
IG II²
10, **184, 185**
24, **185**
47, *III 27,* **194, 230**
124, **187**
141, **193**
212, **201**
215, **196**
244, **197, 220, 222**
337, *III 6,* **74, 108, 112, 127, 228, 235**
338, **196, 211**
342, **201**
351, **192, 193**
360, **192, 201**

Index locorum

References to the pages of this book appear in **bold** type.

General index

References to figure numbers are given at the end of the relevant entries.